UNDERSTANDING PUBLIC POLICY

Fourteenth Edition

Thomas R. Dye
MCKENZIE PROFESSOR OF GOVERNMENT *EMERITUS*
FLORIDA STATE UNIVERSITY

Boston   Columbus   Indianapolis   New York   San Francisco   Upper Saddle River
Amsterdam   Cape Town   Dubai   London   Madrid   Milan   Munich   Paris   Montréal   Toronto
Delhi   Mexico City   São Paulo   Sydney   Hong Kong   Seoul   Singapore   Taipei   Tokyo

Assistant Editor: Stephanie Chaisson
Director of Development: Eileen Calabro
Executive Marketing Manager: Wendy Gordon
Media Editor: Lisa Dotson
Production Manager: S.S. Kulig
Project Coordination, Text Design, and Electronic
  Page Makeup: PreMediaGlobal

Cover Designer: Suzanne Behnke
Cover Art: Stillfx/Veer
Senior Manufacturing Buyer: Dennis J. Para
Printer/Binder: Quad/Graphics-Taunton
Cover Printer: Lehigh-Phoenix Color Corp.

Credits and acknowledgments borrowed from other sources and reproduced, with permission, in this textbook appear on the appropriate page within text and also on page 368.

Library of Congress Cataloging-in-Publication Data

Dye, Thomas R.
  Understanding public policy / Thomas R. Dye. — 14th ed.
      p. cm.
  Includes bibliographical references and index.
  ISBN-13: 978-0-205-23882-8 (alk. paper)
  ISBN-10: 0-205-23882-3 (alk. paper)
  1. Political planning—United States. 2. United States—Politics and government. 3. Policy sciences. I. Title.
  JK468.P64D95 2013
  320.60973—dc23

                                                                                    2011045837

10 9 8 7 6 5 4 3 2 1—QGT—16 15 14 13 12

www.pearsonhighered.com

ISBN-13: 978-0-205-23882-8
ISBN-10:   0-205-23882-3

Contents

3 The Policymaking Process: Decision-Making Activities   32

4 Policy Evaluation: Finding Out What Happens After a Law Is Passed   62

5 Federalism and State Policies: Institutional Arrangements and Policy Variations   82

6 Criminal Justice: Rationality and Irrationality in Public Policy   106

10 Economic Policy: Challenging Incrementalism   206

11 Tax Policy: Battling the Special Interests   228

12 International Trade and Immigration: Elite–Mass Conflict   248

13 Energy and the Environment: Externalities and Interests   268

14 Civil Rights: Elite and Mass Interaction   292

15 Defense Policy: Strategies for Serious Games   324

16 Homeland Security: Terrorism and Nondeterrable Threats   352

Preface

Policy analysis is concerned with "who gets what" in politics and, more important, "why" and "what difference it makes." We are concerned not only with what policies governments pursue, but why governments pursue the policies they do, and what the consequences of these policies are.

Political Science, like other scientific disciplines, has developed a number of concepts and models to help describe and explain political life. These models are not really competitive in the sense that any one could be judged as the "best." Each focuses on separate elements of politics, and each helps us understand different things about political life.

We begin with a brief description of eight analytic models in political science and the potential contribution of each to the study of public policy:

Process model   Group model
Institutional model   Elite model
Rational model   Public choice model
Incremental model   Game theory model

Most public policies are a combination of rational planning, incrementalism, competition among groups, elite preferences, public choice, political processes, and institutional influences. Throughout this volume we employ these models, both singly and in combination, to describe and explain public policy. However, certain chapters rely more on one model than another. The policy areas studied are:

Criminal justice   Energy and Environment
Welfare   Civil rights
Health Care   Defense policy
Education   Homeland security
Economic policy   International trade
Tax policy   and immigration

In short, this volume is not only an introduction to the study of public policy but also an introduction to the models political scientists use to describe and explain political life.

NEW TO THIS EDITION

The fourteenth edition of *Understanding Public Policy* focuses on the policy challenges confronting the Obama administration.

Can America's health care system be transformed according to a rational-comprehensive plan? A new chapter describes earlier incremental changes in health care—Medicare for the aged,

Medicaid for the poor, and SCHIP for children—and then describes the conditions inspiring more comprehensive reform. Prior to health care reform, many working Americans and their dependents, roughly 15 percent of the population, were without health insurance. The cost of health care in America consumes a larger share of the nation's economic resources (about 15 percent of the gross domestic product) than in any other country. Yet the United States ranks well below other nations in many common measures of national health, including life expectancy and infant mortality. The Patient Protection and Affordable Care Act of 2010 represents a rational-comprehensive approach to transforming health care in America. The health care chapter covers the Act's individual mandate, employer mandate, Medicaid expansion, health-care exchanges, taxes and costs. It also describes the controversies surrounding "Obamacare," notably the constitutionality of the individual mandate.

The economic policies of the Obama administration defy the traditional incremental model. The economic chapter describes the Wall Street bailout, the TARP program, the stimulus package, mortgage modification, and new financial regulations. But the demise of the incremental model is especially evident in the explosive growth of federal spending under President Obama and the resulting unprecedented annual federal deficits. The chapter describes the recommendations of the president's deficit reduction commission—recommendations ignored by the president—as well as Republican efforts to cut federal spending. The chapter ends with a discussion of a balanced budget amendment to the Constitution.

The policy effects of the Republican capture of control of the House of Representatives in the midterm congressional elections of 2010 are reflected in several chapters. The tax chapter describes the tax compromise package in the "lame duck" session of Congress in 2010, in which President Obama was obliged to give up his efforts to raise the top marginal income tax rate to 39.6 percent. The energy and environment chapter describes the demise of the comprehensive "cap and trade" program in the Congress, as well as the attempts by the Environmental Protection Agency to achieve by regulation what the Obama administration was unable to achieve by legislation, namely the regulation of carbon dioxide emissions. The international trade and immigration chapter describes the gridlock over immigration reform, and the president's inability to win the enactment of the Dream Act.

The institutional model is strengthened with added coverage of state policies in the federalism chapter. Federalism allows policy variation among the states, notably in educational spending, the costliest function of state government. And states display a wide variation in tax policies, including differences in their reliance on income versus sales taxation. Federalism also envisions conflict between the national government and states. The chapter covers federal intervention in traditional state policy domains with grants-in-aid, preemptions, and mandates. But it also covers state challenges to national policies, including state medical marijuana laws, Arizona's immigration law, and state opposition to "Obamacare." Direct democracy, in the form of the initiative and referenda, is available only in state and local government. State referenda voting provides information on popular policy preferences.

The defense policy chapter describes the Obama administration's shift in priorities from Iraq to Afghanistan. The announced mission in Afghanistan is not nationbuilding but rather to "disrupt, dismantle, and defeat" Al Qaeda. The transition to Afghan security control "will begin in 2011 and conclude in 2014." U.S. troops are combined with NATO forces in an International Security Assistance Force (ISAF) committed primarily to counterinsurgency operations in Afghanistan. The chapter also continues the discussion of when to use military force: U.S. intervention in Libya illustrates the contrast between advocates of using force only when vital interests of the United States are at stake, versus Obama's justification of using force for the humanitarian purpose of protecting the civilian population of Libya.

Finally, the homeland security chapter describes the Obama administration's reversal of its earlier decisions to close the Guantánamo prison and to try terrorists in civilian courts. The Obama administration now argues that it has the authority to hold enemy combatants who pose a danger to national security until the cessation of hostilities. The president has also ordered new military commission trials for certain Guantánamo detainees, including the self-proclaimed mastermind of the 9/11 attacks, Kalid Sheikh Mohammed.

I wish to thank the following reviewers for their helpful comments: Michael Bordelon, Houston Baptist University; Euel Elliott, University of Texas at Dallas; Kim Geron, California State University—East Bay; Jon D. Holstine, American Military University; Jesse Horton, San Antonio College; Kathryn Mohrman, Arizona State University; Ira Reed, Trinity University, Washington D.C.; Bruce Rocheleau, Northern Illinois University; Jessica Ice, Florida State University; Chad Long, St. Edwards University; Olga Smiranova, Eastern Carolina University; Minzi Su, Tennessee State University.

Thomas R. Dye

GIVE YOUR STUDENTS CHOICES

In addition to the traditional printed text, *Understanding Public Policy, 14th Edition* is available in the following format to give you and your students more choices—and more ways to save.

The **CourseSmart eTextbook** offers the same content as the printed text in a convenient online format—with highlighting, online search, and printing capabilities. Visit **www.coursesmart.com** to learn more.

MySearchLab®

MySearchLab is an interactive website that features an eText, access to the EBSCO Content-Select database and multimedia, and step-by-step tutorials which offer complete overviews of the entire writing and research process. MySearchLab is designed to amplify a traditional course in numerous ways or to administer a course online. Additionally, MySearchLab offers course specific tools to enrich learning and help students succeed.

- **eText:** Identical in content and design to the printed text, the Pearson eText provides access to the book wherever and whenever it is needed. Students can take notes and highlight, just like a traditional book. The Pearson eText is also available on the iPad for all registered users of MySearchLab.

- **Flashcards:** These review important terms and concepts from each chapter online. Students can search by chapters or within a glossary and also access drills to help them prepare for quizzes and exams. Flashcards can be printed or exported to your mobile devices.

- **Chapter-specific Content:** Each chapter contains Learning Objectives, Quizzes, Media, and Flashcards. These can be used to enhance comprehension, help students review key terms, prepare for tests, and retain what they have learned. To order this book with MySearchLab access at no extra charge, use ISBN 0205861164.

  Learn more at www.mysearchlab.com

INSTRUCTOR RESOURCES

A comprehensive Instructor's Manual and Test Bank, as well as a PowerPoint Presentation will accompany this new edition of *Understanding Public Policy*. These resources are available for download at www.pearsonhighered.com/irc (access code required).

Expanding the Scope of Public Policy President Barack Obama signs the Patient Protection and Affordable Care Act in the East Room of the White House, March 30, 2010. This health care reform bill greatly expands the scope of public policy in America. Under the Obama Administration, federal government spending has increased from about 20 percent of the gross domestic product (GDP) to over 25 percent. The nation's state and local governments combined add about 13 percent, for a total size of government of approximately 37 percent of the GDP. (© Brooks Kraft/Corbis)

Policy Analysis
What Governments Do, Why They Do It, and What Difference It Makes

WHAT IS PUBLIC POLICY?

This book is about public policy. It is concerned with what governments do, why they do it, and what difference it makes. It is also about political science and the ability of this academic discipline to describe, analyze, and explain public policy.

Definition of Policy

Public policy is whatever governments choose to do or not to do.[1] Governments do many things. They regulate conflict within society; they organize society to carry on conflict with other societies; they distribute a great variety of symbolic rewards and material services to members of the society; and they extract money from society, most often in the form of taxes. Thus, public policies may regulate behavior, organize bureaucracies, distribute benefits, or extract taxes—or all of these things at once.

Policy Expansion and Government Growth

Today people expect government to do a great many things for them. Indeed there is hardly any personal or societal problem for which some group will not demand a government solution—that is, a public policy designed to alleviate personal discomfort or societal unease. Over the years, as more and more Americans turned to government to resolve society's problems, government grew in size and public policy expanded in scope to encompass just about every sector of American life.

Throughout most of the twentieth century, government grew in both absolute size and in relation to the size of the national economy. The size of the economy is usually measured by the gross domestic product (GDP), the sum of all the goods and services produced in the United States in a year (see Figure 1–1). Government spending amounted to only about 8 percent of the GDP at the beginning of the last century, and most governmental activities were carried out by state and local governments. Two world wars, the New Deal programs devised during the Great Depression of the 1930s, and the growth of the Great Society programs of the 1960s and 1970s all greatly expanded the size of government, particularly

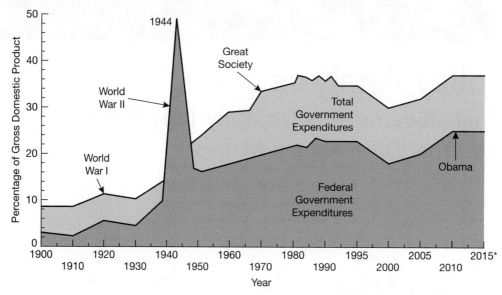

FIGURE 1-1 The Growth of Government The size of government can be measured in relation to the size of the economy. Total federal, state, and local government spending now exceeds 37 percent of the GDP, the size of the economy.
*Estimate from *Budget of the United States Government 2012.*

the federal government. The rise in government growth relative to the economy leveled off during the Reagan presidency (1981–1989). The economy in the 1990s grew faster than government spending, resulting in a modest decline in the size of government *relative to the economy*. Federal spending costs less than 20 percent of the GDP.

The Obama Administration brought about a dramatic increase in federal spending, much of it in response to the "Great Recession" of 2008–2009. Federal spending in 2009 soared to 28 percent of the GDP; this spending included a "stimulus" package designed to jumpstart the economy (see Chapter 10). But it is expected that continued increases in federal spending under President Barack Obama will keep federal spending close to 25 percent of the GDP, the highest figure since World War II. The nation's 50 state governments and 87,000 local governments (cities, counties, towns and townships, school districts, and special districts) combined to account for over 12 percent of the GDP. *Total* government spending—federal, state, and local—now amounts to about 37 percent of GDP.

Scope of Public Policy

Not everything that government does is reflected in governmental expenditures. *Regulatory activity*, for example, especially environmental regulations, imposes significant costs on individuals and businesses; these costs are *not* shown in government budgets. Nevertheless, government spending is a common indicator of governmental functions and priorities. For example, Figure 1–2 indicates that the *federal government* spends more on senior citizens—in Social Security and Medicare outlays—than on any other function, including national defense. Federal welfare and health programs account for substantial budget outlays, but federal financial support of education

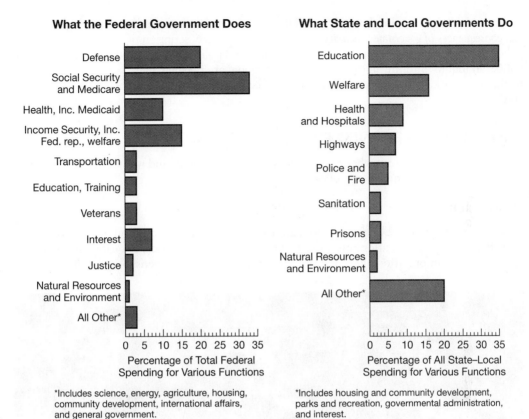

What the Federal Government Does

What State and Local Governments Do

0 5 10 15 20 25 30 35
Percentage of Total Federal
Spending for Various Functions

0 5 10 15 20 25 30 35
Percentage of All State–Local
Spending for Various Functions

*Includes science, energy, agriculture, housing,
community development, international affairs,
and general government.

*Includes housing and community development,
parks and recreation, governmental administration,
and interest.

FIGURE 1–2   Public Policy: What Governments Do Government spending figures indicate that Social Security and Medicare consume the largest share of federal spending, while education is the largest item in state and local government spending.

SOURCES: *Budget of the United States Government, 2012; Statistical Abstract of the United States, 2011.*

is very modest. *State and local governments* in the United States bear the major burden of public education. Welfare and health functions consume larger shares of their budgets than highways and law enforcement do.

WHY STUDY PUBLIC POLICY?

Political science is the study of politics—the study of "who gets what, when, and how?"[2] It is more than the study of governmental institutions, that is, federalism, separation of powers, checks and balances, judicial review, the powers and duties of Congress, the president, and the courts. "Traditional" political science focuses primarily on these institutional arrangements, as well as the philosophical justification of government. And political science is more than the study of political processes, that is, campaigns and elections, voting, lobbying, legislating, and adjudicating. Modern "behavioral" political science focuses primarily on these processes.

Political science is also the study of public policy—*the description and explanation of the causes and consequences of government activity.* This focus involves a description of the content of public policy; an analysis of the impact of social, economic, and political forces on the content of public policy; an inquiry into the effect of various institutional arrangements and political processes on public policy; and an evaluation of the consequences of public policies on society, both intended and unintended.

WHAT CAN BE LEARNED FROM POLICY ANALYSIS?

Policy analysis is finding out what governments do, why they do it, and what difference, if any, it makes. What can be learned from policy analysis?

Description

First, we can describe public policy—we can learn what government is doing (and not doing) in welfare, defense, education, civil rights, health, the environment, taxation, and so on. A factual basis of information about national policy is really an indispensable part of everyone's

Setting Budget Priorities of the President Policy analysis begins by finding out what government is doing. The annual *Budget of the United States Government* is the single most comprehensive policy document of the federal government. It sets forth the policy priorities of the president with price tags attached. It sets the parameters of the debate in Congress over spending and deficit levels. The photo shows copies of the budget for 2012 being delivered to the Senate Budget Committee in February 2011.   (© Michael Reynolds/epa/Corbis)

education. What does the Civil Rights Act of 1964 actually say about discrimination in employment? What did the Supreme Court rule in the *Bakke* case about affirmative action programs? What do the Medicaid and Medicare programs promise for the poor and the aged? What agreements have been reached between the United States and Russia regarding nuclear weapons? How much money are we paying in taxes? How much money does the federal government spend each year, and what does it spend it on? These are examples of descriptive questions.

Causes

Second, we can inquire about the causes, or determinants, of public policy. Why is public policy what it is? Why do governments do what they do? We might inquire about the effects of political institutions, processes, and behaviors on public policies (Linkage B in Figure 1–3). For example, does it make any difference in tax and spending levels whether Democrats or Republicans control the presidency and Congress? What is the impact of lobbying by the special interests on efforts to reform the federal tax system? We can also inquire about the effects of social, economic, and cultural forces in shaping public policy (Linkage C in Figure 1–3). For example: What are the effects of changing public attitudes about race on civil rights policy? What are the effects of recessions on government spending? What is the effect of an increasingly older population on the Social Security and Medicare programs? In scientific terms, when we study the *causes* of public policy, policies become the *dependent* variables, and their various political, social, economic, and cultural determinants become the *independent* variables.

Consequences

Third, we can inquire about the consequences, or impacts, of public policy. Learning about the consequences of public policy is often referred to as *policy evaluation*. What difference, if any, does public policy make in people's lives? We might inquire about the effects of public policy on political institutions and processes (Linkage F in Figure 1–3). For example, what is the effect of continuing high unemployment on Republican party fortunes in Congressional elections? What is the impact of economic policies on the president's popularity? We also want to examine the impact of public policies on conditions in society (Linkage D in Figure 1–3). For example, does capital punishment help to deter crime? Does cutting cash welfare benefits encourage people to work? Does increased educational spending produce higher student achievement scores? In scientific terms, when we study the *consequences* of public policy, policies become the *independent* variables, and their political, social, economic, and cultural impacts on society become the *dependent* variables.

POLICY ANALYSIS AND POLICY ADVOCACY

It is important to distinguish policy analysis from policy advocacy. *Explaining* the causes and consequences of various policies is not equivalent to *prescribing* what policies governments ought to pursue. Learning *why* governments do what they do and what the consequences of their actions are is not the same as saying what governments *ought* to do or bringing about changes in what

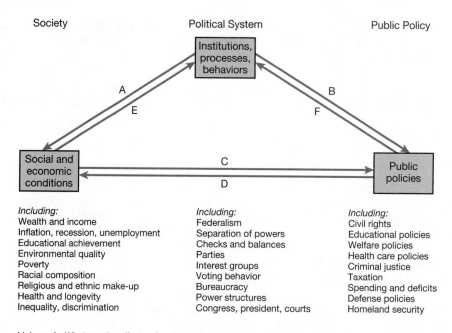

Linkage A: What are the effects of social and economic conditions on political and governmental institutions, processes, and behaviors?

Linkage B: What are the effects of political and governmental institutions, processes, and behaviors on public policies?

Linkage C: What are the effects of social and economic conditions on public policies?

Linkage D: What are the effects (feedback) of public policies on social and economic conditions?

Linkage E: What are the effects (feedback) of political and governmental institutions, processes, and behaviors on social and economic conditions?

Linkage F: What are the effects (feedback) of public policies on political and governmental institutions, processes, and behaviors?

FIGURE 1–3   Studying Public Policy, its Causes and Consequences This diagram (sometimes referred to as the "systems model") classifies societal conditions, political system characteristics, and public policies, and suggests possible linkages between them.

they do. Policy advocacy requires the skills of rhetoric, persuasion, organization, and activism. Policy analysis encourages scholars and students to attack critical policy issues with the tools of systematic inquiry. There is an implied assumption in policy analysis that developing scientific knowledge about the forces shaping public policy and the consequences of public policy is itself a socially relevant activity, and that policy analysis is a *prerequisite* to prescription, advocacy, and activism.

Specifically, policy analysis involves:

1. *A primary concern with explanation rather than prescription.* Policy recommendations— if they are made at all—are subordinate to description and explanation. There is an implicit judgment that understanding is a prerequisite to prescription and that understanding is best achieved through careful analysis rather than rhetoric or polemics.

2. *A rigorous search for the causes and consequences of public policies.* This search involves the use of scientific standards of inference. Sophisticated quantitative techniques may be helpful in establishing valid inferences about causes and consequences, but they are not essential.

3. *An effort to develop and test general propositions about the causes and consequences of public policy and to accumulate reliable research findings of general relevance.* The object is to develop general theories about public policy that are reliable and that apply to different government agencies and different policy areas. Policy analysts clearly prefer to develop explanations that fit more than one policy decision or case study—explanations that stand up over time in a variety of settings.

However, it must be remembered that policy issues are decided not by analysts but by political actors—elected and appointed government officials, interest groups, and occasionally even voters. Social science research often does not fare well in the political arena; it may be interpreted, misinterpreted, ignored, or even used as a weapon by political combatants. Policy analysis sometimes produces unexpected and even politically embarrassing findings. Public policies do not always work as intended. And political interests will accept, reject, or use findings to fit their own purposes.

POLICY ANALYSIS AND THE QUEST FOR SOLUTIONS TO AMERICA'S PROBLEMS

It is questionable that policy analysis can ever "solve" America's problems. Ignorance, crime, poverty, racial conflict, inequality, poor housing, ill health, pollution, congestion, and unhappy lives have afflicted people and societies for a long time. Of course, this is no excuse for failing to work toward a society free of these maladies. But our striving for a better society should be tempered with the realization that solutions to these problems may be very difficult to find. There are many reasons for qualifying our enthusiasm for policy analysis.

Limits on Government Power

First, it is easy to exaggerate the importance, both for good and for ill, of the policies of governments. It is not clear that government policies, however ingenious, can cure all or even most of society's ills. Governments are constrained by many powerful social forces—patterns of family life, class structure, child-rearing practices, religious beliefs, and so on. These forces are not easily managed by governments, nor could they be controlled even if it seemed desirable to do so. Some of society's problems are very intractable.

Disagreement over the Problem

Second, policy analysis cannot offer solutions to problems when there is no general agreement on what the problems are. For example, in educational policy some researchers assume that raising achievement levels (measures of verbal and quantitative abilities) is the problem to which our efforts should be directed. But educators often argue that the acquisition of verbal and quantitative skills is not the only, or even the most important, goal of the public schools. They contend that schools must also develop positive self-images among pupils of all races and backgrounds, encourage social awareness and the appreciation of multiple cultures, teach children to respect one another and to resolve their differences peacefully, raise children's awareness of the dangers of drugs and educate them about sex and sexually transmitted diseases, and so on. In other words, many educators define the problems confronting schools more broadly than raising achievement levels.

Policy analysis is not capable of resolving value conflicts. If there is little agreement on what values should be emphasized in educational policy, there is not much that policy research can contribute to policymaking. At best it can advise on how to achieve certain results, but it cannot determine what is truly valuable for society.

Subjectivity in Interpretation

Third, policy analysis deals with very subjective topics and must rely on interpretation of results. Professional researchers frequently interpret the results of their analyses differently. Social science research cannot be value-free. Even the selection of the topic for research is affected by one's values about what is important in society and worthy of attention.

Limitations on Design of Human Research

Another set of problems in systematic policy analysis centers around inherent limitations in the design of social science research. It is not really possible to conduct some forms of controlled experiments on human beings. For example, researchers cannot order children to go to overcrowded or underfunded schools for several years just to see if it adversely impacts their achievement levels. Instead, social researchers must find situations in which educational deprivation has been produced "naturally" in order to make the necessary observations about the causes of such deprivation. Because we cannot control all the factors in a real-world situation, it is difficult to pinpoint precisely what causes educational achievement or nonachievement. Moreover, even where some experimentation is permitted, human beings frequently modify their behavior simply because they know that they are being observed in an experimental situation. For example, in educational research it frequently turns out that children perform well under *any* new teaching method or curricular innovation. It is difficult to know whether the improvements observed are a product of the new teaching method or curricular improvement or merely a product of the experimental situation.

Complexity of Human Behavior

Perhaps the most serious reservation about policy analysis is the fact that social problems are so complex that social scientists are unable to make accurate predictions about the impact of proposed policies. *Social scientists simply do not know enough about individual and group behavior to be able to give reliable advice to policymakers.* Occasionally policymakers turn to social scientists for "solutions," but social scientists do not have any. Most of society's problems are shaped by so many variables that a simple explanation of them, or remedy for them, is rarely possible. The fact that social scientists give so many contradictory recommendations is an indication of the absence of reliable scientific knowledge about social problems. Although some scholars argue that no advice is better than contradictory or inaccurate advice, policymakers still must make decisions, and it is probably better that they act in the light of whatever little knowledge social science can provide than that they act in the absence of any knowledge at all. Even if social scientists cannot predict the impact of future policies, they can at least attempt to measure the impact of current and past public policies and make this knowledge available to decision makers.

POLICY ANALYSIS AS ART AND CRAFT

Understanding public policy is both an art and a craft. It is an art because it requires insight, creativity, and imagination in identifying societal problems and describing them, in devising public policies that might alleviate them, and then in finding out whether these policies end up making things better or worse. It is a craft because these tasks usually require some knowledge of economics, political science, public administration, sociology, law, and statistics. Policy analysis is really an applied subfield of all of these traditional academic disciplines.

We doubt that there is any "model of choice" in policy analysis—that is, a single model or method that is preferable to all others and that consistently renders the best solutions to public problems. Instead we agree with political scientist Aaron Wildavsky, who wrote:

> Policy analysis is one activity for which there can be no fixed program, for policy analysis is synonymous with creativity, which may be stimulated by theory and sharpened by practice, which can be learned but not taught.[3]

Wildavsky goes on to warn students that solutions to great public questions are not to be expected:

> In large part, it must be admitted, knowledge is negative. It tells us what we cannot do, where we cannot go, wherein we have been wrong, but not necessarily how to correct these errors. After all, if current efforts were judged wholly satisfactory, there would be little need for analysis and less for analysts.

There is no one model of choice to be found in this book, but if anyone wants to begin a debate about different ways of understanding public policy, this book is a good place to begin.

SUMMARY

There are a variety of definitions of public policy. But we say simply that public policy is whatever governments choose to do or not to do.

1. Policy analysis is finding out what governments do, why they do it, and what difference it makes.

2. The scope of public policy has expanded as governments do more things and grow in size.

3. A systems model relates societal conditions to political institutions and processes, and to policy outcomes.

4. Policy analysis is often limited by disagreements over the nature of societal problems, by subjectivity in the interpretation of results, by limitations to the design of policy research, and by the complexity of human behavior.

MySearchLab® EXERCISES

Apply what you learned in this chapter on MySearchLab (www.mysearchlab.com).

NOTES

1. This book discourages elaborate academic discussions of the definition of public policy—we say simply that public policy is whatever governments choose to do or not to do. Even the most elaborate definitions of public policy, on close examination, seem to boil down to the same thing. For example, political scientist David Easton defines public policy as "the authoritative allocation of values for the whole society"—but it turns out that only the government can "authoritatively" act on the "whole" society, and everything the government chooses to do or not to do results in the "allocation of values."

   Political scientist Harold Lasswell and philosopher Abraham Kaplan define policy as a "a projected program of goals, values, and practices," and political scientist Carl Friedrick says, "It is essential for the policy concept that there be a goal, objective, or purpose." These definitions imply a difference between specific government actions and an overall program of action toward a given goal. But the problem raised in insisting that government actions must have goals in order to be labeled "policy" is that we can never be sure whether or not a particular action has a goal, or if it does, what that goal is. Some people may assume that if a government chooses to do something there must be a goal, objective, or purpose, but all we can really observe is what governments choose to do or not to do. Realistically, our notion of public policy must include *all actions* of government, and not what governments or officials say they are going to do. We may wish that governments act in a "purposeful, goal-oriented" fashion, but we know that all too frequently they do not.

   Still another approach to defining public policy is to break down this general notion into various component parts. Political scientist Charles O. Jones asks that we consider the distinction among various proposals (specified means for achieving goals), programs (authorized means for achieving goals), decisions (specific actions taken to implement programs), and effects (the measurable impacts of programs). But again we have the problem of assuming that decisions, programs, goals, and effects are linked. Certainly in many policy areas we will see that the decisions of government have little to do with announced "programs," and neither are connected with national "goals." It may be unfortunate that our government does not function neatly to link goals, programs, decisions, and effects, but, as a matter of fact, it does not.

   So we shall stick with our simple definition: *public policy is whatever governments choose to do or not to do.* Note that we are focusing not only on government action but also on government inaction, that is, what government chooses *not* to do. We contend that government *inaction* can have just as great an impact on society as government action.

   See David Easton, *The Political System* (New York: Knopf, 1953), p. 129; Harold D. Lasswell and Abraham Kaplan, *Power and Society* (New Haven, CT: Yale University Press, 1970), p. 71; Carl J. Friedrich, *Man and His Government* (New York: McGraw-Hill, 1963), p. 70; Charles O. Jones, *An Introduction to the Study of Public Policy* (Boston: Duxbury, 1977), p. 4.

2. Harold Lasswell, *Politics: Who Gets What, When and How* (New York: McGraw Hill, 1936).

3. Aaron Wildavsky, *Speaking Truth to Power* (New York: John Wiley, 1979), p. 3.

BIBLIOGRAPHY

ANDERSON, JAMES E. *Public Policymaking*, 7th ed. Cengage Learning, 2011.

COCHRAN, CLARKE E., et al. *American Public Policy: An Introduction*, 10th ed. Belmont, CA: Wadsworth, Cengage Learning, 2011.

DUNN, WILLIAM N. *Public Policy Analysis*, 4th ed. New York: Pearson Education, 2008.

KRAFT, MICHAEL E., and SCOTT R. FURLONG. *Public Policy: Politics, Analysis and Alternatives*, 3rd ed. Washington, DC: CQ Press, 2009.

PETERS, B. GUY. *American Public Policy: Promise and Performance*, 8th ed. Washington, DC: CQ Press, 2009.

RUSHEFSKY, MARK E. *Public Policy in the United States*, 4th ed. Armonk, NY: M. E. Sharpe, 2008.

WEINER, DAVID and ALDEN R. VINING. *Policy Analysis: Concepts and Practice*, 5th ed. New York: Longman, 2011.

WILDAVSKY, AARON. *Speaking Truth to Power*. New York: John Wiley, 1979.

WEB SITES

OFFICE OF THE PRESIDENT. White House home page, with president's policy positions, speeches, press releases, etc. *www.whitehouse.gov*

U.S. HOUSE OF REPRESENTATIVES. Official House Web site, with links to individual House members' Web sites. *www.house.gov*

U.S. SENATE. Official Senate Web site, with links to individual senators' Web sites. *www.senate.gov*

U.S. CONGRESS ON THE INTERNET. Library of Congress Thomas search engine for finding bills and tracing their progress through Congress. *http://thomas.loc.gov*

FEDERAL STATISTICS ONLINE. Links to federal statistical reports, listed by topic A–Z. *www.fedstats.gov*

U.S. CENSUS BUREAU. The official site of the Census Bureau, with access to all current reports—population, income and poverty, government finances, etc. *www.census.gov*

FIRST GOV. U.S. government's official portal to all independent agencies and government corporations. *www.firstgov.gov*

FEDERAL JUDICIARY. U.S. judiciary official site, with links to all federal courts. *www.uscourts.gov*

SUPREME COURT CASES. Compilation of all key U.S. Supreme Court decisions. *www.supct.law.cornell.edu*

LIBRARY OF CONGRESS. Compilation of the laws of the United States. *http://thomas.loc.gov*

Federal "stimulus" spending Airport construction funded by the American Recovery and Reinvestment Act of 2009. This legislation, known in Washington as the "stimulus package," was designed to pump $787 billion into the American economy to offset the "Great Recession." This bill was a decidedly "non-incremental" addition to federal spending and deficits. Indeed, the 2009 federal budget included the largest single increase in spending and deficit levels incurred in any year in history.   (© Rick D'Elia/Corbis)

2

Models of Politics
Some Help in Thinking About Public Policy

MODELS FOR POLICY ANALYSIS

A model is a simplified representation of some aspect of the real world. It may be an actual physical representation—a model airplane, for example, or the tabletop buildings that planners and architects use to show how things will look when proposed projects are completed. Or a model may be a diagram—a road map, for example, or a flow chart that political scientists use to show how a bill becomes law.

Uses of Models

The models we shall use in studying policy are *conceptual models*. These are word models that try to

- Simplify and clarify our thinking about politics and public policy.
- Identify important aspects of policy problems.
- Help us to communicate with each other by focusing on essential features of political life.
- Direct our efforts to understand public policy better by suggesting what is important and what is unimportant.
- Suggest explanations for public policy and predict its consequences.

Selected Policy Models

Over the years, political science, like other scientific disciplines, has developed a number of models to help us understand political life. Among these models are the following:

- Process model
- Institutional model
- Rational model
- Incremental model

- Group model
- Elite model
- Public choice model
- Game theory model

Each of these terms identifies a major conceptual model that can be found in the literature of political science. None of these models was derived especially to study public policy, yet each offers a separate way of thinking about policy and even suggests some of the general causes and consequences of public policy.

These models are not competitive in the sense that any one of them could be judged "best." Each one provides a separate focus on political life, and each can help us to understand different things about public policy. Although some policies appear at first glance to lend themselves to explanation by one particular model, most policies are a combination of rational planning, incrementalism, interest group activity, elite preferences, game playing, public choice, political processes, and institutional influences. Following is a brief description of each model, with particular attention to the separate ways in which public policy can be viewed.

PROCESS: POLICY AS POLITICAL ACTIVITY

Today political processes and behaviors are a central focus of political science. Since World War II, modern "behavioral" political science has studied the activities of voters, interest groups, legislators, presidents, bureaucrats, judges, and other political actors. One of the main purposes has been to discover patterns of activities—or "processes." Political scientists with an interest in policy have grouped various activities according to their relationship with public policy. The result is a set of *policy processes*, which usually follow the general outline shown in Table 2–1. In short, one can

TABLE 2–1 The Policy Process

- *Problem Identification.* The identification of policy problems through demand from individuals and groups for government action.

- *Agenda Setting.* Focusing the attention of the mass media and public officials on specific public problems to decide what will be decided.

- *Policy Formulation.* The development of policy proposals by interest groups, White House staff, congressional committees, and think tanks.

- *Policy Legitimation.* The selection and enactment of policies through actions by Congress, the president, and the courts.

- *Policy Implementation.* The implementation of policies through government bureaucracies, public expenditures, regulations, and other activities of executive agencies.

- *Policy Evaluation.* The evaluation of policies by government agencies themselves, outside consultants, the media, and the general public.

view the policy process as a series of political activities—problem identification, agenda setting, formulation, legitimation, implementation, and evaluation.

The process model is useful in helping us to understand the various activities involved in policymaking. We want to keep in mind that *policymaking* involves agenda setting (capturing the attention of policymakers), formulating proposals (devising and selecting policy options), legitimating policy (developing political support; winning congressional, presidential, or court approval), implementing policy (creating bureaucracies, spending money, enforcing laws), and evaluating policy (finding out whether policies work, whether they are popular).

Processes: Applying the Model
Political processes and behaviors are considered in each of the policy areas studied in this book. Additional commentary on the impact of political activity on public policy is found in Chapter 3, "The Policymaking Process: Decision-Making Activities," and Chapter 4, "Policy Evaluation: Finding Out What Happens After a Law Is Passed."

INSTITUTIONALISM: POLICY AS INSTITUTIONAL OUTPUT

Government institutions have long been a central focus of political science. Traditionally, political science was defined as the study of government institutions. Political activities generally center around particular government institutions—Congress, the presidency, courts, bureaucracies, states, municipalities, and so on. Public policy is authoritatively determined, implemented, and enforced by these institutions.

The relationship between public policy and government institutions is very close. Strictly speaking, a policy does not become a *public* policy until it is adopted, implemented, and enforced by some government institution. Government institutions give public policy three distinctive characteristics. First, government lends *legitimacy* to policies. Government policies are generally regarded as legal obligations that command the loyalty of citizens. People may regard the policies of other groups and associations in society—corporations, churches, professional organizations, civic associations, and so forth—as important and even binding. But only government policies involve legal obligations. Second, government policies involve *universality*. Only government policies extend to all people in a society; the policies of other groups or organizations reach only a part of the society. Finally, government monopolizes *coercion* in society—only government can legitimately imprison violators of its policies. The sanctions that can be imposed by other groups or organizations in society are more limited. It is precisely this ability of government to command the loyalty of all its citizens, to enact policies governing the whole society, and to monopolize the legitimate use of force that encourages individuals and groups to work for enactment of their preferences into policy.

The Constitution of the United States establishes the fundamental institutional structure for policymaking. It is "the supreme Law of the Land" (Article VI). Its key structural components—separation of powers and checks and balances among the legislative, executive, and judicial branches of the national government—together with federalism—dividing power between the nation and the states—were designed by the Founders in part "to form a more perfect Union." These institutional arrangements have changed significantly over more than two centuries, yet no other written constitution in the world has remained in place for so long. Throughout this volume we will be

Institutionalism: Applying the Model
In Chapter 5, "Federalism and State Policies: Institutional Arrangements and Policy Variations," we shall examine some of the problems of American federalism—the distribution of money and power among federal, state, and local governments.

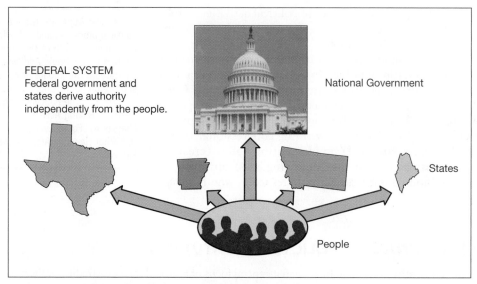

FIGURE 2–1   An Institutional Model: American Federalism Governmental institutional arrangements affect public policy, including federalism—the distribution of money and power among federal, state, and local governments.   (Fotalia)

concerned with the effect of these institutional arrangements on public policy. And in Chapter 5 we shall explore in some detail the effect of federalism.

Federalism recognizes that both the national government and the state governments derive independent legal authority from their own citizens (Figure 2–1): both can pass their own laws, levy their own taxes, and maintain their own courts. The states also have important roles in the selection of national officeholders—in the apportionment of congressional seats, in the alloca-tion of two U.S. senators to each state, and in the allocation of electoral votes for president. Most important, perhaps, both the Congress and three-quarters of states must consent to any changes in the Constitution itself.

RATIONALISM: POLICY AS MAXIMUM SOCIAL GAIN

A rational policy is one that achieves "maximum social gain"; that is, governments should choose policies resulting in gains to society that exceed costs by the greatest amount, and governments should refrain from policies if costs exceed gains.

Note that there are really two important guidelines in this definition of maximum social gain. First, no policy should be adopted if its costs exceed its benefits. Second, among policy alterna-tives, decision makers should choose the policy that produces the greatest benefit over cost. In other words, a policy is rational when the difference between the values it achieves and the values it sacrifices is positive and greater than any other policy alternative. One should *not* view rational-ism in a narrow dollars-and-cents framework, in which basic social values are sacrificed for dollar savings. Rationalism involves the calculation of *all* social, political, and economic values sacrificed or achieved by a public policy, not just those that can be measured in dollars.

To select a rational policy, policymakers must (1) know all the society's value preferences and their relative weights, (2) know all the policy alternatives available, (3) know all the consequences of each policy alternative, (4) calculate the ratio of benefits to costs for each policy alternative, and (5) select the most efficient policy alternative. This rationality assumes that the value preferences of *society as a whole* can be known and weighted. It is not enough to know and weigh the values of some groups and not others. There must be a complete understanding of societal values. Rational policymaking also requires *information* about alternative policies, the *predictive capacity* to foresee accurately the consequences of alternate policies, and the *intelligence* to calculate correctly the ratio of costs to benefits. Finally, rational policymaking requires a *decision-making system* that facilitates rationality in policy formation. A diagram of such a system is shown in Figure 2–2.

However, there are many barriers to rational decision making, so many, in fact, that it rarely takes place at all in government. Yet the model remains important for analytic purposes because it helps to identify barriers to rationality. It assists in posing the question, Why is policymaking *not* a more rational process? At the outset we can hypothesize several important *obstacles to rational policymaking*:

- Many conflicting benefits and costs cannot be compared or weighed; for example, it is difficult to compare or weigh the value of individual life against the costs of regulation.

- Policymakers may not be motivated to make decisions on the basis of societal goals but instead try to maximize their own rewards—power, status, reelection, and money.

- Policymakers may not be motivated to maximize net social gain but merely to satisfy demands for progress; they do not search until they find "the one best way"; instead they halt their search when they find an alternative that will work.

- Large investments in existing programs and policies (sunk costs) prevent policymakers from reconsidering alternatives foreclosed by previous decisions.

Rationalism: Applying the Model
Chapter 6, "Criminal Justice: Rationality and Irrationality in Public Policy," shows that rational policies to deter crime—policies ensuring certainty, swiftness, and severity of punishment—have seldom been implemented. The problems of achieving rationality in public policy are also discussed in Chapter 7, "Welfare: The Search for Rational Strategies," and in Chapter 8, "Health Care: Attempting a Rational-Comprehensive Transformation."

- There are innumerable barriers to collecting all the information required to know all possible policy alternatives and the consequences of each, including the cost of information gathering, the availability of the information, and the time involved in its collection.

- Neither the predictive capacities of the social and behavioral sciences nor those of the physical and biological sciences are sufficiently advanced to enable policymakers to understand the full benefits or costs of each policy alternative.

- Policymakers, even with the most advanced computerized analytical techniques, do not have sufficient intelligence to calculate accurately costs and benefits when a large number of diverse political, social, economic, and cultural values are at stake.

- Uncertainty about the consequences of various policy alternatives compels policymakers to stick as closely as possible to previous policies to reduce the likelihood of unanticipated negative consequences.

- The segmentalized nature of policymaking in large bureaucracies makes it difficult to coordinate decision making so that the input of all the various specialists is brought to bear at the point of decision.

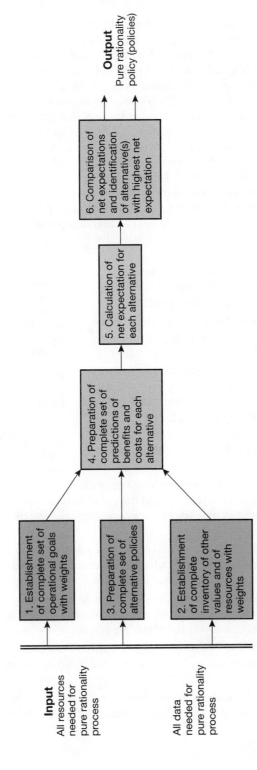

FIGURE 2–2   A Rational Model of a Decision System The rational model assumes complete agreement on goals, knowledge of alternative policies, and the ability to calculate and select the policies with the greatest benefits and least costs.

INCREMENTALISM: POLICY AS VARIATIONS ON THE PAST

Incrementalism views public policy as a continuation of past government activities with only incremental modifications. Political scientist Charles E. Lindblom first presented the incremental model in the course of a critique of the rational model of decision making.[1] According to Lindblom, decision makers do *not* annually review the whole range of existing and proposed policies, identify societal goals, research the benefits and costs of alternative policies in achieving these goals, rank order of preferences for each policy alternative in terms of the maximum net benefits, and then make a selection on the basis of all relevant information. On the contrary, constraints of time, information, and cost prevent policymakers from identifying the full range of policy alternatives and their consequences. Constraints of politics prevent the establishment of clear-cut societal goals and the accurate calculation of costs and benefits. The incremental model recognizes the impractical nature of "rational-comprehensive" policymaking, and describes a more conservative process of decision making.

Incrementalism is conservative in that existing programs, policies, and expenditures are considered as a *base*, and attention is concentrated on new programs and policies and on increases, decreases, or modifications of current programs. (For example, budgetary policy for any government activity or program for 2015 might be viewed incrementally, as shown in Figure 2–3.) Policymakers generally accept the legitimacy of established programs and tacitly agree to continue previous policies.

They do this because they do not have the time, information, or money to investigate all the alternatives to existing policy. The cost of collecting all this information is too great. Policymakers do not have sufficient predictive capacities to know what all the consequences of each alternative will be. Nor are they able to calculate cost–benefit ratios for alternative policies when many diverse political, social, economic, and cultural values are at stake. Thus, completely "rational" policy may turn out to be "inefficient" (despite the contradiction in terms) if the time and cost of developing a rational policy are excessive.

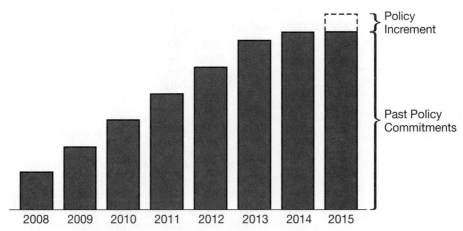

FIGURE 2–3 The Incremental Model The incremental model assumes that policymakers rarely examine past policy commitments, but rather focus their attention on changes in policies and expenditures.

Moreover, incrementalism is politically expedient. Agreement comes easier in policymaking when the items in dispute are only increases or decreases in budgets or modifications of existing programs. Conflict is heightened when decision making focuses on major policy shifts involving great gains or losses, or "all-or-nothing," "yes-or-no" policy decisions. Because the political tension involved in getting new programs or policies passed every year would be very great, past policy victories are continued into future years unless there is a substantial political realignment. Thus, incrementalism is important in reducing conflict, maintaining stability, and preserving the political system itself.

Incrementalism: Applying the Model
Special attention to incrementalism is given in the discussion of government budgeting in Chapter 10, "Economic Policy: Challenging Incrementalism."

But *the incremental model may fail when policymakers are confronted with crises.* When faced with potential collapse of the nation's financial markets in 2008, the president, Congress, the Treasury Department, and the Federal Reserve Board came together to agree on an unprecedented, *nonincremental* expansion of federal power (see Chapter 10, "Economic Policy: Challenging Incrementalism"). Overall, federal spending and deficits increased dramatically, well beyond any levels that might have been predicted by the incremental model. The Treasury Department was given unprecedented authority and $700 billion to "bail out" the nation's major financial institutions. The Federal Reserve Board reduced interest rates to their lowest in history and provided unprecedented amounts of credit to the financial system. Congress itself passed a "stimulus package," the largest single spending bill in the nation's history. Incrementalism was abandoned.

GROUP THEORY: POLICY AS EQUILIBRIUM IN THE GROUP STRUGGLE

Group theory begins with the proposition that interaction among groups is the central fact of politics.[2] Individuals with common interests band together formally or informally to press their demands on government. According to political scientist David Truman, an interest group is "a shared-attitude group that makes certain claims upon other groups in the society"; such a group becomes political "if and when it makes a claim through or upon any of the institutions of government."[3] Individuals are important in politics only when they act as part of, or on behalf of, group interests. The group becomes the essential bridge between the individual and the government. Politics is really the struggle among groups to influence public policy. The task of the political system is to *manage group conflict* by (1) establishing rules of the game in the group struggle, (2) arranging compromises and balancing interests, (3) enacting compromises in the form of public policy, and (4) enforcing these compromises.

Group Theory: Applying the Model
Throughout this volume we will describe struggles over public policy. In Chapter 9, "Education: Group Struggles," we will examine group conflict over public policy in the discussions of education and school issues. In Chapter 11, "Tax Policy: Battling Special Interests," we will observe the power of interest groups in obtaining special treatments in the tax code and obstructing efforts to reform the nation's tax laws.

According to group theorists, public policy at any given time is the equilibrium reached in the group struggle (see Figure 2–4). This equilibrium is determined by the relative influence of various interest groups. Changes in the relative influence of any interest group can be expected to result in changes in public policy; policy will move in the direction desired by the groups gaining influence and away from the desires of groups losing influence. The influence of

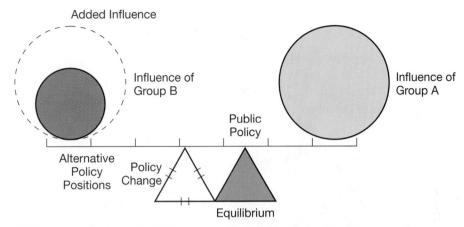

FIGURE 2–4   The Group Model The group model assumes that public policy is a balance of interest group influence; policies change when particular interest groups gain or lose influence.

groups is determined by their numbers, wealth, organizational strength, leadership, access to decision makers, and internal cohesion.[4]

The whole interest group system—the political system itself—is held together in equilibrium by several forces. First, there is a large, nearly universal, *latent group* in American society that supports the constitutional system and prevailing rules of the game. This group is not always visible but can be activated to administer overwhelming rebuke to any group that attacks the system and threatens to destroy the equilibrium.

Second, *overlapping group membership* helps to maintain the equilibrium by preventing any one group from moving too far from prevailing values. Individuals who belong to any one group also belong to other groups, and this fact moderates the demands of groups who must avoid offending their members who have other group affiliations.

Finally, the *checking and balancing resulting from group competition* also helps to maintain equilibrium in the system. No single group constitutes a majority in American society. The power of each group is checked by the power of competing groups. "Countervailing" centers of power function to check the influence of any single group and protect the individual from exploitation.

ELITE THEORY: POLICY AS ELITE PREFERENCE

Public policy may also be viewed as the preferences and values of a governing elite.[5] Although it is often asserted that public policy reflects the demands of "the people," this may express the myth rather than the reality of American democracy. Elite theory suggests that the people are apathetic and ill informed about public policy, that elites actually shape mass opinion on policy questions more than masses shape elite opinion. Thus, public policy really turns out to be the preferences of elites. Public officials and administrators merely carry out the policies decided on by the elite. Policies flow downward from elites to masses; they do not arise from mass demands (see Figure 2–5).

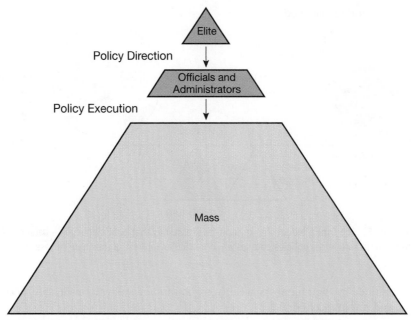

FIGURE 2–5   The Elite Model The elite model implies that public policy does not flow upward from demands by the people, but rather downward from the interests, values, and preferences of elites.

Elite theory can be summarized briefly as follows:

- Society is divided into the few who have power and the many who do not. Only a small number of persons allocate values for society; the masses do not decide public policy.
- The few who govern are not typical of the masses who are governed. Elites are drawn disproportionately from the upper socioeconomic strata of society.
- The movement of nonelites to elite positions must be slow and continuous to maintain stability and avoid revolution. Only nonelites who have accepted the basic elite consensus can be admitted to governing circles.
- Elites share consensus on behalf of the basic values of the social system and the preservation of the system. In America, the bases of elite consensus are the sanctity of private property, limited government, and individual liberty.
- Public policy does not reflect the demands of masses but rather the prevailing values of the elite. Changes in public policy will be incremental rather than revolutionary.
- Active elites are subject to relatively little direct influence from apathetic masses. Elites influence masses more than masses influence elites.

What are the implications of elite theory for policy analysis? Elitism implies that public policy does not reflect the demands of the people so much as it does the interests, values, and preferences of elites. Therefore, change and innovations in public policy come about as a result of redefinitions by elites of their own values. Because of the general conservatism of elites—that is, their interest in preserving the system—change in public policy will be incremental rather than revolutionary. Changes in the political system occur when events threaten the system, and elites, acting on the basis of enlightened self-interest, institute reforms to preserve the system and their place in it. The values of elites may be very "public regarding." A sense of *noblesse oblige* may permeate elite values, and the welfare of the masses may be an important element in elite decision making. Elitism does not necessarily mean that public policy will be hostile toward mass welfare but only that the responsibility for mass welfare rests on the shoulders of elites, not masses.

Elite Theory: Applying the Model
Chapter 12, "International Trade and Immigration: Elite–Mass Conflict," expands on the elite model by arguing that when elite preferences differ from those of the masses, the preferences of elites prevail. Chapter 14, "Civil Rights: Elite and Mass Interaction," portrays the civil rights movement as an effort by established national elites to extend equality of opportunity to blacks. Opposition to civil rights policies is found among white masses in the states.

PUBLIC CHOICE THEORY: POLICY AS COLLECTIVE DECISION MAKING BY SELF-INTERESTED INDIVIDUALS

Public choice is the economic study of nonmarket decision making, especially the application of economic analyses to public policymaking. Traditionally, economics studied behavior in the marketplace and assumed that individuals pursued their private interests; political science studied behavior in the public arena and assumed that individuals pursued their own notion of the public interest. Thus, separate versions of human motivation developed in economics and political science: the idea of *homo economicus* assumed a self-interested actor seeking to maximize personal benefits; that of *homo politicus* assumed a public-spirited actor seeking to maximize societal welfare.

But public choice theory challenges the notion that individuals act differently in politics from the way they do in the marketplace. This theory assumes that all political actors—voters, taxpayers, candidates, legislators, bureaucrats, interest groups, parties, and governments—*seek to maximize their personal benefits in politics as well as in the marketplace*. James Buchanan, the Nobel Prize–winning economist and leading scholar in modern public choice theory, argues that individuals come together in politics for their own mutual benefit, just as they come together in the marketplace; and by agreement (contract) among themselves they can enhance their own well-being, in the same way as by trading in the marketplace.[6] In short, people pursue their self-interest in both politics and the marketplace, but even with selfish motives they can mutually benefit through collective decision making.

Government itself arises from a *social contract* among individuals who agree for their mutual benefit to obey laws and support the government in exchange for protection of their own lives, liberties, and property. Thus, public choice theorists claim to be intellectual heirs to the English political philosopher John Locke, as well as to Thomas Jefferson, who incorporated this social contract notion into the American Declaration of Independence. Enlightened self-interest leads individuals to a constitutional contract establishing a government to protect life, liberty, and property.

Public choice theory recognizes that government must perform certain functions that the marketplace is unable to handle; that is, it must remedy certain "market failures." First, government must provide *public goods*—goods and services that must be supplied to everyone if they are supplied to anyone. The market cannot provide public goods because their costs exceed their value to any single buyer, and a single buyer would not be in a position to keep nonbuyers

Pollution as an Ugly "Externality" Beach litter at the Pembrookshire National Park creates an ugly scene. Public choice theory views pollution as an "externality," a failure of the marketplace and a justification for government intervention. Externalities are created when persons, firms, or governments impose uncompensated costs on others.   (© Andrew Davies/Specialist Stock/Corbis)

Public Choice: Applying the Model
The public choice theory is employed in Chapter 13, "Energy and the Environment: Externalities and Interests," to aid in recognizing environmental pollution as a problem in the control of externalities in human activity. Public choice theory also helps us to understand the behavior of environmental interest groups in dramatizing and publicizing their cause.

from using it. National defense is the most common example: protection from foreign invasion is too expensive for a single person to buy, and once it is provided no one can be excluded from its benefits. So people must act collectively through government to provide for the common defense. Second, *externalities* are another recognized market failure and justification for government intervention. An externality occurs when an activity of one individual, firm, or local government imposes uncompensated costs on others. The most common examples are air and water pollution: the discharge of air and water pollutants imposes costs on others. Governments respond by either regulating the activities that produce externalities or imposing penalties (fines) on these activities to compensate for their costs to society.

Public choice theory helps to explain why political parties and candidates generally fail to offer clear policy alternatives in election campaigns. Parties and candidates are not interested in advancing principles but rather in winning elections. They formulate their policy positions to win elections; they do not win elections to formulate policy. Thus, each party and candidate seeks policy positions that will attract the greatest number of voters.[7] *Given a unimodal distribution of opinion on any policy question* (see Figure 2–6), *parties and candidates will move toward the*

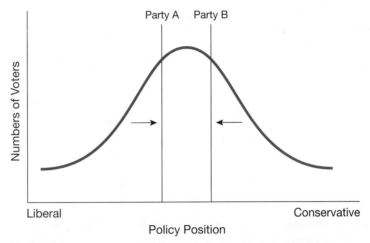

FIGURE 2–6   Public Choice: A Vote-Maximizing Model of Party Competition Public choice theory assumes that individuals and organizations seek to maximize their own benefits in politics; for example, parties and candidates whose policy views may be distinctly liberal or conservative move to the center at election time to win the most votes.

center to maximize votes. Only "ideologues" (irrational, ideologically motivated people) ignore the vote-maximizing centrist strategy.

GAME THEORY: POLICY AS RATIONAL CHOICE IN COMPETITIVE SITUATIONS

Game theory is the study of decisions in situations in which two or more *rational* participants have choices to make and the outcome depends on the choices made by each. It is applied to areas in policymaking in which there is no independently "best" choice that one can make—in which the "best" outcomes depend upon what others do.

The idea of "game" is that rational decision makers are involved in choices that are interdependent. "Players" must adjust their conduct to reflect not only their own desires and abilities but also their expectations about what others will do. Perhaps the connotation of a "game" is unfortunate, suggesting that game theory is not really appropriate for serious conflict situations. But just the opposite is true: game theory can be applied to decisions about war and peace, the use of nuclear weapons, international diplomacy, bargaining and coalition building in Congress or the United Nations, and a variety of other important political situations. A "player" may be an individual, a group, or a national government—indeed, anybody with well-defined goals who is capable of rational action.

Consider the game of "chicken." Two adolescents drive their cars toward each other at a high speed, each with one set of wheels on the center line of the highway. If neither veers off course they will crash. Whoever veers is "chicken." Both drivers prefer to avoid death, but they also want to avoid the "dishonor" of being "chicken." The outcome depends on what both drivers

The game theorist himself or herself supplies the numerical values to the payoffs. If Driver A chooses to stay on course and Driver B chooses to stay on course also, the result might be scored as –10 for both players, who wreck their cars. But if Driver A chooses to stay on course and Driver B veers, then Driver A might get +5 ("courage") and Driver B –5 ("dishonor"). If Driver A veers but Driver B stays on course, the results would be reversed. If both veer, each is dishonored slightly (–1), but not as much as when one or the other stayed on course.

		DRIVER A'S CHOICES	
		Stay on Course	Veer
	Stay on course	A: –10	A: –5
		B: –10	B: +5
DRIVER B'S CHOICES			
	Veer	A: +5	A: –1
		B: –5	B: –1

FIGURE 2–7 A Game-Theoretic Matrix for the Game of Chicken Game theory suggests that policymakers, or "players," adjust their conduct to reflect not only their own preferences but also the likely choices of opponents.

do, and each driver must try to predict how the other will behave. This form of "brinkmanship" is common in international relations (see Figure 2–7). Inspection of the payoff matrix suggests that it would be better for both drivers to veer in order to minimize the possibility of a great loss (–10). But the matrix is too simple. One or both players may place a different value on the outcomes than is suggested by the numbers. For example, one player may prefer death to dishonor in the game. Each player must try to calculate the values of the other, and neither has complete information about the values of the opponent. Moreover, bluffing or the deliberate misrepresentation of one's values or resources to an opponent is always a possibility. For example, a possible strategy in the game of chicken is to allow your opponent to see you drink heavily before the game, stumble drunkenly toward your car, and mumble something about having lived long enough in this rotten world. The effect of this communication on your opponent may increase his or her estimate of your likelihood of staying on course, and hence provide incentive for your opponent to veer and allow you to win.

An important component of game theory is the notion of *deterrence*. Deterrence is the effort to prevent an opponent from undertaking an action by inspiring fear of the consequences of the action. Players engage in deterrence when they threaten their opponents with retaliatory actions that promise to impose costs on their opponents that are far in excess of any benefits their opponents might envision by taking these actions. *Deterrence is really a psychological defense: it tries to prevent opponents from undertaking a particular action by creating in their minds the fear of costly retaliation.*

The success of deterrence depends on the credibility of the retaliatory threat and on the rationality of the opponent. Opponents must truly believe that their actions will result in retaliatory responses that inflict unacceptable costs on themselves, their people, or their nation. Opponents who do not really believe a retaliatory attack will occur are not deterred. Moreover, opponents must

Game Theory: Applying the Model
Game theory is frequently applied in international conflicts. We will explore the utility of game theory, especially the notion of deterrence, in Chapter 15, "Defense Policy: Strategies for Serious Games." We will also explore the weakness of deterrence in defending against terrorism in Chapter 16, "Homeland Security: Terrorism and Nondeterrable Threats."

be *rational*—opponents must weigh the potential costs and benefits of their actions and choose a course of action that does not result in costs that exceed gains. Opponents who are irrational—who do not consider the costs of their actions to themselves, or their people, or their nation—are not deterred.

MODELS: HOW TO TELL IF THEY ARE HELPING OR NOT

A model is merely an abstraction or representation of political life. When we think of political systems or elites or groups or rational decision making or incrementalism or games, we are abstracting from the real world in an attempt to simplify, clarify, and understand what is really important about politics. Before we begin our study of public policy, let us set forth some general criteria for evaluating the usefulness of concepts and models.

Order and Simplify Reality

Certainly the utility of a model lies in its ability to order and simplify political life so that we can think about it more clearly and understand the relationships we find in the real world. Yet too much simplification can lead to inaccuracies in our thinking about reality. On the one hand, if a concept is too narrow or identifies only superficial phenomena, we may not be able to use it to explain public policy. On the other hand, if a concept is too broad and suggests overly complex relationships, it may become so complicated and unmanageable that it is not really an aid to understanding. In other words, some theories of politics may be too complex to be helpful, while others may be too simplistic.

Identify What Is Significant

A model should also identify the really significant aspects of public policy. It should direct attention away from irrelevant variables or circumstances and focus on the real causes and significant consequences of public policy. Of course, what is "real," "relevant," or "significant" is to some extent a function of an individual's personal values. But we can all agree that the utility of a concept is related to its ability to identify what it is that is really important about politics.

Be Congruent with Reality

Generally, a model should be congruent with reality—that is, it ought to have real empirical referents. We would expect to have difficulty with a concept that identifies a process that does not really occur or symbolizes phenomena that do not exist in the real world. However, we must not be too quick to dismiss unrealistic concepts *if* they succeed in directing our attention to why they are unrealistic. For example, no one contends that government decision making is completely rational—public officials do not always act to maximize societal values and minimize societal costs. Yet the concept of rational decision making may still be useful, albeit unrealistic, if it makes us realize how irrational government decision making really is and prompts us to inquire why.

Provide Meaningful Communication

A concept or model should also communicate something meaningful. If too many people disagree over the meaning of a concept, its utility in communication is diminished. For example, if no one really agrees on what constitutes an elite, the concept of an elite does not mean the same thing to everyone. If one defines an elite as a group of democratically elected public officials who are representative of the general public, one is communicating a different idea in using the term than one who defines an elite as an unrepresentative minority that makes decisions for society based on its own interests.

Direct Inquiry and Research

A model should help to direct inquiry and research into public policy. A concept should be operational—that is, it should refer directly to real-world phenomena that can be observed, measured, and verified. A concept, or a series of interrelated concepts (which we refer to as a model), should suggest relationships in the real world that can be tested and verified. If there is no way to prove or disprove the ideas suggested by a concept, the concept is not really useful in developing a science of politics.

Suggest Explanations

Finally, a model should suggest an explanation of public policy. It should suggest hypotheses about the causes and consequences of public policy—hypotheses that can be tested against real-world data. A model that merely *describes* public policy is not as useful as one that *explains* public policy, or at least suggests some possible explanations.

SUMMARY

Political science uses a variety of conceptual models to help explain political life and public policy.

1. The process model views policymaking as a series of political activities.

2. The institutional model focuses attention on the effects of political and governmental institutions on public policy.

3. A rational model implies that government should choose policies that maximize societal gains and minimize costs.

4. An incremental model views public policy largely as a continuation of past government activities with only incremental modifications.

5. Group theory views public policy as the outcome of the struggle among societal groups.

6. The elite model views public policy as the preferences and values of the nations governing elite.

7. Public choice theory applies economic analysis to the study of public policy.

8. Game theory portrays policy as the outcome of interaction between two or more rational participants.

MySearchLab® EXERCISES

Apply what you learned in this chapter on MySearchLab (www.mysearchlab.com).

NOTES

1. See Charles E. Lindblom,"The Science of Muddling Through," *Public Administration Review,* 19 (Spring 1959), 79–88; Aaron Wildavsky, *The Politics of the Budgetary Process* (Boston: Little, Brown, 1964).

2. The classic statement on group theory is David B. Truman, *The Governmental Process* (New York: Knopf, 1951).

3. Ibid., p. 37.

4. Earl Latham,"The Group Basis of Politics," in *Political Behavior*, ed. Heinz Eulau, Samuel J. Eldersveld, and Morris Janowitz (New York: Free Press, 1956), p. 239.

5. Elite theory is explained at length in Thomas R. Dye and Harmon Zeigler, *The Irony of Democracy,* 14th ed. (Belmont, CA: Wadsworth, 2009).

6. James M. Buchanan and Gordon Tullock, *The Calculus of Consent* (Ann Arbor: University of Michigan Press, 1962).

7. Anthony Downs, *An Economic Theory of Democracy* (New York: Harper & Row, 1957).

BIBLIOGRAPHY

BUCHANAN, JAMES M., and GORDON TULLOCK. *The Calculus of Consent.* Ann Arbor: University of Michigan Press, 1962.

DAHL, ROBERT A., and BRUCE STINEBRICKNER. *Modern Political Analysis,* 6th ed. New York: Longman, 2003.

DOWNS, ANTHONY. *An Economic Theory of Democracy.* New York: Harper & Row, 1957.

DYE, THOMAS R. *Top Down Policymaking.* Washington, DC: CQ Press, 2000.

LINDBLOM, CHARLES E., and EDWARD J. WOODHOUSE. *The Policy-Making Process,* 3rd ed. New York: Longman, 1993.

TRUMAN, DAVID B. *The Government Process.* New York: Knopf, 1954.

WATSON, JOEL. *Strategy: An Introduction to Game Theory.* New York: W. W. Norton, 2001.

WILDAVSKY, AARON. *The New Politics of the Budgetary Process,* 2nd ed. New York: HarperCollins, 1992.

WEB SITES

AMERICAN POLITICAL SCIENCE ASSOCIATION. Home page of academic political scientists' professional organization. *www.apsanet.org*

PUBLIC AGENDA ONLINE. Brief guide to a variety of policy issues, including public opinion surveys on these issues. *www.publicagenda.org*

ALMANAC OF POLICY ISSUES. Background information on a variety of issues with links to sources. *www.policy-almanac.org*

POLLING REPORT. Compilation of recent public opinion polls on policy issues, political actors, government institutions, etc. *www.pollingreport.com*

THE GALLUP ORGANIZATION. Home page of the Gallup public opinion organization. *www.gallup.com*

NATIONAL CENTER FOR POLICY RESEARCH. Conservative policy research organization, with studies on a variety of policy issues. *www.nationalcenter.org*

PROGRESSIVE POLICY INSTITUTE. Liberal policy research organization, with policy briefs on a variety of issues. *www.ppionline.org*

NATIONAL ISSUES. Collection of current articles on a variety of policy issues. *www.nationalissues.com*

Presidential Policy "Initiation"   President Barack Obama delivers the annual State of the Union Address to the Congress of the United States in 2010. The State of the Union Address, together with the Budget of the United States Government, sets forth the president's policy proposals for the coming year. This constitutional obligation recognizes the president as the chief initiator of policy, with the Congress playing a deliberative role—accepting, amending, or rejecting the president's proposals. Only occasionally does the Congress attempt to assume policy leadership.   (© Brooks Kraft/Corbis)

3

The Policymaking Process
Decision-Making Activities

THE POLICY PROCESS: HOW POLICIES ARE MADE

Policy studies often focus on *how policies are made* rather than on their content or their causes and consequences. The study of how policies are made generally considers a series of activities, or *processes*, that occur within the political system. These processes, together with the activities involved and likely participants, may be portrayed as in Table 3–1.

Although it may be helpful to think about policymaking as a series of processes, in the real world these activities seldom occur in a neat, step-by-step sequence. Rather these processes often occur simultaneously, each one collapsing into the others. Different political actors and institutions—politicians, interest groups, lobbyists and legislators, executives and bureaucrats, reporters and commentators, think tanks, lawyers and judges—may be engaged in different processes at the same time, even in the same policy area. Policymaking is seldom as neat as the process model. Nonetheless, it is often useful for analytical purposes to break policymaking into component units in order to understand better how policies are made.

PROBLEM IDENTIFICATION AND AGENDA SETTING

Who decides what will be decided? The power to decide what will be a policy issue is crucial to the policymaking process. Deciding what will be the problems is even more important than deciding what will be the solutions. Many civics textbooks imply that agenda setting just "happens." It is sometimes argued that in an open plural society such as ours, channels of access and communication to government are always open, so that any problem can be discussed and placed on the agenda of national decision making. Individuals and groups, it is said, can organize themselves to assume the tasks of defining problems and suggesting solutions. People can define their own interests, organize themselves, persuade others to support their cause, gain access to government officials, influence decision making, and watch over the implementation of government policies and programs. Indeed, it is sometimes argued that the absence of political activity such as this is an indicator of satisfaction.

But, in reality, policy issues do not just "happen." Creating an issue, dramatizing it, calling attention to it, and pressuring government to do something about it are important political tactics. These tactics are employed by influential individuals, organized interest groups, policy-planning organizations, political

TABLE 3–1　Policymaking as a Process Policymaking can be seen as a process—*how* policies are made—in a step-by-step sequence; but in reality these processes overlap and intertwine.

Process	Activity	Participants
Problem Identification	Publicizing societal problems Expressing demands for 　government action	Mass media Interest groups Citizen initiatives Public opinion
⇩	⇩	⇩
Agenda Setting	Deciding what issues will be 　decided, what problems will be 　addressed by government	Elites, including president, 　Congress Candidates for elective office Mass media
⇩	⇩	⇩
Policy Formulation	Developing policy proposals to 　resolve issues and ameliorate 　problems	Think tanks President and executive office Congressional committees Interest groups
⇩	⇩	⇩
Policy Legitimation	Selecting a proposal Developing political support for it Enacting it into law Deciding on its constitutionality	Interest groups President Congress Courts
⇩	⇩	⇩
Policy Implementation	Budgeting and appropriations Organizing departments and agencies Providing payments or services Levying taxes	President and White House staff Executive departments and agencies Independent agencies and 　government corporations
⇩	⇩	⇩
Policy Evaluation	Reporting outputs of government 　programs	Executive departments and 　agencies
	Evaluating impacts of policies on 　target and nontarget groups	Congressional oversight 　committees
	Proposing changes and "reforms"	Mass media Think tanks

candidates and office-holders, and perhaps most important, the mass media. These are the tactics of "agenda setting."

AGENDA SETTING FROM THE BOTTOM UP

The prevailing model of policymaking in American political science is a popularly driven, "bottom-up" portrait of decision making. This "democratic-pluralist" model assumes that any problem can be identified by individuals or groups, by candidates seeking election, by political leaders seeking to enhance their reputation and prospects for reelection, by political parties seeking to define their principles and/or create favorable popular images of themselves, by the mass media seeking to "create" news, and even by protest groups deliberately seeking to call attention to their problems. And, of course, various crises and disasters—from natural disasters such as hurricanes and droughts to man-made tragedies such as school shootings and airplane crashes—attract public attention and compel public officials to respond.

Public Opinion and Agenda Setting

Events, and the media's reporting of them, can focus public attention on issues, problems, and "crises." Concern over terrorism dominated the public's mind following the horrific televised attacks on the World Trade Center and the Pentagon on September 11, 2001. Later, the war in Iraq became "the most important problem facing the country" according to opinion polls. Iraq appeared to be the nation's top policy issue during the congressional elections of 2006 in which opposition Democrats captured control of both houses of Congress.

But the threat of financial collapse and deep recession soon replaced all other issues on the public's agenda. The nation's "top priority" for President Barack Obama became jobs and the economy (see Table 3–2). Defending against future terrorist attacks fell to second place in the policy priorities of most Americans. Other issues—Social Security, education, healthcare, budget deficits, the poor, crime, defense, taxes—followed behind. A minority of Americans listed the environment, immigration, lobbying, and international trade as top priority issues. Global warming was last on the nation's list.

AGENDA SETTING FROM THE TOP DOWN

When V. O. Key, Jr., wrestled with the same problem confronting us—namely, the determination of the impact of popular preferences on public policy—he concluded that "the missing piece of the puzzle" was "that thin stratum of persons referred to variously as the political elite, the political activists, the leadership echelons, or the influentials."

> The longer one frets with the puzzle of how democratic regimes manage to function, the more plausible it appears that a substantial part of the explanation is to be found in the motives that activate the *leadership echelon*, the values that it holds, the rules of the political game to which it adheres, in the expectations which it entertains about its own status in society, and perhaps in some of the objective circumstances, both material and institutional, in which it functions.[1]

Popular Perceptions of Policymaking

It is interesting to note that most Americans believe that the government pays very little attention to their views on public policy and that people in government have little understanding of what people think (see Table 3–3). An overwhelming majority of Americans believe that their government is "run by a few big interests looking out for themselves" rather than "for the benefit of all of the people." And an overwhelming majority believe that the nation would be better off if public policy followed the views of citizens more closely. While policymakers often publicly express disdain for opinion polls, most Americans believe that they should pay *more* attention to them.

TABLE 3–2   Policy Priorities of the American Public I'd like to ask you some questions about priorities for President Obama and Congress this year. As I read from a list, tell me if you think the item should be a top priority, important but lower priority, not too important, or should it not be done?

	Percent Saying Top Priority
Economy	83
Jobs	81
Terrorism	80
Social Security	66
Education	65
Medicare	63
Deficit Reduction	60
Healthcare	57
Helping the Poor	53
Military	49
Energy	49
Health Insurance	49
Crime	49
Moral Decline	45
Finance Regulation	45
Environment	44
Tax Cuts	42
Immigration	40
Lobbyists	36
Trade Policy	32
Global Warming	28

SOURCE: *Pew Research Center Survey*, January 2011, *www.pollingreport.com.*

In short, most Americans believe that policy is made from the top down but should be made from the bottom up.

Elite Agenda Setting

The elitist model of agenda setting focuses on the role of leaders in business, finance, and the media, as well as in government. These leaders may observe societal developments they perceive as threatening to their own values or interests; or they may perceive opportunities to advance their own values and interests or their own careers.

According to sociologist G. William Domhoff, agenda setting "begins informally in corporate boardrooms, social clubs, and discussion groups, where problems are identified as 'issues' to be solved by new policies. It ends in government, where policies are enacted and implemented."[2] This model suggests that the initial impetus for policy change and initial resources for research, planning, and

TABLE 3–3 Popular Attitudes Toward Government Policymaking The American public is highly skeptical of politicians and people in government, believing that they should pay more attention to the public's views.

How much say do you think people like yourself have about what the government does—a good deal, some, or not much?	
A good deal	10%
Some	25
Not much	64
Would you say the government is pretty much run by a few big interests looking out for themselves or that it is run for the benefit of all the people?	
A few big interests	64%
All of the people	28
Do you think that quite a few of the people running the government are crooked, not very many are, or do you think hardly any of them are crooked?	
Quite a few	52%
Not very many	28
Hardly any	10
All (volunteered)	5
If the leaders of the nation followed the views of the public more closely, do you think that the nation would be better off or worse off than it is today?	
Better	81%
Worse	10%
Please tell me which statement you agree with most: (A) When members of Congress are thinking about how to vote on an issue, they should read up on the polls, as this can help them get a sense of the public's view on the issue. (B) When members of Congress are thinking about how to vote on an issue, they should not read the polls, because this will distract them from thinking about what is right.	
Should read the polls	67%
Should not read the polls	26%

SOURCE: *The Polling Report* (2010), *www.pollingreport.com*.

formulation of national policy are derived from corporate and personal wealth. This wealth is channeled into foundations, universities, and policy-oriented think tanks in the form of endowments, grants, and contracts. Moreover, corporate presidents, directors, and top wealth-holders also sit on the governing boards of these institutions and oversee the general direction of their work.

Political Entrepreneurship

Candidates for public office at all levels must keep their names and faces before the voters—in public appearances, interviews, speeches, and press releases. In order to do so, they must say something; that is, deliver a message or theme that creates a favorable image of themselves. Most of these campaign messages, themes, and images are largely devoid of any specific policy content, except in very general terms, for example, "stands up against the special interests," "fights for the taxpayer," or "change you can believe in." But occasionally candidates focus their campaigns on what they perceive to be issues that will motivate voters. Political challengers as well as officials seeking reelection may seize upon particular problems, publicize them, and even propose solutions. If they win the election, they may even claim a "mandate" from the people to pursue the policy direction emphasized in their campaign. Whether or not their success was in fact a product of their policy position, they may believe that they have a responsibility to put forth policy proposals consistent with their campaign messages and themes.

Opinion–Policy Linkage

The problem in assessing the independent effect of mass opinion on the actions of decision makers is that their actions help to mold mass opinion. Even when public policy is in accord with mass opinion, we can never be sure whether mass opinion shaped public policy or public policy shaped mass opinion. The distinguished American political scientist V. O. Key, Jr., wrote, "Government, as we have seen, attempts to mold public opinion toward support of the programs and policies it espouses. Given that endeavor, perfect congruence between public policy and public opinion could be government of public opinion rather than government *by* public opinion."[3]

Policy Effects

Public policy shapes public opinion more often than opinion shapes policy, for several reasons. First, few people have opinions on the great bulk of policy questions confronting the nation's decision makers. Second, public opinion is very unstable. It can change in a matter of days in response to news events precipitated by leaders. Third, leaders do not have a clear perception of mass opinion. Most communications received by decision makers are from other elites—newspersons, interest group leaders, and other influential persons—and not from ordinary citizens.

Media Effects

We must not assume that the opinions expressed in the news media are public opinion. Frequently, this is a source of confusion. Newspersons believe *they* are the public, often confusing their own opinions with public opinion. They even tell the mass public what its opinion is, thus actually helping to mold it to conform to their own beliefs. Decision makers, then, may act in response to news stories or the opinions of influential newspersons in the belief that they are responding to public opinion.

Communicating with Policymakers

Decision makers can easily misinterpret public opinion because the communications they receive have an elite bias. Members of the mass public seldom call or write their senators or representatives, much less converse with them at dinners, cocktail parties, or other social occasions. Most of the communications received by decision makers are *intraelite*, from newspersons, organized group leaders, influential constituents, wealthy political contributors, and personal friends—people who, for the most part, share the same views. It is not surprising, therefore, that members of Congress say that most of their mail is in agreement with their own position; their world of public opinion is self-reinforcing. Moreover, persons who initiate communication with decision makers, by writing or calling or visiting their representatives, are decidedly more educated and affluent than the average citizen.

The President and White House Staff

The president and the executive branch are generally expected to be the "initiators" of policy proposals, with members of Congress in the role of "arbiters" of policy alternatives. (The same division of labor is usually found at the state and local levels, with governors, mayors, and even city managers expected to formulate policy proposals and state legislators and city councils to approve, amend, or reject them.) The Constitution of the United States appears to endorse this arrangement in Article II, Section 3: "[The president] shall from time to time give to Congress information of the State of the Union, and recommend to their consideration such measures as he shall judge necessary and expedient." Each year the principal policy statements of the president come in the State of the Union message, and more importantly, in the *Budget of the United States Government*, prepared by the Office of Management and Budget (see Chapter 10). Many other policy proposals are developed by executive departments in their specialized areas; these proposals are usually transmitted to the White House for the president's approval before being sent to Congress.

Presidents have many motivations to seize the initiative in policymaking. First-term presidents must build a record of success that later can be used in their reelection campaign. They must show that they can "get things done in Washington." They must build and maintain their electoral coalition. They must show that they are capable of following through on at least some of their campaign promises. Second-term presidents are often motivated by a concern for their "place in history." They seek policy achievements that will contribute to their presidential "greatness" in history.

Congress and Legislative Staff

While Congress is generally portrayed as the "arbiter" of policy proposals initiated by others, occasionally leaders in the Congress will try to set forth their own agendas. Perhaps the most well-publicized effort in the Congress to seize the initiative in policymaking was the 1994 "Contract with America" led by then Speaker of the House Newt Gingrich. Republican House candidates across the country united behind a comprehensive set of proposals, including a balanced budget constitutional amendment, term limits for Congress, welfare reform, and so on. But despite a stunning GOP victory in the 1994 congressional elections, enthusiasm for the Contract with America quickly dissipated, and President Bill Clinton soon regained policy leadership.

Nonetheless, members of Congress sometimes serve as agenda setters. They may do so to challenge a president of the opposing party, to gain a reputation as a power broker themselves, or indeed to place on the national agenda an issue they feel requires attention. Committee chairs enjoy a special advantage in congressional agenda setting; they control the agenda of their committees' hearings. And these hearings offer the best opportunity for congressional involvement in agenda setting. Congressional staffs—committee staffs, staffs of the legislative leadership, and aides to individual legislators—often play an important role in bringing issues to the attention of their bosses.

Interest Groups

Interest groups may initiate their own policy proposals, perhaps in association with members of Congress or their staffs who share the same interest. Interest group staffs often bring valuable technical knowledge to policy formation, as well as political information about their group's position on the issues. Because Congress members and their staffs value both kinds of information, interest groups can often provide the precise language they desire in proposed bills and amendments. Thus, interest group staffs often augment the work of congressional staffs. Interest groups also provide testimony at congressional hearings as well as technical reports and analyses used by congressional staffs.

AGENDA SETTING: THE MASS MEDIA

Television is the major source of information for the vast majority of Americans. More than two-thirds report that they receive all or most of their news from television. Television is really the first form of *mass* communication, that is, communication that reaches nearly everyone, including children. More important, television presents a visual image, not merely a printed word. The visual quality of television—the emotional impact that is conveyed by pictures—enables the TV networks to convey emotions as well as information.

Media Power

The media are both players and referees in the game of politics. They not only report to the people on the struggles for power in society, but they also participate in those struggles themselves. They are an elite group, competing for power alongside the more traditional leadership groups from business, labor, government, and other sectors of society. As political journalist Theodore White once observed, "The power of the press in America is a primordial one. It sets the agenda of public discussion; and this sweeping power is unrestrained by any law. It determines what people will talk about and think about—an authority that in other nations is reserved for tyrants, priests, parties, and mandarins."[4]

The Media Focus on the President   President Barack Obama confronts the media on Air Force One. The president is in near constant contact with the press and television; more media space and time are devoted to the president than any other figure in America. Presidents and politicians are said to have a "love/hate" relationship with the media, as they try to use the media for their own purposes, even as the media pursues its own agenda.   (© Brooks Kraft/Corbis)

Media power is concentrated in the hands of a relatively small number of people: the editors, producers, anchors, reporters, and columnists of the leading television networks (ABC, CBS, NBC, FOX, and CNN) and the prestigious press (*New York Times, Washington Post, Wall Street Journal*). Producers and editors generally work behind the scenes, and many influential print journalists are known only by their bylines. But most Americans have come to recognize the faces of the television network anchors and leading reporters. These media people are courted by politicians, treated as celebrities, studied by scholars, and known to millions of Americans by their television images.

Newsmaking

Newsmaking involves all-important decisions about what is "news" and who is "newsworthy." Television executives and producers and newspaper and magazine editors must decide what people, organizations, and events will be given attention—attention that makes these topics matters of general public concern and political action. Without media coverage the general public would not know about these personalities, organizations, or events. They would not become objects of political discussion, nor would they be likely to be considered important by government officials.

Media attention can create issues and personalities. Media inattention can doom issues and personalities to obscurity. The TV camera cannot be "a picture of the world" because the whole world cannot squeeze into the picture. News executives must sort through a tremendous surplus of information and decide what is to be "news."

In addition to deciding what is and what is not news, news executives provide cues to mass audiences about the importance of an issue, personality, or event. Some matters are covered prominently by the media, with early placement on a newscast and several minutes of time, or with front-page newspaper coverage, including big headlines and pictures. The amount of coverage tells us what is important and what is not.

Of course, politicians, professional public relations people, interest group spokespersons, and various aspiring celebrities all know that the decisions of the media are vital to the success of their issue, their organization, and themselves. So they try to attract media attention by deliberately engaging in behavior or manufacturing situations that are likely to win coverage. The result is the "media event"—an activity arranged primarily to stimulate coverage and thereby attract public attention to an issue or individual. Generally, the more bizarre, dramatic, and sensational it is, the more likely it is to attract coverage. A media event may be a press conference to which reporters from the television stations and newspapers are invited by public figures—even when there is really no news to announce. Or it may be a staged debate, confrontation, or illustration of injustice. Political candidates may visit coal mines, ghetto neighborhoods, and sites of fires or other disasters. Sometimes protests, demonstrations, and even violence have been staged primarily as media events to dramatize and communicate grievances.

Media Bias

In exercising their judgment regarding which stories should be given television time or newspaper space, media executives must rely on their own political values and economic interests as guidelines. In general, these executives are more liberal in their views than other segments of the nation's leadership. Topics selected weeks in advance for coverage reflect, or often create, current liberal issues: concern for problems affecting the poor and minorities, women's issues, opposition to defense spending, environmental concerns, and so forth. But liberalism is not the major source of bias in the news.

The principal source of distortion in the news is caused by the need for drama, action, and confrontation to hold audience attention. Television must entertain. To capture the attention of jaded audiences, news must be selected on the basis of emotional rhetoric, shocking incidents, dramatic conflict, overdrawn stereotypes. Race, sex, violence, and corruption in government are favorite topics because of popular interest. More complex problems such as inflation, government spending, and foreign policy must either be simplified and dramatized or ignored. To dramatize an issue, news executives must find or create a dramatic incident; tape it; transport, process, and edit the tape; and write a script for the introduction, the "voice-over," and the "recapitulation." All this means that most "news" must be created well in advance of scheduled broadcasting.

Media Effects

Media effects can be categorized as (1) identifying issues and setting the agenda for policymakers, (2) influencing attitudes and values toward policy issues, and (3) changing the behavior of voters and decision makers. These categories are ranked by the degree of influence the media are likely to have over their audiences. The power of television does not really lie in persuading viewers to take one side of an issue or another. Instead, *the power of television lies in setting the agenda for decision making*—deciding what issues will be given attention and what issues will be ignored.

The media can create new opinions more easily than they can change existing ones. They can often suggest how we feel about new events or issues—those for which we have no prior feelings or experiences. And the media can reinforce values and attitudes that we already hold. But there is very little evidence that the media can change existing values.

The viewer's psychological mechanism of *selective perception* helps to defend against bias in news and entertainment programming. Selective perception means mentally screening out information or images with which one disagrees. It causes people to tend to see and hear only what they want to see and hear. It reduces the impact of television bias on viewers' attitudes and behavior.

FORMULATING POLICY

Policy formulation is the development of policy alternatives for dealing with problems on the public agenda. Policy formulation occurs in government bureaucracies; interest group offices; legislative committee rooms; meetings of special commissions; and policy-planning organizations, otherwise known as think tanks. The details of policy proposals are usually formulated by staff members rather than by their bosses, but staffs are guided by what they know their leaders want.

Think Tanks

Policy-planning organizations are central coordinating points in the policy-making process. Certain policy-planning groups—for example, the Council on Foreign Relations, the American Enterprise Institute, the Heritage Foundation, Center for American Progress, and the Brookings Institution—are influential in a wide range of key policy areas.

These organizations bring together the leadership of corporate and financial institutions, the foundations, the mass media, the leading intellectuals, and influential figures in the government. They review the relevant university and foundation-supported research on topics of interest, and more important, they try to reach a consensus about what action should be taken on national problems under study. Their goal is to develop action recommendations—explicit policies or programs designed to resolve national problems. These policy recommendations of the key policy-planning groups are distributed to the mass media, federal executive agencies, and Congress. The purpose is to lay the groundwork for making policy into law.

The following are among the more influential think tanks:

The Brookings Institution.   The Brookings Institution has long been the dominant policy-planning group for American domestic policy, despite the growing influence of competing think tanks over the years. Brookings staffers dislike its reputation as a liberal think tank, and they deny that Brookings tries to set national priorities. Yet the Brookings Institution has been very influential in planning the War on Poverty, welfare reform, national defense, and taxing and spending policies. The *New York Times* columnist and Harvard historian writing team, Leonard Silk and Mark Silk, describe Brookings as the central locus of the Washington "policy network," where it does "its communicating: over lunch, whether informally in the Brookings cafeteria or at the regular Friday lunch around a great oval table at which the staff and their guests keen over the events of the week like the chorus of an ancient Greek tragedy; through consulting, paid or unpaid, for government or business at conferences, in the advanced studies program; and, over time, by means of the revolving door of government employment."[5]

The American Enterprise Institute.   For many years Republicans dreamed of a "Brookings Institution for Republicans" that would help offset the liberal bias of Brookings itself. In the late 1970s, that role was assumed by the American Enterprise Institute (AEI). The AEI appeals to both Democrats and Republicans who have doubts about big government. President William Baroody, Jr., distinguished the AEI from Brookings: "In confronting societal problems those who tend to gravitate to the AEI orbit would be inclined to look first for a market solution . . . while the other orbit people have a tendency to look for a government solution."[6]

The Heritage Foundation.   Conservative ideologues have never been welcome in the Washington establishment. Yet influential conservative businesspersons gradually came to understand that without an institutional base in Washington, they could never establish a strong and continuing influence in the policy network. So they set about the task of "building a solid institutional base" and "establishing a reputation for reliable scholarship and creative problem solving."[7] The result of their efforts was the Heritage Foundation.

Center for American Progress.   On the left of the political spectrum is the newly influential Center for American Progress (CAP), the intellectual source of policy "change" in the Obama Administration. CAP is funded largely by George Soros, the billionaire sponsor of MoveOn.org and other flourishing left-liberal outlets. It was founded in 2003 by John Podesta, former chief of staff to President Bill Clinton, and designed to give the "progressive" movement the same ideological influence in the Obama Administration as the Heritage Foundation exercised in the Reagan Administration.[8] CAP promises to "engage in a war of ideas with conservatives," and to be more active on behalf of progressive policies than the more scholarly Brookings Institution.

The Council on Foreign Relations.   Political scientist Lester Milbraith observes that the influence of the Council on Foreign Relations (CFR) throughout government is so pervasive that it is difficult to distinguish the CFR from government programs: "The Council on Foreign Relations, while not financed by government, works so closely with it that it is difficult to distinguish Council actions stimulated by government from autonomous actions."[9] The CFR itself, of course, denies that it exercises any control over U.S. foreign policy. Indeed, its bylaws declare, "The Council shall not take any position on questions of foreign policy and no person is authorized to speak or purport to speak for the Council on such matters."[10] But policy initiation and consensus building do not require the CFR to officially adopt policy positions. Many foreign policy decisions are first aired in the CFR's prestigious publication, *Foreign Affairs.*[11]

INTEREST GROUPS AND POLICYMAKING

Washington is awash in special interest groups, lawyers and law firms, lobbyists, and influence peddlers. Interest groups are active in both policy formulation and policy legitimating. Organized interests frequently develop policy proposals of their own and forward them to the White House or to members of Congress or the mass media to place on the agenda of decision making. And they are even more active in policy legitimating. Indeed, political life in Washington is a blur of "lobbying," "fund-raising," "opening doors," "mobilizing grassroots support," "rubbing elbows," and "schmoozing."

Interest groups influence government policy in a variety of ways. It is possible to categorize efforts to influence government policy as follows:

1. Direct lobbying, including testifying at committee hearings, contacting government offices directly, presenting research results, and assisting in the writing of legislation
2. Campaign contributions made through political action committees (PACs)
3. Interpersonal contacts, including travel, recreation, entertainment, and general "schmoozing," as well as the "revolving door" exchange of personnel between government offices and the industries and organizations representing them
4. Litigation designed to force changes in policies through the court system, wherein interest groups and their lawyers bring class-action suits on behalf of their clients or file *amicus curiae* (friend of the court) arguments in cases in which they are interested
5. Grassroots mobilization efforts to influence Congress and the White House by encouraging letters, calls, and visits by individual constituents and campaign contributors

Lobbying

Washington's influence industry is a billion-dollar business. Each year lobbyists spend almost $3 billion trying to influence policy—more than $5 million for each member of Congress![12]

The U.S. Chamber of Commerce regularly ranks at the top of the lobbying spenders. At the industry group level, pharmaceutical and health product manufacturers spend a great deal on lobbying. The insurance industry also ranks high in direct lobbying expenditures, followed by telephone utilities, the oil and gas industry, the defense industry, and electric utilities (see Table 3–4).

**TABLE 3–4   Washington's Top Lobbying Spenders*
Lobbying is a $3 billion business in Washington.

Rank*	Organization
1	US Chamber of Commerce
2	American Medical Assn
3	General Electric
4	Pharmaceutical Rsrch & Mfrs of America
5	AARP
6	American Hospital Assn
7	AT&T Inc
8	Northrop Grumman
9	Blue Cross/Blue Shield
10	National Assn of Realtors
11	Exxon Mobil
12	Verizon Communications
13	Edison Electric Institute
14	Business Roundtable
15	Boeing Co
16	Lockheed Martin
17	PG&E Corp
18	Southern Co
19	General Motors
20	Pfizer Inc

SOURCE: Center for Responsive Politics, accessed January, 2011, *www.crp.org*.
*Rankings are for 1998 through 2010.   (OpenSecrets.org)

It is important to note that direct lobbying expenditures provide only one indicator of an industry's or corporation's clout in Washington. Effective lobbying also requires backup by campaign contributions and in-kind services, election endorsements, and grassroots political support. For example, a survey of Washington insiders conducted by *Fortune* ranked the AARP, the American Israel Public Affairs Committee, and the AFL-CIO as the three most powerful lobbies in Congress.[13] Indeed, only about one-half of the magazine's designated "Power Twenty-Five" were industry lobbies; others included the National Rifle Association, the Christian Coalition, the National Right to Life Committee, independent unions (NEA, AFSCME, Teamsters), and veterans' groups.

Occasionally, when Congress is embarrassed by media reports on extravagant lobbyist-paid travel, vacations, dinners, parties, and other perks, cries are heard for new restrictions on lobbying expenditures. Another reform frequently advocated is the elimination of "earmarking" of particular spending items in larger appropriations bills—items that are heavily lobbied for, yet often are overlooked by most members of Congress when voting on appropriations bills.

PACs

Contributions virtually ensure access to government decision makers. It is highly unlikely that any member of Congress will fail to meet with representatives of groups that helped to fund his or her election. And top White House staff and cabinet officials, if not the president, are almost always prepared to meet with interests that have made significant contributions to the presidential campaign. Contributions do not guarantee a favorable decision, but they can be counted on to guarantee a hearing.

Political action committees (PACs) solicit and receive contributions from members of organizations—unions, corporations, professional and trade associations, as well as ideological, environmental, and issue-oriented groups—and then distribute these funds to political candidates. PACs are regulated by the Federal Elections Commission, which requires them to register their finances and political contributions, and limits their contributions to $5,000 to any candidate per election.

PAC contributions are heavily weighted toward incumbents running for reelection. Usually two-thirds of all PAC contributions go to incumbents; this is true for corporate as well as union and other PACs. PACs are well aware that more than 90 percent of incumbent members of Congress seeking reelection win. Labor unions make heavy use of PACs; union PAC money is heavily weighted toward Democrats (see Table 3–5).

Assessing Interest Group Influence

Most Americans believe that interest group PACs, as well as big corporations, the news media, and lobbyists, "have too much power and influence on Washington."[14] But it is difficult to assess exactly how much power interest groups actually wield in the nation's capital. First of all, the views of members of Congress may coincide with the positions of interest groups independently of any direct lobbying efforts or campaign contributions. Second, the most important effects of interest group efforts may not be found on roll call votes but rather on various earlier stages of the legislative process, including behind-the-scenes negotiations over specific provisions, the drafting of amendments, and the markup of bills in committees and subcommittees. Third, interest group lobbying may have its greatest effect on the details of specific legislation rather than on overall policy directions. Finally, party leadership, constituency influence, and the personal views of the members of Congress all combine to modify the independent effect of interest group activities.

POLICY LEGITIMATION: THE PROXIMATE POLICYMAKERS

What is the role of the "proximate policymakers"? The activities of these policymakers—the president, Congress, courts, federal agencies, congressional committees, White House staff, and interest groups—have traditionally been the central focus of political science and are usually portrayed as the whole of the policymaking process. But the activities of the proximate policymakers are only the final phase of a much more complex process. This final stage is the open, public stage of the policymaking process, and it attracts the attention of the mass media and most political scientists. The activities of the proximate policymakers are much easier to study than the private actions of corporations, foundations, the mass media, and the policy-planning organizations.

Formal Lawmaking Process

Congress is designated in the U.S. Constitution as the principal instrument of policy legitimation. Article I describes the national government's powers (for example, "to lay and collect Taxes, Duties, Imposts and Excises") as powers of *Congress*. It is important to note, however, that

TABLE 3–5 Top PAC Spenders* In addition to lobbying spending, businesses, trade associations, and labor unions contribute billions to political campaigns through political action committees (PACs).

Rank	PAC Name	Percentage Given to:	
		Democrats	Republicans
1	National Assn of Realtors	57%	43%
2	Honeywell International	55%	45%
3	AT&T Inc	47%	53%
4	Intl Brotherhood of Electrical Workers	98%	2%
5	National Beer Wholesalers Assn	56%	44%
6	American Assn for Justice (trial lawyers)	97%	3%
7	American Bankers Assn	33%	66%
8	American Federation of Teachers	99%	0%
9	American Fedn of St/Cnty/Munic Employees	99%	0%
10	Operating Engineers Union	90%	10%
11	Teamsters Union	97%	2%
12	National Auto Dealers Assn	47%	53%
13	Credit Union National Assn	58%	41%
14	Boeing Co	54%	45%
15	Laborers Union	96%	4%
16	Carpenters & Joiners Union	87%	13%
17	American Crystal Sugar	68%	32%
18	International Assn of Fire Fighters	83%	16%
19	Plumbers/Pipefitters Union	96%	2%
20	Machinists/Aerospace Workers Union	98%	2%

SOURCE: Center for Responsive Politics, accessed January 2011, *www.crp.org.*
*Rankings are for 2009–2010.   (OpenSecrets.org)

Congress is not the exclusive repository of policy legitimacy. Courts also bear a heavy responsibility to maintain the legitimacy of governmental authority, and to a somewhat lesser extent, so do administrative bureaucracies. By focusing attention on the Congress in the policy legitimation process, we do not mean to detract from the importance of other governmental institutions in maintaining legitimacy.

Congress has developed highly institutionalized rules and procedures to help legitimate its actions. Indeed, its rules and procedures have become so elaborate that proposed policy changes are extremely difficult. Very few of the bills introduced in Congress are passed; in a typical two-year session more than 10,000 bills will be introduced, but fewer than 800 (less than 10 percent) will be enacted in any form. Congress is accurately perceived more as an obstacle to, than a facilitator of, policy change.

The formal process of lawmaking is outlined in Figure 3–1. The familiar path is taught in virtually every high school and college government class in America. But this outline of the formal lawmaking process fails to describe the role of parties and leadership in guiding legislation in the

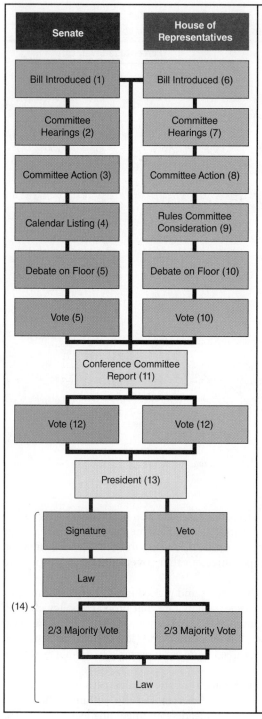

1. **Introduction.** Most bills can be introduced in either house. (In this example, the bill is first introduced in the Senate.) It is given a number and referred to the proper committee.

2. **Hearings.** The committee may hold public hearings on the bill.

3. **Committee action.** The full committee meets in executive (closed) session. It may kill the bill, approve it with or without amendments, or draft a new bill.

4. **Calendar.** If the committee recommends the bill for passage, it is listed on the calendar.

5. **Debate, amendment, vote.** The bill goes to the floor for debate. Amendments may be added. The bill is voted on.

6. **Introduction to the second house.** If the bill passes, it goes to the House of Representatives, where it is referred to the proper committee.

7. **Hearings.** Hearings may be held again.

8. **Committee action.** The committee rejects the bill, prepares a new one, or accepts the bill with or without amendments.

9. **Rules Committee consideration.** If the committee recommends the bill, it is listed on the calendar and sent to the Rules Committee. The Rules Committee can block a bill or clear it for debate before the entire House.

10. **Debate, amendment, vote.** The bill goes before the entire body and is debated and voted upon.

11. **Conference Committee.** If the bill as passed by the second house contains major changes, either house may request a conference committee. The conference—five persons from each house, representing both parties—meets and tries to reconcile its differences.

12. **Vote on conference report.** When committee members reach an agreement, they report back to their respective houses. Their report is either accepted or rejected.

13. **Submission to the president.** If the report is accepted by both houses, the bill is signed by the Speaker of the House and the president of the Senate and is sent to the president of the United States.

14. **Presidential action.** The president may sign or veto the bill within ten days. If the president does not sign and Congress is still in session, the bill automatically becomes law. If Congress adjourns before the ten days have elapsed, it does not become law. (This is called the "pocket veto.") If the president returns the bill with a veto message, it may still become a law if passed by a two-thirds majority in each house.

FIGURE 3–1   How a Bill Becomes a Law The formal process by which a bill becomes a law is complex, making it easier to defeat a bill than to pass a bill.

House and Senate, the influence of constituents and interest groups, the influence of the president and White House staff, and, above all, the continuing pressing need of members of Congress to raise money for their reelection campaigns.

Party Influence

Party loyalty is stronger among members of Congress and other political activists than it is among voters. Party votes—roll call votes in the House and Senate on which a majority of Democrats vote in opposition to a majority of Republicans—occur on more than half the roll call votes in Congress. Indeed, party votes appear to have risen in recent years, indicating an increase in partisanship in Washington. Party unity in Congress—the average percentage of support among members of each party for their party's position on party votes—is also fairly high. On average, both the Democratic and Republican parties can expect more than 80 percent of their members to support their party on a party line vote.

It is true, of course, that party loyalty and party line voting in the Congress may not necessarily be a product of party loyalty or discipline. They may result more from ideological or issue agreement among members of each party.

The social bases in the electorate of the Democratic and Republican parties are slightly different. Both parties draw support from all social groups in America, but the Democrats draw disproportionately from labor, big-city residents, ethnic voters, blacks, Jews, and Catholics; Republicans draw disproportionately from rural, small-town, and suburban Protestants, businesspeople, and professionals. To the extent that the policy orientations of these two broad groups differ, the thrust of party ideology also differs.

What are the issues that cause conflict between the Democratic and Republican parties? In general, Democrats have favored federal action to assist low-income groups through public assistance, housing, and antipoverty programs, and generally a larger role for the federal government in launching new projects to remedy domestic problems. Republicans, in contrast, have favored less government involvement in domestic affairs, lower taxes, and greater reliance on private action.

Presidential Influence

Presidents are expected to set forth policy initiatives in speeches, in messages to the Congress (including the annual State of the Union message), and in the annual Budget of the United States Government. Presidents and their chief advisers regularly sift through policies formulated in think tanks and policy-planning organizations, developed in the offices of interest groups, law firms, and lobbyists, and suggested by heavy campaign contributors in the course of preparing a White House legislative agenda.

But a president's success in getting legislation enacted into law is closely tied to party control of the Congress. Presidents are far more successful when they can work with a Congress controlled by their own party. Presidential "box scores"—the percentage of policy initiatives on which the president took a clear-cut position that is enacted into law by the Congress—depend primarily on whether or not the president's party controls one or both houses of Congress (see Figure 3–2). President Barack Obama's success in Congress was closely tied to the large Democratic majorities in both the House and Senate in his first two years. The capture of control of the House of Representatives by Republicans in the midterm congressional election of 2010 promises a slowdown of the Obama policy agenda.

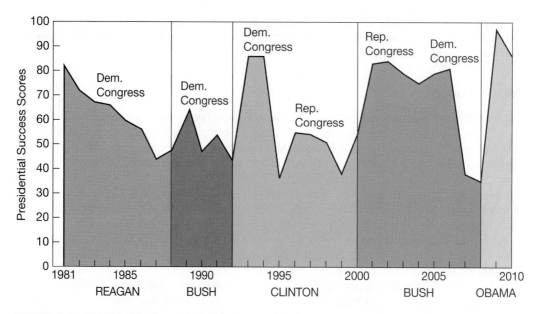

FIGURE 3–2 Presidential Support in Congress A president's success in getting his legislation enacted by Congress is most heavily influenced by whether or not his party controls the House or Senate or both bodies. SOURCE: *Congressional Quarterly,* various issues.

Presidents are more successful in stopping legislation they oppose than in getting legislation they support passed by the Congress. The veto is the president's most important weapon in dealing with Congress. Even the threat of the veto greatly enhances the president's legislative power. A bill vetoed by the president can be passed into law only by the two-thirds vote of both houses of Congress. Seldom is a president so weak that he cannot hold the loyalty of at least one-third of either the House or the Senate. From George Washington to Barack Obama, more than 96 percent of all presidential vetoes have been sustained.

Constituency Influence

Members of Congress like to think of themselves as independent-minded, public-spirited "trustees" rather then merely message-carrying "delegates" sent to Washington by their districts' voters. The philosophical justification for this notion was offered by the English parliamentarian Edmund Burke more than 200 years ago in a speech to his constituents: "Your representative owes you, not his industry only, but his judgment; and betrays, instead of serving you, if he sacrifices it to your opinion."[15]

But the rationale for Congress members' independence from constituency influence may not be so noble as that implied by Burke. Members know that their constituents are largely unaware of their voting records in Congress. Only occasionally, on a highly publicized vote, where home state or district feelings are intense, will a member defer to constituents' views over those of their party's leadership and campaign-cash-contributing interest groups. On most issues, members are free to ignore their constituents: "They don't know much about my votes. Most of what they know is what I tell them. They know more of what kind of a guy I am. It comes through in my letters: 'You care about the little guy.'"[16] A long record of "home-style" politics—doing casework for constituents, performing favors, winning pork-barrel projects for the district, making frequent visits back home to "press the flesh"—can protect members from any opposition that might be generated by their voting records.

Contributor Influence

The cost of running for Congress today virtually guarantees the dependency of its members on heavy campaign contributors. The average incumbent House member now spends nearly $1.5 million running for office *every two years*. The average incumbent U.S. senator spends more than $10 million to maintain his or her seat, and the price tag in some big states can run $50 million or more.

Corporations, interest group PACs, and individual "fat cats" have become the real constituents of Congress (see Table 3–6). Large corporate and individual donors, together with interest group PACs, constitute more than two-thirds of the campaign cash flowing into congressional elections. Small individual donors ($500 or less) provide less than one-third of campaign funds. Most members of Congress spend hours each day making fund-raising calls from their offices on Capitol Hill. "Making your calls" is a basic responsibility of the job.

Throughout the lawmaking process, big campaign contributors expect to be able to call or visit and present their views directly to the officeholders they supported. At the presidential level, major contributors expect to get a meeting with the president or at least with high-level White House staff or cabinet members. At the congressional level, major contributors usually expect to meet directly with representatives and senators. Members of Congress frequently boast of responding to letters, calls, or visits by any constituent. But big contributors expect "face time" with the political leaders they help keep in office.

Campaign contributions are rarely made on a direct quid pro quo basis—that is, direct dollar payments in exchange for sponsoring a bill in Congress or for voting for or against a bill in committee or on the floor. Such direct trade-offs risk exposure as bribery and may be prosecuted under law. Bribery, where it occurs, is probably limited to very narrow and specific policy actions: payments to intervene in a particular case before an administrative agency, payments to insert a very specific break in a tax law or a specific exemption in a trade bill, payments to obtain a specific contract with the government. Bribery on major issues is very unlikely; there is simply too much publicity and too much risk of exposure. But Congress members are smart enough to know what issues concern the contributors and how to vote in order to keep the contributions coming in the future.

THE BUDGETARY AND APPROPRIATIONS PROCESSES

A great deal of policymaking occurs in the budgetary and appropriations processes. Congress may *authorize* policies and programs in legislation, but congress must separately *appropriate* funds to implement the legislation.

The Constitution gives the president no formal powers over taxing and spending. Constitutionally all the president can do is "make recommendations" to Congress. It is difficult to imagine that prior to 1921 the president played no direct role in the budget process. The Secretary of the Treasury compiled the estimates of the individual agencies, and these were sent, without revision, to Congress for its consideration. It was not until the Budget and Accounting Act of 1921 that the president acquired responsibility for budget formulation and thus developed a means of directly influencing spending policy.

TABLE 3–6   All-Time Big-Money Contributors   The cost of running for Congress has skyrocketed, making Congress members ever more dependent on contributions from big corporations and labor unions.

Rank	Organization Name	1989–2010		Rank	Organization Name	1989–2010	
		Dems	Repubs			Dems	Repubs
1	ActBlue (Democratic Party)	99%	0%	25	EMILY's List	99%	0%
2	AT&T Inc	44%	55%	26	National Beer Wholesalers Assn	33%	66%
3	American Fedn of State, County & Municipal Employees	98%	1%	27	Microsoft Corp	53%	46%
4	National Assn of Realtors	49%	50%	28	National Assn of Letter Carriers	88%	10%
5	Goldman Sachs	62%	37%	29	JPMorgan Chase & Co	50%	48%
6	American Assn for Justice (trial lawyers)	90%	8%	30	Time Warner	72%	27%
7	Intl Brotherhood of Electrical Workers	97%	2%	31	Morgan Stanley	44%	54%
8	National Education Assn	93%	6%	32	Lockheed Martin	43%	56%
9	Laborers Union	92%	7%	33	General Electric	51%	48%
10	Service Employees International Union	95%	3%	34	Verizon Communications	40%	58%
11	Teamsters Union	93%	6%	35	AFL-CIO	95%	4%
12	Carpenters & Joiners Union	89%	10%	36	Credit Union National Assn	48%	50%
13	American Federation of Teachers	98%	0%	37	FedEx Corp	40%	58%
14	Communications Workers of America	98%	0%	38	Bank of America	46%	53%
15	Citigroup Inc	50%	49%	39	National Rifle Assn	17%	82%
16	American Medical Assn	39%	59%	40	Ernst & Young	44%	55%
17	United Auto Workers	98%	0%	41	Blue Cross/Blue Shield	39%	60%
18	Machinists & Aerospace Workers Union	98%	0%	42	Sheet Metal Workers Union	97%	1%
19	National Auto Dealers Assn	32%	67%	43	American Hospital Assn	53%	45%
20	United Parcel Service	36%	62%	44	Plumbers & Pipefitters Union	94%	4%
21	United Food & Commercial Workers Union	98%	1%	45	Deloitte Touche Tohmatsu	35%	64%
22	Altria Group	27%	72%	46	American Dental Assn	46%	53%
23	American Bankers Assn	40%	59%	47	International Assn of Fire Fighters	82%	17%
24	National Assn of Home Builders	35%	63%	48	PricewaterhouseCoopers	37%	62%
				49	Operating Engineers Union	85%	13%
				50	Air Line Pilots Assn	84%	15%

SOURCE: Center for Responsive Politics, "Top All-Time Donor Profiles," *www.opensecrets.org*.

OMB—Preparing the Presidential Budget

The president, through the Office of Management and Budget (OMB), located in the Executive Office, has the key responsibility for budget preparation. Work on the fiscal budget starts more than a year before the beginning of the fiscal year for which it is intended. After preliminary consultation with the executive agencies and in accord with presidential policy, the OMB develops targets or ceilings within which the agencies are encouraged to build their requests. This work begins a full sixteen to eighteen months before the beginning of the fiscal year for which the budget is being prepared. (In other words, work would begin in January 2002 on the budget for the fiscal year beginning October 1, 2013, and ending September 30, 2014.) Budgets are named for the fiscal year in which they end, so this example describes the work on the *Budget of the United States Government, 2014* or more simply, "FY14."

Budget materials and instructions go to the agencies with the request that the forms be completed and returned to the OMB. The heads of agencies are expected to submit their completed requests to the OMB by mid-September or early October. Occasionally a schedule of "over ceiling" items (requests above the suggested ceilings) will be included.

With the requests of the spending agencies at hand, the OMB begins its own budget review. Hearings are given to each agency. Top agency officials support their requests as convincingly as possible. On rare occasions dissatisfied agencies may ask the budget director to take their cases to the president.

In December, the president and the OMB director will devote time to the document, which by now is approaching its final stages of assembly. They and their staffs will "blue-pencil," revise, and make last-minute changes as well as prepare the president's message, which accompanies the budget to Congress. After the budget is in legislative hands, the president may recommend further alterations as needs dictate.

Although the completed document includes a revenue plan with general estimates for taxes and other income, it is primarily an expenditure budget. Revenue and tax policy staff work centers in the Treasury Department and not in the OMB. In late January or early February the president presents the *Budget of the United States Government* for the fiscal year beginning October 1 to Congress.

House and Senate Budget Committees

In an effort to consider the budget as a whole, Congress established House and Senate budget committees and a Congressional Budget Office (CBO) to review the president's budget after its submission to Congress. These committees draft a first budget resolution (due May 15) setting forth target goals to guide committee actions on specific appropriation and revenue measures. If appropriations measures exceed the targets in the budget resolution, it comes back to the floor in a reconciliation measure. A second budget resolution (due September 15) sets binding budget figures for committees and subcommittees considering appropriations. In practice, however, these two budget resolutions have been folded into a single measure because Congress does not want to reargue the same issues.

Appropriations Acts

Congressional approval of each year's spending is usually divided into thirteen separate appropriations bills, each covering separate broad categories of spending. These appropriations bills are drawn up by the House and Senate appropriations committees and their specialized subcommittees.

Indeed, House appropriations subcommittees function as overseers of the agencies included in their appropriations bill. The appropriations committees must stay within the overall totals set forth in the budget resolutions adopted by Congress.

An *appropriations* act provides money for spending, and no funds can be spent without it. An *authorization* is an act of Congress establishing a government program and defining the amount of money that it may spend. Authorizations may be for several years. However, the authorization does not actually provide the money that has been authorized; only an appropriations act can do that. Appropriations acts are almost always for a single fiscal year. Congress has its own rule that does not allow appropriations for programs that have not been authorized. However, appropriations frequently provide less money for programs than earlier authorizations.

Appropriations acts include both obligational *authority* and *outlays*. An obligation of authority permits a government agency to enter into contracts calling for payments into future years (new obligated authority). Outlays are to be spent in the fiscal year for which they are appropriated.

Appropriations Committees

Considerations of specific appropriations measures are functions of the appropriations committees in both houses. Committee work in the House of Representatives is usually more thorough than it is in the Senate; the committee in the Senate tends to be a "court of appeal" for agencies opposed to House action. Each committee, moreover, has about ten largely independent subcommittees to review the requests of a particular agency or a group of related functions. Specific appropriations bills are taken up by the subcommittees in hearings. Departmental officers answer questions on the conduct of their programs and defend their requests for the next fiscal year; lobbyists and other witnesses testify.

Supplemental Appropriations

The appropriations acts often fail to anticipate events that require additional federal spending during the fiscal year. For example, the Iraq War and Hurricane Katrina both incurred government spending well above the original appropriations acts for defense and homeland security. It is common for the president to request Congress to appropriate additional funds in such cases—funds not in the original budget for the fiscal year or in the original congressional appropriations acts.

Revenue Acts

The House Committee on Ways and Means and the Senate Finance Committee are the major instruments of Congress for consideration of taxing measures. Through long history and jealous pride they have maintained formal independence of the appropriations committees, further fragmenting legislative consideration of the budget.

Presidential Veto

In terms of aggregate amounts, Congress does not regularly make great changes in the executive budget. It is more likely to shift money among programs and projects. The budget is approved by Congress in the form of appropriations bills, usually thirteen of them, each ordinarily providing for several departments and agencies. The number of revenue measures is smaller. As with other bills that are passed by Congress, the president has ten days to approve or veto appropriations legislation.

Although Congress authorized the president to exercise a "line-item veto" in 1996, the U.S. Supreme Court declared it to be an unconstitutional violation of the separation of powers. The line-item veto would have given the president the authority to "cancel" specific spending items and specific limited tax benefits in an overall appropriations act. But the Court held that this procedure would transfer legislative power—granted by the Constitution only to Congress—to the president.[17]

Continuing Resolutions and "Shutdowns"

All appropriations acts *should* be passed by both houses and signed by the president into law before October 1, the date of the start of the fiscal year. However, it is rare for Congress to meet this deadline, so the government usually finds itself beginning a new fiscal year without a budget. Constitutionally, any U.S. government agency for which Congress does not pass an appropriations act may not draw money from the Treasury and thus is obliged to shut down. To get around this problem, Congress adopts a "continuing resolution" that authorizes government agencies to keep spending money for a specified period, usually at the same level as in the previous fiscal year.

A continuing resolution is supposed to grant additional time for Congress to pass, and the president to sign, appropriations acts. But occasionally this process has broken down in the heat of political combat over the budget. The time period specified in a continuing resolution has expired without agreement on appropriations acts or even on a new continuing resolution. In theory, the absence of either appropriations acts or a continuing resolution should cause the entire federal government to "shut down," that is, to cease all operations and expenditures for lack of funds. (Shutdown occurred during the bitter battle between President Bill Clinton and the Republican-controlled Congress over the Fiscal Year 1996 budget.) But in practice, shutdowns have been only partial, affecting only "nonessential" government employees and causing relatively little disruption.

POLICY IMPLEMENTATION: THE BUREAUCRACY

"Implementation is the continuation of politics by other means."[18] Policymaking does not end with the passage of a law by Congress and its signing by the president. Rather, it shifts from Capitol Hill and the White House to the bureaucracy—to the departments, agencies, and commissions of the executive branch (see Figure 3–3). The bureaucracy is not constitutionally empowered to decide policy questions, but it does so, nonetheless, as it performs its task of implementation.

Implementation and Policymaking

Implementation involves all of the activities designed to carry out the policies enacted by the legislative branch. These activities include the creation of new organizations—departments, agencies, bureaus, and so on—or the assignment of new responsibilities to existing organizations. These organizations must translate laws into operational rules and regulations. They must hire personnel, draw up contracts, spend money, and perform tasks. All of these activities involve decisions by bureaucrats—decisions that determine policy.

As society has grown in size and complexity, the bureaucracy has increased its role in the policymaking process. The standard explanation for the growth of bureaucratic power is that Congress and the president do not have the time, energy, or technical expertise to look after the details of environmental protection or occupational safety or equal employment opportunity or transportation safety or hundreds of other aspects of governance in a modern society. Bureaucratic agencies

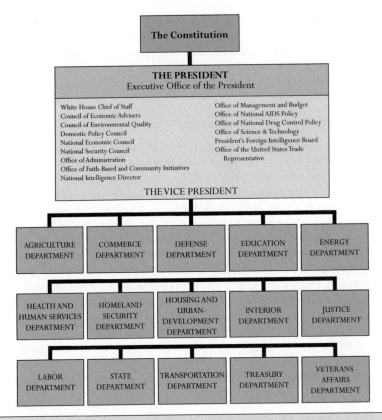

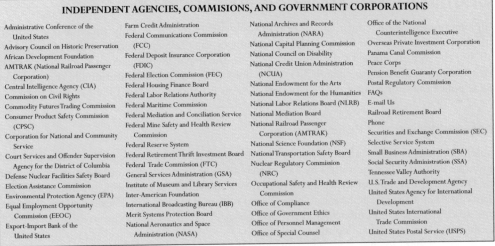

FIGURE 3–3 The Federal Bureaucracy Policymaking continues in the vast federal bureaucracy even after the passage of a law by Congress and its signing by the president.

receive only broad and general policy directions in the laws of Congress. They must decide themselves on important details of policy. This means that much of the actual policymaking process takes place *within* the Environmental Protection Agency (EPA), the Occupational Safety and Health Administration (OSHA), the Equal Employment Opportunity Commission (EEOC), the National Transportation Safety Board, and hundreds of other bureaucratic agencies.

Bureaucratic power in policymaking is also explained by political decisions in Congress and the White House to shift responsibility for many policies to the bureaucracy. Congress and the president can take political credit for laws promising "safe and effective" drugs, "equal opportunity" employment, the elimination of "unfair" labor practices, and other equally lofty, yet vague and ambiguous, goals. It then becomes the responsibility of bureaucratic agencies, for example, the Food and Drug Administration (FDA), the EEOC, and the National Labor Relations Board (NLRB), to give practical meaning to these symbolic measures. Indeed, if the policies developed by these agencies turn out to be unpopular, Congress and the president can blame the bureaucrats.

Regulation and Policymaking

Policy implementation often requires the development of formal rules and regulations by bureaucracies. Federal executive agencies publish about 60,000 pages of rules in the *Federal Register* each year. The rule-making process for federal agencies is prescribed by the Administrative Procedures Act, which requires agencies to

- Announce in the *Federal Register* that a new rule or regulation is being proposed.
- Hold hearings to allow interest groups to present evidence and assignments regarding the proposed rule.
- Conduct research on the proposed rule's economic impact, environmental impact, and so on.
- Solicit "public comments" (usually the arguments of interest groups).
- Consult with higher officials, including the Office of Management and Budget.
- Publish the new rule or regulation in the *Federal Register*.

Rule making by the bureaucracy is central to the policymaking process. Formal rules that appear in the *Federal Register* have the force of law. Bureaucratic agencies may levy fines and penalties for violations of these regulations, and these fines and penalties are enforceable in the courts. Congress itself can only amend or repeal a formal regulation by passing a new law and obtaining the president's signature. Controversial bureaucratic regulations (policies) may remain in effect when Congress is slow to act, when legislation is blocked by key congressional committee members, or when the president supports the bureaucracy and refuses to sign bills overturning regulations. The courts usually do not overturn bureaucratic regulations unless they exceed the authority granted to the agency by law or unless the agency has not followed the proper procedure in adopting them.

Adjudication and Policymaking

Policy implementation by bureaucracies often involves adjudication of individual cases. (While rule making resembles the legislative process, adjudication resembles the judicial process.) In adjudication, bureaucrats must decide whether a person, firm, corporation, and so on has complied with laws and regulations and, if not, what penalties or corrective actions are to be applied. Federal regulatory agencies—for example, the EPA, the EEOC, the Internal Revenue Service (IRS), the Federal Trade Commission (FTC), the Securities and Exchange Commission (SEC)—are heavily engaged in adjudication. They have established procedures for investigation, notification, hearing, decision, and appeal; individuals and firms involved in these proceedings often hire lawyers specializing in the field of regulation. Administrative hearings are somewhat less formal than a court trial, and the "judges" are employees of the agency itself. Losers may appeal to the federal courts, but the history of agency successes in the courts discourages many appeals. The record of agency decisions in individual cases is a form of public policy. Just as previous court decisions reflect judicial policy, previous administrative decisions reflect bureaucratic policy.

Bureaucratic Discretion and Policymaking

It is true that much of the work of bureaucrats is administrative routine—issuing Social Security checks, collecting and filing income tax returns, delivering the mail. But bureaucrats almost always have some discretion in performing even routine tasks. Often individual cases do not exactly fit established rules; often more than one rule might be applied to the same case, resulting in different outcomes. For example, the IRS administers the U.S. tax code, but each auditing agent has considerable discretion in deciding which rules to apply to a taxpayer's income, deductions, business expenses, and so on. Indeed, identical tax information submitted to different IRS offices almost always results in different estimates of tax liability. But even in more routine tasks, from processing Medicare applications to forwarding mail, individual bureaucrats can be friendly and helpful, or hostile and obstructive.[19]

Policy Bias of Bureaucrats

Generally bureaucrats believe strongly in the value of their programs and the importance of their tasks. EPA officials are strongly committed to the environmental movement; officials in the Central Intelligence Agency (CIA) believe strongly in the importance of good intelligence to the nation's security; officials in the Social Security Administration are strongly committed to maintaining the benefits of the retirement system. But in addition to these professional motives, bureaucrats, like everyone else, seek higher pay, greater job security, and added power and prestige for themselves.

Professional and personal motives converge to inspire bureaucrats to expand the powers, functions, and budgets of their agencies. (Conversely, bureaucrats try to protect their "turf" against reductions in functions, authority, and budgets.) "Budget maximization"—expanding the agency's budget as much as possible—is a driving force in government bureaucracies.[20] This is especially true regarding discretionary funds in an agency's budget—funds that bureaucrats have flexibility in deciding how to spend, rather than funds committed by law to specific purposes. The bureaucratic bias toward new functions and added authority and increases in personnel and budgets helps explain the growth of government over time.

POLICY EVALUATION: IMPRESSIONISTIC VERSUS SYSTEMATIC

The policy process model implies that evaluation is the final step in policymaking. It implies that policymakers—Congress, the president, interest groups, bureaucrats, the media, think tanks, and so on—seek to learn whether or not policies are achieving their stated goals; at what costs; and with what effects, intended and unintended, on society. Sophisticated versions of the model portray a "feedback" linkage—evaluations of current policy identify new problems and set in motion the policymaking process once again.

However, most policy evaluations in Washington, state capitols, and city halls are unsystematic and impressionistic. They come in the form of interest group complaints about the inadequacies of laws or budgets in protecting or advancing their concerns; in media stories exposing waste or fraud or mismanagement in a program or decrying the inadequacies of government policies in dealing with one crisis or another; in legislative hearings in which executive officials are questioned and occasionally badgered by committee members or their staffs about policies or programs; and sometimes even in citizens' complaints to members of Congress, the White House, or the media. Yet these "evaluations" often succeed in stimulating reform—policy changes designed to remedy perceived mistakes, inadequacies, wasteful expenditures, and other flaws in existing policy.

SUMMARY

The policy process model focuses on *how* policies are made, rather than on the substance or content of policies. The model identifies a variety of activities that occur within the political system, including identification of problems and agenda setting, formulating policy proposals, legitimating policies, implementing policies, and evaluating their effectiveness.

1. Agenda setting is deciding what will be decided; that is, what issues will be covered by the media, brought to the attention of decision makers, and identified as problems requiring government solutions.

2. A "bottom-up" portrayal of policymaking emphasizes the role of public opinion in setting the agenda for policymakers. Events, and media reporting of them, can focus public opinion on issues, problems, and "crises." But it is not always clear whether opinion molds policy or policy creates opinion.

3. A "top-down" model of policymaking emphasizes the role of national leadership in creating issues and formulating policy. The general public does not have opinions on many specific policy questions. In opinion polls, Americans express doubt about whether the government understands their thinking or acts for the benefit of all.

4. The mass media, particularly the television networks, play a major role in agenda setting. By deciding what will be news, the media set the agenda for political discussion. The continuing focus on the dramatic, violent, and negative aspects of American life may unintentionally create apathy and alienation—television malaise.

5. A great deal of policy formulation occurs outside the formal governmental process. Prestigious, private, policy-planning organizations—such as the Council on Foreign Relations—explore policy alternatives, advise governments, develop policy consensus, and even supply top governmental leaders. The policy-planning organizations bring together the leadership of the corporate and financial worlds, the mass media, the foundations, the leading intellectuals, and top government officials.

6. The activities of the proximate policymakers—the president, Congress, executive agencies, and so forth—attract the attention of most commentators and political scientists. But nongovernmental leaders, in business and finance, foundations, policy-planning organizations, the mass media, and other interest groups, may have already set the policy agenda and selected major policy goals. The activities of the proximate policymakers tend to center around the means, rather than the ends, of public policy.

7. Congress is designated in the Constitution as the principal instrument of policy legitimation. Congress members are influenced by the views of their cash constituents as much or more than by the views of their voting constituents back home. Big-money campaign contributors usually enjoy direct

access to members of Congress during the lawmaking process.

8. Partisanship is on the rise in Congress. Party line voting now occurs on more than half of all roll call votes in Congress. Party divisions have occurred on many key votes in Congress in recent years.

9. Presidents are expected to provide the initiative for congressional lawmaking. Presidential initiatives are usually outlined in the annual State of the Union message and followed up in the presidential Budget of the United States Government. Presidents aremore successful in getting their legislative proposals enacted when their own party controls Congress.

10. A great deal of policymaking occurs in the budgetary and appropriations processes. The president, through the Office of Management and Budget (OMB), has the responsibility for preparation of the *Budget of the United States Government* each year for submission to Congress. Congress may have authorized policies and programs in legislation, but it must continually appropriate funds to implement legislation.

11. Policy implementation is an important component of the policymaking process. Bureaucrats make policy as they engage in the tasks of implementation—making regulations, adjudicating cases, and exercising their discretion. Professional and personal motives combine to bias bureaucrats toward expanding the powers and functions of their agencies and increasing their budgets, especially their discretionary funds.

MySearchLab® EXERCISES

Apply what you learned in this chapter on MySearchLab (www.mysearchlab.com).

NOTES

1. V. O. Key, Jr., *Public Opinion and American Democracy* (New York: Knopf, 1967), p. 537.

2. G. William Domhoff, *Who Rules America? Power and Politics in the Year 2000* (Mountain View, CA: Mayfield, 1998), p. 127.

3. V. O. Key, Jr., *Public Opinion and American Democracy* (New York: Knopf, 1967), pp. 422–423.

4. Theodore White, *The Making of the President, 1972* (New York: Bantam, 1973), p. 7.

5. Leonard Silk and Mark Silk, *The American Establishment* (New York: Basic Books, 1980), p. 160.

6. Ibid., p. 179.

7. *Heritage Foundation Annual Report 1985* (Washington, DC: Heritage Foundation, 1985).

8. See Mark Green and Michele Jolin, eds., *Change for America: A Progressive Blueprint for the 44th President* (New York: Basic Books, 2009).

9. Lester Milbraith, "Interest Groups in Foreign Policy," in *Domestic Sources of Foreign Policy,* ed. James Rosenau (New York: Free Press, 1967), p. 247.

10. Council on Foreign Relations, *Annual Report,* 1988, p. 160.

11. Serious students of public policy are advised to read the books and journals published by these leading policy-planning organizations, especially *The Brookings Review* (published quarterly by the Brookings Institution, 1775 Massachusetts Avenue NW, Washington, DC 20036); *The American Enterprise* (published bimonthly by the American Enterprise Institute, 1150 17th Street NW, Washington, DC 20036); *Policy Review* (published quarterly by the Heritage Foundation, 214 Massachusetts Avenue NE, Washington, DC 20002); *Foreign Affairs* (published five times annually by the Council on Foreign Relations, 58 East 68th Street, New York, NY 10021).

12. Center for Responsive Politics (2009) *www.crp.org*

13. *Fortune,* December 1997.

14. *Polling Report*, March 1999. *www.pollingreport.com*

15. "Speech to the Electors of Bristol," November 3, 1774.

16. Richard F. Fenno, Home Style (Boston: Little, Brown, 1978); also quoted in Roger H. Davidson and Walter T. Oleszek, *Congress and Its Members* (Washington, DC: CQ Press, 2000), p. 149.

17. *Clinton v. City of New York*, 524 U.S. 417 (1998).

18. Donald S. Van Meter and Carl E. VanHorn, "The Policy Implementation Process," *Administration and Society*, 6 (February 1975), p. 447.

19. See James Q. Wilson, *Bureaucracy: What Governments Do and Why They Do It* (New York: Basic Books, 1989).

20. William Niskanen, *Bureaucracy and Representative Government* (Chicago: Aldine, 1971).

BIBLIOGRAPHY

ANDERSON, JAMES E. *Public Policymaking* 7th ed. Cengage Learning, 2011.

CIGLAR, ALLAN J., and BURDETT A. LOUIS. *Interest Group Politics*, 8th ed. Washington, DC: CQ Press, 2011.

DAVIDSON, ROGER H., WALTER J. OLESZEK, and FRANCES E. LEE. *Congress and Its Members*, 12th ed. Washington, DC: CQ Press, 2009.

GORMLEY, WILLIAM T., and STEVEN T. BALA. *Bureaucracy and Democracy: Accountability and Performance*, 2nd ed. Washington, DC: CQ Press, 2007.

GRABER, DORIS A. *Mass Media and American Politics*, 8th ed. Washington, DC: CQ Press, 2009.

HETHERINGTON, MARK T., and WILLIAM O. KEEFE. *Parties, Politics, and Public Policy in America*, 11th ed. Washington, DC: CQ Press, 2009.

KERWIN, CORNELIUS, M. *Rulemaking: How Government Agencies Write Law and Make Policy*, 4th ed. Washington, DC: CQ Press, 2010.

KINGDON, JOHN W. *Agendas, Alternatives, and Public Policies*. Boston: Little, Brown, 1984.

SMITH, JAMES A. *The Idea Brokers: Think Tanks and the Rise of the New Policy Elite*. New York: Macmillan, 1991.

WEB SITES

CENTER FOR RESPONSIVE POLITICS. Source of information on campaign finances—contributions, recipients, PACs, lobbyists, etc. *www.opensecrets.org*

FEDERAL ELECTIONS COMMISSION. Official government site for campaign finance reports. *www.fec.gov*

REPUBLICAN NATIONAL COMMITTEE. Official site of the RNC, including GOP policy positions, press releases, news, etc. *www.rnc.org*

DEMOCRATIC NATIONAL COMMITTEE. Official site of the DNC, including Democratic Party policy positions, press releases, news, etc. *www.democrat.org*

THE BROOKINGS INSTITUTION. Liberal think tank for policy research, with policy studies, press briefings, etc. *www.brookings.org*

AMERICAN ENTERPRISE INSTITUTE. Moderate think tank for policy research, with policy studies, press briefings, etc. *www.aei.org*

HERITAGE FOUNDATION. Conservative think tank for policy research, with policy briefs, news about issues currently being debated in Congress, press releases, etc. *www.heritage.org*

COUNCIL ON FOREIGN RELATIONS. Leading foreign relations think tank, with task force reports and access to its journal, *Foreign Affairs. www.cfr.org*

CATO INSTITUTE. Libertarian (minimal government) think tank, with policy studies, press releases, etc. *www.cato.org*

U.S. Office of Management and Budget (OMB). Official site of OMB, with the current Budget of the United States Government.

Policy Evaluation through Congressional Testimony Secretary of the Treasury Timothy Geithner testifies before a Congressional Oversight Panel evaluating the effectiveness of the Troubled Asset Relief Program (TARP) June 22, 2010. Geithner argued that the TARP program, often criticized as the "Wall Street bailout," was successful in stabilizing the financial community and that taxpayers were recovering a major portion of their investment.   (© Benjamin J. Myers/Corbis)

4

Policy Evaluation
Finding Out What Happens After a Law Is Passed

Americans often assume that once we pass a law, create a bureaucracy, and spend money, the purpose of the law, the bureaucracy, and the expenditure will be achieved. We assume that when Congress adopts a policy and appropriates money for it, and when the executive branch organizes a program, hires people, spends money, and carries out activities designed to implement the policy, the effects of the policy will be felt by society and will be those intended. Unfortunately, these assumptions are not always warranted. The national experiences with many public programs indicate the need for careful appraisal of the real impact of public policy.

Does the government really know what it is doing? Generally speaking, no. Governments usually know how much money they spend; how many persons ("clients") are given various services; how much these services cost; how their programs are organized, managed, and operated; and, perhaps, how influential interest groups regard their programs and services. But even if programs and policies are well organized, efficiently operated, widely utilized, adequately financed, and generally supported by major interest groups, we may still want to ask, So what? Do they work? Do these programs have any beneficial effects on society? Are the effects immediate or long range? Positive or negative? What is the relationship between the costs of the program and the benefits to society? Could we be doing something else with more benefit to society with the money and work force devoted to these programs? Unfortunately, governments have done very little to answer these more basic questions.

POLICY EVALUATION: ASSESSING THE IMPACT OF PUBLIC POLICY

Policy evaluation is learning about the consequences of public policy. Other, more complex, definitions have been offered: "Policy evaluation is the assessment of the overall effectiveness of a national program in meeting its objectives, or assessment of the relative effectiveness of two or more programs in meeting common objectives."[1] "Policy evaluation research is the objective, systematic, empirical examination of the effects ongoing policies and public programs have on their targets in terms of the goals they are meant to achieve."[2]

Some definitions tie evaluation to the stated "goals" of a program or policy. But since we do not always know what these "goals" really are, and because we know that some programs and policies pursue conflicting "goals," we will not limit our notion of policy evaluation to their achievement. Instead, we will concern ourselves with all of the consequences of public policy, that is, with "policy impact."

The impact of a policy is all its *effects on real-world conditions*, including:

- Impact on the target situation or group
- Impact on situations or groups other than the target (spillover effects)
- Impact on future as well as immediate conditions
- Direct costs, in terms of resources devoted to the program
- Indirect costs, including loss of opportunities to do other things

Ideally, all the benefits and costs, both immediate and future, should be measured.

Measuring Impact, Not Output

"Policy impact" is not the same as "policy output." In assessing policy impact, we cannot be content simply to measure government activity. For example, the number of dollars spent per member of a target group (per pupil educational expenditures, per capita welfare expenditures, per capita health expenditures) is not really a measure of the impact of a policy on the group. It is merely a measure of government activity—that is, a measure of *policy output*. Unfortunately many government agencies produce reams of statistics measuring outputs—such as welfare benefits paid, criminal arrests and prosecutions, Medicare payments, and school enrollments. But this "bean counting" tells us little about poverty, crime, health, or educational achievement. We cannot be satisfied with measuring how many times a bird flaps its wings; we must know how far the bird has flown. In describing public policy, or even in explaining its determinants, measures of policy output are important. But in assessing *policy impact*, we must identify changes in society that are associated with measures of government activity.

Target Groups

The target group is that part of the population for whom the program is intended—such as the poor, the sick, the ill-housed. Target groups must first be identified and then the desired effect of the program on the members of these groups must be determined. Is it to change their physical or economic circumstances—for example, the percentage of minorities or women employed in professional or managerial jobs, the income of the poor, the infant death rate? Or is it to change their knowledge, attitudes, awareness, interests, or behavior? If multiple effects are intended, what are the priorities among different effects? What are the possible unintended effects (side effects) on target groups?

Nontarget Groups

All programs and policies have differential effects on various segments of the population. Identifying important nontarget groups for a policy is a difficult process. For example, what is the impact of the welfare reform on groups *other* than the poor—government bureaucrats, social workers, local political figures, working-class families who are not on welfare, taxpayers, and others? Nontarget effects may be expressed as benefits as well as costs, such as the benefits to the construction industry of public housing projects.

TABLE 4–1 Assessing Policy Impact A rational approach to policy evaluation tries to calculate the difference between all present and future, target and nontarget, costs and benefits.

	BENEFITS		COSTS	
	Present	**Future**	**Present**	**Future**
Target Groups	Benefits	Benefits	Costs	Costs
Nontarget Groups	Benefits	Benefits	Costs	Costs
	Sum	Sum	Sum	Sum
	Present	Future	Present	Future
	Benefits	Benefits	Costs	Costs
	Sum All Benefits	Minus	Sum All Costs	
	=	Net Policy Impact		

Short-Term and Long-Term Effects

When will the benefits or the costs be felt? Is the program designed for short-term emergencies? Or is it a long-term, developmental effort? If it is short term, what will prevent the processes of incrementalism and bureaucratization from turning it into a long-term program, even after the immediate need is met? Many impact studies show that new or innovative programs have short-term positive effects—for example, Operation Head Start and other educational programs. However, the positive effects frequently disappear as the novelty and enthusiasm of new programs wear off. Other programs experience difficulties at first, as in the early days of Social Security, but turn out to have "sleeper" effects, as in the widespread acceptance of Social Security today. Not all programs aim at the same degree of permanent or transient change.

Calculating Net Benefits and Costs

The task of calculating the *net* impact of a public policy is truly awesome. It would be all the benefits, both immediate and long range, minus all the costs, both immediate and future (see Table 4–1). Even if all these costs and benefits are known (and everyone agrees on what is a "benefit" and what is a "cost"), it is still very difficult to come up with a net balance.

THE SYMBOLIC IMPACT OF POLICY

The impact of a policy may also include its symbolic effects. Its symbolic impact deals with the perceptions that individuals have of government action and their attitudes toward it. Even if government policies do not succeed in eliminating poverty, preventing crime, and so on, the failure of government to *try* to do these things would be even worse. Individuals, groups, and whole societies frequently judge public policy in terms of its *good intentions* rather than *tangible accomplishments*. Sometimes very popular programs have little positive tangible impact.

The policies of government may tell us more about the aspirations of a society and its leadership than about actual conditions. Policies do more than effect change in societal conditions; they also help hold people together and maintain an orderly state.

Once upon a time politics was described as "who gets what, when, and how." Today it seems that politics centers on "who *feels* what, when, and how." What governments say is as important as what governments do. Television has made the image of public policy as important as the policy itself. Systematic policy analysis concentrates on what governments do, why they do it, and what difference it makes. It devotes less attention to what governments say. Perhaps this is a weakness in policy analysis. Our focus is primarily on activities of governments rather than their rhetoric.

PROGRAM EVALUATION: WHAT GOVERNMENTS USUALLY DO

Most government agencies make some effort to review the effectiveness of their own programs. These reviews usually take one of the following forms:

Hearings and Reports

The most common type of program review involves hearings and reports. Government administrators are asked by chief executives or legislators to give testimony (formally or informally) on the accomplishments of their own programs. Frequently, written annual reports are provided by program administrators. But testimonials and reports of administrators are not very objective means of program evaluation. They frequently magnify the benefits and minimize the costs of the program.

Site Visits

Occasionally teams of high-ranking administrators, expert consultants, legislators, or some combination of these people will decide to visit agencies or conduct inspections in the field. These teams can pick up impressionistic data about how programs are being run, whether they are following specific guidelines, whether they have competent staffs, and sometimes whether or not the clients (target groups) are pleased with the services.

Program Measures

The data developed by government agencies themselves generally cover policy output measures: the number of recipients in various welfare programs, the number of persons in work-force training programs, the number of public hospital beds available, the tons of garbage collected, or the number of pupils enrolled. But these program measures rarely indicate what impact these numbers have on society: the conditions of life confronting the poor, the success of work-force trainees in finding and holding skilled jobs, the health of the nation's poor, the cleanliness of cities, and the ability of graduates to read and write and function in society.

Comparison with Professional Standards

In some areas of government activity, professional associations have developed standards of excellence. These standards are usually expressed as a desirable level of output: for example, the number of pupils per teacher, the number of hospital beds per one thousand people, the number of cases for each welfare worker. Actual government outputs can then be compared with ideal outputs. Although such an exercise can be helpful, it still focuses on government outputs and not on the impact of government activities on the conditions of target or nontarget groups. Moreover, the standards themselves are usually developed by professionals who are really guessing at what ideal levels of benefits and services should be. There is rarely any hard evidence that ideal levels of government output have any significant impact on society.

Evaluation of Citizens' Complaints

Another common approach to program evaluation is the analysis of citizens' complaints. But not all citizens voluntarily submit complaints or remarks about governmental programs. Critics of government programs are self-selected, and they are rarely representative of the general public or even of the target groups of government programs. There is no way to judge whether the complaints of a vocal few are shared by the many more who have not spoken up. Occasionally, administrators develop questionnaires for participants in their program to learn what their complaints may be and whether they are satisfied or not. But these questionnaires really test public opinion toward the program and not its real impact on the lives of participants.

Surveys of Public Opinion

Occasionally governments undertake to survey citizens about their satisfaction or dissatisfaction with various programs and services. This is more common at the local level of government. Yet even polls focused on federal government services can be instructive (see Table 4–2).

PROGRAM EVALUATION: WHAT GOVERNMENTS CAN DO

None of the common evaluative methods just mentioned really attempts to weigh *costs* against *benefits*. Indeed, administrators seldom calculate the ratio of costs to services—the dollars required to train one worker, to provide one hospital bed, to collect and dispose of one ton of garbage. It is even more difficult to calculate the costs of making specific changes in society—the dollars required to raise student reading levels by one grade, to lower the infant death rate by one point, to reduce the crime rate by one percent. To learn about the real impact of governmental programs on society, more complex and costly methods of program evaluation are required.

Systematic program evaluation involves comparisons—comparisons designed to estimate what changes in society can be attributed to the program rather than nonprogram factors. Ideally, this means comparing what "actually happened" to "what would have happened if the program had never been implemented." It is not difficult to measure what happened; unfortunately too much program evaluation stops there. The real problem is to measure what would have happened without a program and then compare the two conditions of society. The difference must be attributable to the program itself and not to other changes that are occurring in society at the same time.

Before Versus After Comparisons

There are several common research designs in program evaluation. The most common is the before-and-after study, which compares results in a jurisdiction at two times—one before the program was implemented and the other some time after. Usually only target groups are examined.

TABLE 4–2 Public Satisfaction/Dissatisfaction with Federal Government Programs Polls can reflect general satisfaction or dissatisfaction with federal programs. Often the military ranks at or near the top of public esteem; the public is decidedly less satisfied with energy policy, health care, poverty programs, and the nation's finances.

Next we are going to name some major areas the federal government handles. For each one please say whether you are satisfied or dissatisfied with the work the government is doing.

	Satisfied	Dissatisfied	Unsure
National parks	71	27	2
Military and national defense	59	40	1
Agriculture and farming	56	38	5
Transportation	56	42	2
Homeland security	50	49	1
Environmental issues	48	51	1
Public housing/urban development	47	49	4
Criminal justice	47	52	1
Labor and employment issues	44	54	2
Foreign affairs	41	58	1
Education	41	59	0
Job creation/economic growth	39	60	1
Responding to natural disasters	33	66	1
Energy policy	27	71	2
Health care	24	75	1
Poverty programs	24	75	1
The nation's finances	23	76	1

SOURCE: *The Polling Report*, accessed January 2011, www.pollingreport.com.

These before-and-after comparisons are designed to show program impacts, but it is very difficult to know whether the changes observed, if any, came about as a result of the program or as a result of other changes that were occurring in society at the same time (see Design 1, Figure 4–1).

Projected Trend Line Versus Postprogram Comparisons

A better estimate of what would have happened without the program can be made by project-ing past (preprogram) trends into the postprogram time period. Then these projections can be compared with what actually happened in society after the program was implemented. The differ-ence between the projections based on preprogram trends and the actual postprogram data can be attributed to the program itself. Note that data on target groups or conditions must be obtained for several time periods before the program was initiated, so that a trend line can be established (see Design 2, Figure 4–1). This design is better than the before-and-after design, but it requires more effort by program evaluators.

Design 1

Before vs. After

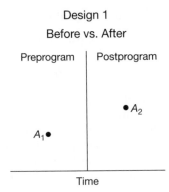

Time

■ $A_2 - A_1$ = Estimated Program Effect

Design 2

Projected vs. Postprogram

Time

■ $A_2 - A_1$ = Estimated Program Effect

Design 3

With vs. Without Program

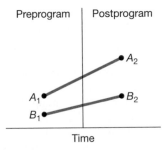

Time

■ A has Program; B does not.
■ $(A_2 - A_1) - (B_2 - B_1)$ = Estimated Program Effect.
■ Or difference between A and B in rate of change equals Estimated Program Effect.

Design 4

The Classic Research Design:
Control vs. Experimental Groups

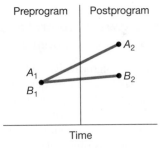

Time

■ A has Program; B does not.
■ A and B identical in preprogram period.
■ $A_2 - B_2$ = Estimated Program Effect

FIGURE 4–1   Policy Evaluation Research Designs Policy evaluation can utilize a variety of research designs.

Consider, for example, efforts at evaluating welfare reform (see the section "Evaluation: Is Welfare Reform Working?" in Chapter 7). To date, most evaluations of welfare reform have followed the trend line research design. If the goal of the reform is to reduce welfare rolls, there is ample evidence that the program has contributed to that goal (see Figure 7-6). The "target group" (recipients of cash welfare payments) has been reduced by over half since the ending of the federal cash entitlement program, Aid to Families with Dependent Children, and its substitution with the federally aided state program, Temporary Assistance for Needy Families, in 1996. But it is not clear exactly what proportion of this reduction is due to the policy itself and what proportion is due to other economic factors. All we really know is that the welfare rolls declined.

Comparisons Between Jurisdictions With and Without Programs

Another common evaluation design is to compare individuals who have participated in programs with those who have not, or to compare cities, states, or nations which have programs with those that do not. Comparisons are sometimes made in the postprogram period only; for example, comparisons of the job records of those who have participated in work-force training programs with those who have not, or comparisons of homicide rates in states that have the death penalty with the homicide rates in states without the death penalty. But so many other differences exist between individuals or jurisdictions that it is difficult to attribute differences in their conditions to differences in government programs. For example, persons who voluntarily enter a work-force training program may be more motivated to find a job or have different personal characteristics than those who do not. States with the death penalty may tend to be rural states, which have lower homicide rates than urban states, which may or may not have the death penalty.

Some of the problems involved in comparing jurisdictions with and without programs can be resolved if we observe both kinds of jurisdictions before and after the introduction of the program. This enables us to estimate differences between jurisdictions before program efforts are considered. After the program is initiated, we can observe whether the differences between jurisdictions have widened or not (see Design 3, Figure 4–1). This design provides some protection against attributing differences to a particular program when underlying socioeconomic differences between jurisdictions are really responsible for different outcomes.

Comparisons Between Control and Experimental Groups Before and After Program Implementation

The classic research design involves the careful selection of control and experimental groups that are identical in every way, the application of the policy to the experimental group only, and the comparison of changes in the experimental group with changes in the control group after the application of the policy. Initially, control and experimental groups must be identical, and the preprogram performance of each group must be measured and found to be the same. The program must be applied only to the experimental group. The postprogram differences between the experimental and control groups must be carefully measured (see Design 4, Figure 4–1). This classic research design is preferred by scientists because it provides the best opportunity of estimating changes that derived from the effects of other forces in society.

EXPERIMENTAL POLICY RESEARCH

Many policy analysts argue that policy experimentation offers the best opportunity to determine the impact of public policies. This opportunity rests on the main characteristics of experimental research: the systematic selection of experimental and control groups, the application of the policy under study to the experimental group only, and the careful comparison of differences between the experimental and the control groups after the application of the policy. But government-sponsored experimental policy research raises a series of important questions.

A Bias Toward Positive Results

First, are government-sponsored research projects predisposed to produce results supportive of popular reform proposals? Are social scientists, whose personal political values are generally liberal and reformist, inclined to produce findings in support of liberal reform measures? Moreover, successful experiments—in which the proposed policy achieves positive results—will receive more acclaim and produce greater opportunities for advancement for social scientists and administrators than will unsuccessful experiments—in which the policy is shown to be ineffective. Liberal, reform-oriented social scientists expect liberal reforms to produce positive results. When reforms appear to do so, the research results are immediately accepted and published; but when results are unsupportive or negative, the social scientists may be inclined to go back and recode their data, redesign their research, or reevaluate their results because they believe a "mistake" must have been made. The temptation to "fudge the data," "reinterpret" the results, coach participants on what to say or do, and so forth will be very great. In the physical and biological sciences, the temptation to "cheat" in research is reduced by the fact that research can be replicated and the danger of being caught and disgraced is very great. But social experiments can seldom be replicated perfectly, and replication seldom brings the same distinction to a social scientist as does the original research.

The Hawthorne Effect

People behave differently when they know they are being watched. Students, for example, generally perform at a higher level when something—anything—new and different is introduced into the classroom routine. This "Hawthorne effect" may cause a new program or reform to appear more successful than the old, but it is the newness itself that produces improvement. The term is taken from early experiments at the Hawthorne plant of Western Electric Company in Chicago in 1927. It was found that worker output increased with *any* change in routine, even decreasing the lighting in the plant.[3]

Generalizing Results to the Nation

Another problem in policy research is that results obtained with small-scale experiments may differ substantially from those that would occur if a large-scale nationwide program were adopted. For example, years ago a brief experiment involving a small number of families purported to show that a government-guaranteed income did not change the work behavior of recipients; they continued to behave as their neighbors did—searching for jobs and accepting employment when it was offered.[4] Subsequent studies of the effects of a guaranteed government income challenged even these experimental group findings but also predicted that a *nationwide* program would produce much more dramatic changes in working behavior. If everyone in the nation were guaranteed a minimum annual income, cultural standards might be changed nationwide; the resulting work disincentives might "seriously understate the expected cost of an economy-wide program."[5]

Ethical and Legal Issues

Experimental strategies in policy impact research raise still other problems. Do government researchers have the right to withhold public services from individuals simply to provide a control group for experimentation? In the medical area, where giving or withholding treatment can result in death or injury, the problem is obvious and many attempts have been made to formulate a code of ethics. But in the area of social experimentation, what are we to say to control groups who are chosen to be similar to experimental groups but denied benefits in order to serve as a base for comparison? Setting aside the legal and ethical issues, it will be politically difficult to provide services for some people and not others.

Evaluation as a Partisan Activity House Budget Committee member Paul Ryan (R.-WI) points to the 2000-plus page Obama health care reform bill still in markup binders. The bill became the Patient Protection and Affordable Care Act of 2010 on strictly partisan votes in the House and Senate. Few legislators knew what was in the bill when they voted on it. Full implementation, including the mandate that every American obtain health insurance, occurs in 2014.   (Washington Post/Getty Images)

Political Interpretations of Results

Finally, we must acknowledge that the political milieu shapes policy research. Politics helps decide what policies and policy alternatives will be studied in the first place. Politics can also affect findings themselves, and certainly the interpretations and uses of policy research are politically motivated.

Despite these problems, the advantages of policy experimentation are substantial. It is exceedingly costly for society to commit itself to large-scale programs and policies in education, welfare, housing, health, and so on without any real idea about what works.

FEDERAL EVALUATION: THE OFFICE OF MANAGEMENT AND BUDGET

Among its many responsibilities, the Office of Management and Budget (OMB) in the Executive Office of the President undertakes program evaluations and encourages executive agencies to do so as well. It advises executive agencies to "embrace a culture where performance measurement and evaluation are regularly used." It further recommends:

Rigorous evaluations using experimental or quasi-experimental methods that identify the effects of programs in situations where doing so is difficult using other methods; and rigorous qualitative evidence that complement what can be learned from empirical evidence and provide greater insight into the contexts where programs and practices are implemented more or less successfully.[6]

OMB funds some "rigorous program evaluations" through a competitive review process. But it emphasizes the development of agency infrastructure for undertaking their own program evaluations.

Benefit-Cost Analysis of Federal Regulations

As early as 1936, Congress required the Army Corps of Engineers to undertake benefit-cost analysis in their flood control projects, to ensure that projects would produce benefits in excess of costs. Subsequently, the Corps of Engineers led the way in the development of government benefit-cost analysis. The Reagan Administration was the first to establish a broad commitment to benefit-cost analysis in regulatory decision making. Agencies were ordered to undertake regulatory action only on the basis of "reasoned determination" that benefits justify the costs and that the regulatory action maximized net societal benefits (benefits minus costs). Subsequent presidential administrations have reaffirmed their commitment to applying benefit cost analysis to federal regulatory actions.

Ideally, government agencies should (a) propose or adopt a regulation only upon a reasoned determination that its benefits justify its costs (recognizing that some benefits and costs are difficult to quantify); (b) tailor its regulations to impose the least burden on society consistent with obtaining regulatory objectives; (c) select, in choosing among alternative regulatory approaches, those approaches that maximize net benefits (including potential economic, environmental, public health, safety, and equity impacts; (d) identify and assess available alternatives to direct regulation, including providing economic incentives to encourage the desired behavior; and (e) use the best available techniques to quantify anticipated present and future benefits and costs as accurately as possible. These criteria are set forth in various presidential executive orders.

Value of a Statistical Life

Among the controversies in benefit-cost analysis is the valuation of a human life, often required in the design of evaluations of health and safety regulations. Among the agencies that have developed a value for a statistical life are the Environmental Protection Agency, Department of Transportation, Food and Drug Administration, Occupational Safety and Health Administration, and Department of Homeland Security. Recent valuations have fluctuated between $5 million and $7 million. These calculations are required in monetarizing mortality risks; they do not suggest the value of any individual's life.

FEDERAL EVALUATION: THE GENERAL ACCOUNTABILITY OFFICE

The General Accountability Office (GAO) is an arm of Congress. It has broad authority to audit the operations and finances of federal agencies, to evaluate their programs, and to report its findings to Congress. For most of its history, the GAO confined itself to financial auditing and management and administrative studies. Over time, however, it has increasingly undertaken evaluative research on government programs.

The GAO was established by Congress as an independent agency in 1921, in the same Budget and Accounting Act that created the first executive budget; its authority to undertake evaluation studies was expanded in the Congressional Budget and Impoundment Control Act of 1974, the same act that established the House and Senate Budget Committees and the Congressional Budget Office (see Chapter 7). The GAO is headed by the Comptroller General of the United States. Most GAO reports are requested by Congress, although the office can also undertake studies on its own initiative.

According to the GAO, "Program evaluation—when it is available and of high quality—provides sound information about what programs are actually delivering, how they are being managed, and the extent to which they are cost-effective."[7] The GAO believes that evaluation efforts by federal agencies fall woefully short of what is required for rational decision making. It has been especially critical of the Defense Department for failing to test weapons systems adequately, to monitor defense contractors and their charges, or to adjust its future plans to expected reductions in defense spending (see Chapter 15). The GAO has criticized the Environmental Protection Agency for measuring its own success in terms of input measures—numbers of inspections performed and enforcement actions undertaken—rather than actual improvements in environmental conditions, such as in water quality or air quality (see Chapter 13). The GAO has also reported on the Social Security trust fund and the dangers of spending trust fund money on current governmental operations (see Chapter 7). It has reported on the high and growing cost of medical care in the United States, especially Medicaid and Medicare, and noted the lack of correlation between medical spending and measures of the nation's health (see Chapter 8). It has undertaken to assess the overall impact of drug control policies (see Chapter 6), and it has studied the default rate on student loans and recommended collection of overdue loans by withholding tax refunds (see Chapter 9). In short, the GAO has been involved in virtually every major policy question confronting the nation.[8]

PROGRAM EVALUATION: WHY IT FAILS SO OFTEN

Occasionally, government agencies attempt their own policy evaluations. Government analysts and administrators report on the conditions of target groups before and after their participation in a new program, and some effort is made to attribute observed changes to the new program itself. Policy experimentation is less frequent; seldom do governments systematically select experimental and control groups of the population, introduce a new program to the experimental group only, and then carefully compare changes in the conditions of the experimental group with a control group that has not benefited from the program. Some of the problems confronting policy evaluation include:

- The first task confronting anyone who wants to evaluate a public program is to determine what the goals of the program are. What are the target groups, and what are the desired effects? But governments often pursue incompatible goals to satisfy diverse groups. Overall policy planning and evaluation may reveal inconsistencies in public policy and force reconsideration of fundamental societal goals. Where there is little agreement on the goals of a public program, evaluation studies may engender a great deal of political conflict.

Government agencies generally prefer to avoid conflict, and hence to avoid studies that would raise such questions.

- Many programs and policies have primarily symbolic value. They do not actually change the conditions of target groups but merely make these groups feel that the government "cares." A government agency does not welcome a study that reveals that its efforts have no tangible effects; such a revelation itself might reduce the symbolic value of the program by informing target groups of its uselessness.

- Government agencies have a strong vested interest in "proving" that their programs have a positive impact. Administrators frequently view attempts to evaluate the impact of their programs as attempts to limit or destroy the programs or to question the competence of the administrators.

- Government agencies usually have a heavy investment—organizational, financial, physical, psychological—in current programs and policies. They are predisposed against finding that these policies do not work.

- Any serious study of policy impact undertaken by a government agency would involve some interference with ongoing program activities. The press of day-to-day business generally takes priority over study and evaluation. More important, the conduct of an experiment may necessitate depriving individuals or groups (control groups) of services to which they are entitled under law; this may be difficult, if not impossible, to do.

- Program evaluation requires funds, facilities, time, and personnel, which government agencies do not like to sacrifice from ongoing programs. Policy impact studies, like any research, cost money. They cannot be done well as extracurricular or part-time activities. Devoting resources to studies may mean a sacrifice in program resources that administrators are unwilling to make.

HOW BUREAUCRATS EXPLAIN NEGATIVE FINDINGS

Government administrators and program supporters are ingenious in devising reasons why negative findings about policy impacts should be rejected. Even in the face of clear evidence that their favorite programs are useless or even counterproductive, they will argue that:

- The effects of the program are long range and cannot be measured at the present time.

- The effects of the program are diffuse and general in nature; no single criterion or index adequately measures what is being accomplished.

- The effects of the program are subtle and cannot be identified by crude measures or statistics.

- Experimental research cannot be carried out effectively because to withhold services from some persons to observe the impact of such withholding would be unfair to them.

- The fact that no difference was found between persons receiving the services and those not receiving them means that the program is not sufficiently intensive and indicates the need to spend *more* resources on the program.

- The failure to identify any positive effects of a program is attributable to inadequacy or bias in the research itself, not in the program.

Political scientist James Q. Wilson formulated two general laws to cover all cases of social science research on policy impact:

Wilson's First Law: All policy interventions in social problems produce the intended effect—if the research is carried out by those implementing the policy or by their friends.

Wilson's Second Law: No policy intervention in social problems produces the intended effect—if the research is carried out by independent third parties, especially those skeptical of the policy.

Wilson denies that his laws are cynical. Instead he reasons that:

Studies that conform to the First Law will accept an agency's own data about what it is doing and with what effect; adopt a time frame (long or short) that maximizes the probability of observing the desired effect; and minimize the search for other variables that might account for the effect observed. Studies that conform to the Second Law will gather data independently of the agency; adopt a short time frame that either minimizes the chance for the desired effect to appear or, if it does appear, permits one to argue that the results are "temporary" and probably due to the operation of the "Hawthorne Effect" (i.e., the reaction of the subjects to the fact that they are part of an experiment); and maximize the search for other variables that might explain the effects observed.[9]

WHY GOVERNMENT PROGRAMS ARE SELDOM TERMINATED

Government programs are rarely terminated. Even when evaluative studies produce negative findings; even when policymakers themselves are fully aware of fraud, waste, and inefficiency; even when highly negative benefit-cost ratios are reported, government programs manage to survive. Once policy is institutionalized within a government, it is extraordinarily difficult to terminate.

Why is it so difficult for governments to terminate failed programs and policies? The answer to this question varies from one program to another, but a few generalizations are possible.

Concentrated Benefits, Dispersed Costs

Perhaps the most common reason for the continuation of inefficient government programs and policies is that their limited benefits are concentrated in a small, well-organized constituency, while their greater costs are dispersed over a large, unorganized, uninformed public. Although few in number, the beneficiaries of a program are strongly committed to it; they are concerned, well-informed, and active in their support. If the costs of the program are spread widely among all taxpayers, no one has a strong incentive to become informed, organized, or active in opposition to it. Although the costs of a failed program may be enormous, if they are dispersed widely enough so that no one individual or group bears a significant burden, there will be little incentive to organize an effective opposition. (Consider the case of a government subsidy program for peanut growers. If $300 million per year were distributed to 5,000 growers, each would average $60,000 in subsidy income. If each grower would contribute 10 percent of this subsidy to a political fund to reward friendly legislators, the fund could distribute $30 million in campaign contributions. If the costs of the program could be dispersed evenly among 300 million Americans, each would pay only $1. No one would have a sufficient incentive to become informed, organized, or active in opposition to the subsidy program. So it would continue, regardless of its limited benefits and extensive costs to society.) When program costs are widely dispersed, it is irrational for individuals, each of whom bears only a tiny fraction of these costs, to expend the time, energy, and money to counter the support of the program's beneficiaries.

Legislative and Bureaucratic Interests

Among the beneficiaries of any government program are those who administer and supervise it. Bureaucratic jobs depend on a program's continuation. Government positions with all of their benefits, pay, prerequisites, and prestige are at stake. Strong incentives exist for bureaucrats to resist or undermine negative evaluations of their programs, to respond to public criticism by making only marginal changes in their programs, or even by claiming that their programs are failing because not enough is being spent on them.

Legislative systems, both in Congress and in state capitals, are structured so that legislators with the most direct control over programs are usually the most friendly to them. The committee system, with its fragmentation of power and invitation to logrolling ("You support my committee's report, and I'll support yours") favors retention of existing programs and policies. Legislators on committees with jurisdiction over the programs are usually the largest recipients of campaign contributions from the organized beneficiaries of the programs. These legislators can use their committee positions to protect failed programs, to minimize reform, and to block termination. Even without the incentives of bureaucratic position and legislative power, no public official wants to acknowledge failure publicly.

Incrementalism at Work

Governments seldom undertake to consider any program as a whole in any given year. Active consideration of programs is made at the margin—that is, attention is focused on proposed changes in existing programs rather than on the value of programs in their entirety. Usually this attention comes in the budgetary process, when proposed increases or decreases in funding are under discussion in the bureaucracy and legislature. Negative evaluative studies can play a role in the budgetary process—limiting increases for failed programs or perhaps even identifying programs ripe for budget cutting. But attention is almost always focused on changes or reforms, increases or decreases, rather than on the complete termination of programs. Even mandating "sunset" legislation, used in many states (requiring legislatures periodically to reconsider and reauthorize whole programs), seldom results in program termination.

POLITICS AS A SUBSTITUTE FOR ANALYSIS

Policy analysis, including systematic policy evaluation, is a rational process. It requires some agreement on what problems the government should undertake to resolve; some agreement on the nature of societal benefits and costs and the weights to be given to them; and some agreement on the formulation of a research design, the measurement of benefits and costs, and the interpretation of the results. Value conflicts intrude at almost every point in the evaluation process, but policy analysis cannot resolve value conflicts.

Politics is the management of conflict. People have different ideas about what the principal problems confronting society are and about what, if anything, the government should do about them. Value conflicts explain why policymakers rely so little on systematic policy analysis in the formulation, selection, or evaluation of policy. Instead, they must rely on political processes.

A political approach to policy analysis emphasizes:

- The search for common concerns that might form the basis for identification of societal problems
- Reasonable trade-offs among conflicting values at each stage of the policymaking process
- The search for mutually beneficial outcomes for diverse groups; attempting to satisfy diverse demands
- Compromise and conciliation and a willingness to accept modest net gains (half a loaf) rather than suffer the loss of more comprehensive proposals
- Bargaining among participants, even in separate policy areas, to win allies ("I'll support your proposals if you support mine.")

At best, policy analysis plays only a secondary role in the policymaking process. But it is an important role, nonetheless. Political scientist Charles E. Lindblom explains "the intelligence of democracy":

> Strategic analysis and mutual adjustment among political participants, then, are the underlying processes by which democratic systems achieve the level of intelligent action that they do....
>
> There is never a point at which the thinking, research, and action is "objective," or "unbiased." It is partisan through and through, as are all human activities, in the sense that the expectations and priorities of those commissioning and doing the analysis shape it, and in the sense that those using information shape its interpretation and application.
>
> Information seeking and shaping must intertwine inextricably with political interaction, judgment, and action. Since time and energy and brainpower are limited, strategic analysis must focus on those aspects of an issue that participating partisans consider to be most important for persuading each other. There is no purely analytical way to do such focusing; it requires political judgments: about what the crucial unknowns are, about what kind of evidence is likely to be persuasive to would-be allies, or about what range of alternatives may be politically feasible.[10]

THE LIMITS OF PUBLIC POLICY

Never have Americans expected so much of their government. Our confidence in what governments can do seems boundless. We have come to believe that they can eliminate poverty, end racism, ensure peace, prevent crime, restore cities, clean the air and water, and so on, if only they will adopt the right policies.

Perhaps confidence in the potential effectiveness of public policy is desirable, particularly if it inspires us to continue to search for ways to resolve societal problems. But any serious study of public policy must also recognize the limitations of policy in affecting these conditions.

1. Some societal problems are incapable of solution because of the way in which they are defined. If problems are defined in *relative* rather than *absolute* terms, they may never

be resolved by public policy. For example, if the poverty line is defined as the line that places one-fifth of the population below it, poverty will always be with us regardless of how well off the "poor" may become. Relative disparities in society may never be eliminated. Even if income differences among classes were tiny, tiny differences may come to have great symbolic importance, and the problem of inequality would remain.

2. Expectations may always outrace the capabilities of governments. Progress in any policy area may simply result in an upward movement in expectations about what policy should accomplish. Public education never faced a dropout problem until the 1960s, when for the first time a majority of boys and girls were graduating from high school. At the turn of the century, when high school graduation was rare, there was no mention of a dropout problem.

3. Policies that solve the problems of one group in society may create problems for other groups. In a plural society, one person's solution may be another person's problem. For example, solving the problem of inequality in society may mean redistributive tax and spending policies, which take from persons of above-average wealth to give to persons with below-average wealth. The latter may view this as a solution, but the former may view it as creating serious problems. There are *no* policies that can simultaneously attain mutually exclusive ends.

4. It is quite possible that some societal forces cannot be harnessed by governments, even if it is desirable to do so. It may turn out that the government cannot stop urban location patterns of whites and blacks, even if it tries to do so. Whites and blacks may separate themselves regardless of government policies in support of integration. Some children may not be able to learn much in public schools no matter what is done. In other words, governments may not be *able* to bring about some societal changes.

5. Frequently, people adapt themselves to public policies in ways that render the policies useless. For example, we may solve the problem of poverty by government guarantees of a high annual income, but by so doing we may reduce incentives to work and thus swell the number of dependent families beyond the fiscal capacities of government to provide guarantees. The possibility always exists that adaptive behavior may frustrate policy.

6. Societal problems may have multiple causes, and a specific policy may not be able to eradicate the problem. For example, job training may not affect the hardcore unemployed if their employability is also affected by chronic poor health.

7. The solution to some problems may require policies that are more costly than the problem. For example, it may turn out that certain levels of public disorder—including riots, civil disturbances, and occasional violence—cannot be eradicated without the adoption of very repressive policies—the forceable breakup of revolutionary parties, restrictions on the public appearances of demagogues, the suppression of hate literature, the addition of large numbers of security forces, and so on. But these repressive policies would prove too costly in democratic values—freedom of speech and press, rights of assembly, freedom to form opposition parties. Thus, a certain level of disorder may be the price we pay for democracy. Doubtless, there are other examples of societal problems that are simply too costly to solve.

8. The political system is not structured for completely rational decision making. The solution of societal problems generally implies a rational model, but government may not be capable of formulating policy in a rational fashion. Instead, the political system may reflect group interests, elite preferences, institutional forces, or incremental change, more than rationalism. Presumably, a democratic system is structured to reflect mass influences, whether these are rational or not. Elected officials respond to the demands of their constituents, and this may inhibit completely rational approaches to public policy.

SUMMARY

Policy evaluation is learning about the consequences of public policy.

1. Policy evaluation involves assessing the impact of policy on target and nontarget groups, future as well as immediate impacts, and direct as well as indirect costs.

2. Government agencies themselves usually report policy output measures, rather than the effects of these outputs on societal conditions.

3. Systematic policy evaluation may involve before and after comparisons, projected trend line versus post program comparisons, and comparisons of governments with and without programs.

4. The classic research design involves comparisons between control and experimental groups both before and after program implementation.

5. The Office of Management and Budget (OMB) and the General Accountability Office (GAO) undertake evaluations of federal programs.

6. There are many political and bureaucratic obstacles to effective policy evaluation.

MySearchLab® EXERCISES

Apply what you learned in this chapter on MySearchLab (www.mysearchlab.com).

NOTES

1. Joseph S. Wholey, et al., *Federal Evaluation Policy* (Washington, DC: Urban Institute, 1970), p. 25.

2. David Nachmias, *Public Policy Evaluation* (New York: St. Martin's Press, 1979), p. 4.

3. See David L. Sills, ed., *International Encyclopedia of the Social Sciences*, vol. 7 (New York: Free Press, 1968), p. 241.

4. David Kershaw and Jerelyn Fair, eds., *Final Report of the New Jersey Graduated Work Incentive Experiment* (Madison: University of Wisconsin, Institute for Research on Poverty, 1974).

5. John F. Cogan, *Negative Income Taxation and Labor Supply: New Evidence from the New Jersey–Pennsylvania Experiment* (Santa Monica, CA: Rand Corporation, 1978). See also SRI International, *Final Report of the Seattle–Denver Income Maintenance Experiment* (Washington, DC: U.S. Government Printing Office, 1983), for experimental results suggesting that government job training has no effect on a person's subsequent earnings or employment and that a guaranteed income significantly lowers earnings and hours of work and contributes to marital dissolutions.

6. Office of Management and Budget, *Budget of the United States Government 2012*, Analytical Perspectives, Chapter 8 Program Evaluation, p. 83.

7. *Federal Evaluation Issues* (Washington, DC: General Accounting Office, 1989).

8. *Annual Index of Reports Issued* (Washington, DC: General Accountability Office, annually).

9. James Q. Wilson, "On Pettigrew and Armor," *The Public Interest* 31 (Spring 1973), pp. 132–134.

10. Charles E. Lindblom and Edward J. Woodhouse, *The Policy-Making Process*, 3rd ed. (Englewood Cliffs, NJ: Prentice Hall, 1993), pp. 31–32.

BIBLIOGRAPHY

AMMONS, DAVID N. *Tools for Decision-Making: A Practical Guide for Local Government.* Washington, DC: CQ Press, 2002.

BARDACH, EUGENE. *A Practical Guide for Policy Analysis*, 3rd ed. Washington, DC: CQ Press, 2008.

BINGHAM, RICHARD D., and CLAIRE L. FELBINGER. *Evaluation in Practice*, 2nd ed. Washington, DC: CQ Press, 2002.

HEINEMAN, ROBERT A., et al. *The World of the Policy Analyst*, 3rd ed. Washington, DC: CQ Press, 2001.

O'SULLIVAN, ELIZABETHANN, et al. *Research Methods for Public Administrators*, 5th ed. New York: Longman, 2008.

POSAVAC, EMIL J. *Program Evaluation*, 8th ed. New York: Pearson, 2011.

PRESSMAN, JEFFREY L., and AARON WILDAVSKY. *Implementation.* Berkeley: University of California Press, 1974.

WEIMER, DAVID, L., and AIDAN R. VINING. *Policy Analysis: Concepts and Practices*, 5th ed. New York: Longman, 2011.

WILDAVSKY, AARON. *Speaking Truth to Power.* New York: John Wiley, 1979.

WEB SITES

GENERAL ACCOUNTABILITY OFFICE. The GAO is the investigative and evaluative arm of the Congress. Its purpose is to hold the executive branch accountable to the Congress. Its reports cover a wide variety of issues. *www.gao.gov*

OFFICE OF MANAGEMENT AND BUDGET. In addition to preparing the Budget of the United States, OMB performs management studies, including reports on financial management and regulatory matters. *www.whitehouse.gov/omb*

ASSOCIATION FOR PUBLIC POLICY ANALYSIS AND MANAGEMENT. Academic organization that publishes the *Journal of Policy Analysis and Management*, with articles on public administration and management. *www.appam.org*

AMERICAN SOCIETY FOR PUBLIC ADMINISTRATION. Organization of academic and professional public administrators, with news, job listings, and publication—*Public Administration Review. www.aspanet.org*

RAND CORPORATION. Originally devoted almost exclusively to research on defense and weapons systems, RAND studies now include space research, Internet technology, information protection, and assessments of government programs across a wide spectrum. *www.rand.org*

CATO INSTITUTE, *Regulation magazine.* Articles assessing the costs and effectiveness of government programs, especially regulatory programs and agencies. *www.cato.org/pubs/regulation*

When State and Federal Laws Clash Supporters and opponents of California Proposition 19, which would have legalized marijuana for recreational use, hold opposing signs on the ballot referendum. Proposition 19 failed in November 2010, and California avoided a direct conflict with federal law which classifies marijuana as an illegal substance. Nonetheless, several states allow marijuana for medical use. The federal Drug Enforcement Administration (DEA) has announced that it will not prosecute medical users in states where it is permitted, thus avoiding a federal-state conflict. (© Ted Soqui/Corbis)

5

Federalism and State Policies
Institutional Arrangements and Policy Variations

AMERICAN FEDERALISM

Virtually all nations of the world have some units of local government—states, provinces, regions, cities, counties, towns, villages. Decentralization of policymaking is required almost everywhere. But nations are not truly *federal* unless both national and subnational governments exercise separate and autonomous authority, both elect their own officials, and both tax their own citizens for the provision of public services. Moreover, federalism requires the powers of the national and subnational governments to be guaranteed by a constitution that cannot be changed without the consent of both national and subnational populations.[*]

The United States, Canada, Australia, India, Germany, and Switzerland are generally regarded as federal systems, but Great Britain, France, Italy, and Sweden are not. Although these latter nations have local governments, they depend on the national government for their powers. They are considered *unitary* rather than federal systems because their local governments can be altered or even abolished by the national government acting alone. In contrast, a system is said to be *confederal* if the power of the national government is dependent on local units of government. While these terms—*federal, unitary,* and *confederal*—can be defined theoretically, in the real world of policymaking it is not so easy to distinguish between governments that are truly federal and those that are not. Indeed, it is not clear whether government in the United States today retains its federal character.

There are more than 89,000 separate governments in the United States, more than 60,000 of which have the power to levy their own taxes. There are states, counties, municipalities (cities, boroughs, villages), school districts, and special districts (see Table 5–1). However, only the national government and the states are recognized in the U.S. Constitution; all local governments are subdivisions of states. States may create, alter, or abolish these governments by amending state laws or constitutions.

---

[*]Other definitions of federalism in American political science: "Federalism refers to a political system in which there are local (territorial, regional, provincial, state, or municipal) units of government, as well as a national government, that can make final decisions with respect to at least some governmental authorities and whose existence is especially protected." James Q. Wilson and John J. DiIulio, Jr., *American Government*, 7th ed. (Boston: Houghton Mifflin, 1998), p. 52. "Federalism is the mode of political organization that unites smaller polities within an overarching political system by distributing power among general and constituent units in a manner designed to protect the existence and authority of both national and subnational systems enabling all to share in the overall system's decision making and executing processes." Daniel J. Elazar, *American Federalism: A View from the States* (New York: Thomas Y. Crowell, 1966), p. 2.

TABLE 5–1   Governments in the United States There are more than 87,000 governments in the United States.

U.S. government	1
State governments	50
Counties	3,033
Municipalities	19,492
Townships	16,579
School districts	13,051
Special districts	37,381
Total	89,587

SOURCE: *Census of Governments, 2007.*

WHY FEDERALISM?

Why have state and local governments anyway? Why not have a centralized political system with a single government accountable to national majorities in national elections—a government capable of implementing uniform policies throughout the country? A variety of arguments are made on behalf of federalism.

Protection Against Tyranny

The nation's Founders understood that "republican principles"—periodic elections, representative government, political equality—would not be sufficient in themselves to protect individual liberty. These principles may make governing elites more responsive to popular concerns, but they do not protect minorities or individuals, "the weaker party or an obnoxious individual," from government deprivations of liberty or property. Indeed, according to the Founders, "the great object" of constitution writing was both to preserve popular government and, at the same time, to protect individuals from "unjust and interested" *majorities*. "A dependence on the people is, no doubt, the primary control of government, but experience has taught mankind the necessity of auxiliary precautions."[1]

Among the most important "auxiliary precautions" devised by the Founders to control government was federalism, which was viewed as a source of constraint on big government. They sought to construct a governmental system incorporating the notion of "opposite and rival interests." Governments and government officials could be constrained by competition with other governments and other government officials.[2]

Policy Diversity

Today, federalism continues to permit policy diversity. The entire nation is not straitjacketed with a uniform policy to which every state and community must conform. State and local governments may be better suited to deal with specific state and local problems. Washington bureaucrats do not always know best about what to do in Commerce, Texas, for example.

Conflict Management

Federalism helps manage policy conflict. Permitting states and communities to pursue their own policies reduces the pressures that would build up in Washington if the national government had to decide everything. Federalism permits citizens to decide many things at the state and local levels of government and avoid battling over single national policies to be applied uniformly throughout the land.

Dispersal of Power

Federalism disperses power. The widespread distribution of power is generally regarded as an added protection against tyranny. To the extent that pluralism thrives in the United States, state and local governments have contributed to its success. They also provide a political base for the survival of the opposition party when it has lost national elections.

Increased Participation

Federalism increases political participation. It allows more people to run for and hold political office. Nearly a million people hold some kind of political office in counties, cities, townships, school districts, and special districts. These local leaders are often regarded as closer to the people than Washington officials. Public opinion polls show that Americans believe that their local governments are more manageable and responsive than the national government.

Improved Efficiency

Federalism improves efficiency. Even though we may think of 89,000 governments as an inefficient system, governing the entire nation from Washington would be even worse. Imagine the bureaucracy, red tape, delays, and confusion if every government activity in every community in the nation—police, schools, roads, firefighting, garbage collection, sewage disposal, street lighting, and so on—were controlled by a central government in Washington.

Ensuring Policy Responsiveness

Federalism encourages policy responsiveness. Multiple, competing governments are more sensitive to citizens' views than a centralized, monopolistic government. The existence of multiple governments offering different packages of benefits and costs allows a better match between citizens' preferences and public policy. People and businesses can vote with their feet by relocating to those states and communities that most closely conform to their own policy preferences. Mobility not only facilitates a better match between citizens' preferences and public policy, it also encourages competition among states and communities to offer improved service at lower costs.

Encouraging Policy Innovation

Federalism encourages policy experimentation and innovation. Federalism may be perceived today as a conservative idea, but it was once viewed as the instrument of progressivism. A strong argument can be made that the groundwork for the New Deal was built in state policy experimentation during the Progressive Era. Federal programs as diverse as income tax, unemployment compensation, counter-cyclical public works, Social Security, wage and hour legislation, bank deposit insurance, and food stamps all had antecedents at the state level. Much of the current liberal policy agenda—health insurance, child-care programs, government support of industrial research and development—has been embraced by various states. Indeed, the compelling phrase "laboratories of democracy" is generally attributed to the great progressive jurist Supreme Court Justice Louis D. Brandeis, who used it in defense of state experimentation with new solutions to social and economic problems.

POLITICS AND INSTITUTIONAL ARRANGEMENTS

Political conflict over federalism—over the division of responsibilities and finances between national and state/local governments—has tended to follow traditional liberal and conservative political cleavages. Generally, liberals seek to enhance the power of the *national* government. Liberals believe that people's lives can be changed by the exercise of government power to end discrimination, abolish poverty, eliminate slums, ensure employment, uplift the downtrodden, educate the masses, and cure the sick. The government in Washington has more power and resources than state and local governments have, and liberals have turned to it to cure America's ills. State and local governments are regarded as too slow, cumbersome, weak, and unresponsive. It is difficult to achieve change when reform-minded citizens must deal with 50 state governments or 89,000 local governments. Moreover, liberals argue that state and local governments contribute to inequality in society by setting different levels of services in education, welfare, health, and other public functions. A strong national government can ensure uniformity of standards throughout the nation. The government in Washington is seen as the principal instrument for liberal social and economic reform.

Generally, conservatives seek to return power to *state and local* governments. They are more skeptical about the good that Washington can do. Adding to the power of the national government is not an effective way of resolving society's problems. On the contrary, conservatives often argue that "government is the problem, not the solution." Excessive government regulation, burdensome taxation, and inflationary government spending combine to restrict individual freedom, penalize work and savings, and destroy incentives for economic growth. Government should be kept small, controllable, and close to the people.

Institutional Arenas and Policy Preferences

Debates about federalism are seldom constitutional debates; rather, they are debates about policy. People decide which level of government—national, state, or local—is most likely to enact the policy they prefer. Then they argue that that level of government should have the responsibility for enacting the policy. Political scientist David Nice explains "the art of intergovernmental politics" as "trying to reduce, maintain, or increase the scope of conflict in order to produce the policy decisions you want." Abstract debates about federalism or other institutional arrangements, devoid of policy implications, hold little interest for most citizens or politicians. "Most people have little interest in abstract debates that argue which level of government should be responsible for a given task. What people care about is getting the policies they want."[3]

Thus, the case for centralizing policy decisions in Washington is almost always one of substituting the policy preferences of national elites for those of state and local officials. It is not seriously argued on constitutional grounds that national elites better reflect the policy preferences of the American people. Rather, federal intervention is defended on policy grounds—the assertion that the goals and priorities that prevail in Washington should prevail throughout the nation.

Concentrating Benefits to Organized Interests

The national government is more likely to reflect the policy preferences of the nation's strongest and best-organized interest groups than are 89,000 state and local governments. This is true, first, because the costs of "rent seeking"—lobbying government for special subsidies, privileges, and protections—are less in Washington in relation to the benefits available from national legislation than the combined costs of rent seeking at 89,000 subnational centers. Organized interests, seeking concentrated benefits for themselves and dispersed costs to the rest of society, can concentrate their own resources in Washington. Even if state and local governments individually are more vulnerable to the lobbying efforts of wealthy, well-organized special interests, the prospect of influencing all 50 separate state governments or, worse, 89,000 local governments is discouraging to them. The costs of rent seeking at 50 state capitols, 3,000 county courthouses, and tens of thousands of city halls, while not multiplicative by these numbers, are certainly greater than the costs of rent seeking in a single national capitol.

Moreover, the benefits of national legislation are comprehensive. A single act of Congress, a federal executive regulation, or a federal appellate court ruling can achieve what would require the combined and coordinated action by hundreds, if not thousands, of state and local government agencies. Thus, the benefits of rent seeking in Washington are greater in relation to the costs.

Dispersing Costs to Unorganized Taxpayers

Perhaps more important, the size of the national constituency permits interest groups to disperse the costs of specialized, concentrated benefits over a very broad constituency. Cost dispersal is the key to interest group success. If costs are widely dispersed, it is irrational for individuals, each of whom bears only a tiny fraction of these costs, to expend time, energy, and money to counter the claims of the special interests. Dispersal of costs over the entire nation better accommodates the strategies of special interest groups than the smaller constituencies of state and local government.

In contrast, state and local government narrows the constituencies over which costs must be spread, thus increasing the burdens to individual taxpayers and increasing the likelihood that they will take notice of them and resist their imposition. Economist Randall G. Holcombe explains: "One way to counteract this [interest group] effect is to provide public goods and services at the smallest level of government possible. This concentrates the cost on the smallest group of taxpayers possible and thus provides more concentrated costs to accompany the concentrated benefits."[4] He goes on to speculate whether the tobacco subsidies granted by Washington to North Carolina farmers would be voted by the residents of that state if they had to pay their full costs.

The rent-seeking efficiencies of lobbying in Washington are well known to the organized interests. As a result, the policies of the national government are more likely to reflect the preferences of the nation's strongest and best-organized interests.

AMERICAN FEDERALISM: VARIATIONS ON THE THEME

American federalism has undergone many changes in the more than 200 years since the Constitution of 1787. That is, the meaning and practice of federalism have transformed many times.

State-Centered Federalism (1787–1865)

From the adoption of the Constitution of 1787 to the end of the Civil War, the states were the most important units in the American federal system. People looked to the states for the resolution of most policy questions and the provision of most public services. Even the issue of slavery was decided by state governments. The supremacy of the national government was frequently questioned, first by the Antifederalists (including Thomas Jefferson) and later by John C. Calhoun and other defenders of slavery and secession.

Dual Federalism (1865–1913)

The supremacy of the national government was decided on the battlefields of the Civil War. Yet for nearly a half-century after that conflict, the national government narrowly interpreted its delegated powers and the states continued to decide most domestic policy issues. The resulting pattern has been described as dual federalism, in which the state and the nation divided most government functions. The national government concentrated its attention on the delegated powers—national defense, foreign affairs, tariffs, commerce crossing state lines, money, standard weights and measures, post office and post roads, and admission of new states. State governments decided the important domestic policy issues—education, welfare, health, and criminal justice. The separation of policy responsibilities was once compared to a "layer cake," with local governments at the base, state governments in the middle, and the national government at the top.[5]

Cooperative Federalism (1913–1964)

The distinction between national and state responsibilities gradually eroded in the first half of the twentieth century. American federalism was transformed by the Industrial Revolution and the development of a national economy; the federal income tax in 1913, which shifted financial resources to the national government; and the challenges of two world wars and the Great Depression. In response to the Great Depression of the 1930s, state governors welcomed massive federal public works projects under President Franklin D. Roosevelt's New Deal. In addition, the federal government intervened directly in economic affairs, labor relations, business practices, and agriculture. Through its grants-in-aid, the national government cooperated with the states in public assistance, employment services, child welfare, public housing, urban renewal, highway building, and vocational education.

This new pattern of federal–state relations was labeled cooperative federalism. Both the nation and the states exercised responsibilities for welfare, health, highways, education, and criminal justice. This merging of policy responsibilities was compared to a marble cake: "As the colors are mixed in a marble cake, so functions are mixed in the American federal system."[6]

Yet even in this period of shared national–state responsibility, the national government emphasized cooperation in achieving common national and state goals. Congress generally acknowledged that it had no direct constitutional authority to regulate public health, safety, or welfare. It relied primarily on its powers to tax and spend for the general welfare in order to provide financial assistance to state and local governments to achieve shared goals. Congress did not legislate directly on local matters. For example, Congress did not require the teaching of vocational education in public high schools because public education was not an "enumerated power" of the national government in the U.S. Constitution. But Congress could offer money to states and school districts to assist in teaching vocational education and even threaten to withdraw the money if federal standards were not met. In this way the federal government involved itself in fields "reserved" to the states.

Centralized Federalism (1964–1980)

Over the years it became increasingly difficult to maintain the fiction that the national government was merely assisting the states in performing their domestic responsibilities. By the time President Lyndon B. Johnson launched the Great Society in 1964, the federal government had clearly set forth its own "national" goals. Virtually all problems confronting American society— from solid waste disposal and water and air pollution to consumer safety, street crime, preschool education, and even rat control—were declared to be national problems. Congress legislated directly on any matter it chose, without regard to its "enumerated powers." The Supreme Court no longer concerned itself with the "reserved" powers of the states, and the Tenth Amendment lost most of its meaning. The pattern of national–state relations became centralized. As for the cake analogies, one commentator observed, "The frosting had moved to the top, something like a pineapple upside-down cake."[7]

The states' role under centralized federalism is that of responding to federal policy initiatives and conforming to federal regulations established as conditions for federal grant money. The administrative role of the states remained important; they helped implement federal policies in welfare, Medicaid, environmental protection, employment training, public housing, and so on. But the states' role was determined not by the states themselves but by the national government.

Bureaucracies at the federal, state, and local levels became increasingly indistinguishable. Coalitions of professional bureaucrats—whether in education, public assistance, employment training, rehabilitation, natural resources, agriculture, or whatever—worked together on behalf of shared goals, whether they were officially employed by the federal government, the state government, or a local authority. State and local officials in agencies receiving a large proportion of their funds from the federal government felt very little loyalty to their governor or state legislature.

New Federalism (1980–1985)

Efforts to reverse the flow of power to Washington and return responsibilities to state and local government have been labeled the *new federalism*. The phrase originated in the administration of President Richard M. Nixon, who used it to describe general revenue sharing, that is, federal sharing of tax revenues with state and local governments, with few strings attached. Later, the phrase "new federalism" was used by President Ronald Reagan to describe a series of proposals designed to reduce federal involvement in domestic programs and encourage states and cities to undertake greater policy responsibilities themselves. These efforts included the consolidation of many categorical grant programs into fewer block grants, an end to general revenue sharing, and less reliance by the states on federal revenue.

Coercive Federalism (1985–1995)

It was widely assumed before 1985 that Congress could not directly legislate how state and local governments should perform their traditional functions. Congress was careful not to issue direct orders to the states; instead, it undertook to grant or withhold federal aid money, depending on whether states and cities abided by congressional "strings" attached to these grants. In theory, at least, the states were free to ignore conditions established by Congress for federal grants and forgo the money.

However, in its 1985 *Garcia* decision, the U.S. Supreme Court appeared to remove all barriers to direct congressional legislation in matters traditionally "reserved" to the states.[8] The case arose after Congress directly ordered state and local governments to pay minimum wages to their employees. The Court reversed earlier decisions that Congress could not directly legislate state and local government matters. It also dismissed arguments that the nature of American federalism and the Reserved Powers Clause of the Tenth Amendment prevented Congress from directly legislating state affairs. It said that the only protection for state powers was to be found in the states' role in electing U.S. senators, members of Congress, and the president—a concept known as "representational federalism."

Representational Federalism

The idea behind representational federalism is that there is *no* constitutional division of powers between states and nation—federalism is defined by the role of the states in electing members of Congress and the president. The United States is said to retain a federal system because its national officials are selected from subunits of government—the president through the allocation of electoral college votes to the states, and the Congress through the allocation of two Senate seats per state and the apportionment of representatives based on state population. Whatever protection exists for state power and independence must be found in the national political process—in the influence of state and district voters on their senators and members of Congress.

The Supreme Court rhetorically endorsed a federal system in the *Garcia* decision but left it up to the national Congress, rather than the Constitution or the courts, to decide what powers should be exercised by the states and the national government. In a strongly worded dissenting opinion, Justice Lewis Powell argued that if federalism is to be retained, the Constitution must divide powers, not the Congress. "The states' role in our system of government is a matter of constitutional law, not legislative grace... [This decision] today rejects almost 200 years of the understanding of the constitutional status of federalism."[9]

However, in 1995 the Supreme Court appeared to revive the original notion of a Congress with limited, enumerated powers.

FEDERALISM REVIVIED?

Controversies over federalism are as old as the nation itself. And while over time the flow of power has been toward Washington, occasionally Congress and even the Supreme Court have reasserted the constitutional division of power between the federal government and the states.

Welfare Reform and "Devolution"

In 1995, with Republican majorities in both houses of Congress, "Devolution" became a popular catch word. Devolution meant the passing down of responsibilities from the national government to the states, and welfare reform turned out to be the key to devolution. Since Franklin D. Roosevelt's New Deal, with its federal guarantee of cash Aid to Families with Dependent Children (AFDC), low-income mothers and children had enjoyed a federal "entitlement" to welfare benefits. But in 1996 the welfare reform bill passed by Congress and signed by President Clinton (after two earlier vetoes) turned over responsibility for determining eligibility for cash aid to the states, ending the sixty-year federal entitlement. The Temporary Assistance to Needy Families established block grants to the states and gave them broad responsibility for determining eligibility and benefits levels. But Congress did add some "strings" to these grants: states must place a two-year limit on continuing cash benefits and a five-year lifetime limit. This was a major change in federal welfare policy (see Chapter 7).

Supreme Court Revival of Federalism (1995–Present)

Recent decisions of the U.S. Supreme Court suggest at least a partial revival of the original constitutional design of federalism.

In 1995, the Supreme Court issued its first opinion in more than 60 years that recognized a limit on Congress's power over interstate commerce and reaffirmed the Founders' notion of a national government with only the powers enumerated in the Constitution. The Court found that the federal Gun-Free School Zones Act was unconstitutional because it exceeded Congress's powers under the Interstate Commerce Clause. Chief Justice William H. Rehnquist, writing for the majority in a 5-to-4 decision in *United States* v. *Lopez,* even cited James Madison with approval: "The powers delegated by the proposed Constitution are few and defined. Those which are to remain in the state governments are numerous and indefinite."[10]

The Supreme Court invalidated a provision of a popular law of Congress, the Brady Handgun Violence Protection Act. The Court decided in 1997 that the law's command to local law enforcement officers to conduct background checks on gun purchasers violated "the very principle of separate state sovereignty." The Court affirmed that the federal government may "neither issue directives requiring the states to address particular problems, nor command the states' officers, or those of their political subdivisions, to administer or enforce the federal regulatory program."[11]

These decisions run counter to most of the Court's twentieth-century holdings that empowered the national government to do just about anything it wished under a broad interpretation of the Interstate Commerce Clause. The narrowness of the Court votes in these decisions (5–4) suggested that this revival of federalism might be short-lived. But in 2000, to the surprise of many observers, the Supreme Court held that Congress's Violence Against Women Act was an unconstitutional extension of federal power into the reserved police powers of states. Citing its earlier *Lopez* decision, the Court held that noneconomic crimes are beyond the power of the national government under the Interstate Commerce Clause. "Gender-motivated crimes of violence are not, in any sense, economic activity." The Court rejected Congress's argument that the aggregate impact of crime nationwide has a substantial effect on interstate commerce. "The Constitution requires a distinction between what is truly national and what is truly local, and there is no better example of the police power, which the Founders undeniably left reposed in the States and denied the central government, than the suppression of violent crime and vindication of its victims."[12] But this decision, too, was made by a 5–4 vote of the justices, suggesting the replacement of justices might reverse this trend toward federalism by the Supreme Court.

MONEY AND POWER FLOW TO WASHINGTON

Money and power go together. As institutions acquire financial resources, they become more powerful. The centralization of power in Washington has come about largely as a product of growth in the national government's financial resources—its ability to tax, spend, and borrow money.

Federal Grants-in-Aid

The federal grant-in-aid has been the principal instrument for the expansion of national power. As late as 1952, federal intergovernment transfers amounted to about 10 percent of all state and local government revenue. Federal transfers creeped up slowly for a few years; rose significantly after 1957 with the National Defense (Interstate) Highway Program and a series of post-Sputnik educational programs; and then surged in the welfare, health, housing, and community development fields under President Lyndon B. Johnson's Great Society programs (1965–1968). President Nixon not only expanded these Great Society transfers but also added his own general revenue-sharing program. Federal financial interventions continued to grow despite occasional rhetoric in Washington about state and local responsibility. By 1980, more than 27 percent of all state and local revenue came from the federal government. So dependent had state and local governments become on federal largess that the most frequently voiced rationale for continuing federal grant programs was that states and communities had become accustomed to federal money and could not survive without it (see Figure 5–1).

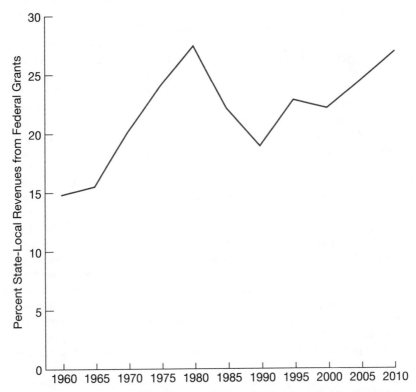

FIGURE 5–1   State and Local Government Dependency on Federal Grants State and local government dependency on federal money rose sharply prior to 1980; during the Reagan presidency federal grants were curtailed, but have risen again in recent years.

President Ronald Reagan briefly challenged the nation's movement toward centralized government. The Reagan administration ended general revenue sharing. It also succeeded in consolidating many categorical grant programs in larger block grants, allowing for greater local control over revenue allocation. Categorical grants are awarded to specific projects approved by a federal department distributing designated funds. A block grant is a payment to a state or local government for a general function, such as community development or education. State and local officials may use such funds for their stated purposes without seeking the approval of federal agencies for specific projects.

Today, federal grants again account for about one-quarter of all state and local government spending. It is unlikely that centralizing tendencies in the American federal system can ever be permanently checked or reversed. It is not likely that presidents or members of Congress will ever be moved to restrain national power. People expect them to "Do something!" about virtually every problem that confronts individuals, families, communities, states, or the nation. Politicians risk appearing "insensitive" if they respond by saying that a particular problem is not a federal concern.

Federal Grant Purposes

Federal grants are available in nearly every major category of state and local government activity. So numerous and diverse are they that there is often a lack of information about their availability, purpose, and requirements. In fact, federal grants can be obtained for the preservation of historic buildings, the development of minority-owned businesses, aid to foreign refugees, the drainage of abandoned mines, riot control, and school milk. However, health (including Medicaid for the poor) and welfare (including family cash aid and food stamps) account for more than two-thirds of federal aid money (see Figure 5–2).

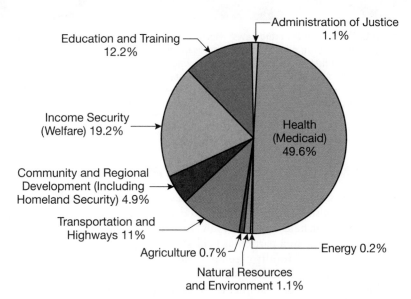

FIGURE 5–2   Purposes of Federal Grant-in-Aid Money Medicaid is the largest category of federal grant money, followed by welfare, education, and transportation. SOURCE: *Statistical Abstract of the United States, 2010.*

Achieving National Uniformity in Drinking Laws   Mothers Against Drunk Driving (MADD) sponsor a crash truck as part of a continuing youth education program regarding the dangers of drinking and driving. In 2010 MADD celebrated the twenty-first anniversary of the Lifesaving 21 Minimum Drinking Age Act for which MADD was largely responsible. The Act conditions federal highway grants-in-aid to the states on the states' enacting 21-year-old drinking laws. Setting conditions on grants-in-aid money is the primary method by which the federal government influences the policies of state and local governments.   (© prettyfoto/Alamy)

FEDERAL PREEMPTIONS AND MANDATES

The supremacy of federal laws over those of the states, spelled out in the National Supremacy Clause of the Constitution, permits Congress to decide whether or not there is *preemption* of state laws in a particular field by federal law. In *total preemption*, the federal government assumes all regulatory powers in a particular field—for example, copyrights, railroads, and airlines. No state regulations in a totally preempted field are permitted. *Partial preemption* stipulates that a state law on the same subject is valid as long as it does not conflict with the federal law in the same area. For example, the Occupational Safety and Health Act of 1970 specifically permits state regulation of any occupational safety or health issue on which the federal Occupational Safety and Health Administration (OSHA) has *not* developed a standard; but once OSHA enacts a standard, all state standards are nullified. Yet another form of the partial preemption, the *standard partial preemption*, permits states to regulate activities in a field already regulated by the federal government, as long as state regulatory standards are at least as stringent as those of the federal government. Usually states must submit their regulations to the responsible federal agency for approval; the federal agency may revoke a state's regulating power if it fails to enforce the approved standards. For example, the federal Environmental Protection Agency (EPA) permits state environmental regulations that meet or exceed EPA standards.

Federal Mandates

Federal mandates are direct orders to state and local governments to perform a particular activity or service, or to comply with federal laws in the performance of their functions. Federal mandates occur in a wide variety of areas, from civil rights to minimum wage regulations. Their range is reflected in some examples of federal mandates to state and local governments:

- *Age Discrimination Act of 1986* Outlaws mandatory retirement ages for public as well as private employees, including police, firefighters, and state college and university faculty.
- *Asbestos Hazard Emergency Act of 1986* Orders school districts to inspect for asbestos hazards and remove asbestos from school buildings when necessary.
- *Safe Drinking Water Act of 1986* Establishes national requirements for municipal water supplies; regulates municipal waste treatment plants.
- *Clean Air Act of 1990* Bans municipal incinerators and requires auto emission inspections in certain urban areas.
- *Americans with Disabilities Act of 1990* Requires all state and local government buildings to promote handicapped access.
- *National Voter Registration Act of 1993* Requires states to register voters at driver's license, welfare, and unemployment compensation offices.
- *No Child Left Behind Act of 2001* Requires states and their school districts to test public school pupils.
- *Help America Vote Act of 2002* Requires states to modernize registration and voting procedures.
- *Real ID Act of 2005* Requires that each state produce a "Real ID" driver's license that meets standards set by the Department of Homeland Security.
- *Patient Protection and Affordable Care Act of 2010* Establishes various mandates, including a requirement that state Medicaid programs serve all persons and families with incomes below 133 percent of the federal poverty level.

"Unfunded" Mandates

Federal mandates often impose heavy costs on states and communities. When no federal monies are provided to cover these costs, the mandates are said to be *unfunded mandates*. Governors, mayors, and other state and local officials have often urged Congress to halt the imposition of unfunded mandates on states and communities. Private industries have long voiced the same complaint. Regulations and mandates allow Congress to address problems while pushing the costs of doing so onto others.

STATES BATTLE BACK

The American states are battling back on several fronts, in efforts to retain their powers against federal encroachment.

Health Insurance Individual Mandate

The comprehensive Patient Protection and Affordable Care Act of 2010 (President Obama's health care reform) includes a mandate that every individual in the country obtain government approved health insurance. Failure to comply will result in an annual tax penalty to be enforced by the Internal Revenue Service. (For more information, see Chapter 8.) Attorneys General in several states have undertaken legal action in federal court challenging this "individual mandate" as an unconstitutional expansion of federal power over the citizens of their states. Never before has the federal government mandated that individuals buy a product. Are there any "reserved powers" of the states under the 10th Amendment? What remains of the notion of a national government of limited and enumerated powers?

Supporters of the individual mandate claim that it is justified under the Interstate Commerce Clause of the Constitution. Historically this Clause has been given broad interpretation by the Supreme Court; Congress can regulate any economic activity that "taken in the aggregate substantially affects interstate commerce."[13] Health insurance, supporters argue, is an integral part of interstate commerce. The health insurance industry must pool all individuals, including the young and healthy, if the industry is to cover the ill and persons with preexisting conditions. They also argue that the individual mandate is constitutional because it is structured as a tax on income, which is authorized under the 16th Amendment.

Arguments over the individual mandate and the Patient Protection and Affordable Care Act are highly partisan. The Act was passed in Congress without a single Republican vote in either the House or Senate. The issue of the constitutionality of the individual mandate is likely to be decided by the Supreme Court. (See also "Repealing Obamacare?" in Chapter 8.)

Arizona's Immigration Law

Frustrated by the failure of the federal government to enforce existing federal immigration laws, Arizona passed its own illegal-immigration law in 2010. (For more information, see Chapter 12.) The Arizona law mirrors federal law dealing with aliens, requiring them to carry valid immigration documents. It makes it a *state* crime to be in the country illegally. Police are given broad powers to detain anyone suspected of being an illegal alien.

The U.S. Justice Department filed suit against the Arizona law arguing that it violates the Supremacy Clause of the Constitution: "A state may not establish its own immigration policy or enforce state laws in a manner that interferes with federal immigration laws. The Constitution and federal immigration laws do not permit the development of a patchwork of state and local immigration policy throughout the country."[14] (A separate constitutional question is whether the Arizona law poses a threat to the 14th Amendment's Equal Protection Clause by encouraging racial profiling in its enforcement.)

Supporters of the law argue that it is not in conflict with federal laws on immigration. When the federal government fails in its own responsibility to protect the nation's borders, states may intervene to do so themselves. Federal courts must answer the question, "Do federal laws totally preempt state laws in the area of immigration?"

Marijuana for Medical Use

The federal government prohibits the sale, possession, or growth of marijuana for any purpose. Federal law does not recognize a medical exception. The Food and Drug Administration lists marijuana as a "Schedule 1 substance under the Controlled Substance Act, classified as having a high potential for abuse and no currently accepted medical use."

But a number of states have undertaken to legalize marijuana for medical use. Many have done so through ballot propositions. Majorities of Americans approve the use of marijuana for medical purposes. (However, in 2010, California voters defeated a ballot proposition that would have allowed marijuana use for recreational purposes.) There is a clear conflict between federal and state laws over medical marijuana.

In partial recognition of this conflict, Attorney General Eric Holder announced in 2009 "clarifying guidelines… for the use of federal investigative and prosecutorial resources." The Drug Enforcement Administration (DEA) will not arrest or prosecute individual marijuana users who are in compliance with state laws authorizing marijuana for medical purposes. "These guidelines do not legalize marijuana. [BUT] it is not the practice of the DEA to target individuals with serious medical conditions who comply with state laws authorizing their use for medical purposes."[15] In other words, the federal government will not enforce federal law in states which have passed laws approving the use of marijuana for medical purposes.

STATE POLICYMAKING BY INITIATIVE AND REFERENDA

The U.S. Constitution has no provision for direct voting by the people on national policy questions. The nation's Founders were profoundly skeptical of direct democracy—citizens themselves initiating and deciding policy questions. They had read about direct democracy in the ancient Greek city state of Athens and believed the "follies" of direct democracy outweighed any virtues it might possess. The Founders believed that government rests ultimately on the consent of the governed. However, their notion of "republicanism" envisioned decision making by representatives of the people, not the people themselves—representative democracy rather than direct democracy.

But 100 years later, a strong populist movement developed in the American states, attacking railroads, corporate "trusts," and politicians under their sway. Populists believe that elected representatives were ignoring the needs of farmers, debtors, and laborers. They sought to bypass politicians and have the people directly initiate and vote on policy issues. Today the initiative and referenda for state constitutional amendments exists in 18 states (see Table 5–2).

Initiative

The initiative is a device whereby a specific number or percentage of voters, through the use of a petition, may propose policy changes, either as constitutional amendments or as state laws to be placed on the ballot for adoption or rejection by the electorate of a state. This process bypasses the legislature and allows citizens to propose laws and constitutional amendments.

Referendum

The referendum is a device by which the electorate must approve laws or constitutional amendments. Referenda may be submitted by the legislature, or referenda may be demanded by popular petition through the initiative device.

TABLE 5–2 Citizen Initiatives in the States Initiative for Constitutional Amendments (Signatures Required to Get on Ballot)[a]

Arizona (15%)
Arkansas (10%)
California (8%)
Colorado (5%)
Florida (8%)[b]
Illinois (8%)
Massachusetts (3%)
Michigan (10%)
Mississippi (12%)
Missouri (8%)
Montana (10%)
Nebraska (10%)
Nevada (10%)
North Dakota (4% of state population)
Ohio (10%)
Oklahoma (15%)
Oregon (8%)
South Dakota (10%)

[a]Figures expressed as percentage of vote in last governor's election unless otherwise specified; some states also require distribution of votes across counties and districts.
[b]Florida requires referenda to pass by a supermajority (60 percent).

Proponents of direct democracy make several strong arguments on behalf of the initiative and referendum device. It enhances government responsiveness and accountability; even the threat of a successful initiative and referendum drive sometimes encourages officials to take popular actions. It allows groups that are not especially well represented in state capitals, taxpayers for example, to place their concerns on the public agenda. It stimulates voter interest and improves election day turnout. Controversial issues on the ballot—the death penalty, abortion, gay marriage, gun control, taxes—bring out additional voters. Finally, it can secure the passage of constitutional amendments and laws ignored or rejected by elected officials.

Opponents of direct democracy, from our nation's Founders to the present, argue that representative democracy offers far better protection for individual liberty and the rights of minorities than direct democracy. The Founders constructed a system of checks and balances not so much to protect against the oppression of a ruler, but rather to protect against the tyranny of the majority. It is also argued that voters are not sufficiently informed to cast intelligent ballots on many issues. Moreover, a referendum does not allow consideration of alternative policies or modifications or amendments to the proposition set forth on the ballot. In contrast, legislators devote a great deal of attention to writing, rewriting and amending bills, and seeking out compromises among interests.

TABLE 5-3   Selected State Ballot Propositions 2010

Marijuana. California's Proposition 19 that would have legalized recreational use of marijuana was one of the highest profile initiatives in 2010. But it ended up failing by a 46–54 vote in that state. Voters rejected medical marijuana use in Arizona, Oregon, and South Dakota. In prior years most medical marijuana use referenda had won approval on state ballots.

Labor Unions. Voters in Arizona, South Carolina, and Utah passed propositions requiring secret ballots for union elections. These measures are intended to overcome the "card check," allowing workers to unionize without a secret ballot by signing cards stating they support unionization.

Income Tax. Voters in the state of Washington firmly rejected, 35–66, a proposal to enact an income tax on individuals earning more than $200,000. Voters appeared to be in no mood to soak the rich. Or they may have believed that once an income tax was enacted, the income threshold would gradually fall, extending the tax to lower income individuals.

Racial Preferences. Arizona voters approved a proposition that prohibits the state from discriminating for or against individuals on the basis of race and ethnicity by a 59–41 margin. The state joins California, Michigan, Nebraska, and Washington that had previously approved such measures. The effect of these measures is to limit affirmative action programs.

Politics of State Initiatives and Referenda

National surveys report overwhelming support for "laws which allow citizens to place initiatives directly on the ballot by collecting petition signatures." Both liberal and conservative interests have used the initiative and referendum devices (see Table 5–3).

COMPARING PUBLIC POLICIES OF THE STATES

An overview of state and local government spending suggests the variety of policy areas in which these governments are active. Education is by far the most expensive function of state and local governments: Education accounts for about 35 percent of all state–local spending. Most of this money goes to elementary and secondary schools, but about nine percent nationwide goes to state universities and community colleges. Welfare, health and hospitals (including Medicaid), and highways place a heavy financial burden on states and communities (see Figure 5–3).

The American states provide an excellent setting for comparative analysis and the testing of hypotheses about the determinants of public policies. Policies in education, taxation, welfare, health, highways, natural resources, public safety, and many other areas vary a great deal from state to state, which allows us to inquire about the causes of divergent policies.

Variations in State Tax Policy

State governments rely principally upon sales taxes and income taxes to fund their services, while local governments rely principally upon property taxes. Currently only five states do *not* impose a general sales tax (AK, DE, MT, NH, OR). Sales taxes in the states range from five to nine percent; groceries, rent, and medicines are usually exempted, in an effort to make sales taxes less regressive (see "Taxation, Fairness and Growth" in Chapter 11).

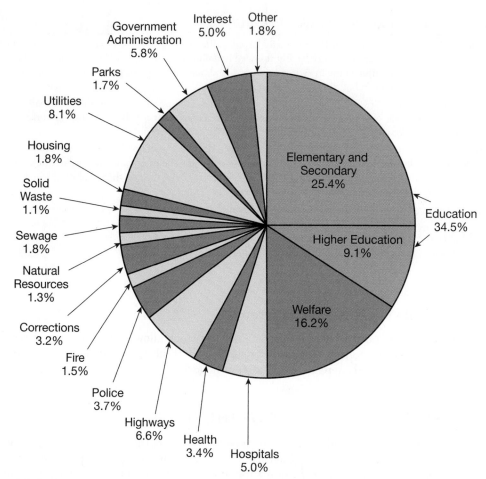

FIGURE 5–3 State–Local Government Expenditures by Function State and local governments spend more money on education than any other function.
SOURCE: Data from U.S. Bureau of Census, *Governmental Finances 2002*, April 28, 2005.

The decision to place primary reliance upon income versus sales taxation is one of the most important policy choices facing state government. Today all but seven states tax individual income (see Table 5–4). Some state income taxes are progressive with top marginal rates exceeding 10 percent; other states have adopted flat rate income taxes. In 2010 Washington state voters rejected a proposition that would have imposed an income tax on high-income earners.

Variations in State Educational Spending

Spending for elementary and secondary education varies a great deal among the states (see Table 5-5). Some states (for example, New Jersey, New York, Connecticut) spend well over twice as much as other states (for example, Utah, Idaho, Arizona, Oklahoma) for the education of the average pupil in public schools. How can we explain such policy variation among the states?

TABLE 5–4   Income Taxes in the States Federalism results in wide variations in tax policies among the states.

States Without Income Taxes		
Alaska	New Hampshire[a]	Texas
Florida	South Dakota	Washington
Nevada	Tennessee[a]	Wyoming
States Taxing Individual Income (rate ranges in parentheses)		
Alabama (2.0–5.0)	Kentucky (2.0–6.0)	North Carolina (6.0–8.25)
Arizona (2.8–5.0)	Louisiana (2.0–6.0)	North Dakota (2.1–15.6)
Arkansas (1.0–7.0)	Maine (2.0–8.5)	Ohio (0.7–7.5)
California (1.0–9.3)	Maryland (2.0–4.8)	Oklahoma (0.5–6.75)
Colorado (4.6)	Massachusetts (5.0)	Oregon (5.0–9.0)
Connecticut (3.0–5.0)	Michigan (4.0)	Pennsylvania (2.8)
Delaware (2.2–6.0)	Minnesota (5.3–7.8)	Rhode Island (26% federal)[b]
Georgia (1.0–6.0)	Mississippi (3.0–5.0)	South Carolina (2.5–7.0)
Hawaii (1.4–8.25)	Missouri (1.5–6.0)	Utah (2.3–7.0)
Idaho (1.6–7.8)	Montana (2.0–11.0)	Vermont (3.6–9.5)
Illinois (3.0)	Nebraska (2.5–6.8)	Virginia (2.0–5.75)
Indiana (3.4)	New Jersey (1.4–6.4)	West Virginia (3.0–6.5)
Iowa (0.4–9.0)	New Mexico (1.7–6.8)	Wisconsin (4.6–6.8)
Kansas (3.5–6.5)	New York (4.0–7.7)	

[a]State income tax is limited to dividends and interest only, and excludes wage income.
[b]State income taxes determined as a percentage of federal income tax liability.
SOURCE: Data from Council of State Governments, *Book of the States,* 2008 (Lexington, KY: Council of State Governments, 2008).

TABLE 5–5   Policy Variation among the States Federalism allows wide variation among the states in public policies including spending for public schools.
Per Pupil Spending for Public Elementary and Secondary Education

1	Rhode Island	$18,729	12	Maryland	12,281
2	New Jersey	16,967	13	Hawaii	11,968
3	New York	16,769	14	Virginia	11,672
4	Vermont	15,466	15	Michigan	11,579
5	Wyoming	15,459	16	Minnesota	11,447
6	Connecticut	14,472	17	Wisconsin	11,299
7	Maine	13,978	18	Arkansas	11,171
8	Massachusetts	13,804	19	Illinois	11,142
9	Delaware	13,496	20	Alaska	11,137
10	New Hampshire	13,112	21	West Virginia	11,043
11	Pennsylvania	12,541	22	New Mexico	10,551

(continued)

TABLE 5-5   continued

23	Oregon	10,381	37	Kentucky	9,325
24	Georgia	10,182	38	Texas	9,288
25	Louisiana	10,158	39	Missouri	9,076
26	Washington	10,082	40	North Carolina	8,974
27	Indiana	10,037	41	Florida	8,930
28	South Dakota	9,858	42	North Dakota	8,687
29	Colorado	9,828	43	Tennessee	8,617
30	Nebraska	9,781	44	California	8,520
31	Montana	9,676	45	Oklahoma	8,348
32	Kansas	9,662	46	Nevada	7,951
33	Iowa	9,472	47	Idaho	7,875
34	Ohio	9,445	48	Mississippi	7,752
35	Alabama	9,418	49	Arizona	6,170
36	South Carolina	9,375	50	Utah	6,095

SOURCE: National Education Association, 2010. Used by permission.

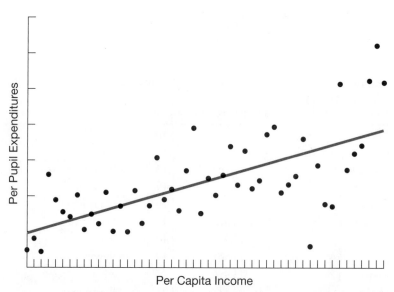

FIGURE 5-4   Fifty States Arranged According to per Capita Personal Income and per Pupil Educational Expenditures Personal income is the principal determinant of how much states spend on the education of each pupil.

Economic Resources and Public Policy

Economic research very early suggested that public policies were closely related to the level of economic resources in a society. We can picture this relationship by viewing a "plot" between per capita personal income and per pupil spending in public schools, as shown in Figure 5–4. Per capita income is measured on the horizontal, or X, axis, and per pupil spending is measured on the vertical, or Y, axis. Each state is plotted in the graph according to its values on these two measures. The resulting pattern—states arranged from the lower left to the upper right—shows that increases in income are associated with increases in educational spending. The diagonal line is a representation of the hypothesis that income largely determines educational spending.

SUMMARY

American federalism creates unique problems and opportunities in public policy. For 200 years, since the classic debates between Alexander Hamilton and Thomas Jefferson, Americans have argued the merits of policymaking in centralized versus decentralized institutions. The debate continues today.

1. Eighty-seven thousand separate governments— states, counties, cities, towns, boroughs, villages, special districts, school districts, and authorities—make public policy.

2. Proponents of federalism since Thomas Jefferson have argued that it permits policy diversity in a large nation, helps to reduce conflicts, disperses power, increases political participation, encourages policy innovation, and improves governmental efficiency.

3. Opponents of federalism argue that it allows special interests to protect positions of privilege, frustrates national policies, distributes the burdens of government unevenly, hurts poorer states and communities, and obstructs action toward national goals.

4. The nature of American federalism has changed radically over two centuries, with the national government steadily growing in power. "Coercive federalism" refers to Washington's direct mandates to state governments in matters traditionally reserved to the states. "Representational federalism" contends that there is no constitutional division of powers between nation and states, and federalism is defined only by the states' role in electing the president and Congress.

5. Over time, power has flowed toward Washington and away from the states, largely as a result of the greater financial resources of national government and its involvement in grant-in-aid programs to state and local governments. These governments are obliged to abide by federal regulations as a condition of receiving federal money. And these governments have become increasingly reliant on federal aid. Today federal aid constitutes over one-quarter of state–local government revenue.

6. Federalism, however, has enjoyed a modest revival in recent years. Congress strengthened federalism in the Welfare Reform Act of 1996 by ending a 60-year-old federal guarantee of cash assistance and "devolving" the responsibility for cash welfare aid to the states. Nonetheless, Congress attached many "strings" to its welfare grants to the states in the Temporary Assistance to Needy Families program.

7. Federalism has also been strengthened by a series of (narrow 5–4) decisions by the Supreme Court limiting the national government's power under the Commerce Clause and reasserting the authority of the states in the exercise of their police powers.

8. Federal preemptions of policy areas are justified under the Supremacy Clause of the Constitution. Powers delegated to the Congress under Article I may be totally preempted, where no state laws are permitted, or partially preempted, where federal law allows state laws which do not conflict with federal law. Federal mandates are direct orders to state governments to perform a particular activity or service. When no federal monies are made available to cover costs, the mandates are said to be "unfunded mandates."

9. States have tried to resist federal encroachment on their powers in several areas. States have undertaken legal actions in federal courts contending that the requirement for all Americans to purchase health insurance under the Patient Protection and Affordable Care Act of 2010 is an unconstitutional expansion of federal power. Supporters of the Act contend that it is constitutional under the Interstate Commerce Clause. Arizona has enacted its own immigration law; the U.S. Justice Department contends that immigration law is preempted by federal statutes. The federal government has retreated on state medical marijuana laws, the Justice Department indicating that it would not prosecute medical marijuana users who are in compliance with state laws.

10. Considerable policy variations exist among the 50 states. For example, tax burdens in some states are more than twice as high as other states, and educational spending per pupil is almost three times greater in some states than others. Economic resources are an important determinant of overall levels of taxing, spending, and services in the states.

MySearchLab® EXERCISES

Apply what you learned in this chapter on MySearchLab (www.mysearchlab.com).

NOTES

1. James Madison, Alexander Hamilton, John Jay, *The Federalist,* Number 51 (New York: Modern Library, 1958).
2. See Thomas R. Dye, *American Federalism: Competition among Governments* (Lexington, MA: Lexington Books, 1990).
3. David C. Nice, *Federalism: The Politics of Intergovernmental Relations* (New York: St. Martin's Press, 1987), p. 24.
4. Randall G. Holcombe, *An Economic Analysis of Democracy* (Carbondale: Illinois University Press, 1986), p. 174.
5. Morton Grodzins, *The American System* (Chicago: Rand McNally, 1966), pp. 8–9.
6. Ibid., p. 265.
7. Charles Press, *State and Community Governments in the Federal System* (New York: John Wiley, 1979), p. 78.
8. *Garcia v. San Antonio Metropolitan Transit Authority,* 469 U.S. 528 (1985).
9. Justice Lewis Powell, Minority Opinion, *Garcia v. San Antonio Metropolitan Transit Authority.*
10. Quoting from *The Federalist,* Number 45, in *United States v. Lopez,* 514 U.S. 549 (1995).
11. *Printz v. United States,* 521 U.S. 890 (1997).
12. *United States v. Morrison,* 529 U.S. 598 (2000).
13. *Gonzales v. Raich,* 545 U.S. 1 (2005).
14. *United States v. State of Arizona,* Federal District Court B. cf (July 28, 2010).
15. www.justice.gov/usao/reports/medical-marijuana

BIBLIOGRAPHY

DYE, THOMAS R. *American Federalism: Competition among Governments.* Lexington, MA: Lexington Books, 1990.

DYE, THOMAS R., and SUSAN A. MACMANUS. *Politics in States and Communities,* 13th ed. New York: Longman, 2009.

ELAZAR, DANIEL J. *The American Mosaic.* Boulder, CO: Westview, 1994.

GRAY, VIRGINIA, and RUSSELL L. Harrison. *Politics in the American States,* 9th ed. Washington, DC: CQ Press, 2007.

KEY, V. O., JR. *American State Politics: An Introduction*. New York: Knopf, 1956.

——.*Southern Politics in State and Nation*. New York: Knopf, 1951.

O'TOOLE, LAURENCE J., JR. *American Intergovernmental Relations*, 4th ed. Washington, DC: CQ Press, 2006.

WEB SITES

NATIONAL ASSOCIATION OF STATE INFORMATION RESOURCE EXECUTIVES. Information on state governments by category, for example, "criminal justice," "education," and "finance," as well as access to state home pages. *www.nasire.org*

COUNCIL OF STATE GOVERNMENTS. Organization of state governments providing comparative information on the states, especially in its annual publication *The Book of the States*. *www.csg.org*

NATIONAL CONFERENCE OF STATE LEGISLATURES. Home page of NCSL providing information on state legislatures, membership, partisan composition, and overview of key issues confronting state legislatures. *www.ncsl.org*

NATIONAL LEAGUE OF CITIES. Official organization of 18,000 cities in the nation, with information on policy positions, including grant-in-aid programs. *www.nlc.org*

NATIONAL CIVIC LEAGUE. Reform organization supporting nonpartisan local government, manager system, etc., with information on local government issues. *www.ncl.org*

INTERNATIONAL CITY/COUNTY MANAGEMENT ASSOCIATION. Official organization of professional city and county managers, with data on city and county government in annual *Municipal Yearbook*. *www.icma.org*

GOVERNING. Home page of *Governing* magazine, the nation's leading monthly publication directed at state and local government officials, contains information on politics, public affairs, and policy issues. *www.governing.com*

NATIONAL GOVERNORS ASSOCIATION. Official Web site of the nation's governors, with news releases and policy positions. *www.nga.org*

U.S. DEPARTMENT OF HOUSING AND URBAN DEVELOPMENT. Official HUD site, with information on grant programs, federal aid, etc. *www.hud.gov*

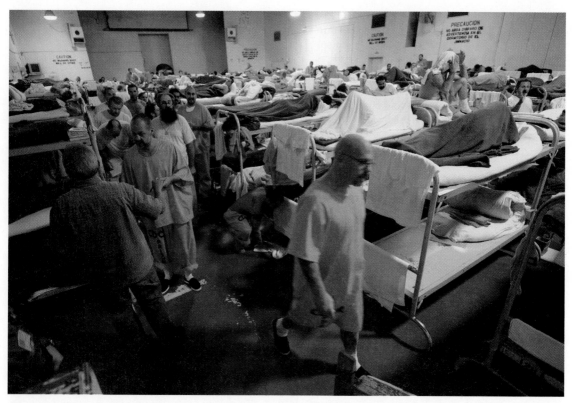

Incapacitating Criminals Incurs Costs Prison overcrowding in California's Chino State Prison in 2010. During the 1990s the incarceration rate (prisoners as a percent of the population) rose in America, while the crime rate fell. This suggests that incapacitating criminals may be an effective method of reducing crime. But prison overcrowding and the costs of imprisonment now inspire calls for alternative (non-prison) sentencing, especially for nonviolent crimes. (Getty Images)

6

Criminal Justice
Rationality and Irrationality in Public Policy

CRIME IN AMERICA

Crime is a central problem confronting any society. The rational strategy of crime fighting is known as *deterrence*. The goal of deterrence is to make the costs of committing crimes far greater than any benefits potential criminals might derive from their acts. With advanced knowledge of these costs, rational individuals should be deterred from committing crimes. But before we describe the deterrence model and assess its effectiveness, let us examine the nature and extent of crime in America.

Measuring Crime

It is not easy to learn exactly how much crime occurs in society. The official crime rates are based on the Federal Bureau of Investigation's Uniform Crime Reporting Program, but the FBI reports are based on figures supplied by state and local police agencies (see Table 6–1). The FBI has established a uniform classification of the number of serious crimes per 100,000 people that are reported to the police: *violent crimes* (crimes against persons)—murder and nonnegligent manslaughter, forcible rape, robbery, aggravated assault; and *property crimes* (crimes committed against property only)—burglary, larceny, arson, and theft, including auto theft. But one should be cautious in interpreting official crime rates. They are really a function of several factors: (1) the willingness of people to report crimes to the police, (2) the adequacy of the reporting system that tabulates crime, and (3) the amount of crime itself.

Trends in Crime Rates

Crime is no longer at the top of the nation's policy agenda. Since peaking in the early 1990s, crime rates have actually declined (see Figure 6–1). Law enforcement officials often attribute successes in crime fighting to police "crackdowns," more aggressive "community policing," and longer prison sentences for repeat offenders, including "three strikes you're out" laws. (All are discussed later in this chapter.) In support

TABLE 6–1   Crime Rates in the United States Official crime rates (offenses reported to police) are compiled and published each year by the FBI, enabling us to follow the rise and fall of various types of crimes.

	Offenses Reported to Police per 100,000 Population								
	1960	1970	1980	1985	1990	1995	2000	2005	2010
Violent Crimes	160	360	597	557	730	685	507	459	403
Murder	5	8	10	8	9	8	6	6	5
Forcible Rape	9	18	37	37	41	37	32	32	27
Robbery	60	172	251	209	256	221	145	141	120
Assault	85	162	298	303	423	418	324	291	253
Property Crimes	1,716	3,599	5,353	4,666	5,073	4,591	3,618	3,482	2,951

SOURCE: Federal Bureau of Investigation, *Crime in the United States* (annual).

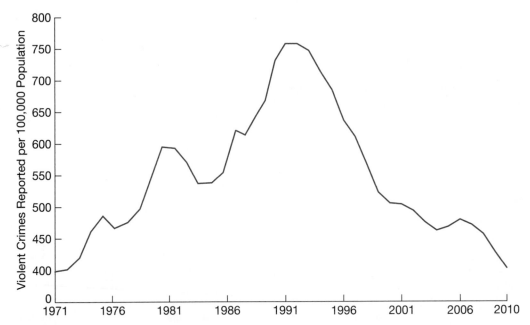

FIGURE 6–1   Violent Crime Rate Contrary to popular perceptions, violent crime has declined dramatically over the past 20 years.
SOURCES: U.S. Department of Justice, Bureau of Justice Statistics, *Sourcebook of Criminal Justice Statistics*, 1999; Federal Bureau of Investigation, *Crime in the United States*, 2010.

of this claim, they observe that the greatest reductions in crime occurred in the nation's largest cities, especially those such as New York that adopted tougher law enforcement practices.

Violence attributed to terrorism is now separately reported by the FBI. (Thus, the murder rate reported for 2001 in the FBI's Uniform Crime Reporting Program does *not* include the deaths that resulted from the terrorist attacks on America on September 11, 2001.) In all, there were 3,047 deaths from the 9/11 terrorist attack on New York's World Trade Center, the Pentagon in Washington, and the airliner crash in Somerset County, Pennsylvania (see Chapter 16).

Victimization

FBI official crime rates understate the real amount of crime. Many crimes are not reported to the police and therefore cannot be counted in the official rate. In an effort to learn the real amount of crime in the nation, the U.S. Justice Department regularly surveys a national sample, asking people whether they have been a victim of a crime during the past year.[1] These surveys reveal that the victimization rate is much higher than the official crime rate. The number of forcible rapes, as well as burglaries, assaults, and robberies, is twice the number reported to police. And property crimes are three times higher. Only auto theft and murder statistics are reasonably accurate, indicating that most people call the police when their car is stolen or someone is murdered.

The victimization rate for violent crime, although over twice as high as the reported crime rate, has generally risen and fallen over the years in the same fashion as the crime rate. That is, the victimization rate for violent crime peaked in the early 1990s, and has fallen dramatically since then. Why do people fail to report crime to the police? The most common reason given by interviewees is the belief that the police cannot be effective in dealing with the crime. Other reasons include the feeling that the crime is "a private matter" or that the victim does not want to harm the offender. Fear of reprisal is mentioned much less frequently, usually in cases of assault and family crimes.

Juvenile Crime

The juvenile system is not designed for deterrence. Children are not held fully responsible for their actions, in the belief that they do not possess the ability to understand the nature or consequences of their behavior or its rightness or wrongness. Yet juvenile crime, most of which is committed by 15- to 17-year-olds, accounts for about 20 percent of the nation's overall crime rate. Offenders under 18 years of age are usually processed in a separate juvenile court.

Juvenile courts rarely impose serious punishment. Available data suggest that about 13 percent of juveniles charged with *violent* crimes are sent to adult court; 16 percent are sent to juvenile detention centers; and the remaining 71 percent are either dismissed, placed on probation, given suspended sentences, or sent home under supervision of a parent.[2] Very few juveniles who are sentenced to detention facilities stay there very long. Even those convicted of murder are not usually kept in detention facilities beyond the age of 21. Moreover, the names of juveniles arrested, charged, or convicted are withheld from publication or broadcast, eliminating whatever social stigma might be associated with their crimes. Their juvenile criminal records are expunged when they become adults, so that they can begin adulthood with "clean" records. Whatever the merits of the juvenile system in the treatment of young children, it is clear that the absence of deterrence contributes to criminal behavior among older youths—15-, 16-, and 17-year-olds. Indeed these years are among the most crime-prone ages.

Only in the last few years have states begun to change their juvenile systems to incorporate the notion of deterrence. All 50 states now try some juvenile offenders age 14 and over in the adult system for serious crimes. In most states decisions to transfer juveniles to the adult court system are made by either judges or prosecutors. However, relatively few juveniles are tried as adults.

Nonserious and Victimless Crimes

The FBI's Uniform Crime Reporting Program does not count nonserious or victimless crimes, including drug violations, prostitution, gambling, driving while intoxicated, and liquor law violations. These crimes vastly outnumber the FBI's indexed serious crimes. There are five times as many arrests for nonserious as for serious crimes.

Some crimes are labeled "victimless" because participation by all parties to the crime is presumed to be voluntary. For example, prostitution is considered a victimless crime because both the buyer and seller voluntarily engage in it. Most drug crimes—the sale and use of modest amounts of drugs—are voluntary and considered victimless. Nonetheless, there is a close relationship between these nonserious crimes and more serious FBI index crimes. Prostitutes are vulnerable to violence and theft because perpetrators know that they are unlikely to report crime to the police for fear of prosecution themselves. Drug dealers have no way to enforce agreements by going to the courts. They must resort to violence or intimidation to conclude deals, and they too are unlikely to report crimes to the police. It is sometimes argued that if drugs and prostitution were legalized, their association with serious crime would diminish, just as the end of prohibition largely ended crime associated with the sale of alcohol.

White-Collar Crime

Most white-collar crime does not appear in the FBI's index of crimes. Nonetheless, white-collar crime is estimated to cost the American public more in lost dollars than all of the "serious" index crimes put together. Fraud (the perversion of the truth in order to cause others to part with their money), as well as forgery, perjury (lying under oath), tax evasion, and conspiring with others to commit these crimes, are all part of white-collar crime.

Corruption in Government

It is widely believed that "politics is corrupt," but it is difficult to measure the full extent of corruption in government. Part of the problem is in defining terms: what is "corrupt" to one observer may be "just politics" to another. The line between unethical behavior and criminal activity is a fuzzy one. Unethical behavior may include favoritism toward relatives, friends, and constituents, or conflicts of interest, in which public officials decide issues involving a personal financial interest. Not all unethical behavior is criminal conduct. But *bribery* is a criminal offense—soliciting or receiving anything of value in exchange for the performance of a governmental duty. And *perjury* is lying under oath.

The U.S. Justice Department reports on *federal* prosecutions of public officials for violations of federal criminal statutes. These reports do not include state prosecutions, so they do not cover all of the criminal indictments brought against public officials each year. Nonetheless, these figures indicate that over 1,100 public officials are indicted by the Justice Department each year.[3]

It is not uncommon for special interests to contribute to the campaign chests of elected officeholders from whom they are seeking favorable governmental actions. Indeed, public officials may come to expect contributions from contractors, developers, unions, and others doing business with government. A "pay to play" culture develops in many cities and states. But the key difference between merely rewarding supporters and engaging in bribery is the *quid pro quo*: if a payment or contribution is made for a specific governmental action, it risks criminal prosecution as bribery. So prudent interests make sure that their contributions are made well in advance of the governmental actions they seek. Prudent politicians avoid any communications that suggest that a particular official action was made in exchange for a payment or contribution.

Hate Crimes

Hate crimes are offenses motivated by hatred against a victim or a group based upon race, religion, sexual orientation, ethnicity or national origin, or disability. A hate crime is bias-motivated criminal *conduct*; it is not the mere *expression* of bias or hatred.

Since the official reporting of hate crimes began in the 1990s, roughly 8,000 incidents of hate crimes have been reported annually to the FBI. This is a small proportion of the more than 12 million crimes reported each year. A majority of reported hate crimes are motivated by race, with most of these crimes directed at African-Americans (see Figure 6–2). Of religious hate crimes, most are anti-Jewish. Of ethnicity-motivated crimes, most are anti-Hispanic. And of sexual orientation hate crimes, most are anti-male homosexual.

Bias-motivated crimes cause greater harm to society than crimes committed with other motivations, for example, greed, passion, etc. The U.S. Supreme Court, in upholding a Wisconsin law that increased the penalty for crimes intentionally inflicted upon victims based upon their race, religion, sexual orientation, national origin, or disability, observed that "bias-motivated crimes are more likely to provoke retaliatory crimes, inflict distinct emotional harms on their victims, and incite community unrest . . . the State's desire to redress these perceived wrongs provides an adequate explanation for its penalty enhancement provision over and above mere disagreement with offenders' beliefs or biases".[4] Motivation has always been an element in criminal cases. It does not violate the First Amendment freedom of expression to consider motivation in a criminal case, but there must be a crime committed, independent of the defendant's beliefs or biases.

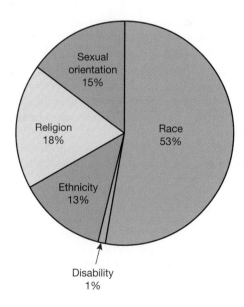

FIGURE 6–2   Bias Motivation in Hate Crimes Bias-motivated crimes are a small proportion of total crimes committed each year, but they are considered to be especially harmful to society.
SOURCE: Data from *Statistical Abstract of the United States, 2010,* p. 199.

Historically the Supreme Court viewed prohibitions on offensive speech as unconstitutional infringements of First Amendment freedoms. "The remedy to be applied is more speech, not enforced silence." The Supreme Court was called upon to review prohibitions on hate speech in 1992 when the city of St. Paul, Minnesota, enacted an ordinance prohibiting any communication that "arouses anger, alarm, or resentment among others on the basis of race, color, creed, religion, or gender." But the Supreme Court, in a unanimous decision, struck down the city's effort to prohibit expressions only because they "hurt feelings."[5] Speech expressing racial, gender, or religious intolerance is still speech and is protected by the First Amendment.

While upholding enhanced penalties for bias-motivated crimes, the Supreme Court has held that a criminal defendant's "abstract beliefs, however obnoxious to most people, may not be taken into consideration by a sentencing judge."[6] But the defendants motive for committing a particular criminal act has traditionally been a factor in sentencing, and a defendant's verbal statements can be used to determine motive.

CRIME AND DETERRENCE

The deterrence strategy in criminal justice policy focuses on punishment—its certainty, swiftness, and severity. The effectiveness of deterrence depends on:

- The *certainty* that a crime will be followed by costly punishment. Justice must be sure.
- The *swiftness* of the punishment following the crime. Long delays between crime and punishment break the link in the mind of the criminal between the criminal act and its consequences. And a potential wrongdoer must believe that the costs of a crime will occur within a meaningful timeframe, not in a distant, unknowable future. Justice must be swift.
- The *severity* of the punishment. Punishment that is perceived as no more costly than the ordinary hazards of life on the streets, which the potential criminal faces anyhow, will not deter. Punishment must clearly outweigh whatever benefits might be derived from a life of crime in the minds of potential criminals. Punishment must be severe.

These criteria for an effective deterrent policy are ranked in the order of their probable importance. That is, it is most important that punishment for crime be certain. The severity of punishment is probably less important than its swiftness or certainty.

Social Heterogeneity

Of course, there are many other conflicting theories of crime in America. For example, it is sometimes argued that this nation's crime rate is a product of its social heterogeneity—the multiethnic, multiracial character of the American population. Low levels of crime in European countries, Japan, and China are often attributed to their homogeneous populations and shared cultures. African-Americans in the United States are both victims and perpetrators of crime far more frequently than whites. Whereas African-Americans constitute only 12.7 percent of the population, they account for nearly 40 percent of all persons in federal and state prisons (see Table 6–2).

African-Americans are also much more likely to be victims of crime; the murder victimization rate for African-American males is almost ten times greater than for white males (see Table 6–3).

TABLE 6–2 Federal and State Prisoners by Race Blacks and Hispanics comprise a majority of federal and state prisoners; these groups are also far more likely than whites to be victims of crime.

Race	Percent
White	42.8
Black	39.6
Hispanic	16.6
Other races	1.0

SOURCE: *Statistical Abstract of the United States, 2010*, p. 210.

TABLE 6–3 Murder: Victims and Weapons Black males are almost eight times more likely to be murdered than white males; most murders are committed with guns.

	Victims (Murder Rate, 2006)	Weapons (Percent, 2007)	
Total	6.2	Guns, total	68
		Handguns	50
		Stabbing	13
White			
Male	5.4	Blunt object	4
Female	1.9	Strangulation	1
Black		Beating	6
Male	40.6	Arson	1
Female	6.6	Other	7

SOURCE: *Statistical Abstract of the United States, 2010*, pp. 193–194.

Socialization and Control

Yet another explanation of crime focuses on the erosion of social institutions—families, schools, churches, communities—that help to control behavior. These are the institutions that transmit values to children and socially censure impermissible behavior among adults. When ties to family, church, and community are loosened or nonexistent, individuals are less constrained by social mores. Older juveniles turn to peer groups, including gangs, for status and recognition. Defiance of authority, including arrest and detention, and other "macho" behaviors become a source of pride among young males. The deterrent effect of the criminal justice system is minimized. In contrast, when family oversight of behavior is close or when young people find status and recognition in school activities, sports or recreation, or church affairs, social mores are reinforced.

Irrational Crime

It is also argued that crime is irrational—that the criminal does not weigh benefits against potential costs before committing the act. Many acts of violence are committed by persons acting in blind rage—murders and aggravated assaults among family members, for example. Many rapes are acts of violence, inspired by hatred of women, rather than efforts to obtain sexual pleasure. More murders occur in the heat of argument than in the commission of other felonies. These are crimes of passion rather than calculated acts. Thus, it is argued, *no* rational policies can be devised to deter these irrational acts.

Deterrence Versus Liberty

Finally, we must recognize that the reduction of crime is not the overriding value of American society. Americans cherish individual liberty. Freedom from repression—from unlawful arrests, forced confessions, restrictions on movement, curfews, arbitrary police actions, unlimited searches of homes or seizures of property, punishment without trial, trials without juries, unfair procedures, brutal punishments, and so on—is more important to Americans than freedom from crime. Many authoritarian governments boast of low crime rates and criminal justice systems that ensure certain, swift, and severe punishment, but these governments fail to protect the personal liberties of their citizens. Indeed, given the choice of punishing all of the guilty, even if some innocents are also punished by mistake, or taking care that innocent persons not be punished, even if some guilty people escape, most Americans would choose the second alternative—protecting the innocent.

DOES CRIME PAY?

While we acknowledge that there are multiple explanations for crime, we shall argue that the frequency of crime in America is affected by rational criminal justice policy: *crime is more frequent when deterrence is lax, and crime declines with the movement toward stricter deterrence policy.*

Lack of Certainty

The best available estimates of the certainty of punishment for serious crime suggests that very few crimes actually result in jail sentences for the perpetrators. Yearly 12 million serious crimes are reported to the police, but less than two million persons are arrested for these crimes (see Figure 6–3). Some of those arrested are charged with committing more than one crime, but it is estimated that the police "clear" less than 20 percent of reported crimes by arresting the offender. Some offenders are handled as juveniles; some are permitted to plead guilty to minor offenses; others are released because witnesses fail to appear or evidence is weak or inadmissible in court. Convicted felons are three times more likely to receive probation than a prison sentence. Thus, even if punishment could deter crime, our current criminal justice system does *not* ensure punishment for crime.

Lack of Swiftness

The deterrent effect of a criminal justice system is lost when punishment is so long delayed that it has little relationship to the crime. The bail system, together with trial delays, allows criminal defendants to escape the consequences of their acts for long, indefinite periods of time. Most criminal defendants are free on bail shortly after their arrest; only those accused of the most serious crimes, or adjudged to be likely to flee before trial, are held in jail without bond. In preliminary hearings held shortly after arrest, judges release most defendants pending trial; even after a trial and a guilty

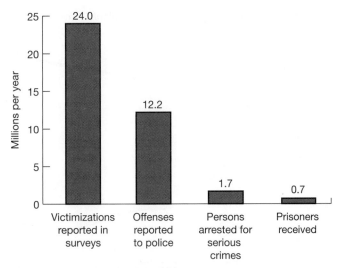

FIGURE 6–3   Crime and Punishment Many crimes are not reported to police, many crimes do not result in arrests, and relatively few criminals are imprisoned; this lack of certainty of punishment for crime undermines deterrence.
SOURCE: Data from *Statistical Abstract of the United States, 2010.*

verdict, many defendants are free on bail pending the outcome of lengthy appeals. The Constitution guarantees persons accused of crimes freedom from "excessive bail" (Eighth Amendment).

The court system works very slowly, and delays favor the criminal defendant. Defendants request delays in court proceedings to remain free as long as possible. Moreover, they know that witnesses against them will lose interest, move away, grow tired of the hassle, and even forget key facts, if only the case can be postponed long enough.

Justice delayed destroys the deterrent effect, especially in the minds of youthful offenders, who may be "present oriented" rather than "future oriented." They may consider the benefits of their criminal acts to be immediate, while the costs are so far in the future that they have no real meaning. Or the costs may be estimated to be only the arrest itself and a night in jail before release on bail. For deterrence to work, the perceived costs of crime must be greater than the perceived benefits in *the minds of potential wrongdoers*.

The Question of Severity

State and federal prisons currently hold over 1,600,000 prisoners, up from 320,000 in 1980. Not only are there more inmates in the nation's prisons, but also the percentage of the nation's population behind bars, the incarceration rate, is much higher today than 20 years ago. Roughly three percent of the nation's population is under correctional supervision—in prison, jail, probation, or parole.[7]

In recent years, prison sentences lengthened dramatically. Prison-building programs, begun in the states in the 1980s, expanded the nation's prison capacity and resulted in fewer early releases of prisoners. Many state legislatures enacted mandatory minimum prison terms for repeat offenders (including popular "three strikes you're out" laws mandating life sentences for third violent felonies). And many states enacted determinant sentencing or sentencing guidelines (legally prescribed specific prison terms for specified offenses) limiting judicial discretion in sentencing.

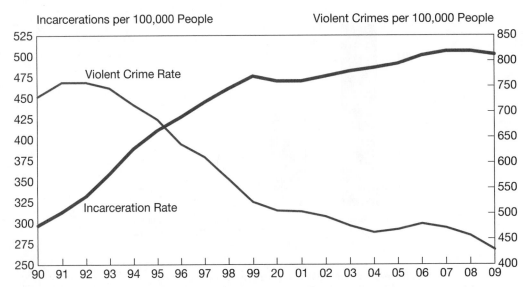

FIGURE 6-4   As the Incarceration Rate Rose, Violent Crime Declined The incarceration rate (the number of prisoners in relation to the nation's population) has risen dramatically, while the violent crime rate has declined dramatically, suggesting that imprisoning criminals reduces crime.
*Includes prisoners in federal and state prisons at year's end.
SOURCE: Bureau of Justice Statistics, 2010. *http//bjs.ojp.usdoj.gov*

The result of these changes was a dramatic increase in the time served for violent offenses. The average time served for such offenses doubled since 1990, and the average percentage of sentences served rose from less than 50 percent to more than 80 percent.

However, the economic recession beginning in 2008, and the burdens it placed on state finances, brought new pressures to reduce prison populations. In 2009 the incarceration rate fell for the first time in 20 years. Liberal voices advocating diversion programs—drug treatment, probation, and judicial supervision in lieu of incarceration—were heard once again in state capitols.

Deterrence or Incapacitation?

Even if stricter criminal justice policies are partly or primarily responsible for declining crime rates, it is not clear whether these policies are creating a deterrent effect or simply incapacitating wrongdoers and thereby preventing them from committing crimes outside prison walls.

There is a close correlation between *rising* incarceration rates and *declining* rates of violent crime (see Figure 6–4). Perhaps the nation succeeded in getting more violent criminals off the streets (incapacitation). Or perhaps the increased severity of punishment had a deterrent effect.

POLICE AND LAW ENFORCEMENT

The principal responsibility for law enforcement in America continues to rest with state and local governments. The major *federal* law enforcement agencies—the FBI and the Drug Enforcement Administration (DEA) in the Department of Justice, and the Bureau of Alcohol, Tobacco, and

Firearms (ATF) in the Treasury Department—are charged with enforcing federal laws. Although the role of the federal government in law enforcement is growing, state and local governments continue to carry the major burdens of police protection, judicial systems, and prison and parole programs.

Police Functions

At least three important functions in society are performed by police: enforcing laws, keeping the peace, and furnishing services. Actually, law enforcement may take up only a small portion of a police officer's daily activity. The service function is far more common—attending accidents, directing traffic, escorting crowds, assisting stranded motorists, and so on. The function of peace-keeping is also very common—breaking up fights, quieting noisy parties, handling domestic or neighborhood quarrels, and the like. It is in this function that police exercise the greatest discretion in the application of the law. In most of these incidents, it is difficult to determine blame, and the police must use personal discretion in handling each case.

The police are on the front line of society's efforts to resolve conflict. Indeed, instead of a legal or law enforcement role, the police are more likely to adopt a peace-keeping role. They are generally lenient in their arrest practices; that is, they use their arrest powers less often than the law allows. Rather than arresting people, the police prefer first to reestablish order. Of course, the decision to be more or less lenient in enforcing the law gives the police a great deal of discretion—they exercise decision-making powers on the streets.

Police Discretion

What factors influence police decision making? Probably the first factor is the attitude of the other people involved in police encounters. If a person adopts an acquiescent role, displays deference and respect for the police, and conforms to police expectations, he or she is much less likely to be arrested than a person who shows disrespect or uses abusive language.[8] This is not just an arbitrary response. The police learn through training and experience the importance of establishing their authority on the streets.

Community Policing

Most police activity is "reactive": typically two officers in a patrol car responding to a radio dispatcher who is forwarding reports of incidents. Police agencies frequently evaluate themselves in terms of the number and frequency of patrols, the number of calls responded to, and the elapsed time between the call and the arrival of officers on the scene. But there is little evidence that any of these measures affect crime rates or even citizens' fear of crime or satisfaction with the police.[9]

An alternative strategy is for police to become more "proactive": typically by becoming more visible in the community by walking or bicycling the sidewalks of high crime areas; learning to recognize individuals on the streets and winning their confidence and respect; deterring or scaring away drug dealers, prostitutes, and their customers by a police presence. But this "community policing" is often expensive.

Police Crackdowns

Police crackdowns—beefed-up police actions against juvenile gangs, prostitutes, and drug traffickers; the frisking of likely suspects on the street for guns and drugs; and arrests for (often ignored) public drinking, graffiti, and vandalism—can reduce crime only if supported by the community as well as prosecutors and judges. Crime rates, even murder rates, have been significantly reduced during periods of police crackdowns in major cities.[10] But these efforts are often sporadic; enthusiasm ebbs as jails fill up and the workload of prosecutors and courts multiplies.

Broken Windows

New York City's experience suggests what can be accomplished by stepped-up police activity. In 1993 the city's newly elected mayor Rudolph Giuliani began to implement what became known as the "broken windows" strategy in law enforcement. The strategy is based on the notion that one neglected broken window in a building will soon lead to many other broken windows. In crime fighting, this theory translates into more arrests for petty offenses (for example, subway turnstile jumping, graffiti, vandalism, and aggressive panhandling, including unwanted automobile window washing) in order not only to improve the quality of life in the city but also to lead to the capture of suspects wanted for more serious crimes. This strategy was coupled with the use of the latest computer mapping technology to track crime statistics and pinpoint unusual activity in specific neighborhoods. Each police precinct was regularly evaluated on the number and types of crimes occurring in it.

The introduction of these hard-line tactics created more than a little controversy. Civil libertarians, as well as many minority-group leaders, complained that these police tactics fell disproportionately on minorities and the poor. It was alleged that Mayor Giuliani's hard-nosed attitude toward crime created an atmosphere that led to increased police brutality.

But the "broken windows" strategy appears to have made New York City, once among the highest crime rate cities in the nation, now the safest large city in America. Over a five-year period following the introduction of Mayor Giuliani's tough policies, the city's overall crime rate fell by an unprecedented 50 percent, and murders fell by 70 percent.[11]

FEDERALIZING CRIME

Politicians in Washington are continually pressured to make "a federal crime" out of virtually every offense in society. Neither Democrats nor Republicans, liberals nor conservatives, are willing to risk their political futures by telling their constituents that crime fighting is a state and local responsibility. So Washington lawmakers continue to add common offenses to the ever lengthening list of federal crimes.

The Federal Role in Law Enforcement

Traditionally, the federal government's responsibilities were limited to the enforcement of a relatively narrow range of federal criminal laws, including laws dealing with counterfeiting and currency violations; tax evasion, including alcohol, tobacco, and firearm taxes; fraud and embezzlement; robbery or theft of federally insured funds, including banks; interstate criminal activity; murder or assault of a federal official; and federal drug laws. While some federal criminal laws overlapped state laws, most criminal activity—murder, rape, robbery, assault, burglary, theft, auto theft, gambling, prostitution, drug offenses, and so on—fell under state jurisdiction. Indeed, the *police power* was believed to be one of the "reserved" powers states referred to in the Tenth Amendment.

But over time Congress has made more and more offenses *federal* crimes. Today federal crimes range from drive-by shootings to obstructing sidewalks in front of abortion clinics. Any violent offense motivated by racial, religious, or ethnic animosity is a "hate crime" subject to federal investigation and prosecution. "Racketeering" and "conspiracy" (organizing and communicating with others about the intent to commit a crime) is a federal crime. The greatest impact of federal involvement in law enforcement is found in drug-related crime. Drug offenders may be tried in either federal or state courts or both. Federal drug laws, including those prohibiting possession, carry heavier penalties than those of most states.

Constitutional Constraints

Only recently has the U.S. Supreme Court recognized that federalizing crime may impinge upon the reserved powers of states. In 1994 Congress passed a popular Violence Against Women Act that allowed victims of gender-motivated violence, including rape, to sue their attackers for monetary damages in federal court. Congress defended its constitutional authority to involve itself in crimes against women by citing the Commerce Clause, arguing that crimes against women interfered with interstate commerce, the power over which is given to the national government in Article 1 of the Constitution. But in 2000 the Supreme Court said, "If accepted, this reasoning would allow Congress to regulate any crime whose nationwide, aggregate impact has substantial effects on employment, production, transit, or consumption. Moreover, such reasoning will not limit Congress to regulating violence, but may be applied equally as well, to family law and other areas of state regulation since the aggregate effect of marriage, divorce, and childbearing on the national economy is undoubtedly significant. The Constitution requires a distinction between what is truly national and what is truly local, and there's no better example of the police power, which the Founders undeniably left reposed in the states and denied the central government, than the suppression of violent crime in vindication of its victims."[12] In Justice Scalia's opinion, allowing Congress to claim that violence against women interfered with interstate commerce would open the door to federalizing *all* crime: this "would allow general federal criminal laws, because all crime affects interstate commerce."

Multiple Federal Agencies

The U.S. Department of Justice, headed by the attorney general, handles all criminal prosecutions for violation of federal laws. The Justice Department succeeds in convicting nearly 75,000 offenders in federal district courts, about one-third of these convictions are for drug offenses. The federal government's principal investigative agencies are the Federal Bureau of Investigation (FBI) and the Drug Enforcement Administration (DEA), both units of the Department of Justice, and the Bureau of Alcohol, Tobacco, and Firearms (ATF) in the Treasury Department.

Efforts to combine these federal law enforcement agencies have consistently foundered in bureaucratic turf battles. (The Central Intelligence Agency (CIA) is an independent agency, which, prior to the passage of the USA Patriot Act in 2001, was constrained in sharing intelligence information with domestic law enforcement agencies.) The Department of Homeland Security includes the Transportation Security Administration; Immigration and Customs Enforcement (ICE); the Border Patrol; the Secret Service; and the U.S. Coast Guard, all of which exercise some law enforcement responsibilities (see Chapter 16). This proliferation of federal law enforcement organizations does little to help fight crime.

CRIME AND GUNS

Gun control legislation is a common policy initiative following highly publicized murders or assassination attempts on prominent figures. The federal Gun Control Act of 1968 was a response to the assassinations of Senator Robert F. Kennedy and Martin Luther King, Jr., in that year, and efforts to legislate additional restrictions occurred after attempts to assassinate Presidents Gerald

Ford and Ronald Reagan. The rationale for restricting gun purchases, licensing gun owners, or banning guns altogether is that fewer crimes would be committed with guns if guns were less readily available. Murders, especially crimes of passion among family members or neighbors, would be reduced, if for no other reason than that it is physically more difficult to kill someone with only a knife, a club, or one's bare hands. Most murders are committed with guns (see Table 6–3).

Federal Gun Laws

Various federal gun control acts[13] include the following:

- A ban on interstate and mail-order sales of handguns
- Prohibition of the sale of any firearms to convicted felons, fugitives, illegal aliens, drug users, or adjudicated mental defectives
- A requirement that all firearms dealers must be licensed by the federal Bureau of Alcohol, Tobacco, and Firearms
- A requirement that manufacturers record by serial number all firearms, and dealers record all sales. (Dealers must require proof of identity and residence of buyers, and buyers must sign a statement certifying their eligibility to purchase.)
- Continued restrictions of private ownership of automatic weapons, military weapons, and other heavy ordinance

Federal regulations also ban the importation of "assault weapons," which are generally defined as automatic weapons.

The Brady Law

The federal Brady Law of 1993 requires a five-day waiting period for the purchase of a handgun. The national law is named for James S. Brady, former press secretary to President Ronald Reagan, who was severely wounded in the 1981 attempted assassination of the president. Brady and his wife, Sarah, championed the bill for many years before its adoption. Under the law's provisions, handgun dealers must send police agencies a form completed by the buyer (which is also required in most states); police agencies have five days to make certain the purchaser is not a convicted felon, fugitive, drug addict, or mentally ill person. Supporters believe the law is a modest step in keeping handguns from dangerous people. Opponents, including the National Rifle Association lobby, believe that the law is an empty political gesture at fighting crime that erodes the Second Amendment right to bear arms.

The rejection rate of Brady gun applications is less than two percent.

Gun Ownership

Gun ownership is widespread in the United States. Estimates vary, but there are probably 200 million firearms in the hands of the nation's 308 million people. In public opinion surveys half of all American families admit to owning guns. A majority of gun owners say their guns are for hunting and sports; about one-third say the purpose of their gun ownership is self-defense. Interestingly, both those who favor a ban on handguns and those who oppose such a ban cite crime as the reason for their position. Those who want to ban guns say they contribute to crime and violence. Those who oppose a ban feel they need guns for protection against crime and violence.

There are about 30,000 gun-related deaths in the United States each year. A majority of these deaths (58 percent) are suicides; over one-third (38 percent) are homicides; and the remaining (four percent) are accidental. It is relatively easy to count gun-related deaths, but it is very difficult to estimate the number of deaths, injuries, or crimes that are prevented by citizens using guns. *Protective uses of guns against murder, burglary, assault, and robbery have been estimated to be as high as two million per year.*[14] If this estimate is correct, then guns are used more for self-protection than for crime.

State Laws

State laws, and many local ordinances, also govern gun ownership. Handgun laws are common. Most states require that a record of sale be submitted to state or local government agencies; some states require an application and a waiting period before the purchase of a handgun; a few states

Gun Control Remains a Hot Button Issue Bumper stickers on display at a meeting of the National Rifle Association. The NRA is a powerful lobby in Congress in opposition to gun control legislation. The Supreme Court has affirmed an individual's right to possess a gun under the Second Amendment of the Constitution. But various government restrictions on guns may still be constitutional.   (© Shannon Stapleton/Reuters/Corbis)

require a license or a permit to purchase one; most states require a license to carry a "concealed weapon" (hidden gun). Private gun sales are largely unregulated. Until recently, most states allowed unregulated private sales at "gun shows." Private sales are not covered by the Brady Act.

Gun Laws and Crime

There is no systematic evidence that gun control laws reduce violent crime. If we compare violent crime rates in jurisdictions with very restrictive gun laws (for example, New York, Massachusetts, New Jersey, Illinois, and the District of Columbia) to those in jurisdictions with very loose controls, we find no differences in rates of violent crime that cannot be attributed to social conditions. Gun laws, including purchase permits, waiting periods, carrying permits, and even complete prohibitions, seem to have no effect on violent crime, or even crimes committed with guns.[15] Indeed, gun laws do not even appear to have any effect on gun ownership. Even the Massachusetts ban on handguns, which calls for a mandatory prison sentence for unlicensed citizens found carrying a firearm, did not reduce gun-related crime.[16] The total number of persons imprisoned for gun crimes was essentially unchanged; however, more persons without criminal records were arrested and charged with gun law violations. To date we must conclude that "there is little evidence to show that gun ownership among the population as a whole is, per se, an important cause of criminal violence."[17]

Indeed, some criminologists argue that guns in the hands of law-abiding citizens may reduce violent crime.[18] It is difficult to obtain evidence of "nonevents," in this case crimes averted by citizens with weapons, or crimes uncommitted by potential offenders fearing confrontation with armed citizens. Proponents of gun control have ready access to data on the number of murders committed with handguns. But there is also some evidence that as many or more crimes against both persons and property are foiled or deterred by gun ownership.[19]

The Right to Bear Arms

The gun control debate also involves constitutional issues. The Second Amendment to the U.S. Constitution states, "A well regulated militia, being necessary to the security of a free state, the right of the people to keep and bear arms, shall not be infringed." For many years arguments over gun control centered on whether "the right to bear arms" was an individual right like the First Amendment freedom of speech, or whether the prefatory clause referring to "a well regulated militia" meant that the Second Amendment protected only the collective right of the states to form militias; that is, the right of states to maintain National Guard units.

Proponents of gun control often cited a Supreme Court decision, *United States* v. *Miller* (1939).[20] In this case, the Court considered the constitutionality of the federal National Firearms Act of 1934, which, among other things, prohibited the transportation of sawed-off shotguns in interstate commerce. The defendant claimed that Congress could not infringe on his right to keep and bear arms. But the Court responded that a sawed-off shotgun had no "relationship to the preservation or efficiency of a well-regulated militia." The clear implication of this decision was that the right to bear arms referred only to a state's right to maintain a militia.

Opponents of gun control argued that the rights set forth in the Bill of Rights ought to be interpreted as individual rights. The history surrounding the adoption of the Second Amendment reveals the concern of citizens with the attempt by a despotic government to confiscate their arms and render them helpless to resist tyranny. James Madison wrote in *The Federalist*, No. 46, that "the advantage of being armed which the Americans possess over the people of almost every other nation . . . forms a barrier against the enterprise of [tyrannical] ambition." Early American political rhetoric was filled with praise for an armed citizenry able to protect its freedoms with force if necessary. And the "militia" was defined as every adult free male able to carry a weapon. Even early English common law recognized the right of individuals "to have and use arms for self-protection and defense."[21]

The Supreme Court finally resolved the underlying issue in *District of Columbia* v. *Heller* (2008) by holding that "The Second Amendment protects an individual right to possess a firearm unconnected with service in a militia, and to use that arm for traditionally lawful purposes, such as self-defense within the home."[22] The Court held that the District of Columbia's complete ban on handguns in the home violated the individual's right under the Second Amendment "to keep and bear arms." The Court observed that many bills of rights in state constitutions at the time of the Second Amendment's ratification contained an individual right to bear arms. And it noted that the earlier case, *United States* v. *Miller,* applied only to a type of weapon not commonly used for lawful purposes. The Court also held that the District's requirement that all guns in the home be either disassembled or guarded with a trigger lock violated the right of self-defense by rendering guns nonfunctional.

But the Supreme Court went on to observe that "Like most rights, the Second Amendment right is not unlimited. It is not a right to keep and carry any weapon whatsoever in any manner whatsoever and for whatever purpose." Justice Scalia, writing for a 5–4 majority, wrote that various government restrictions on guns may be constitutional, including restrictions on carrying concealed weapons, prohibitions on the possession of firearms by felons and the mentally ill, or laws forbidding the carrying of firearms in sensitive places, such as schools and government buildings. Thus, the Supreme Court left open the issue of exactly which gun controls are constitutional and which are not. It is likely that arguments over the constitutionality of various gun-control measures will occupy the courts for some time to come.

THE DRUG WAR

Americans have long harbored ambivalent attitudes toward drug use. Alcohol and tobacco are legal products. The manufacture, sale, or possession of heroin and cocaine are criminal offenses under both state and federal laws. Marijuana has been "decriminalized" in several states, making its use or possession a misdemeanor comparable to a traffic offense; a majority of states, however, retain criminal sanctions against the possession of marijuana, and its manufacture and sale are still prohibited by federal law. However, popular referenda votes in several states, including California, indicate that voters approve of the use of marijuana for medical purposes.

Drug Use

Overall drug use in the United States today appears to be below levels of two or three decades ago. However, since the mid-1990s, drug use has crept upward. These conclusions are drawn from national surveys on drug use regularly undertaken by the federal government (see Figure 6–5).

Marijuana is the most commonly used drug in the United States. Roughly nine percent of the population over 12 years old report that they have used marijuana in the past month. There is conflicting evidence as to whether or not marijuana is more or less dangerous to health than alcohol or tobacco. The White House Office of National Drug Control Policy contends that the effects of marijuana include frequent respiratory infections, impaired memory and learning, and increased heart rate. It defines marijuana as an addictive drug because it causes physical dependence, and

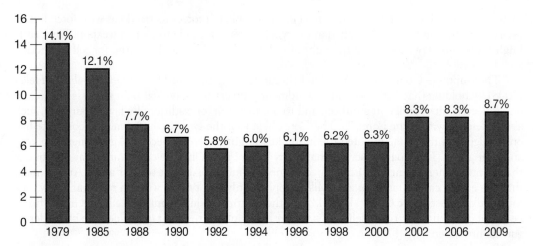

FIGURE 6–5 Drug Use in America* Drug use today is less than it was in the 1970s, although there has been a rise in recent years.
SOURCE: Substance Abuse and Mental Health Services (SAMHSA), National Survey of Drug Use and Health. www.samhsa.gov
*Current (past-month) use of any illicit drug.

some people report withdrawal symptoms. In contrast, the National Organization for the Reform of Marijuana Laws (NORML) argues that marijuana is nontoxic; it cannot cause death by overdose; and its "responsible use" is "far less dangerous than alcohol or tobacco." The real problem, it contends, is that marijuana's prohibition creates an environment for criminal activity, wastes criminal justice resources, and invites government to invade our private lives.

Cocaine use is much more limited than marijuana use. About one percent of the population over 12 years of age report using cocaine in the past month. Cocaine is not regarded as physically addictive, although the psychological urge to continue its use is strong. It is made from coca leaves and imported into the United States. Originally, its high cost and celebrity use made it favored in upper-class circles. However, cocaine spread rapidly in the streets with the introduction of "crack" in the 1980s. Crack cocaine can be smoked and a single "hit" purchased for a few dollars. The health problems associated with cocaine use are fairly serious, as reported by the National Institute on Drug Abuse. Death, although rare, can occur from a single ingestion. The power of the coca leaf has been known for hundreds of years; Coca-Cola originally contained cocaine, though the drug was removed from the popular drink in 1903.

Heroin use is relatively rare. The Harrison Narcotic Act of 1916 made the manufacture, sale, or possession of heroin in the United States a federal crime. Various "designer" drugs, for example, "ecstasy," occasionally appear in clubs and on the streets. Some are prepared in underground laboratories where hallucinogens, stimulants, and tranquilizers are mixed in various combinations. Drugs that are injected intravenously, rather than inhaled, pose additional health dangers. Intravenous injections with contaminated needles are a major contributor to the spread of the HIV-AIDS virus.

Prescription Drugs

Prescription drug abuse is now perceived as a major concern in the war on drugs. Past month use of prescription drugs for nonmedical purposes is currently estimated to exceed the use of marijuana. This use appears to be especially prevalent among young people, who often obtain these drugs

TABLE 6–4 Drug Use by Age Young Americans are much more likely to use illicit drugs and to binge drink than older Americans.

	18–25	26–34	35 and Over
Any illicit[a]	19.7%	10.9%	4.6%
marijuana	16.4	7.9	3.0
cocaine	1.7	1.4	0.6
Alcohol[a]	61.2	52.8	50.1
binge use[b]	41.8	20.0	21.2
Cigarettes[a]	36.2	24.1	24.6

[a] Current (within the past month) use
[b] Five or more drinks on the same occasion
SOURCE: National Survey of Drug Use and Health, *Statistical Abstract of the United States, 2010*, p. 131.

from their parents' medicine cabinets. A number of factors may contribute to the increased use of prescription drugs: the belief that they are safer than illicit street drugs; the relative ease with which they can be obtained from family and friends; and a lack of awareness of potentially serious consequences of their nonmedical use, especially when mixed with alcohol.

Drugs and Youth

Drug use varies considerably by age group. Younger people are much more likely to use illicit drugs than older people, and young people are more likely to "binge" drink (see Table 6–4).

Drug Trafficking

It is very difficult to estimate the total size of the drug market. The U.S. Office of Drug Control Policy estimates that Americans spend about $65 billion on illicit drugs each year. This would suggest that the drug business is comparable in size to one of the ten largest U.S. industrial corporations. More important, perhaps, drugs produce a huge profit margin. Huge profits in turn allow drug traffickers to corrupt police and government officials as well as private citizens in the United States and other nations.

DRUG POLICY OPTIONS

Antidrug efforts can be categorized as (a) interdiction, including international attacks on the supply of drugs; (b) domestic law enforcement, including federal and state incarceration for the possession and sale of drugs; (c) treatment, including rehabilitation centers, drug courts, and methadone; (d) prevention, including school-based, community, and media-centered antidrug education. The bulk of federal antidrug spending is concentrated on interdiction and law enforcement (see Figure 6–6).

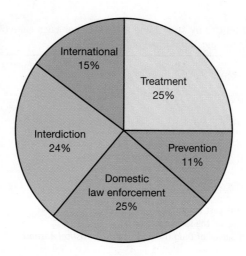

FIGURE 6–6   Federal Antidrug Spending About
two-thirds of federal antidrug spending is directed at interdiction and
law enforcement; only about one-third at treatment and prevention.
SOURCE: Office of National Drug Control policy, 2011.

Interdiction

Efforts to seal U.S. borders against the importation of drugs have been frustrated by the sheer volume of smuggling. Each year increasingly large drug shipments are intercepted by the U.S. Drug Enforcement Administration, the U.S. Customs Service, the U.S. Coast Guard, and state and local agencies. Yet each year the volume of drugs entering the country seems to increase. Drug "busts" are considered just another cost of doing business to the traffickers.

Federal drug policy also includes efforts to destroy the sources of drugs. U.S. military as well as drug enforcement officers are sent abroad to assist foreign governments (Colombia, for example) in destroying coca crops and combating drug cartels. But these activities often result in strained relationships with foreign countries. Our neighbors wonder why the U.S. government directs its efforts at the suppliers, when the demand for drugs arises within the United States itself. The continued availability of drugs on the nation's streets—drugs at lower prices and higher purities—suggests that interdiction has largely failed.

Education

Efforts aimed at educating the public about the dangers of drugs have inspired many public and private campaigns over the years, from the Advertising Council's TV ads "This is your brain on drugs" to local police–sponsored DARE (drug abuse resistance education) programs.

The decline in overall drug use from the levels of the 1970s is often overlooked in political debates over drug policy. Culturally, drug use went from being stylish and liberating to being unfashionable and unhealthy. Perhaps educational campaigns contributed to drug use decline, as well as the onset of HIV-AIDS, and the well-publicized drug-related deaths of celebrity athletes and entertainers. Recent fluctuations in reported drug use, however, suggest that educational campaigns may grow stale over time.

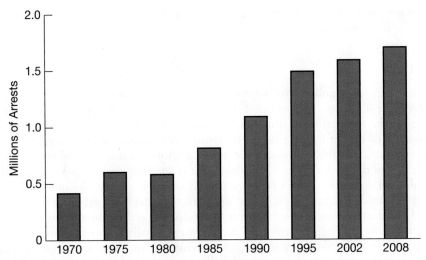

FIGURE 6–7   Drug Arrests Drug arrests, relatively low in the 1970s, have more than tripled in recent years. Arrests for drug offenses exceed those for any other crime.
SOURCE: Federal Bureau of Investigation, *Uniform Crime Reports*, 2010.

Enforcement

The FBI and state and local law enforcement agencies already devote a major portion of their efforts toward combating drugs. Over 1.5 *million* persons are arrested for drug violations each year (see Figure 6–7). Federal and state prisons now hold a larger percentage of the nation's population than ever before. Sentences have been lengthened for drug trafficking.

Federal law calls for a mandatory minimum sentence of five years for the possession or sale of various amounts of heroin, cocaine, or marijuana. Drug offenders account for 59 percent of the federal prison population and 21 percent of state prison populations. It costs about $25,000 per year to house each federal prison inmate.

The U.S. Drug Enforcement Administration (DEA) in the Department of Justice was created by Congress in 1973. Because it has the authority to enforce federal drug laws both in the United States and abroad, DEA officers may go abroad to collect international intelligence and to cooperate with foreign authorities. The U.S. Customs Service has the responsibility for stopping the entry of narcotics at U.S. borders. The U.S. Coast Guard cooperates in drug interception. The FBI monitors drug trafficking that contributes to other federal crimes. Surveillance of low-level buying and selling of drugs is usually left to state and local authorities.

Congress created a "drug czar" position in 1988 (officially the National Drug Control Policy Director) to develop and coordinate antidrug policy in the United States. The national "war on drugs" has included federal funds for prison construction, state and local drug law enforcement activity, and state and local drug treatment programs.

Treatment

Special "drug courts" and diversion programs developed in the states often give nonviolent drug users a choice between entering treatment programs or going to jail. While some users benefit from treatment, the overall success of treatment programs is very poor; most heavy drug users have been through treatment programs more than once. An estimated 60 to 80 percent of heavy cocaine users return to heavy use after treatment.[23]

Legalization?

The failure of antidrug policies to significantly reduce the drug supply or demand, coupled with the high costs of enforcement and the loss of civil liberties, has caused some observers to propose the legalization of drugs and government control of their production and sale. Prohibition failed earlier in the twentieth century to end alcohol consumption, and crime, official corruption, and the enormous cost of futile efforts to stop individuals from drinking eventually forced the nation to end Prohibition. It is similarly argued that the legalization of drugs would end organized crime's profit monopoly over the drug trade; raise billions of dollars by legally taxing drugs; end the strain on relations with Latin American nations caused by efforts to eradicate drugs; and save additional billions in enforcement costs, which could be used for education and drug treatment.[24] If drugs were legally obtainable under government supervision, it is argued that many of society's current problems would be alleviated: the crime and violence associated with the drug trade, the corruption of public officials, the spread of diseases associated with drug use, and the many infringements of personal liberty associated with antidrug wars.

California Votes Against Legalizing Marijuana

California voters rejected ballot Proposition 19 to "Regulate, Control and Tax Cannabis Act" in 2010. Opponents argued that legalizing marijuana for recreational purposes (California had already passed a medical marijuana law) would help with the state's budget shortfall, deny profits to drug cartels, and redirect law enforcement to more dangerous crimes. Opponents, including most law enforcement groups, argued that it would have negative health consequences, lead to additional substance abuse, and fail to produce much tax revenue or curb drug cartels. Opposition prevailed by a vote of 53 to 46 percent, but this was a closer margin than the 67 to 33 No vote taken in 1972 on the same proposition.

Legalizing marijuana would have created a conflict between federal and state law. The sale, growth, and possession of marijuana remains illegal under the federal Controlled Substance Act, which classifies marijuana as a Schedule 1 substance "with a high potential for abuse and no currently acceptable medical use." Attorney General Eric Holder, acting on behalf of the Obama Administration, had earlier indicated that the Justice Department would not investigate or prosecute medical marijuana users who were in compliance with state laws. However, Holder explicitly threatened to take the state of California to federal court if Proposition 19 had passed.

CRIME AND THE COURTS

The development of rational policies in criminal justice is complicated by conflicting values—our commitment to due process of law and our determination to fight crime. Public opinion has long held that the court system is overly concerned with the rights of accused criminals. A majority of Americans believe that the Supreme Court has gone too far in protecting the rights of defendants in criminal cases, and that the courts are more concerned with protecting these rights than the rights of victims.[25]

Yet although society needs the protection of the police, it is equally important to protect society *from* the police. Arbitrary searches, seizures, and arrests; imprisonment without hearing or trial; forced confessions; beatings and torture; tainted witnesses; excessive punishments; and other human rights violations are all too common throughout the world. The courts function to protect citizens accused of crime as well as to mete out punishment for criminal behavior.

Insufficient Evidence and Dismissal

About half of all felony arrests result in dismissal of the charges against the defendant. This decision is usually made by the prosecutor (the state's attorney, district attorney, or county prosecutor, as the office is variously designated in the states; or a prosecuting attorney in the U.S. Department of Justice in a federal criminal case). The prosecutor may determine that the offense is not serious or that the offender is not a danger to society or that the resources of the office would be better spent pursuing other cases. But the most common reason for dismissal of the charges is insufficient evidence.

Unreasonable Searches and Seizures

Individuals are protected by the Fourth Amendment from "unreasonable searches and seizures" of their private "persons, houses, papers, and effects." The Amendment lays out specific rules for searches and seizures of evidence: "No warrants shall issue but upon probable cause, supported by Oath or affirmation, and particularly describing the place to be searched, and the persons or things to be seized." Judges cannot issue a warrant just to let the police see if an individual has committed a crime; there must be "probable cause" for such issuance. The indiscriminate searching of whole neighborhoods or groups of people is unconstitutional and is prevented by the Fourth Amendment's requirement that the place to be searched must be specifically described in the warrant. This requirement is meant to prevent "fishing expeditions" into an individual's home and personal effects on the possibility that some evidence of unknown illegal activity might crop up. An exception is if police officers, in the course of a valid search for a specified item, find other items whose very possession is a crime, for example, illicit drugs.

However, the courts permit the police to undertake many other "reasonable" searches *without* a warrant: searches in connection with a valid arrest, searches to protect the safety of police officers, searches to obtain evidence in the immediate vicinity and in the suspect's control, searches to preserve evidence in danger of being immediately destroyed, and searches with the consent of a suspect. Indeed, most police searches today take place without a warrant under one or another of these conditions. The Supreme Court has also allowed automobile searches and searches of open fields without warrants in many cases. The requirement of "probable cause" has been very loosely defined; even a "partially corroborated anonymous informant's tip" qualifies as probable cause to make a search, seizure, or arrest.[26] And if the police, while making a warranted search or otherwise lawfully on the premises, see evidence of a crime "in plain view," they may seize such evidence without further authorization.[27]

Self-Incrimination and Right to Counsel

Freedom from self-incrimination originated in English common law; it was originally designed to prevent persons from being tortured into confessions of guilt. It is also a logical extension of the notion that individuals should not be forced to contribute to their own prosecution, that the burden of proof rests upon the state. The Fifth Amendment protects people from both physical and psychological coercion.[28] It protects not only accused persons at their own trial but also witnesses testifying in trials of others, civil suits, congressional hearings, and so on. Thus, "taking the Fifth" has become a standard phrase in our culture: "I refuse to answer that question on the grounds that it might tend to incriminate me." The protection also means that judges, prosecutors, and juries cannot use the refusal of people to take the stand at their own trial as evidence of guilt. Indeed, a judge or attorney is not even permitted to imply this to a jury, and a judge is obligated to instruct a jury *not* to infer guilt from a defendant's refusal to testify.

The Supreme Court under Justice Earl Warren greatly strengthened the Fifth Amendment protection against self-incrimination and the right to counsel in a series of rulings in the 1960s:

Gideon v. *Wainwright* (1963)—Equal protection under the Fourteenth Amendment requires that free legal counsel be appointed for all indigent defendants in all criminal cases.

Escobedo v. *Illinois* (1964)—Suspects are entitled to confer with counsel as soon as a police investigation focuses on them or once "the process shifts from investigatory to accusatory."

Miranda v. *Arizona* (1966)—Before questioning suspects, a police officer must inform them of all their constitutional rights, including the right to counsel (appointed at no cost to the suspect, if necessary) and the right to remain silent. Although suspects may knowingly waive these rights, the police cannot question anyone who at any point asks for a lawyer or declines "in any manner" to be questioned. The Supreme Court reaffirmed in 2000 that "*Miranda* has become embedded in routine police practice to the point where the warnings have become part of our national culture."[29] (See Figure 6–8.)

METROPOLITAN POLICE DEPARTMENT Warning as to Your Rights	WAIVER
You are under arrest. Before we ask you any questions you must understand what your rights are. You have the right to remain silent. You are not required to say anything to us at any time or to answer any questions. Anything you say can be used against you in court. You have the right to talk to a lawyer for advice before we question you and to have him with you during questioning. If you cannot afford a lawyer and want one, a lawyer will be provided for you. If you want to answer questions now without a lawyer present, you will still have the right to stop answering at any time. You also have the right to stop answering at any time until you talk to a lawyer.	1. Have you read or had read to you the warning as to your rights?_____ 2. Do you understand these rights? _____ 3. Do you wish to answer any questions? _____ 4. Are you willing to answer questions without having an attorney present? _____ 5. Signature of defendant on line below. _____ 6. Time _____ Date _____ 7. Signature of officer _____ 8. Signature of witness _____

FIGURE 6–8 The Miranda Warning The Supreme Court, in its 1966 Miranda decision, ruled that police must inform suspects of their constitutional rights before questioning them.

The Exclusionary Rule

Illegally obtained evidence and confessions may not be used in criminal trials. If police find evidence of a crime in an illegal search, or if they elicit statements from suspects without informing them of their rights to remain silent or to have counsel, the evidence or statements produced are not admissible in a trial. This exclusionary rule is one of the more controversial procedural rights that the Supreme Court has extended to criminal defendants. The rule is also unique to the United States: in Great Britain evidence obtained illegally may be used against the accused, although the accused may bring charges against the police for damages.

The rule provides enforcement for the Fourth Amendment guarantee against unreasonable searches and seizures, as well as the Fifth Amendment guarantee against compulsory self-incrimination and the guarantee of counsel. Initially applied only in federal cases, in *Mapp* v. *Ohio* (1961),[30] the Supreme Court extended the exclusionary rule to *all* criminal cases in the United States. A "good faith exception" is made "when law enforcement officers have acted in objective good faith or their transgressions have been minor."[31]

The exclusionary rule is a controversial court policy. Many trial proceedings today are not concerned with the guilt or innocence of the accused but instead focus on possible procedural errors by police or prosecutors. If the defendant's attorney can show that an error was committed, the defendant goes free, regardless of his or her guilt or innocence.

Plea Bargaining

Most convictions are obtained by guilty pleas. Indeed, about 90 percent of the criminal cases brought to trial are disposed of by guilty pleas before a judge, not trial by jury. The Constitution guarantees defendants a trial by jury (Sixth Amendment), but guilty pleas outnumber jury trials by ten to one.[32]

Plea bargaining, in which the prosecution either reduces the seriousness of the charges, drops some but not all charges, or agrees to recommend lighter penalties in exchange for a guilty plea by the defendant, is very common. Some critics of plea bargaining view it as another form of leniency in the criminal justice system that reduces its deterrent effects. Other critics view plea bargaining as a violation of the Constitution's protection against self-incrimination and guarantee of a fair jury trial. Prosecutors, they say, threaten defendants with serious charges and stiff penalties to force a guilty plea. Still other critics see plea bargaining as an under-the-table process that undermines respect for the criminal justice system.

While the decision to plead guilty or go to trial rests with the defendant, this decision is strongly influenced by the policies of the prosecutor's office. A defendant may plead guilty and accept the certainty of conviction with whatever reduced charges the prosecutor offers and/or accept the prosecutor's pledge to recommend a lighter penalty. Or the defendant may go to trial, confronting serious charges with stiffer penalties, with the hope of being found innocent. However, the possibility of an innocent verdict in a jury trial is only one in six. This apparently strong record of conviction occurs because prosecutors have already dismissed charges in cases in which the evidence is weak or illegally obtained. Thus, most defendants confronting strong cases against them decide to "cop a plea."

It is very fortunate for the nation's court system that most defendants plead guilty. The court system would quickly break down from overload if any substantial proportion of defendants insisted on jury trials.

PRISONS AND CORRECTIONAL POLICIES

At least four separate theories of crime and punishment compete for preeminence in guiding correctional policies. *Justice*: First, there is the ancient Judeo-Christian idea of holding individuals responsible for their guilty acts and compelling them to pay a debt to society. Retribution is an expression of society's moral outrage, and it lessens the impulse of victims and their families to seek revenge. *Deterrence*: Another philosophy argues that punishment should be sure, speedy, commensurate with the crime, and sufficiently conspicuous to deter others from committing crimes. *Incapacitation*: Still another philosophy in correctional policy is that of protecting the public from lawbreakers or habitual criminals by segregating them behind prison walls. *Rehabilitation*: Finally, there is the theory that criminals are partly or entirely victims of social circumstances beyond their control and that society owes them comprehensive treatment in the form of rehabilitation.

Prison Populations

More than 10 million Americans are brought to a jail, police station, juvenile home, or prison each year. The vast majority are released within hours or days. There are, however, about 1.5 million inmates in state and federal prisons in the United States. These prisoners are serving time for serious offenses; almost all had a record of crime before they committed the act that led to their current imprisonment. These are persons serving at least one year of prison time; an additional 750,000 persons are held in local jails, serving less than one year of imprisonment. In all, over 2.25 million Americans are currently in prisons or jails.

Failure of Rehabilitation

If correctional systems could be made to work—that is, actually to rehabilitate prisoners as useful, law-abiding citizens—the benefits to the nation would be enormous. Eighty percent of all felonies are committed by repeat offenders—individuals who have had prior contact with the criminal justice system and were not corrected by it. Reformers generally recommend more education and job training, more and better facilities, smaller prisons, halfway houses where offenders can adjust to civilian life before parole, more parole officers, and greater contact between prisoners and their families and friends. But there is no convincing evidence that these reforms reduce what criminologists call "recidivism," the offenders' return to crime.

Recidivism Rate

The Bureau of Justice Statistics reports that the overall recidivism rate for the United States is 67.5 percent.[33] This is the percent of prisoners released who were rearrested within three years of their release.

Prison life does little to encourage good behavior, as noted by policy analyst John DiIulio, Jr.: "For the most part, the nation's adult and juvenile inmates spend their days in idleness punctuated by meals, violence, and weight lifting. Meaningful educational, vocational, and counseling programs are rare. Strong inmates are permitted to pressure weaker prisoners for sex, drugs, and money. Gangs organized along racial and ethnic lines are often the real 'sovereigns of the cellblock.'"[34]

Failure of Probation

In addition to the nation's prison population of 1.5 million, there are over four million people currently on probation (see Table 6–5). But probation has been just as ineffective as prison in reducing crime. Even though people placed on probation are considered less dangerous to society than

TABLE 6–5   Jail, Prison, Probation, and Parole Population
Almost seven million people in the United States are serving on probation or parole, or have been sentenced to jail or prison.

Total	7,225,800
Prison	1,524,500
Jail	766,400
Probation	4,203,900
Parole	819,300

SOURCE: *Bureau of Justice Statistics,* 2010.

those imprisoned, studies indicate that nearly two-thirds of probationers will be arrested and over one-half will be convicted for a crime committed *while on probation*.

Failure of Parole

Over two-thirds of all prisoner releases come about by means of parole. Modern penology, with its concern for reform and rehabilitation, appears to favor parole over unconditional releases. The function of parole and postrelease supervision is to procure information on the parolees' postprison conduct and to facilitate the transition between prison and complete freedom. These functions are presumably oriented toward protecting the public and rehabilitating the offender. However, studies of recidivism indicate that up to three-fourths of the persons paroled from prison will be rearrested for serious crimes. There is no difference in this high rate of recidivism between those released under supervised parole and those released unconditionally. Thus, it does not appear that parole succeeds in its objectives.

CAPITAL PUNISHMENT

Capital punishment has been the topic of a long and heated national debate. Opponents of the death penalty argue that it is "cruel and unusual punishment," in violation of the Eighth Amendment of the Constitution. They also argue that the death penalty is applied unequally. A large proportion of those executed have been poor, uneducated, and non-white. In contrast, a sense of justice among many Americans demands retribution for heinous crimes—a life for a life. A mere jail sentence for a multiple murderer or rapist-murderer seems unjust compared with the damage inflicted on society and the victims. In most cases, a life sentence means less than ten years in prison under the current parole and probation policies of many states. Convicted murderers have been set free, and some have killed again.

Prohibition on Unfair Application

Prior to 1972, the death penalty was officially sanctioned by about half of the states as well as by federal law. However, no one had actually suffered the death penalty since 1967 because of numerous legal tangles and direct challenges to the constitutionality of capital punishment.

In *Furman* v. *Georgia* (1972), the Supreme Court ruled that capital punishment as then imposed violated the Eighth Amendment and Fourteenth Amendment prohibitions against cruel and unusual punishment and due process of law.[35] The reasoning in the case is very complex. Only two justices declared that capital punishment itself is cruel and unusual. The other justices in the majority felt that death sentences had been applied unfairly: a few individuals were receiving the death penalty for crimes for which many others were receiving much lighter sentences. These justices left open the possibility that capital punishment would be constitutional if it were specified for certain kinds of crime and applied uniformly.

After this decision, a majority of states rewrote their death penalty laws to try to ensure fairness and uniformity of application. Generally, these laws mandate the death penalty for murders committed during rape, robbery, hijacking, or kidnapping; murders of prison guards; murder with torture; and multiple murders. Two trials would be held—one to determine guilt or innocence and another to determine the penalty. At the second trial, evidence of "aggravating" and "mitigating" factors would be presented; if there were aggravating factors but no mitigating factors, the death penalty would be mandatory.

Death Penalty Reinstated

In a series of cases in 1976 (*Gregg* v. *Georgia, Profitt* v. *Florida, Jurek* v. *Texas*)[36] the Supreme Court finally held that "the punishment of death does not invariably violate the Constitution." The Court upheld the death penalty, employing the following rationale: the men who drafted the Bill of Rights accepted death as a common sanction for crime. It is true that the Eighth Amendment prohibition against cruel and unusual punishment must be interpreted in a dynamic fashion, reflecting changing moral values. But the decisions of more than half of the nation's state legislatures to reenact the death penalty since 1972 and the decision of juries to impose the death penalty on hundreds of people under these new laws are evidence that "a large proportion of American society continues to regard it as an appropriate and necessary criminal sanction." Moreover, said the Court, the social purposes of retribution and deterrence justify the use of the death penalty. This ultimate sanction is "an expression of society's moral outrage at particularly offensive conduct." The Court affirmed that *Furman* v. *Georgia* struck down the death penalty only where it was inflicted in "an arbitrary and capricious manner." The Court upheld the death penalty in states where the trial was a two-part proceeding and where, during the second part, the judge or jury was provided with relevant information and standards. The Court upheld the consideration of "aggravating and mitigating circumstances." It also upheld automatic review of all death sentences by state supreme courts to ensure that these sentences were not imposed under the influence of passion or prejudice, that aggravating factors were supported by the evidence, and that the sentence was not disproportionate to the crime. However, the Court disapproved of state laws *mandating* the death penalty in first degree murder cases, holding that such laws were "unduly harsh and unworkably rigid."[37]

The Supreme Court has also held that executions of the mentally retarded are "cruel and unusual punishments" prohibited by the Eighth Amendment.[38] In 2005 the Court held that the Eighth Amendment prohibited executions of offenders who were under age 18 when they committed their crimes.[39] And in 2008 the court held that the death penalty for the rape of a child violated the Eighth Amendment; the implication of the decision is that the death penalty can only be imposed for "crimes that take a victim's life."[40]

Racial Bias

The death penalty has also been challenged as a violation of the Equal Protection Clause of the Fourteenth Amendment because of a racial bias in the application of the punishment. White murderers are just as likely to receive the death penalty as black murderers. However, some statistics show that if the *victim* is white, there is a greater chance that the killer will be sentenced to death than if the victim is black. Nonetheless, the Supreme Court has ruled that statistical disparities in the race of victims by itself does not bar the death penalty in all cases. There must be evidence of racial bias against a particular defendant for the Court to reverse a death sentence.[41]

States and the Death Penalty

Currently some 35 states have the death penalty in their laws. The federal government itself has the death penalty, but the execution of Oklahoma City bomber Timothy McVeigh in 2001 marks the first death sentence carried out by the federal government in several decades. U.S. military law also includes the death penalty. Fifteen states have no death penalty, nor does the District of Columbia (see Figure 6–9).

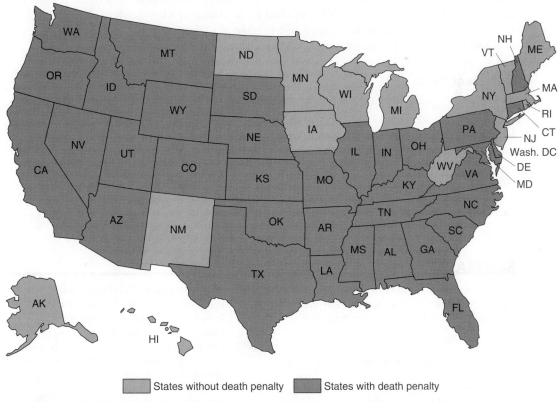

States without death penalty   States with death penalty

FIGURE 6–9   Death Penalty in the United States Currently, 35 states have the death penalty.

Executions

Today, there are about 3,500 prisoners nationwide on death row, that is, persons convicted and sentenced to death. But only about fifty executions are actually carried out each year. The strategy of death row prisoners and their lawyers, of course, is to delay indefinitely the imposition of the death penalty with endless stays and appeals. So far the strategy has been successful for all but a few luckless murderers. As trial judges and juries continue to impose the death penalty and appellate courts continue to grant stays of execution, the number of prisoners on death row grows. The few who have been executed have averaged ten years of delay between trial and execution.

The writ of habeas corpus is guaranteed in the U.S. Constitution, but how many habeas corpus petitions should a condemned prisoner be allowed to submit? The death penalty, of course, is irreversible, and it must not be imposed if there is any doubt whatsoever about the defendant's guilt. But how many opportunities and resulting delays should death row inmates have to challenge their convictions and sentences? In recent years the Supreme Court has limited habeas corpus petitions in federal courts by prisoners who have already filed claims and lost and who have failed to follow rules of appeal. If new evidence is uncovered after all court appeals have been exhausted, the Supreme Court has indicated that appeal lies with governors' powers of pardon.

The potential for wrongful executions has always worried Americans. The development of DNA evidence in recent years has made it possible to review and appeal some death penalty sentences. And indeed, DNA evidence has resulted in the release of a few death row prisoners. Other prisoners have been removed from death row because of trial errors, attorney incompetence, evidence withheld by the prosecution, and other procedural errors.

Deterrent Value

The death penalty as it is employed today—inflicted on so few after so many years following the crime—has little deterrent effect. Nonetheless, it serves several purposes. It gives prosecutors some leverage in plea bargaining with murder defendants. The defendants may choose to plead guilty in exchange for a life sentence when confronted with the possibility that the prosecutor may win a conviction and the death penalty in a jury trial. More important, perhaps, the death penalty is symbolic of the value society places on the lives of innocent victims. It dramatically signifies that society does not excuse or condone the taking of innocent lives. It symbolizes the potential for society's retribution against heinous crime.

SUMMARY

Crime is a central problem in our society. We face a conflict between our desire to retain individual freedoms and our desire to ensure the safety of our people.

1. After dramatic increases in crime rates over many years, crime rates have been falling since 1993. Law enforcement officials frequently attribute this decline to the adoption of public policies designed to deter crime and incapacitate criminals.

2. A rational policy toward crime would endeavor to make its costs far outweigh its benefits and in theory deter potential wrongdoers. Effective deterrence requires that punishment be certain, swift, and severe. However, certainty and swiftness are probably of more importance to deterrence than is severity.

3. But punishment for crime in the United States today is neither certain nor swift. The likelihood of going to jail for any particular

crime is probably less than one in a hundred. Speedy trial and punishment are rare; criminal defendants usually succeed in obtaining long delays between arrest and trial, when most remain free on bail prior to trial.

4. However, incapacitation (placing more criminals in prison for longer terms) appears to be related to lower crime rates. Prison building in the 1980s, together with mandatory sentencing laws and sentencing guidelines in the states, has resulted in higher incarceration rates (numbers of prisoners per 100,000 population).

5. The police provide many services to society in addition to law enforcement. Indeed, only a small proportion of their time is spent in fighting crime. It is difficult to demonstrate conclusively that increased police protection reduces the actual amount of crime.

6. Guns are used in a large number of violent crimes. Public policy on gun control varies throughout the nation. However, states with strict gun control laws do not have lower rates of violent crime, or even of gun-related crime, than states without such laws. The Supreme Court has declared that gun ownership is an individual right guaranteed by the Second Amendment.

7. Public policies toward alcohol and drug use are ambivalent. Although the health dangers of cigarettes, alcohol, marijuana, cocaine, and heroin are widely known, the manufacture, sale, and use of each of these substances are treated differently in law enforcement.

8. Court congestion, increased litigation, excessive delays, endless appeals, variation in sentencing, and excessive plea bargaining all combine to detract from deterrence. The exclusionary rule, which prohibits the use of illegally obtained evidence in court, has generated controversy since it was first announced by the Supreme Court in *Mapp* v. *Ohio* in 1961.

9. About half of all serious charges are dismissed by prosecutors before trial. But most convictions are obtained by guilty pleas without jury trials. Plea bargaining is the most common means of resolving criminal cases. Without plea bargaining, the court system would break down from overload.

10. Prison and parole policies have failed to rehabilitate prisoners. Prisons can reduce crime only by incapacitating criminals for periods of time. Most prisoners are recidivists— persons who previously served a sentence of incarceration before being sentenced again. Parolees—persons released by officials for good behavior—are just as likely to commit new crimes as those released after serving full sentences.

11. Capital punishment as currently imposed—on very few persons and after very long delays—is not an effective deterrent.

MySearchLab® EXERCISES

Apply what you learned in this chapter on MySearchLab (www.mysearchlab.com).

NOTES

1. U.S. Department of Justice, *Criminal Victimization in the United States*, published annually (Washington, DC: Bureau of Justice Statistics).

2. U.S. General Accounting Office, *Juvenile Justice* (Washington, DC: Government Printing Office, 1995), p. 2.

3. Statistical Abstract of the United States, 2010, p. 205.

4. *Wisconsin v. Mitchell*, 508 U.S. 476 (1993).

5. *R.A.V. v. City of St. Paul*, 505 U.S. 377 (1992).

6. *Whitney v. California*, 274 U.S. 357 (1927).

7. Bureau of Justice Statistics, *www.ojp.usdoj. gov/bjs*

8. Stuart A. Sheingold, "Cultural Cleavage and Criminal Justice," *Journal of Politics*, 40 (November 1978), pp. 865–897.

9. See Stuart Sheingold, *The Politics of Law and Order* (New York: Layman, 1984).

10. For a summary, see John J. DiIulio, Jr., "Arresting Ideas: Tougher Law Enforcement Is Driving Down Crime," *Policy Review* (Fall 1995), pp. 12–16.

11. William S. Bratlon, "The New City Police Department's Civil Enforcement of Quality of Life Crimes," *Journal of Law and Policy 1995*, pp. 447–464; also cited by William J. Bennett, John J. DiIulio, Jr., and John P. Walters, *Body Count* (New York: Simon & Schuster, 1996).

12. *United States v. Morrison*, 529 U.S. 598 (2000).

13. Gun Control Act of 1968; Firearms Owners' Protection Act of 1986; Brady Handgun Violence Protection Act of 1993; Omnibus Crime Control Act of 1994.

14. See Gary Kleck and Marc Gertz, "Armed Resistance to Crime: The Prevalence and Nature of Self-Defense with Guns," *Journal of Criminal Law and Criminology*, 86 (Fall 1996), pp. 150–187; Gary Kleck, *Targeting Guns* (New York: Aldine de Gruyter, 1997).

15. Douglas R. Murray, "Handguns, Gun Control Laws and Firearm Violence," *Social Problems*, 23 (1975); James D. Wright and Peter H. Rossi, *Weapons, Crime, and Violence in America* (Washington, DC: U.S. Department of Justice, National Institute of Justice, 1981).

16. David Rossman, *The Impact of the Mandatory Gun Law in Massachusetts* (Boston: Boston University School of Law, 1979).

17. Wright and Rossi, *Weapons, Crime, and Violence*, p. 540.

18. Gary Kleck, *Point Blank: Guns and Violence in America* (New York: Aldine de Gruyter, 1991); Gary Kleck, "The Impact of Gun Control and Gun Ownership Levels on Violence Rates," *Journal of Quantitative Criminology* (1993), pp. 249–287; John

R. Lott, *More Guns, Less Crime*, 2nd ed. (Chicago: University of Chicago Press, 2000).

19. Gary Kleck and Mark Gertz, "Carrying Guns for Protection," *Journal of Research on Crime and Delinquency*, 35 (May 1998), pp. 190–198.

20. *United States v. Miller*, 307 U.S. 174 (1939).

21. William Blackstone, *Commentaries of the Laws of England*, Vol. 1, p. 144.

22. *District of Columbia v. Heller* (June 26, 2008).

23. Various studies cited by William J. Bennett, et al., *Body Count*, pp. 172–180.

24. Ethan A. Nadelmann, "The Case for Legalization," *The Public Interest* (Summer 1988), pp. 3–31.

25. Public Agenda Online, September 2002.

26. *Illinois v. Gates*, 462 U.S. 213 (1983).

27. *Arizona v. Hicks*, 480 U.S. 321 (1987).

28. *Spano v. New York*, 360 U.S. 315 (1959).

29. *Dickerson v. U.S.*, 530 U.S. 428 (2000).

30. *Mapp v. Ohio*, 367 U.S. 643 (1961).

31. *United States v. Leon*, 468 U.S. 897 (1984).

32. U.S. Department of Justice, Bureau of Justice Statistics, *The Prevalence of Guilty Pleas*, December 1984.

33. Bureau of Justice Statistics, "Reentry Trends in the U.S." *www.bjs.ojp.usdoj-gov/recidivism*

34. John J. DiIulio, Jr., "Punishing Smarter," *Brookings Review* (Summer 1989), 8.

35. *Furman v. Georgia*, 408 U.S. 238 (1972).

36. *Gregg v. Georgia, Profitt v. Florida, Jurek v. Texas*, 428 U.S. 153 (1976).

37. *Summer v. Shuman*, 483 U.S. 66 (1987).

38. *Atkins v. Virginia*, 536 U.S. 304 (2002).

39. *Roper v. Simmons*, March 1, 2005.

40. *Kennedy v. Louisiana*, June 25, 2008.

41. *McCluskey v. Kemp*, 481 U.S. 279 (1987).

BIBLIOGRAPHY

BENNETT, WILLIAM J., JOHN J. DIIULIO, JR., and JOHN P. WALTERS. *Body Count*. New York: Simon & Schuster, 1996.

COLE, GEORGE F., and CHRISTOPHER E. SMITH. *The American System of Criminal Justice*, 12th ed. Cengage, 2010.

KLECK, GARY. *Point Blank: Guns and Violence in America*. New York: Aldine de Gruyter, 1991.

SCHMALLEGER, FRANK. *Criminal Justice Today*, 10th ed. New York: Prentice Hall, 2011.

SPITZER, ROBERT J. *The Politics of Gun Control*, 4th ed. Washington DC: CQ Press, 2007.

VIZZARD, WILLIAM J. *Shots in the Dark: The Policy and Politics of Gun Control*. Latham, MD: Rowman and Littlefield, 2000.

WILSON, JAMES Q. *Thinking about Crime*, 2nd ed. New York: Basic Books, 1984.

WILSON, JAMES Q., and RICHARD J. HERRNSTEIN. *Crime and Human Nature*. New York: Simon & Schuster, 1985.

WRIGHT, RICHARD A. *In Defense of Prisons*. Westport, CT: Greenwood Press, 1994.

WEB SITES

FEDERAL BUREAU OF INVESTIGATION. Official Web site of the FBI, including uniform crime reports, "ten most wanted," etc. *www.fbi.gov*

BUREAU OF JUSTICE STATISTICS, U.S. DEPARTMENT OF JUSTICE. Statistics on crime rates, victimization, sentencing, corrections, etc. *www.ojp.usdoj.gov/bjs*

DEATH PENALTY INFORMATION CENTER. Advocacy group opposing death penalty, with information on executions. *www.deathpenalty.org*

NATIONAL RIFLE ASSOCIATION. Advocacy organization defending Second Amendment right to bear arms. *www.nra.org*

AMERICAN CIVIL LIBERTIES UNION. Advocacy organization for civil liberties. *www.aclu.org*

U.S. DRUG ENFORCEMENT ADMINISTRATION. Official DEA Web site, with information on drug laws and enforcement. *www.usdoj.gov/dea*

NATIONAL INSTITUTE ON DRUG ABUSE. Government information about drugs and their effects, including trends and statistics on drug use. *www.nida.nih.gov*

NATIONAL ORGANIZATION FOR THE REFORM OF MARIJUANA LAWS. Advocacy organization supporting the legalization of marijuana. *www.norml.org*

OFFICE OF NATIONAL DRUG CONTROL POLICY. Official site of the government's "Drug Czar," with information on national drug control strategy, etc. *www.whitehousedrugpolicy.gov*

DRUG POLICY ALLIANCE. Advocacy organization opposed to the war on drugs. *www.drugpolicy.org*

Food Lines Lengthen During Hard Times   Food lines in Sacramento, California in 2010 illustrate the continuing effort to provide for people who have fallen on hard times. The number of cash welfare recipients has declined in recent years following welfare reform in 1996. But participation in food programs has increased, especially since the onset of the "Great Recession" 2008–2009. (© Randy Pench/ZUMA Press/Corbis)

7

Welfare
The Search for Rational Strategies

RATIONALITY AND IRRATIONALITY IN THE WELFARE STATE

Why does poverty persist in a nation where total social welfare spending is many times the amount needed to eliminate poverty? The answer is that the poor are *not* the principal beneficiaries of social welfare spending. Most of it, including the largest programs—Social Security and Medicare—goes to the *non*poor. Only about one-sixth of federal social welfare spending is "means-tested" (see Figure 7–1), that is, distributed to recipients based on their low-income or poverty status. The middle class, not the poor, is the major beneficiary of the nation's social welfare spending.

"Entitlements"

Entitlements are government benefits for which Congress has set eligibility criteria—age, income, retirement, disability, unemployment, and so forth. Everyone who meets the criteria is "entitled" by law to the benefit.

Most of the nation's major entitlement programs were launched either in the New Deal years of the 1930s under President Franklin D. Roosevelt (Social Security, Unemployment Compensation; Aid to Families with Dependent Children [AFDC], now called Temporary Assistance to Needy Families [TANF], and Aid to Aged, Blind, and Disabled, now called Supplemental Security Income or SSI); or the Great Society years of the 1960s under President Lyndon B. Johnson (food stamps, Medicare, Medicaid).

Today nearly one-third of the population of the United States is "entitled" to some form of government benefit. *Social insurance* entitlements may be claimed by persons regardless of their income or wealth. Entitlement to Social Security and Medicare is determined by *age*, not income or poverty. Entitlement to unemployment compensation benefits is determined by employment status. Federal employee and veterans' retirement benefits are based on previous government or military service. These *non*–means-tested programs account for the largest number of recipients of government benefits. In contrast, *public assistance* programs (including cash welfare assistance, Medicaid, and food stamps) are means-tested: benefits are limited to low-income recipients (see Table 7–1). Because many programs overlap, with individuals receiving more than one type of entitlement benefit, it is not really possible to know exactly the total number of people receiving government assistance. But it is estimated that *over half of all families in the nation include someone who receives a government check.*

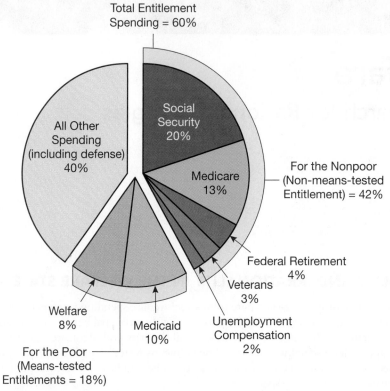

FIGURE 7–1   Federal Entitlement Spending for the poor and Nonpoor
Entitlement spending exceeds 60 percent of the federal budget, but most
entitlement spending goes to the nonpoor.
SOURCE: *Budget of the United States Government, 2012.*

Rational Strategies, Irrational Results

It is not possible in this chapter to describe all the problems of the poor in America or all the difficulties in developing rational social welfare policies. But it is possible to describe the general design of alternative strategies to deal with welfare, to observe how these strategies have been implemented in public policy, and to outline some of the obstacles to a rational approach to social welfare problems.

DEFINING THE PROBLEM: POVERTY IN AMERICA

A rational approach to policymaking requires a clear definition of the problem. But political conflict over the nature and extent of poverty in America is a major obstacle to a rational approach to social welfare policy.

Proponents of programs for the poor frequently make high estimates of that population. They view the problem of poverty as persistent, even in an affluent society; they contend that many millions of people suffer from hunger, exposure, and remedial illness. Their definition of the problem virtually mandates immediate and massive public welfare programs.

TABLE 7–1   Major Federal Entitlement Program   Nearly one-third of the nation's population receives some kind of direct government entitlement.

Social Insurance Programs (No Means Test for Entitlement to Benefits)	Beneficiaries (Millions)
Social Security, OASDI	50.8
Medicare	45.2
Government Retirement	2.6
Veterans' Benefits	3.8
Unemployment Compensation	8.9

Public Assistance Programs (Means-Tested Entitlement)	Beneficiaries (Millions)
Cash Aid	
Temporary Assistance for Needy Families, TANF	4.3
Supplemental Security Income, SSI	7.4
Earned income tax credit, EITC	3.0
Medical Care	
Medicaid	57.1
State Child Health Insurance Program, SCHIP	7.4
Food Benefits	
Food stamps, SNAP	34.6
School lunches	31.0
School breakfasts	10.6
Women, Infants, Children, WIC	8.7
Education Aid	
Federal Family Education Loans	12.7
Pell Grants	5.7
Federal Work Study	0.8
Head Start	0.9

SOURCE: *Statistical Abstract of the United States, 2011.*

In contrast, others minimize the number of poor in America. They believe that the poor are considerably better off than the middle class of fifty years ago and even wealthy by the standards of most other societies in the world. They believe government welfare programs encourage poverty, destroy family life, and rob the poor of incentives to work, save, and assume responsibility for their own well-being. They deny that anyone needs to suffer from hunger, exposure, or remedial illness if they use the services and facilities available to them.

How Many Poor?

How much poverty really exists in America? According to the U.S. Bureau of the Census, there were between 35 and 45 million poor people in the United States in recent years (see Table 7–2), or approximately 12 to 15 percent of the population.[1] This official estimate of poverty includes

TABLE 7–2 Poverty in America In recent years, approximately 12 to 15 percent of the population has lived below the poverty line; poverty is most prevalent among female-headed households; blacks and Hispanics experience more poverty than whites.

Poverty definition for family of four	21,954
Number of poor	44 million
Poverty percentage of total population	14.3
Race (% poor)	
White	9.4
Black	25.8
Hispanic	25.3
Age (% poor)	
Under 18	20.7
Over 65	8.9
Family (% poor)	
Married couple	5.8
Female householder, no husband	29.5

SOURCE: U.S. Bureau of the Census (2011), *www.census.gov*, Data for 2009.

all those Americans whose annual cash income falls below that which is required to maintain a decent standard of living. (The dollar amount of the "poverty line" is flexible to take into account the effect of inflation; the amount rises each year with the rate of inflation.)

Liberal Criticism

This official definition of poverty has many critics. Some liberal critics believe that poverty is underestimated because (1) the official definition includes cash income from welfare and Social Security, and without this government assistance, the number of poor would be much higher, perhaps 20 percent of the total population; (2) the official definition does not count the many "near poor"; there are 57 million Americans, or about 19 percent of the population, who live below 125 percent of the poverty level; (3) the official definition does not take into account regional differences in the cost of living, climate, or accepted styles of living; and (4) the official definition does not consider what people *think* they need to live adequately.

Conservative Criticism

Some conservative critics also challenge the official definition of poverty: (1) it does not consider the value of family assets; people (usually older) who own their own mortgage-free homes, furniture, and automobiles may have current incomes below the poverty line yet not suffer hardship; (2) there are many families and individuals who are officially counted as poor but who do not think of themselves as such—students, for example, who deliberately postpone earning an income to secure an education; (3) many persons (poor and nonpoor) underreport their real income, which leads to overestimates of the number of poor; and (4) more importantly, the official definition of poverty excludes "in-kind" (noncash) benefits given to the poor by governments, for example, food stamps, free medical care, public housing, and school lunches. If these benefits were costed out (calculated as cash income), there may be only half as many poor people as shown in official statistics. This figure might be thought of as the "net poverty" rate, which refers to people who remain poor even after counting their in-kind government benefits. The net poverty rate is only about 8 percent, compared to over 14 percent for the official poverty rate.

Latent Poverty

How many people would be poor if we did *not* have government Social Security and welfare programs? What percentage of the population can be thought of as "latent poor," that is, persons who would be poor without the assistance they receive from federal programs? Latent poverty is well above the official poverty line. It has ranged from about 20 to 25 percent in recent years. So, in the absence of federal social welfare programs, over one-fifth of the nation's population would be poor.

WHO ARE THE POOR?

Poverty occurs in many kinds of families and all races and ethnic groups. However, some groups experience poverty in proportions greater than the national average.

Family Structure

Poverty is most common among female-headed families. The incidence of poverty among these families has ranged between 25 and 30 percent in recent years, compared to only 5 to 6 percent for married couples (see Table 7–2). Nearly half of all female-headed families with children under 18 live in poverty. These women and their children make up more than two-thirds of all the persons living in poverty in the United States. These figures describe "the feminization of poverty" in America. Clearly, poverty is closely related to family structure. Today the disintegration of the traditional husband–wife family is the single most influential factor contributing to poverty.

Race

Blacks experience poverty in much greater proportions than whites. Over the years the poverty rate among blacks in the United States has been over twice as high as that among whites. Poverty among Hispanics is also significantly greater than among whites.

The relationship between race and family structure is a controversial topic. About 50 percent of all black families in the United States in 2010 were headed by females, compared with about 18 percent of all white families.[2]

Age

The aged in the United States experience *less* poverty than the nonaged. The aged are not poor, despite the popularity of the phrase "the poor and the aged." The poverty rate for persons over sixty-five years of age is well below the national average. Moreover, the aged are much wealthier than the nonaged. They are more likely than younger people to own homes with paid-up mortgages. A large portion of their medical expenses are paid by Medicare. With fewer expenses, the aged, even with relatively smaller cash incomes, experience poverty in a different fashion from a young mother with children.

Temporary Versus Persistent Poverty

Most poverty is temporary, and most welfare dependency is relatively brief, lasting less than two years. Tracing poor families over time presents a different picture of the nature of poverty and welfare from the "snapshot" view taken in any one year. For example, we know that over recent decades 11 to 15 percent of the nation's population had been officially classified as poor in any one year (see Figure 7–2). However, over a decade as many as 25 percent of the nation's population may have fallen below the poverty line at one time or another.[3] Only some poverty is persistent: about 6 percent of the population remains in poverty for more than five years. This means that most of the people who experience poverty in their lives do so for only a short period of time.

However, the *persistently poor* place a disproportionate burden on welfare resources. Less than half of the people on welfare rolls at any one time are persistently poor; that is, likely to remain poor for five or more years. Thus, for most welfare recipients, welfare payments are a relatively short-term aid that helps them over life's difficult times. But for some, welfare is a more permanent part of their lives.

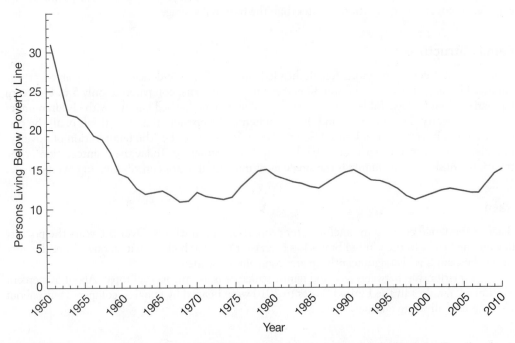

FIGURE 7–2   Persons below Poverty Line (Percentage) Poverty in America declined significantly prior to the 1960s. The enactment of many Great Society programs may have encouraged the continuation of poverty by promoting social dependency. Poverty has varied between 12 and 15 percent of the population since 1970. The "Great Recession" beginning in 2008 increased poverty.
SOURCE: U.S. Census Bureau, *Poverty in the United States: 2003* (Washington, DC: Government Printing Office, 2004), pp. 40–45; and *www.census.gov*.

WHY ARE THE POOR POOR?

Inasmuch as policymakers cannot even agree on the definition of poverty, it comes as no surprise that they cannot agree on its causes. Yet rationality in public policymaking requires some agreement on the causes of social problems.

Low Productivity

Many economists explain poverty in terms of *human capital theory*. The poor are poor because their economic productivity is low. They do not have the human capital—the knowledge, skills, training, work habits, abilities—to sell to employers in a free market. Absence from the labor force is the largest single source of poverty. Over two-thirds of the poor are children, mothers of small children, or aged or disabled people, all of whom cannot reasonably be expected to find employment. No improvement in the general economy is likely to affect these people directly. Since the private economy has no role for them, they are largely the responsibility of government. The poorly educated and unskilled are also at a disadvantage in a free labor market. The demand for their labor is low, employment is often temporary, and wage rates are low.

Economic Stagnation

Economists also recognize that some poverty results from inadequate aggregate demand. Serious recessions with increases in unemployment raise the proportion of the population living below the poverty line. According to this view, the most effective antipoverty policy is to assure continued economic growth and employment opportunity. Historically, the greatest reductions in poverty have occurred during prosperous times.

Discrimination

Discrimination plays a role in poverty that is largely unaccounted for by economic theory. We have already observed that blacks are more likely to experience poverty than whites. It is true that some of the income differences between blacks and whites are a product of educational differences. However, *blacks earn less than whites even at the same educational level*. If the free market operated without interference by discrimination, we would expect little or no difference in income between blacks and whites with the same education.

Culture of Poverty

Yet another explanation focuses on a "culture of poverty." According to this notion, poverty is a "way of life," which is learned by the poor. The culture of poverty involves not just a low income but also indifference, alienation, apathy, and irresponsibility. This culture fosters a lack of self-discipline to work hard, to plan and save for the future, and to get ahead. It also encourages family instability, immediate gratification, and "present-orientedness" instead of "future-orientedness." All of these attitudes prevent the poor from taking advantage of the opportunities available to them. Even cash payments do not change the way of life of these hard-core poor very much. According to this theory, additional money will be spent quickly for nonessential or frivolous items.

Opponents of this idea argue that it diverts attention from the conditions of poverty that *foster* family instability, present-orientedness, and other ways of life of the poor. The question is really whether a lack of money creates a culture of poverty, or vice versa. Reformers are likely to focus on the condition of poverty as the fundamental cause of the social pathologies that afflict the poor.

Disintegrating Family Structure

Poverty is closely associated with family structure. As we have seen, poverty is greatest among female-headed households and least among husband–wife households. It may be fashionable in some circles to view husband–wife families as traditional or even antiquated and to redefine *family* as any household with more than one person. But no worse advice could be given to the poor.

Of all age groups, children are most likely to be poor; about 20 percent of America's children live in poverty. Disintegrating family structure explains most of this: only about 10 percent of children living with married parents currently live in poverty, whereas over 40 percent of those living with single mothers do so.[4]

THE PREVENTIVE STRATEGY: SOCIAL SECURITY

The administration of President Franklin D. Roosevelt brought conscious attempts by the federal government to develop rational programs to achieve societal goals. In the most important piece of legislation of the New Deal, the Social Security Act of 1935, the federal government undertook to establish the basic framework for welfare policies at the federal, state, and local levels and, more important, to set forth a strategy for dealing with poverty. The Great Depression of that era convinced the nation's leadership that poverty could result from forces over which the individual had no control—loss of job, old age, death of the family breadwinner, or physical disability. One solution was to require individuals to purchase insurance against their own indigency resulting from any of these occurrences.

Social Insurance

The social insurance concept devised by the New Deal planners was designed to *prevent* poverty resulting from uncontrollable forces. Social insurance was based on the same notion as private insurance—sharing risks and setting aside money for a rainy day. Social insurance was not to be charity or public assistance; it was to be preventive. It relied on the individual's compulsory contribution to his or her own protection. In contrast, public assistance is only alleviative and relies on general tax revenues from all taxpayers. Indeed, when the Roosevelt administration presented the social insurance plan to Congress in the Social Security Act of 1935, it contended that it would eventually abolish the need for any public assistance program because individuals would be compelled to protect themselves against poverty.

OASDI

The key feature of the Social Security Act of 1935 is the Old Age Survivor's and Disability Insurance (OASDI) program, generally known as Social Security.* This is a compulsory social insurance program financed by regular deductions from earnings, which gives individuals a

---

*The original Social Security Act of 1935 did not include disability insurance; this was added by amendment in 1950. Health insurance for the aged—Medicare—was added by amendment in 1965. Medicare is discussed in Chapter 8.

legal right to benefits in the event of certain occurrences that cause a reduction of their income: old age, death of the head of household, or permanent disability. OASDI now covers about nine out of every ten workers in the United States, including the self-employed. The only large group outside its coverage are federal employees, who have their own retirement system.

FICA

Social Security is financed by FICA (Federal Insurance Contributions Act) deductions from employees' wages with equal contributions taken from employers. The standard rate for OASDI has been 6.2 percent each from employees and employers for a total of 12.4 percent of wages up to a specified top limit ($106,800 in 2011). (However in 2011 Congress reduced the FICA deduction on employees pay by two percentage points, from 6.2 to 4.2 as part of the tax package. See Chapter 11.) Wages above the top limit, and income from other sources, including rents, royalties, pensions, dividends, and capital gains, are *not* subject to FICA.

Payroll tax deductions are also made for hospital insurance under Medicare. Medicare taxes add 1.45 percent tax on employees and employers, bringing the total payroll tax for Social Security and Medicare combined to 7.65 percent on employees and employers, for a total of 15.3 percent of payrolls. The Medicare tax has no top limit on wages.

Retirement Benefits

Upon retirement, an insured worker is entitled to monthly benefit payments based on age at retirement and the amount earned during his or her working years. Retirees may choose reduced benefits at age 63. Full benefits for persons born before 1938 begin at age 65. For persons born after 1938 the age of full retirement benefits gradually increases until it reaches 67 for persons born after 1959.

Benefit payments receive automatic cost-of-living adjustments (COLAs) indexed to inflation each year. The formula for calculating COLAs increases benefits faster than the actual cost of living for the elderly.

Survivor and Disability Benefits

OASDI also provides benefit payments to survivors of an insured worker, including a spouse if there are dependent children. But if there are no dependent children, benefits will not begin until the spouse reaches retirement age. OASDI provides benefit payments to persons who suffer permanent and total disabilities that prevent them from working for more than one year.

INTENDED AND UNINTENDED CONSEQUENCES OF SOCIAL SECURITY

The framers of the Social Security Act of 1935 created a "trust fund" with the expectation that a reserve would be built up from social insurance premiums from working people. The reserve would earn interest, and the interest and principal would be used in later years to pay benefits. Benefits for an individual would be in proportion to his or her contributions. General tax revenues would not be used at all. It was intended that the system would resemble the financing of private insurance, but it turned out not to work that way at all.

The "Trust Fund"

The social insurance system is now financed on a pay-as-you-go, rather than a reserve system. Today, the income from all social insurance premiums (taxes) pays for current Social Security benefits. Today, this generation of workers is paying for the benefits of the last generation, and it is hoped that this generation's benefits will be financed by the next generation of workers. Social Security "trust fund" revenues are lumped together with general tax revenues in the federal budget. Indeed, Social Security payments (FICA deductions from wages) now comprise over 35 percent of total federal revenues.

Social Security FICA taxes appear in the federal budget as current revenues (see Chapter 11). Until recently these taxes *exceeded* payments made to beneficiaries. The surpluses were spent by the federal government; there was no "lockbox" holding these taxes for the exclusive use of the Social Security Administration. But now benefit payments to Social Security recipients exceed the income from FICA taxes. In theory these benefits can still be paid from the "trust fund," but inasmuch as the "trust fund" is merely an accounting gimmick, benefits are actually paid from current federal revenues. Even if a real trust fund was held by the federal government, it would be exhausted by 2040 (see Figure 7–3).

The Generational Compact

Taxing current workers to pay benefits to current retirees may be viewed as a compact between generations. Each generation of workers in effect agrees to pay benefits to an earlier generation of retirees, in the hope that the next generation will pay for their own retirement. But low birth rates (reducing the number of workers), longer life spans (increasing the number of retirees), and generous benefits are straining workers' ability to pay.

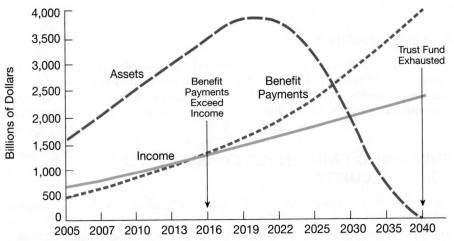

FIGURE 7–3　The Future of Social Security The Social Security fund will be exhausted as the "baby-boom" generation ages; Social Security reform has been put off again and again by Congress.
SOURCE: *Social Security Administration Trustee Report, 2005.*

The Dependency Ratio

Since current workers must pay for the benefits of current retirees and other beneficiaries, the dependency ratio becomes an important component of evaluating the future of Social Security. The dependency ratio for Social Security is the number of recipients as a percentage of the number of contributing workers. Americans are living longer, thereby increasing the dependency ratio. A child born in 1935, when the Social Security system was created, could expect to live only to age 61, four years *less* than the retirement age of 65. The life expectancy of a child born in 2010 is 78 years, 13 years *beyond* the retirement age.[5] In the early years of Social Security, there were ten workers supporting each retiree—a dependency ratio of 10 to 1. But today, as the U.S. population grows older—because of lower birth rates and longer life spans—there are only three workers for each retiree, and by 2030 the dependency ratio will rise to two workers for each retiree.

Generous COLAs

Currently, Social Security annual COLAs (cost-of-living adjustments) are based on the consumer price index (CPI), which estimates the cost of all consumer items each year. There are serious problems with the use of the CPI to provide annual values in Social Security benefits. First of all, cost estimates in the CPI include home buying, mortgage interest, child rearing, and other costs that many retirees do not confront. Most *workers* do not have the same protection against inflation as retirees; that is, average wage rates do not always match the increases in cost of living. Over the years, the COLAs have improved the economic well-being of Social Security recipients relative to American workers. Second, the CPI has been shown to *over*estimate rises in the real cost of living. Overestimates in the CPI result in more generous COLAs each year.

Wealthy Retirees

Social Security benefits are paid to all eligible retirees, regardless of whatever other income they may receive. There is no means test for benefits. The result is that large numbers of affluent Americans receive government checks each month. Of course, they paid into Social Security during their working years and they can claim these checks as a legal "entitlement" under the insurance principle. But currently their benefits far exceed their previous payments.

Since the aged experience *less* poverty than today's workers (see Table 7–2) and possess considerably more wealth, Social Security benefits constitute a "negative" redistribution of income, that is, a transfer of income from poorer to richer people. The elderly are generally better off than the people supporting them.

SOCIAL SECURITY REFORM?

Without significant reform, Social Security will become increasingly burdensome to working taxpayers in the next century. The "baby boom" from 1945 to 1960 produced a large generation of people who crowded schools and colleges in the 1960s and 1970s and who began to retire in 2010. Changes in lifestyle—less smoking, more exercise, better weight control—as well as medical advances, may increase the aged population even more.

"Saving" Social Security

"Saving" Social Security is a popular political slogan in Washington. But agreement on exactly how to reform the system continues to evade lawmakers.

Social Security is such a politically volatile topic that presidents have resorted to independent and nonpartisan commissions to recommend reform, rather than undertake to initiate reforms themselves. In 1983 a National Commission on Social Security Reform, appointed by President Ronald Reagan and made up of equal numbers of Democrats and Republicans, recommended increases in Social Security taxes to build a reserve for the large number of baby-boom generation retirees expected after the year 2010. The commission also recommended, and Congress enacted, a gradual increase in the full retirement age from 65 to 67, beginning in 2000. The Social Security and Medicare tax was also increased to its current combined employer and employee 15.3 percent. However, no real "reserve" was ever created, other than as an accounting gimmick.

Reform Options

There is no lack of reform proposals for Social Security.[6] The problem is that no particular proposal enjoys widespread popular support. In theory, Congress could limit benefits in several ways, for example, by raising the eligibility age for full retirement to 68 or 70, by limiting COLAs to the true increases in the cost of living for retirees, or by reducing benefits for high-income retirees. Or, Congress could increase Social Security revenues by raising the payroll tax rate, or by eliminating the cap on earnings that are taxed. But politically, such reforms are very controversial.

Various proposals to "privatize" all or part of Social Security represent yet another approach to reform. One idea was to allow the Social Security trust fund to invest in the private stock market with the expectation that stock values will increase over time. A related idea is to allow American workers to deposit part of their Social Security payroll tax into individual retirement accounts to buy securities of their own choosing. Of course, such a plan would expose workers to the risk of bad investment decisions. "Privatizing" Social Security does not appear to be very popular with the American people.

The "Third Rail" of American Politics

Social Security is the most expensive program in the federal budget but also the most politically sacrosanct. Politicians regularly call it the "third rail" of American politics—touch it and die.

Senior citizens are the most politically powerful age group in the population. They constitute 28 percent of the voting-age population, but more important, because of their high turnout rates, they constitute nearly one-third of the voters on election day. Moreover, seniors are well represented in Washington; the American Association of Retired Persons (AARP) is the nation's single largest organized interest group. Most seniors, and their lobbyists in Washington, adamantly oppose any Social Security reforms that might reduce benefits.

Unemployment Compensation

A second important feature of the Social Security Act of 1935 was that it induced states to enact unemployment compensation programs through the imposition of the payroll tax on employers. A federal unemployment tax is levied on the payroll of all employers, but employers paying into state insurance programs that meet federal standards may use these state payments to offset most of their federal unemployment tax. In other words, the federal government threatens to undertake an unemployment compensation program and tax if the states do not do so themselves. This federal program succeeded in inducing all fifty states to establish such programs.

In most states, unemployed workers must report in person and show that they are willing and able to work in order to receive unemployment compensation benefits. In practice, this means that unemployed workers must register with the U.S. Employment Service (usually located in the same building as the state unemployment compensation office) as a condition of receiving their unemployment checks. States cannot deny workers benefits for refusing to work as strikebreakers or for rates lower than prevailing rates. But states can deny benefits to workers who refuse to accept "suitable" jobs.

Extended Benefits.   Originally unemployment compensation was designed as a "temporary and partial" replacement of wages for involuntarily unemployed workers. But the "Great Recession" of recent years caused the Congress to extend unemployment payments well beyond the 26 weeks that had been established as the maximum length of compensation. Indeed, by 2011 Congress had extended benefits to three years duration. The payroll tax does not produce sufficient revenues to cover these extensions, so the Congress pays for extensions from general revenues. Nationwide, benefits average about $350 per week. Critics of these extensions note that beneficiaries tend to find jobs near the end of their compensation period, suggesting that compensation has encouraged unemployment. Extensions beyond six months suggest that unemployment compensation is becoming a permanent welfare program rather than a temporary insurance program.

THE ALLEVIATIVE STRATEGY: PUBLIC ASSISTANCE

The Social Security and unemployment compensation programs were based on the insurance strategy to *prevent* poverty, but in the Social Security Act of 1935 the federal government also undertook to help the states provide public assistance to certain needy people. This strategy was designed to *alleviate* the conditions of poverty. The original idea was to provide a minimum level of subsistence to certain categories of needy adults—the aged, blind, and disabled—and to provide for the care of dependent children.

Supplemental Security Income (SSI)

Supplemental Security Income (SSI) is a means-tested, federally administered income assistance program that provides monthly cash payments to needy elderly (65 or older), blind, and disabled people. A loose definition of "disability"—including alcoholism, drug abuse, and attention deficiency among children—has led to a rapid growth in the number of SSI beneficiaries.

Medicaid

Medicaid is a joint federal–state program that provides health services to low-income Americans. Women and children receiving public assistance benefits qualify for Medicaid, as does anyone who gets cash assistance under SSI. States can also offer Medicaid to the "medically needy"—those who face crushing medical costs but whose income or assets are too high to qualify for SSI or Temporary Assistance for Needy Families, including pregnant women and young children not receiving other aid. Medicaid also pays for long-term nursing home care, but only after beneficiaries have used up virtually all of their savings and income.

SCHIP

The State Children's Health Insurance Program (SCHIP) provides federal grants to the states to extend health insurance to children who would not otherwise qualify for Medicaid. The program is generally targeted toward families with incomes below 200 percent of the poverty level. But each state may set its own eligibility limits, and each state has flexibility in the administration of the program.

Food Stamps (SNAP)

The food stamp program provides low-income households with SNAP cards (Supplemental Nutrition Assistance Program) that can be used to purchase food and groceries sufficient for a nutritious family diet. The program is overseen by the federal government but is administered by the states.

Temporary Assistance for Needy Families (TANF)

Today the cash assistance program is a federal block grant to the states for needy families with dependent children. A result of welfare reform legislation passed by a Republican-controlled Congress in 1996 and signed by President Bill Clinton, this program replaced Aid to Families with Dependent Children (AFDC). Adults receiving TANF cash benefits are required to begin working within two years of receiving aid. States may exempt from this work requirement a parent of a child 12 months of age or younger. Federal funds cannot be used for adults who have *received welfare for more than five years*, although state and local funds can be used. States can exempt up to 20 percent of their caseload from this time limit. States can also opt to impose a shorter time limit on benefits. None of the funds can be used for adults who do not work *after receiving welfare for two years*. In addition, states have the option to deny welfare to unwed parents under age 18 unless they live with an adult and attend school.

WELFARE REFORM

Developing a rational strategy to assist the poor is hampered by the clash of values over individual responsibility and social compassion. As Harvard sociologist David Ellwood explains:

> Welfare brings some of our most precious values—involving autonomy, responsibility, work, family, community and compassion—into conflict. We want to help those who are not making it but in so doing, we seem to cheapen the efforts of those who are struggling hard just to get by. We want to offer financial support to those with low incomes, but if we do we reduce the pressure on them and their incentive to work. We want to help people who are not able to help themselves, but then we worry that people will not bother to help themselves. We recognize the insecurity of single-parent families but, in helping them, we appear to be promoting or supporting their formation.[7]

The social insurance programs that largely serve the middle class (Social Security, Medicare, unemployment compensation) are politically popular and enjoy the support of large numbers of politically active beneficiaries. But public assistance programs that largely serve the poor (cash aid, SSI, food stamps, Medicaid) are far less popular and are surrounded by many controversies.

Public Policy as a Cause of Poverty?

Can the government itself encourage poverty by fashioning social welfare programs and policies that destroy incentives to work, encourage families to break up, and condemn the poor to social dependency?

Poverty in America steadily declined from 1950, when about 30 percent of the population was officially poor, to 1970, when about 12 percent of the population was poor. During this period of progress toward the elimination of poverty, government welfare programs were minimal. But the downward trend in poverty ended in the 1970s and early 1980s (see Figure 7–2). This was a period in which AFDC payments were significantly increased and eligibility rules were relaxed. The food stamp program was initiated in 1965 and became a major new welfare benefit. Medicaid was initiated in the same year and by the late 1970s became the costliest of all welfare programs. Federal aid to the aged, blind, and disabled were merged into a new SSI program (Supplement Security Income), which quadrupled in numbers of recipients. Policymakers became obliged to consider the possibility that policy changes—new welfare programs, expanded benefits, and relaxed eligibility requirements—contributed to increased poverty.[8]

Welfare Reform Politics

A consensus grew over the years that long-term social dependency had to be addressed in welfare policy. The fact that most *nonpoor* mothers work convinced many liberals that welfare mothers had no special claim to stay at home with their children. And many conservatives acknowledged that some transitional assistance—education, job training, continued health care, and day care for children—might be necessary to move welfare mothers into the work force.

Although President Bill Clinton had promised "to end welfare as we know it," it was the Republican-controlled Congress elected in 1994 that proceeded to do so. The Republican-sponsored welfare reform bill ended the 60-year-old federal "entitlement" for low-income families with children—the venerable Aid to Families with Dependent Children (AFDC) program. In its place the Republicans devised a "devolution" of responsibility to the states through federal block grants—Temporary Assistance to Needy Families—lump sum allocations to the states for cash welfare payments with benefits and eligibility requirements decided by the states. Conservatives in Congress imposed tough-minded "strings" to state aid, including a two-year limit on continuing cash benefits and a five-year lifetime limit; a "family cap" that would deny additional cash benefits to women already on welfare who bear more children; the denial of cash welfare to unwed parents under 18 years of age unless they live with an adult and attend school. President Clinton vetoed the first welfare reform bill passed by Congress in early 1996, but later he reversed himself and signed the welfare reform act establishing the Temporary Assistance to Needy Families program (described earlier). Food stamps, SSI, and Medicaid were continued as federal "entitlements."

Evaluation: Is Welfare Reform Working?

If welfare reform is evaluated in terms of the numbers of people receiving cash welfare payments, then TANF has been a stunning success. Welfare recipients dropped by two-thirds in the years following welfare reform (see Figure 7–4). Yet during this same period recipients of food stamps, SSI, and Medicaid increased.

Continuing Welfare Needs

While nearly everyone agrees that getting people off of welfare rolls and onto payrolls is the main goal of reform, there are major obstacles to the achievement of this goal. First of all, a substantial portion (perhaps 25 to 40 percent) of long-term welfare recipients have handicaps—physical disabilities, chronic illnesses, learning disabilities, alcohol or drug abuse problems—that prevent them from holding a full-time job. Many long-term recipients have no work experience (perhaps 40 percent), and two-thirds of them did not graduate from high school. Almost half have three or

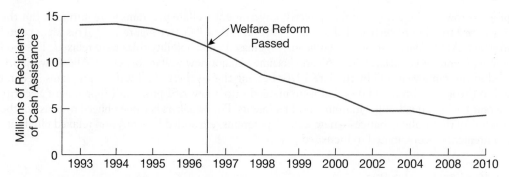

FIGURE 7–4 Evaluating Welfare Reform Since the passage of welfare reform in 1996, the numbers of people receiving cash benefits have declined dramatically. The "Great Recession" beginning in 2008 has brought a modest increase in TANF recipients.
SOURCE: U.S. Department of Health and Human Services.

more children, making daycare arrangements a major obstacle. It is unlikely that any counseling, education, job training, or job placement programs advocated by liberals could ever succeed in getting these people into productive employment. Policymakers argue whether there are 4 million jobs available to unskilled mothers, but even if there are such jobs available, they would be low-paying, minimum-wage jobs that would not lift them out of poverty.

THE WORKING POOR

Significant numbers of people who work part-time or even full-time still fall below the poverty line. These "working poor" constitute about 10 percent of the nation's work force.

The Minimum Wage

The Fair Labor Standards Act of 1937, an important part of President Franklin D. Roosevelt's New Deal, set a standard 40-hour workweek and minimum hourly wage for American workers. Congress periodically raises the minimum wage. (For 2011 the federal minimum wage is set at $7.15 per hour.) Over time, however, larger numbers of workers have become independent "contractors" or "managers" or other classifications of employees that fall outside the protection of federal wage and hour laws.

The Earned Income Tax Credit

Low-income workers in America currently benefit more from the Earned Income Tax Credit (EITC) than the minimum wage. The EITC was enacted in 1975 to provide an incentive to work. The credit does more than eliminate the burden of the federal income tax for low-income people; rather, it results in a "refund" check for those who claim and qualify for the credit. (In 2011 families with two or more children and incomes below $45,373 qualified for the credit and received a check from the government.) The maximum check in 2011 was $4,915. The EITC may be thought of as a "negative income tax." It results in government payments to low-income workers.

The EITC is now the largest means-tested program other than Medicaid. Over 20 million families receive EITC checks. Nonetheless, it is estimated that about one-third of qualifying families fail to take advantage of their EITC benefits.

HOMELESSNESS AND PUBLIC POLICY

Homeless "street people" may be the most visible social welfare problem confronting the nation. The homeless suffer exposure, alcoholism, drug abuse, and chronic mental illness while wandering the streets of the nation's larger cities. No one really knows the true number of homeless.[9] The issue has become so politicized that an accurate assessment of the problem and a rational strategy for dealing with it have become virtually impossible. The term *homeless* is used to describe many different situations. There are the street people who sleep in subways, bus stations, parks, or the streets. Some of them are temporarily traveling in search of work; some have left home for a few days or are youthful runaways; others have roamed the streets for months or years. There are the *sheltered homeless* who obtain housing in shelters operated by local governments or private charities. As the number of shelters has grown in recent years, the number of sheltered homeless has also grown. But most of the sheltered homeless come from other housing, not the streets. These are people who have been recently evicted from rental units or have previously lived with family or friends. They often include families with children; the street homeless are virtually all single persons.

Who Are the Homeless?

Among all homeless, both street people and sheltered homeless, single men make up 41 percent, families with children 44 percent, single women 13 percent, and unaccompanied youth 5 percent.[10] Among single people living on the streets, close to half are chronic alcohol and/or drug abusers, and an additional one-fourth to one-third are mentally ill. Families with children are found among the sheltered homeless, and many of the sheltered homeless are employed. The sheltered homeless remain for an average of six months. Single street people may remain homeless for years.

Public Policy as a Cause of Homelessness

The current plight of many of the street homeless is a result of various "reforms" in public policy, notably the "deinstitutionalization" of care for the mentally ill and the "decriminalization" of vagrancy and public intoxication.

Deinstitutionalization

Deinstitutionalization was a reform advanced by mental health care professionals and social welfare activists in the 1960s and 1970s to release chronic mental patients from state-run mental hospitals. It was widely recognized that aside from drugs, no psychiatric therapies have much success among the long-term mentally ill. Drug therapies can be administered on an outpatient basis; they usually do not require hospitalization. So it was argued that no one could be rightfully kept in a mental institution against his or her will; people who had committed no crimes and who posed no danger to others should be released. Federal and state monies for mental health were to be directed toward community mental health facilities that would treat the mentally ill on a voluntary outpatient basis.

Decriminalization

"Vagrancy" and public intoxication are no longer crimes. Involuntary confinement has been abolished for the mentally ill and for substance abusers, unless a person is adjudged in court to be "a danger to himself or others," which means a person must commit a serious act of violence before the courts will intervene. For many homeless this means the freedom to "die with their rights on." The homeless are victimized by cold, exposure, hunger, the availability of alcohol and illegal drugs, and violent street crimes perpetrated against them, in addition to the ravages of their illness itself.

The Failure of Community Care

Community-based care is largely irrelevant to the plight of the chronic mentally ill and alcohol and drug abusers in the streets. Many are "uncooperative"; they are isolated from society; they have no family members or doctors or counselors to turn to for help. For them, community care is a Salvation Army meal and cot; a night in a city-run refuge for the homeless; or a ride to the city hospital psychiatric ward for a brief period of "observation," after which they must be released again to the streets. The nation's vast social welfare system provides little help. They lose their Social Security, welfare, and disability checks because they have no permanent address. They cannot handle forms, appointments, or interviews; the welfare bureaucracy is intimidating.

SUMMARY

A rational approach to social welfare policy requires a clear definition of objectives, the development of alternative strategies for achieving them, and a careful comparison and weighing of the costs and benefits of each. But there are seemingly insurmountable problems in developing a completely rational policy:

1. Contrasting definitions of poverty constitute one obstacle to rational policymaking. Official government sources define poverty in terms of minimum dollar amounts required for subsistence. In recent years about 12 to 15 percent of the population has fallen below the official poverty line. Latent poverty refers to people who would fall below the poverty line in the absence of government assistance; about 20 percent of the population falls within this definition of poverty. Net poverty refers to people who remain poor even after receiving government assistance; about 8 percent of the population falls within this definition.

2. Contrasting explanations of poverty also make it difficult to formulate a rational policy. Is poverty a product of a lack of knowledge, skills, and training? Or recession and unemployment? Or a culture of poverty? Certainly the disintegration of the traditional husband–wife family is closely associated with poverty. How can the government devise a rational policy to keep families together, or at least not encourage them to dissolve?

3. Government welfare policies themselves may be a significant cause of poverty. Poverty in America had steadily declined before the development of Great Society programs, the relaxation of eligibility requirements for welfare assistance, and the rapid increase of welfare expenditures in the 1970s. To what extent do government programs themselves encourage social dependency and harm the long-term prospects of the poor?

4. The social insurance concept was designed as a preventive strategy to insure people against indigence arising from old age, death of a family breadwinner, or physical disability. But the Social Security "trust fund" idea remains in name only. Today each generation of workers is expected to pay the benefits for the next generation of retirees.

5. Unemployment compensation was designed as a temporary partial replacement of wages for involuntarily unemployed workers. But Congress has extended unemployment payments well beyond the 26 weeks that most states had established as the maximum length of compensation.

6. The federal government also pursues an alleviative strategy in assisting the poor with a variety of direct cash and in-kind benefit programs. The SSI program provides direct federal cash payments to the aged, blind, and disabled. As a welfare program, SSI is paid from general tax revenues, and recipients must prove their need. The largest in-kind welfare programs are federal food stamps and Medicaid.

7. Welfare reform in 1996, including a two-year limit on cash assistance and work and school requirements, appears to have reduced cash welfare rolls substantially. But some people are not capable of moving from welfare to work.

8. "Rational" strategies sometimes produce unintended consequences. Deinstitutionalization of the mentally ill and decriminalization of public intoxication produced many homeless people. It is often difficult to reach these people through conventional welfare programs.

MySearchLab® EXERCISES

Apply what you learned in this chapter on MySearchLab (www.mysearchlab.com).

NOTES

1. U.S. Bureau of the Census, *Statistical Abstract of the United States, 2010*, p. 456.

2. *Statistical Abstract of the United States, 2010*, p. 56.

3. Greg J. Duncan, *Years of Poverty, Years of Plenty* (Ann Arbor, MI: Institute of Social Research, 1984).

4. *Statistical Abstract of the United States, 2010*, p. 459.

5. Ibid, p. 76.

6. See Henry J. Aaron and Robert D. Reischauer, *Countdown to Reform: The Great Social*

Security Debate (Washington, DC: Brookings Institution, 2001).

7. David Ellwood, *Poor Support: Poverty in the American Family* (New York: Basic Books, 1988), p. 6.

8. Charles Murray, *Losing Ground* (New York: Basic Books, 1984).

9. Peter H. Rossi, *Down and Out in America* (Chicago: University of Chicago Press, 1989).

10. U.S. Conference of Mayors, *Report of the Taskforce on Hunger and Homelessness*, December 2002.

BIBLIOGRAPHY

AARON, HENRY J. *Saving Social Security: Which Way to Reform?* Washington, DC: Brookings Institution Press, 2006.

DIAMOND, PETER, and PETER R. ORSZAG. *Saving Social Security*, rev. ed. Washington, DC: Brookings Institution Press, 2005.

DINITTO, DIANA M. *Social Welfare: Politics and Policy*, 7th ed. New York: Pearson, 2011.

JENCKS, CHRISTOPHER, and PAUL E. PETERSON. *The Urban Underclass*. Washington, DC: Brookings Institution Press, 1991.

MACMANUS, SUSAN. *Young versus Old*. Boulder, CO: Westview Press, 1996.

MURRAY, CHARLES. *Losing Ground*. New York: Basic Books, 1984.

ROGERS, HAROLD R., Jr. *American Poverty in a New Age of Reform*. New York: M. E. Sharpe, 2nd ed. 2006.

RYCROFT, ROBERT S. *The Economics of Inequality, Discrimination, Poverty, and Mobility*. New York: M. E. Sharpe, 2009.

WILSON, WILLIAM J. *The Truly Disadvantaged*. Chicago: University of Chicago Press, 1987.

WEB SITES

CHILDREN'S DEFENSE FUND. Advocacy organization for welfare programs, with special emphasis on aid for children. *www.childrensdefense.org*

URBAN INSTITUTE. Think tank with emphasis on welfare issues. *www.urban.org*

AMERICAN ASSOCIATION OF RETIRED PERSONS (AARP). Home page of the leading advocacy group for seniors. *www.aarp.org*

CATO INSTITUTE (SOCIAL SECURITY). Libertarian think tank's special site advocating privatizing Social Security. *www.socialsecurity.org*

NATIONAL COMMITTEE TO PRESERVE SOCIAL SECURITY AND MEDICARE. Advocacy organization for expansion of benefits under Social Security and Medicare. *www.ncpssm.org*

THIRD MILLENNIUM. Advocacy organization for young adults concerned with deficit spending, Social Security reform, etc. *www.millennium.org*

U.S. SOCIAL SECURITY ADMINISTRATION. Official site with information on Social Security—history, statistics, projections for the future, etc. *www.ssa.gov*

Access to Health Care A free dental clinic in the Los Angeles Sports Arena in 2010 attracts thousands of patients. America offers the highest quality of medical care in the world, but not everyone has equal access to it. President Obama's comprehensive health care reform act in 2010 includes an "individual mandate" that every person acquire health insurance by 2014 or face a tax penalty. (© Wendy Stone/Corbis)

8

Health Care
Attempting a Rational-Comprehensive Transformation

HEALTH CARE IN AMERICA

Can America transform its entire health care system according to a rational-comprehensive plan? In 2010 President Barack Obama and a Democratic-controlled Congress acted to transform health care in America with the Patient Protection and Affordable Care Act. National health care had been attempted unsuccessfully by past presidents, including Franklin D. Roosevelt, Harry Truman, and Bill Clinton. According to President Obama: "Moving to provide all Americans with health insurance is not only a moral imperative, but it is also essential to a more effective and efficient health care system."[1] But the question remains whether such a rational-comprehensive approach will improve the quality of health care in America, or reduce its costs, or improve access to health care, or achieve any of these goals.

Perhaps the first obstacle to a rational approach in health care is to define the problem. Is it our goal to have *good health*—that is, whether we live at all (infant mortality), or how well we live (days lost to sickness), or how long we live (average lifespans)? Or is our goal to have *good medical care*—frequent visits to the doctor, well-equipped and accessible hospitals, and equal access to medical care by rich and poor alike?

The first lesson in health policy is understanding that good medical care does not necessarily mean good health. Good health correlates best with factors over which doctors and hospitals have no control: heredity, lifestyle (smoking, obesity, drinking, exercise, worry), and the physical environment (sewage disposal, water quality, conditions of work, and so forth). Most of the bad things that happen to people's health are beyond the reach of doctors and hospitals. In the long run, infant mortality, sickness and disease, and life span are affected very little by the quality of medical care. If you want a long, healthy life, choose parents who have lived a long, healthy life, and then do all the things your mother always told you to do: don't smoke, don't drink, get lots of exercise and rest, don't overeat, relax, and don't worry.

Leading Causes of Death

Historically, most of the reductions in infant and adult death rates have resulted from public health and sanitation, including immunization against smallpox, clean public water supply, sanitary sewage disposal, improved diets, and increased standards of living. Many of the leading causes of death today (see Table 8–1), including heart disease, stroke, cancer, accidents, and suicides, are closely linked to personal habits and lifestyles.

TABLE 8–1 Leading Causes of Death[a]   Many of the leading causes of death today are closely linked to personal habits and life styles; the overall death rate has declined significantly since 1960.

	1960	1970	1980	1990	2000	2008
Heart disease	369.0	362.0	334.3	289.0	257.5	203.1
Stroke (cerebrovascular)	108.0	101.9	80.5	57.9	60.2	44.0
Cancer	149.2	162.8	181.9	201.7	200.5	186.2
Accidents	52.3	56.4	48.4	37.3	33.9	39.9
Pneumonia	37.3	30.9	26.7	31.3	24.3	18.5
Diabetes	16.7	18.9	15.5	19.5	24.9	23.2
Suicide	10.6	11.6	12.5	12.3	10.3	11.8
Homicide	4.7	8.3	9.4	10.2	5.8	5.9
AIDS/HIV	—	—	—	9.6	5.4	4.0
Alzheimer's disease	—	—	—	—	21.8	27.1

[a]Deaths per 100,000 population per year.
SOURCE: *Statistical Abstract of the United States, 2010,* p. 86. Updated at Center for Disease Control, *www.cdc.gov/nchs*

Costs and Benefits: Cross-National Comparisons

The United States spends more of its resources on health care than any other advanced industrialized nation, yet it ranks below other nations in many key measures of the health of its people (see Figure 8–1). Life expectancy in the United States is lower, and the infant death rate is higher, than in many of these nations. The United States offers the most advanced and sophisticated medical care in the world, attracting patients from countries that rank ahead of us in these common health measures. The United States is the locus of the most advanced medical research in the world, drawing researchers from all over the world. This apparent paradox—the highest quality medical care, combined with poor health statistics for the general public—suggests that our nation's health care problems center more on access to care, education, and prevention of health problems than on the quality of care available.

Health Care Costs

The United States spends over $2 trillion on health care each year—over $7,000 per person. These costs represent nearly 16 percent of the GDP and they are growing rapidly. It is estimated that by 2017 almost 20 percent of the GDP—more than $4 trillion—will be spent on health care. The enactment of the Medicare and Medicaid programs in 1965 and their rapid growth since then contribute to this inflation of health care costs. But there are many other causes as well. Advances in medical technology have produced elaborate and expensive equipment. Hospitals that have made heavy financial investment in this equipment must use it as often as possible. Physicians trained in highly specialized techniques and procedures wish to use them. The threat of malpractice suits forces doctors to practice "defensive medicine"—to order multiple tests and consultations to guard against even the most remote medical possibilities. Pharmaceutical companies have driven up spending for drugs by advertising expensive brand-name prescription drugs on television, encouraging patients to ask

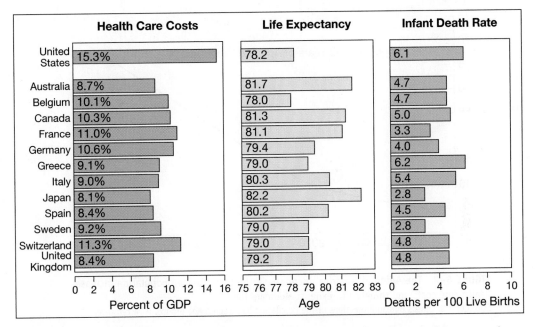

FIGURE 8–1   Health Care Costs and Benefits: A Cross-National Comparison The United States spends a larger proportion of its GDP on health care than any other nation, yet people in other nations enjoy better overall health than Americans.

SOURCE: *Statistical Abstract of the United States, 2010*, pp. 827, 824.

their doctors for these drugs. (Prior to 1997 direct advertising for prescription drugs was not permitted.) Cheaper generic versions of the same drugs receive no such publicity.

An Aging Population

In the not-too-distant future, an aging population (see Figure 8–2) will drive up medical care costs to near astronomical figures. Currently, one-third of all health care expenditures benefit the aged.

Medical Care as a Right

Americans now generally view access to medical care as a right. No one should be denied medical care or suffer pain or remedial illness for lack of financial resources. There is widespread agreement on this ethical principle. The tough questions arise when we seek rational strategies to implement it.

INCREMENTAL STRATEGIES: MEDICARE, MEDICAID, SCHIP

America's national health care policy traditionally reflected an incremental approach. Medicare was enacted in 1965 as an amendment to the Social Security Act of 1935, and it represented an extension of the social insurance principle. It covers persons 65 and over regardless of income. Hospital care is covered from premiums added to the Social Security payroll tax; physician

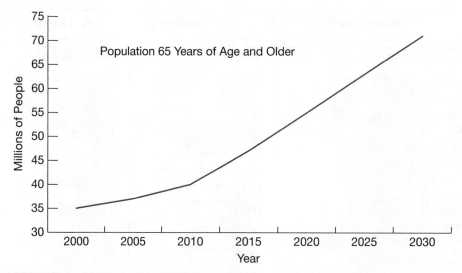

FIGURE 8–2 The Aging of America Increases in the nation's aged population increase health care costs and threaten to exhaust Medicare funds.
SOURCE: U.S. Census Bureau Projections of the Population by Selected Age Groups. *www.census.gov*

services are covered from modest premiums deducted from recipients of Social Security checks. Medicaid was enacted at the same time to provide health care for the poor. It represented an extension of the federally-aided state welfare programs begun in the 1930s. A State Child Health Insurance Program was added in 1997, with bipartisan support in Congress. It offered grants to states to provide health insurance for children whose family income was less than 200 percent of the poverty level.

Medicare: Health Care as Government Insurance

Medicare provides prepaid hospital insurance and low-cost voluntary medical insurance for the aged, directly under federal administration. Medicare includes HI—a compulsory basic health insurance plan covering hospital costs for the aged, which is financed out of payroll taxes collected under the Social Security system—and SMI—a voluntary, supplemental medical insurance program that will pay 80 percent of "allowable" charges for physicians' services and other medical expenses, financed in part by contributions from the aged and in part by general tax revenues.

Only *aged* persons are covered by Medicare provisions. Eligibility is not dependent on income; all aged persons eligible for Social Security are also eligible for Medicare. No physical examination is required, and preexisting conditions are covered. The costs of SMI are so low to the beneficiaries that participation by the elderly is almost universal.

Medicare requires patients to pay small initial charges or "deductibles." The purpose is to discourage unnecessary hospital or physician care. HI generally pays the full charges for the first 60 days of hospitalization each year after a deductible charge equivalent to one day's stay; but many doctors charge higher rates than allowable under SMI. Indeed, it is estimated that only about half of the doctors in the nation accept SMI allowable payments as payment in full. Many doctors bill Medicare patients for charges above the allowable SMI payments. Medicare does not pay for eyeglasses, dental expenses, hearing aids, or routine physical examinations.

Medicaid: Health Care as Welfare

Medicaid is the federal government's largest single welfare program for the poor. Its costs now exceed the costs of all other public assistance programs—including family cash assistance, SSI, and the food stamp program. Medicaid was begun in 1965 and grew quickly.

Medicaid is a combined federal and state program. The states exercise fairly broad administrative powers and carry almost half of the financial burden. Medicaid is a welfare program designed for needy persons: no prior contributions are required, monies come from general tax revenues, and most recipients are already on welfare rolls. Although states differ in their eligibility requirements, they must cover all people receiving federally funded public assistance payments. Most states also extend coverage to other "medically needy"—individuals who do not qualify for public assistance but whose incomes are low enough to qualify as needy.

States also help set benefits. All states are required by the federal government to provide inpatient and outpatient hospital care, physicians' services, laboratory services and X-rays, and nursing and home health care. They must also develop an early and periodic screening, diagnosis, and treatment program for all children under Medicaid. However, states themselves decide on the rate of reimbursement to hospitals and physicians. Low rates can discourage hospitals and physicians from providing good care. To make up for low payments, they may schedule too many patients in too short a time, prescribe unnecessary tests and procedures to make treatment expensive, or shift costs incurred in treating Medicaid patients to more affluent patients with private insurance.

SCHIP: Health Care for Children

Under the State Children's Health Insurance Program (SCHIP) the federal government provides grants to states to extend health insurance to children who would not otherwise qualify for Medicaid. The program is generally targeted toward families with incomes below 200 percent of the poverty level. But each state may set its own eligibility limits and has flexibility in the administration of the program. States may expand their Medicaid programs to include children or develop separate child health programs.

HEALTH CARE MODIFICATIONS

Over the years significant modifications were made in both private and governmental insurance programs.

Managed Care Programs

Skyrocketing costs caused both governments and private insurance companies to promote various types of "managed care" programs. Both Medicare and Medicaid shifted many of their beneficiaries to managed care programs.

Health maintenance organizations (HMOs) are the most common type of managed care program. They try to control costs by requiring patients to use a network of approved doctors and hospitals, and by reviewing what these "preferred" caregivers do. For example, a managed care organization might insist that doctors prescribe cheaper generic drugs in place of brand-name products. In many cases, patients must get the organization's approval before undergoing operations or other treatments. And patients have to pay more to visit a doctor who is not in the network. In contrast, under traditional "fee-for-service" health insurance plans, the patient chooses a doctor, gets treated, and the bill is sent to the insurance company. The patient may have to pay a deductible for a percentage of the total bill—a "co-pay."

Controversies over Managed Care

Efforts of private insurers and government to control costs created new political controversies. Many of the cost-control regulations and restrictions instituted by insurance companies and HMOs frustrate both patients and physicians. For example, both doctors and patients complain that preapproval of treatment by insurance companies removes medical decisions from the physician and patient and places them in hands of insurance company administrators. Patients complain that HMOs refuse to allow them to see specialists, limit the number and variety of tests, and encourage doctors to minimize treatment.

Patients' Bill of Rights

The growth of managed care health plans, with their efforts to control costs, fueled the drive for a "patients' bill of rights." The most common proposals are those allowing patients to see specialists without first obtaining permission from a representative of their health plan; provide emergency care without securing prior approval from their health plan; allowing immediate appeal if the patient is denied coverage for a particular treatment; and giving patients the right to sue their health plans for medical mistakes. Various states have adopted these proposals. But the health care industry, including HMOs, argue that these proposals increase the cost of health insurance and open health care providers to patients' lawsuits.

Portability, Preexisting Conditions

People with preexisting conditions, such as heart disease, hypertension, or cancer, face formidable problems in obtaining and keeping health insurance. Some modest reforms were enacted in 1996 when Congress guaranteed the "portability" of health insurance—allowing workers to maintain their insurance coverage if they change jobs. Their new employer's health insurance company cannot deny them insurance for "preexisting conditions." But the act did not bar increases in premiums, nor did it require the coverage of preexisting conditions in new policies. The failure of insurance companies to address the issue of preexisting conditions contributed heavily to support for more comprehensive reforms.

Prescription Drug Costs

Prescription drugs are more costly in the United States than anywhere else in the developed world. The American pharmaceutical industry argues that the higher prices that Americans pay help to fund research on new drugs, and that drug price controls would curtail the development of new and potentially life-saving drugs. Likewise, they argue that laws mandating the early expiration of drug patents, or laws encouraging the use of generic competition, would adversely affect research and development in pharmaceutics. In effect, Americans are being asked to subsidize drug research that benefits the entire world.

Many Americans have resorted to importing drugs from Canada or other nations that have much lower prices than those being charged in the United States. The Food and Drug Administration contends that this practice is illegal. Drug companies claim that imported drugs may not be safe, a highly dubious claim, inasmuch as they are the same drugs shipped by the American drug companies to Canada and other nations.

Prescription Drug Coverage Under Medicare

The long battle over adding prescription drug coverage to Medicare finally came to an end in 2003 when Congress passed and President George W. Bush signed such a bill. The bill was welcomed by the AARP and most seniors, but it promises to significantly increase the costs of Medicare over the long term. Prescription drugs have been covered by Medicaid since its inception.

THE HEALTH CARE REFORM MOVEMENT

Over the years health care reform efforts centered on two central concerns: controlling costs and expanding access. These concerns are related: expanding access to Americans who are uninsured and closing gaps in coverage increases spending, even while the other thrust of reform is to slow the growth of overall health care costs.

The Single Payer Plan

Liberals have long pressed for a Canadian-style health care system in which the government would provide health insurance for all Americans in a single national plan paid for by increases in taxes. In effect, a single-payer plan would expand Medicare to everyone, not just the aged. The plan boasts of simplicity, savings in administrative costs over multiple insurers, and direct federal control over prices to be paid for hospital and physician services and drugs. Single-payer universal coverage would require major new taxes.

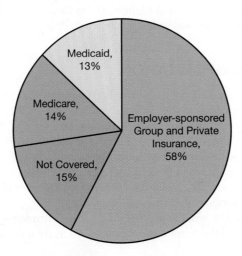

FIGURE 8–3   Health Care Coverage and the Uninsured in 2008
SOURCE: *Statistical Abstract of the United States, 2008*, p. 107.

America's Reliance on the Private Market

"Socialized medicine" was never very popular with the American people. They enjoyed the finest medical care in the world, with the most advanced treatments, state-of-the-art equipped hospitals and clinics, the world's best medical schools, and the best-trained medical specialists. American pharmaceutical companies led the way in research and development of life-saving treatments. The nation relied largely on the private market and individual choice in providing health care. Employer-sponsored private health insurance, together with individually purchased policies, covered over half of the population. Medicare covered the aged, and Medicaid covered the poor. Over 85 percent of Americans were covered by private or government insurance (see Figure 8–3). Heavy majorities of Americans expressed satisfaction in national polls with their own health care.

The Uninsured

Prior to health care reform, many working Americans and their dependents had no health insurance; about 15 percent of the nation's population. Many of these uninsured postponed or went without needed medical care; many were denied medical care by hospitals and physicians except in emergencies. Confronted with serious illness, many were obliged to impoverish themselves to become eligible for Medicaid. Their unpaid medical bills, including emergency room visits, were absorbed by hospitals or shifted to paying patients and their insurance companies. Many uninsured people work for small businesses or were self employed or unemployed.

Costs Versus Outcomes

As described earlier, overall health care costs in America amount to nearly 16 percent of the nation's GDP, the highest in the world. Yet the United States ranks well below other nations in many common measures of national health, including life expectancy and infant mortality (see Figure 8–1). This discrepancy—the most expensive and highest quality medical care, together with poor health statistics for the overall population—was widely attributed to America's unequal access to health care.

HEALTH CARE TRANSFORMATION

President Barack Obama and a Democratic-controlled Congress acted to transform health care in America with the Patient Protection and Affordable Care Act of 2010. Incremental change was rejected in favor of a 2600 page rational-comprehensive plan.

America's health care system will continue to rely primarily on private health insurance companies. However, private insurers will no longer be permitted to deny insurance for preexisting conditions, or to drop coverage when patients get sick, or to place lifetime limits on coverage. Dependent children under age 26 can be covered under their parents' insurance plan. These particular reforms faced no serious opposition in Congress.

But many provisions in the lengthy bill stirred intense controversy. Republicans in both the House of Representatives and the Senate were unanimous in their opposition to the overall bill. Among its many provisions:

Individual Mandate.   Every American will be required to purchase health insurance by 2014 or face a tax penalty up to 2.5 percent of their household income. The Internal Revenue Service is charged with enforcing this individual mandate.

Health Care Reform Becomes a Partisan Issue President Barack Obama campaigned across America in support of a comprehensive health insurance reform bill that Congress eventually enacted as the Patient Protection and Affordable Care Act of 2010. Republicans in Congress were unanimous in their opposition; they pledged to repeal it following their capture of control of the House of Representatives in the midterm congressional elections. But it is unlikely that outright repeal can be achieved with a Democratic-controlled Senate and the threat of a presidential veto. House Republicans are now trying to "defund" the Act—withholding appropriations required for its enforcement. (© Martin H. Simon/Corbis)

Employer Mandate. Employers with 50 or more workers will be obliged to provide health insurance to their employees. Companies that fail to do so will face substantial fines. Small businesses are offered tax credits for offering their employees health insurance.

Medicaid Expansion. State Medicaid eligibility will be expanded to include all individuals with incomes up to 133 percent of the federal poverty level. The federal government will initially fund this new state mandate, but eventually the states must fund increasing shares of it themselves.

Health Insurance Exchanges. The federal government will assist states in creating "exchanges" or marketplaces where individuals and small businesses can purchase health insurance from private companies. Health plans offered through the exchanges must meet federal requirements, including coverage for preventative care. Federal subsidies will be available for individuals who earn between 133 and 400 percent of the federal poverty level. High risk pools will be created to cover individuals with preexisting conditions.

Taxes. A surtax of 3.8 percent is imposed on personal investment income of individuals with adjusted gross income of $200,000 or couples with adjusted gross income of $250,000 or more. An excise tax is placed on high cost ("Cadillac") private health care plans as well as on medical devices. New fees are imposed on health insurance companies and on brand-name drug manufacturers.

No "Public Option."   Congress rejected President Obama's proposed "public option"—a government-run nonprofit health insurance agency that would compete with private insurers. The president had argued that a public option was necessary "to keep them honest" by offering reasonable coverage at affordable prices. But critics warned that the public option threatened a "government takeover" of the nation's health care system. Over time private insurance companies would lose out to the public program, eventually creating a single national health insurance system or "socialized medicine." Liberals in Congress were disappointed when the public option was dropped from the bill.

Costs.   President Obama argued that the cost of health care reform could be recovered in savings from the existing health care system—"a system that is currently full of waste and abuse." The president claimed that eliminating waste and inefficiency in Medicare and Medicaid could pay for most of his plan. But critics doubt that such savings exist. Indeed, the proposal to cut waste and abuse in Medicare inspired critics to claim that health care reform is coming at the expense of the elderly.

Controversy surrounds estimates of the true costs of the Act. The addition of 45 million previously uninsured Americans into the nation's health care system is likely to produce strains on hospitals and physicians. Costs are likely to increase, and there is the possibility that health care will be rationed. End-of-life care accounts for a substantial portion of total health care costs; critics of the Act fear that such care will become the target of cost-cutters.

REPEALING "OBAMACARE"?

Republicans in Congress promised the repeal of "Obamacare." But repeal is not a realistic option with Barack Obama in possession of the presidential veto power. So opponents of the Patient Protection and Affordable Care Act of 2010 must content themselves with efforts to revise the law. Yet even this task is complicated by the many interlocking and interdependent provisions of the health care system created by the Act.

The Constitutionality of the Individual Mandate

At the heart of Obamacare is a requirement that every American obtain health insurance. The health insurance industry supports this provision; it generates customers, including younger and healthier people. It also enables insurers to accept the risks of covering people with costly preexisting conditions.

But Attorneys General in several states have undertaken legal action challenging the Act as an unconstitutional expansion of federal power over the citizens of their states. The 10th amendment to the Constitution states plainly "The powers not delegated to the United States by this Constitution, nor prohibited by it to the States, are reserved to the States respectively, or to the people." Does the 10th Amendment carry any meaning in the twenty-first century? If Congress can force Americans to buy a product, what remains of the notion of a national government of limited and enumerated power?

Supporters claim that the mandate is justified under the Interstate Commerce Clause of the Constitution. This Clause has historically been given broad interpretation by the Supreme Court; Congress can regulate any economic activity that "taken in the aggregate substantially affects interstate commerce."[2] But the Supreme Court has also held that the Commerce Clause cannot justify any federal regulation whatsoever. The Court has ruled that carrying a gun near a school does not significantly affect interstate commerce,[3] and the Court overturned a law making violence against women a federal crime on the same grounds.[4] Supporters of the Act also claim that the mandate is constitutional because it is structured as a tax, which is authorized under the 16th Amendment. The issue is likely to be decided by the U.S. Supreme Court.

Barring IRS Enforcement

Americans who do not purchase health insurance by 2014 are subject to a fine to be levied by the IRS at tax time. The Act authorizes the IRS to determine who is not in compliance, to levy fines, and to withhold the fines from tax refunds. Opponents in Congress may seek to prevent the IRS from enforcing the law, perhaps by "defunding" the costs of administration. But President Obama is pledged to veto any attempt to weaken the individual mandate or its enforcement.

State Participation in Exchanges

States are authorized by the Act to create health insurance exchanges to provide coverage for individuals and small businesses by pooling them into larger groups to purchase insurance from private companies. States can refuse to participate, which might complicate the administration of a key provision of the Act. But the federal government is authorized to step in where the states fail to create these exchanges.

Conflict over Standards

Obamacare sets standards for health insurance plans acceptable in state health insurance exchanges. The federal Department of Health and Human Services is authorized to decide what medical treatments will be covered; it mandates coverage of emergency room visits, maternity care, prescription drugs, hospitalization, and medical tests. Opponents are likely to press for maximum flexibility for the states in deciding what services should be included in the exchanges.

Medicaid Cost

The Act mandates that the states expand their Medicaid programs to include all children and adults living in families with incomes under 133 percent of the federal poverty level. Some Republican governors and attorneys general have challenged the constitutionality of this mandate in federal court. Medicaid is the fastest rising cost in the budgets of state governments across the country, and state lawmakers contend that they do not have the funds to cover this federal mandate.

Medical Loss Ratio

The Act requires health insurance companies to abide by a "medical loss ratio"—a mandate that companies spend 85 percent of the premiums they receive on clinical services and costs related to the quality of care. Only 15 percent of premiums can go to administrative costs, advertising, or profit. It is likely that insurance companies will be in near constant conflict with the federal Department of Health and Human Services over the definition of medical costs versus administrative and other costs.

SUMMARY

The Patient Protection and Affordable Care Act of 2010 represents an attempt to transform the American health care system according to a rational-comprehensive government plan. Prior to 2010, the nation relied primarily on market-based, private, employer-sponsored group and individual insurance, together with Medicaid for the aged and Medicare for the poor. These government programs were amendments to the original Social Security Act of 1935 and represented incremental modifications of social insurance and welfare programs. "Obamacare" is a rational-comprehensive departure from previous policy. It is true that Obamacare retains the private insurance principle, but the federal government now plays the leading role in deciding about health care for all Americans.

1. Is the principal objective of health care policy good health, as defined by lower death rates, less illness, and longer life? Or is it access to good medical care? If good health is the objective, preventative efforts to change people's personal habits and lifestyles are more likely to improve health than anything else. Many of the leading causes of death—heart disease, stroke, cancer, cirrhosis of the liver, accidents, and suicides—are closely linked to personal habits and lifestyles.

2. The United States spends more of its economic resources on health care than any other nation in the world. Currently about 16 percent of the nation's GDP is devoted to health care, a figure that appears to rise each year. An aging population promises to drive up medical costs even further.

3. The United States boasts of the finest medical care in the world, the finest medical schools, and the best-trained medical specialists. Yet despite high costs and quality medical care, the United States ranks well below many other advanced nations in overall health statistics, including life expectancy and infant mortality rate.

4. Medicare was enacted in 1965 as an extension of the nation's Social Security program for the aged. It includes a basic health insurance plan covering hospital costs which is financed out of payroll taxes collected under Social Security payroll deductions. It also includes a voluntary supplemental medical insurance program that pays 80 percent of government approved charges for physicians' services and other medical expenses, financed in part by contributions from the aged.

5. Medicaid is the federal government's largest single welfare program. Medicaid is a federally aided, state-administered welfare program designed for needy persons; no prior contributions are required; financing comes from general tax revenues. States pay about half of the costs of Medicaid, and they have considerable flexibility in its administration. The federal government also provides grants to states to extend health insurance to children under the State Children's Health Insurance Program (SCHIP).

6. Over the years, various incremental modifications were made in both private and government insurance programs, including the growth of health management organizations (HMOs) designed to control costs. Other modest changes included a patient's bill of rights, portability of health insurance, and prescription drug coverage under Medicare.

7. But reformers continued to be concerned with the plight of the uninsured. Employer-sponsored private health insurance, together with individually purchased policies, covered over half of the population. Medicare covered the aged, and Medicaid covered the poor. Over 85 percent of the American people were covered by either private or government insurance. But about 15 percent of the nation's population were uninsured.

8. President Barack Obama and a Democratic-controlled Congress rejected incremental change in favor of a rational-comprehensive government plan—the Patient Protection and Affordable Care Act of 2010. Among its many provisions: an individual mandate requiring every American to purchase health insurance by 2014 or face a tax penalty; a mandate that employers with 50 or more workers provide health insurance to their employees; the mandated expansion of Medicaid to include all individuals

with incomes up to 133 percent of the federal poverty level; the creation of state "exchanges" or marketplaces where individuals and small businesses can purchase government approved health insurance from private companies. Congress rejected President Obama's proposal for a "public option"—a government-run health insurance agency that would compete with private insurers.

9. Republicans in Congress were united in their opposition to the Act. They pledged to repeal "Obamacare" but that strategy is doomed to failure as long as Barack Obama possesses a presidential veto. Rather, Republicans in Congress may try to curtail funding for various provisions of the Act, including IRS enforcement of the tax penalties under the individual mandate.

10. Several states have challenged the constitutionality of the individual mandate. They argue that Congress has no power to force Americans to buy a product. But supporters of the Act argue that it is a constitutional exercise of congressional power under the Interstate Commerce Clause of the Constitution. The issue is likely to be decided by the U.S. Supreme Court.

MySearchLab® EXERCISES

Apply what you learned in this chapter on MySearchLab (www.mysearchlab.com).

NOTES

1. President Barack Obama, *Budget of the United States Government 2010*, p.28.
2. *González v. Raich* 545 U.S. 1 (2005).
3. *U.S. v. Lopez* 514 U.S. 549 (1995).
4. *U.S. v. Morrison* 529 U.S. 598 (2000).

BIBLIOGRAPHY

BLUMENTHAL, DAVID, and JAMES MONRO. *Heart of Power: Health Politics in the Oval Office*, Berkeley: University of California Press, 2010.

BONDENHEIMER, THOMAS S., and KEVIN GRUMBACH. *Understanding Health Policy: A Critical Approach*, 5th ed. New York: Lange, 2010.

JACOBS, LAWRENCE R., and THEDA SKOCPOL. *Health Care Reform in American Politics*, New York: Oxford University Press, 2010.

PATEL, KENT, and MARK E. RUSHEVSKY. *Health Care in America: Separate and Unequal.* New York: M.E. Sharpe, 2008.

WEISSERT, CAROL B., and WILLIAM G. WEISSERT. *Governing Health: the Politics of Health Policy*, 3rd ed. Baltimore: Johns Hopkins University Press, 2006.

WEB SITES

HEALTH INSURANCE ASSOCIATION OF AMERICA. Lobby group for the health insurance industry with research, reports, and news on health insurance. *www.hiaa.org*

KAISER NETWORK. Up-to-date information on health care legislation with links to policy organizations, public opinion polls, and advocacy groups. *www.kaisernetwork.org*

ROBERT WOOD JOHNSON FOUNDATION. Leading research foundation on health care issues. *www.rwjf.org*

U.S. CENTER FOR DISEASE CONTROL. Official site with data on health topics A-Z. *www.cdc.gov*

Controversies over Testing Elementary school pupils in Forsyth County, North Carolina, taking a standardized test. Testing is a key element of the No Child Left Behind Act passed in 2001. But continuing controversy surrounds standardized testing and its use for evaluating schools and teachers. Critics of the Act contend that an emphasis on testing leads to a "test-taking" education rather than broad preparation for life. Supporters argue that teachers and schools must be held accountable for student achievement. (© Will & Deni McIntyre/Corbis)

9

Education
Group Struggles

MULTIPLE GOALS IN EDUCATIONAL POLICY

Perhaps the most widely recommended "solution" to the problems that confront American society is more and better schooling. If there ever was a time when schools were expected only to combat ignorance and illiteracy, that time is far behind us. Today, schools are expected to do many things: resolve racial conflict and inspire respect for "diversity"; provide values, aspirations, and a sense of identity to disadvantaged children; offer various forms of recreation and mass entertainment (football games, bands, choruses, cheerleading, and the like); reduce conflict in society by teaching children to get along well with others and to adjust to group living; reduce the highway accident toll by teaching students to be good drivers; fight disease and poor health through physical education, health training, and even medical treatment; eliminate unemployment and poverty by teaching job skills; end malnutrition and hunger through school breakfast, lunch, and milk programs; fight drug abuse and educate children about sex; and act as custodians for teenagers who have no interest in education but whom we do not permit either to work or to roam the streets unsupervised. In other words, nearly all the nation's problems are reflected in demands placed on the nation's schools. And, of course, these demands are frequently conflicting.

Today over 55 million pupils attend preschool, grade school, and high school in America, about 49 million who attend public schools and about 6 million who attend private schools. Over 18 million students are enrolled in institutions of higher education—community colleges, colleges, and universities.[1]

EDUCATIONAL ATTAINMENT

Educational attainment is measured by the years of schools completed, rather than by student knowledge. In educational attainment, the nation has an enviable record, with 85 percent of the overall population now graduating from high school and 28 percent graduating from college. Discrepancies between white and black educational attainment have diminished (see Figure 9–1). High school graduation rates of blacks and whites are nearing parity. Only Hispanic educational levels still appear to lag.

A college education is now fairly common. The white college graduation rate has reached 30 percent, and the black college graduation rate nearly 20 percent. Again, the Hispanic rate seems to lag. As late as 2000, women's educational attainment rates were below those of men. But that condition has changed; today, women of all races have *higher* educational attainment rates than men.[2]

175

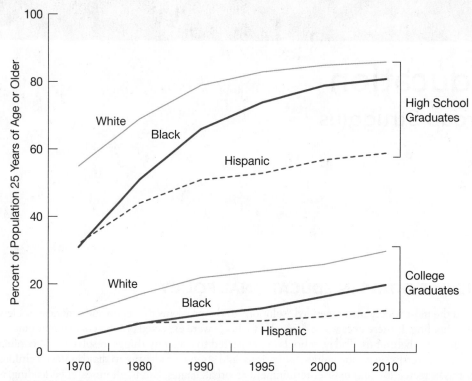

FIGURE 9–1   Educational Attainments by Race Educational attainment has risen for all races in the past three decades, with 85 percent of the overall population now graduating from high school and 28 percent graduating from college.
SOURCE: *Statistical Abstract of the United States, 2010*, p. 149.

THE EDUCATIONAL GROUPS

Interest group activity in education involves a wide array of racial, religious, labor, and civil rights organizations, as well as parents', citizens', and educational groups.

Parents and Citizens Versus Professionals

Many disputes over education pit parents' and citizens' groups against professional educators. Citizens' groups assert that schools are public institutions that should be governed by the local citizenry through their elected representatives. This was the original concept in American public education developed in the nineteenth century. But as school issues became more complex, the knowledge of citizen school boards seemed insufficient to cope with the many problems confronting the schools—teaching innovations, curricular changes, multimillion-dollar building programs, special education programs, and so forth. In the twentieth century, the school superintendent and his or her administrative assistants came to exercise more and more control over day-to-day operations of the schools. Theoretically, the superintendent only implements the policies of the board, but in practice he or she has assumed much of the policymaking in education. The superintendent is a full-time administrator, receiving direct advice from attorneys, architects, accountants, and educational consultants, and generally setting the agenda for school board meetings.

Professional Educators

Professional educators can be divided into at least three distinct groups. Numerically, the largest group (2.5 million) is composed of schoolteachers. But perhaps the most powerful group is that of professional school administrators, particularly the superintendents of schools. A third group consists of the faculties of teachers' colleges and departments of education at universities. This last group often interacts with the state departments of education, diffuses educational innovations and ideologies to each generation of teachers, and influences requirements for teacher certification within the states.

Teachers' Unions

Most of the nation's teachers are organized into either the older and larger National Education Association (NEA), with about 2 million members, or the smaller but more militant American Federation of Teachers (AFT). The NEA maintains a large Washington office and makes substantial campaign contributions to political candidates. The AFT has a smaller membership, concentrated in big-city school districts, but as an affiliate of the AFL-CIO it can call on assistance from organized labor. State and district chapters of both unions have achieved collective bargaining status in most states and large urban school districts. The chapters have shut down schools to force concessions by superintendents, board members, and taxpayers not only in salaries and benefits but also in classroom conditions, school discipline, and other educational matters. Both educational groups lobby Congress as well as the White House and other parts of the executive branch, particularly the Department of Education (DOE). Indeed, the DOE was created in 1979 largely because of President Carter's campaign pledge to educational groups to create a separate education department.

Voters and Taxpayers

School politics at the community level differ from one community to another, but it is possible to identify a number of political groups that appear on the scene almost everywhere. There is, first, the small band of voters who turn out for school elections. On the average, only about 25 to 35 percent of eligible voters bother to cast ballots in school elections. Voter turnout at school bond and tax elections also demonstrates no groundswell of public interest in school affairs. Perhaps even more interesting is the finding that the larger the voter turnout in a school referendum, the more likely the *defeat* of educational proposals. In general, the best way to defeat a school bond referendum is to have a large turnout. Proponents of educational expenditures are better advised *not* to work for a large turnout but rather for a better-informed and more educationally oriented electorate.

Parents

Parents of schoolchildren are somewhat more likely to vote in school board elections. A few active parents even attend school board meetings and voice their opinions. However, Parent–Teacher Associations (PTAs) in most local communities are dominated by teachers and school administrators. Only occasionally are local PTAs "captured" by disgruntled parents and turned into groups opposed to administrative or school board policies.

Parents are generally more supportive of taxing and spending for schools than nonparents, including older voters who have already raised their children. Indeed, in many communities parents of school-age children are pitted against older taxpayers in battles over school spending.

School Boards

School board members constitute another important group of actors in local school politics. They are selected largely from among parents (often with ties to schoolteachers or administrators), as well as among local civic leaders. There is some evidence that people who are interested in education and have some knowledge of what the schools are doing tend to support education more than do the less informed citizens.

Racial and Religious Groups

Because of the frequent involvement of racial and religious issues in education, such groups as the National Association for the Advancement of Colored People (NAACP), the National Catholic Education Conference, the American Jewish Congress, Americans United for the Separation of Church and State, and the American Civil Liberties Union all become involved in educational policy. These well-established national organizations have long led the battles in federal courts over segregation and other racial issues in the schools, prayer and Bible reading in the schools, and public financing of religious schools.

Community-based religious groups are often active on behalf of the restoration of traditional moral values in local schools. Among the well-publicized issues of concern in these community battles are sex education courses that imply approval of premarital sex, distribution of contraceptives in schools, and the teaching of evolution and the exclusion of creationism.

BATTLING OVER THE BASICS

Citizens' groups with an interest in education—parents, taxpayers, and employers—have confronted professional educators—school administrators, state education officials, and teachers' unions—over the vital question of what should be taught in public schools. Public sentiment is strongly in favor of teaching the basic "three Rs" ("reading, 'riting, and 'rithmetic"), enforcing minimum standards with tests, and even testing teachers themselves for their mastery of the basics. Parents are less enthusiastic than professional educators about emotional growth, "getting along with others," self-expression and self-image, cultural enrichment, and various "innovative" programs of education.

The SAT Score Controversy

For many years critics of modern public education cited declining scores on standardized tests, particularly the Scholastic Assessment Test (SAT), required by many colleges and universities, as evidence of the failure of the schools to teach basic reading and mathematics skills. The SAT scores declined significantly during the 1960s and 1970s, even as per pupil educational spending was rising and federal aid to education was initiated (see Figure 9–2). Critics charged that the nation was pouring money into a failed educational system; they pressed their case for a return to the basics. (In 1996, the Scholastic Aptitude Test was replaced by the Scholastic Assessment Test.

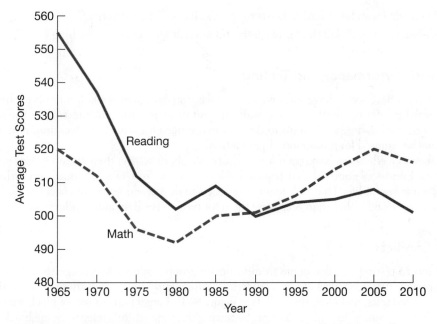

FIGURE 9–2   Average SAT Score Trends Average SAT scores declined dramatically
prior to the 1980s, then began a slow recovery.
SOURCE: The College Board, Princeton, N.J., *www.collegeboard.com*

Scores prior to 1996 were converted to reflect the change. The maximum score in each section is
800: writing [not shown] was added in 2006.)

However, professional educators argued that declining SAT scores were really a function of
how many students took the test. During the years of declining scores, increasing numbers and proportions of students were taking the test—students who never aspired to college in the past whose
test scores did not match those of the earlier, smaller group of college-bound test-takers.

A Nation at Risk

The decline in SAT scores ended in the 1980s. A "back to basics" citizens' reform movement
in education was given impetus by an influential 1983 report by the National Commission on
Excellence in Education entitled "A Nation at Risk."[3]

The commission's recommendations set the agenda for educational policy for many years.
Among the recommendations were these:

- A minimum high school curriculum of four years of English, three years of mathematics,
  three years of social science, and one-half year of computer science
- Four to six years of foreign language study beginning in the elementary grades
- Standardized tests for achievement for all of these subjects
- More homework, a seven-hour school day, and a 200- to 220-day school year

- Reliable grades and standardized tests for promotion and graduation
- "Performance-based" salaries for teachers and rewards for "superior" teaching

Improved Performance and Testing

In recent years SAT scores have improved somewhat. Improvement is likely a result of the movement toward greater emphasis on basic skills and minimum competence testing in the schools. Tests may be used as diagnostic tools to determine the need for remedial education, or minimum scores may be required for promotion or graduation.

Professional educators have been less enthusiastic about testing than citizen groups and state legislators. Educators contend that testing leads to narrow "test-taking" education rather than broad preparation for life. That is, it requires teachers to devote more time to coaching students on how to pass an exam rather than preparing them for productive lives after graduation.

Racial Conflict

Opposition to testing has also come from minority group leaders who charge that the tests are racially biased. Average scores of black students are frequently lower than those of white students on standardized tests, including the SAT (see Figure 9–3). Larger percentages of black students are held back from promotion and graduation by testing than are white students. Some black leaders charge that racial bias in the examination itself, as well as racial isolation in the school, contribute to black–white differences in exam scores. Denying a disproportionate number of black students a diploma because of the schools' failure to teach basics may be viewed as a form of discrimination. However, to date, federal courts have declined to rule that testing requirements for promotion or

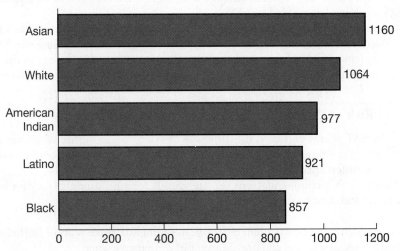

FIGURE 9–3   Average SAT Scores by Race, Ethnicity* SAT scores vary by race and ethnicity.
*Figures for 2010. Combined reading and math scores.
SOURCE: *National Center for Education Statistics, nces.ed.gov/fastfacts*

graduation are discriminatory, as long as sufficient time and opportunity have been provided for all students to prepare for the examinations.

Dropout Rates

Another indicator of educational performance is the dropout rate. Yet school administrators differ with most taxpayers on how to measure it. School administrators, seeking to minimize this embarrassing statistic, count only those students who are officially recorded as having stopped attending school during the tenth, eleventh, or twelfth grade, as a percentage of total attendance in these grades. This measure is very low, nationally between 4 and 5 percent. But the U.S. Census Bureau measures the dropout rate as *persons age 18 to 24 who are not attending school and have not graduated, as a percentage of all 18- to 24-year-olds* (see Figure 9–4). This is a much higher figure, nationally about 13 percent. However measured, national dropout rates are declining very slowly.

Cross-National Comparisons

It is also possible to measure educational performance by comparing scores of American students with those of students of other nations on common school subjects, notably math and science. The results of one such study, published by the U.S. National Center for Educational Statistics, are shown in Figure 9–5. The performance of the U.S. students can only be described as mediocre. In the countries with top-performing students, education appears to have a higher cultural priority; that is, education is highly valued in the family and society generally. Moreover, in all of the

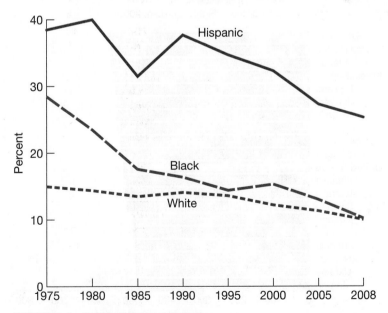

FIGURE 9–4   National Dropout Rates*
*Percentage of persons age 18–24 who are not attending school and have not graduated from high school.
SOURCE: *Statistical Abstract of the United States, 2010*, p. 170.

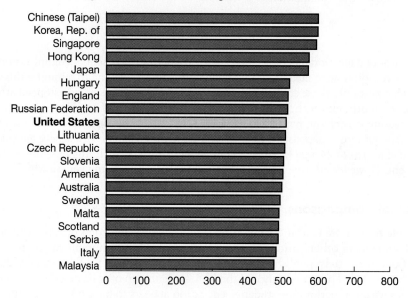

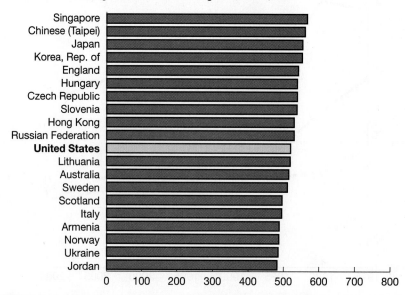

FIGURE 9–5   Educational Achievement: Cross-National Comparisons American students are only mediocre compared to students of other nations in math and science.
SOURCE: National Center for Education Statistics."Trends in International Mathematics and Science Study," December, 2008.

top-performing nations, educational standards and testing are determined at the national level rather than by states and school districts as in the United States. These international comparisons appear to support efforts in the United States to develop national standards and national testing. But educational groups in the states, as well as conservative groups fearing a "federal takeover" of American education, generally resist the imposition of national standards.

THE FEDERAL GOVERNMENT'S ROLE IN EDUCATION

Traditionally, education in the United States was a community responsibility. But over the years, state governments have assumed major responsibility for public education. The federal government remains largely an interested spectator in the area of educational policy. While the U.S. Supreme Court has taken the lead in guaranteeing racial equality in education and separating religion from public schools, the U.S. Congress has never assumed any significant share of the costs of education. State and local taxpayers have always borne over 90 percent of the costs of public elementary and secondary education; the federal share has never exceeded 10 percent. Similarly, federal expenditures for higher education have never exceeded 15 percent of the total costs.

Nonetheless, the federal government's interest in education is a long-standing one. In the famous Northwest Ordinance of 1787, Congress offered land grants for public schools in the new territories and gave succeeding generations words to be forever etched on grammar school cornerstones: "Religion, morality, and knowledge, being necessary to good government and the happiness of mankind, schools, and the means for education should ever be encouraged." The earliest democrats believed that the safest repository of the ultimate powers of society was the people themselves. If the people made mistakes, the remedy was not to remove power from their hands but to help them in forming their judgment through education. If the common people were to be granted the right to vote, they must be educated for the task. This meant that public education had to be universal, free, and compulsory. Compulsory education began in Massachusetts in 1852 and was eventually adopted by Mississippi in 1918.

Early Federal Aid

In 1862, the Morrill Land Grant Act provided grants of federal land to each state for the establishment of colleges specializing in agricultural and mechanical arts. These became known as land-grant colleges. In 1867, Congress established a U.S. Office of Education; in 1979, a separate, cabinet-level Department of Education was created. The Smith-Hughes Act of 1917 set up the first program of federal grants-in-aid to promote vocational education, enabling schools to provide training in agriculture, home economics, trades, and industries. In the National School Lunch and Milk programs, begun in 1946, federal grants and commodity donations were made for nonprofit lunches and milk served in public and private schools. In the Federal Impacted Areas Aid program, begun in 1950, federal aid was authorized for "federally impacted" areas of the nation. These are areas in which federal activities create a substantial increase in school enrollments or a reduction in taxable resources because of a federally owned property. In response to the Soviet Union's success in launching the first satellite into space in 1957, Congress became concerned that the American educational system might not be keeping abreast of advances being made in other nations, particularly in science and technology. In the National Defense Education Act of 1958, Congress provided financial aid to states and public school districts to improve instruction in science, mathematics, and foreign languages. Congress also established a system of loans to undergraduates, fellowships to graduate students, and funds to colleges—all in an effort to improve the training of teachers in America.

ESEA

The Elementary and Secondary Education Act (ESEA) of 1965 established the single largest federal aid to education programs. "Poverty-impacted" schools were the principal beneficiaries of ESEA, receiving instructional materials and educational research and training. Title I of ESEA provided federal financial assistance to "local educational agencies serving areas with concentrations of children from low-income families" for programs "which contribute particularly to meeting the special needs of educationally deprived children."

Educational Block Grants

Early in the Reagan administration, the Education Consolidation and Improvement Act of 1981 consolidated ESEA and other federal educational grant programs into single block grants for states and communities. The purpose was to give states and local school districts greater discretion over the use of federal educational aid. Title I educational aid was retained, but greater flexibility in its use was given to local school officials.

Head Start

The most popular federal educational aid program is Head Start, which emerged from President Lyndon B. Johnson's "War on Poverty" in the 1960s to provide special preschool preparation to disadvantaged children before they enter kindergarten or first grade. Over the years it has enjoyed great popularity among parents, members of Congress, and both Republican and Democratic

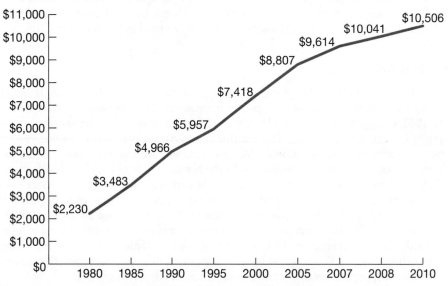

FIGURE 9–6 Public School Spending per Pupil Average spending in public schools has risen dramatically to over $10,000 per pupil, suggesting that money alone cannot raise student performance.

SOURCE: *Digest of Education Statistics*, National Center for Education Statistics, 2011.

presidents. However, despite an avalanche of research by professional educators seeking to prove the value of the program, the results can only be described as mixed at best. Much of the value of Head Start preparation disappears after a few years of schooling; disadvantaged pupils who attended Head Start do not perform much better in middle school than disadvantaged pupils who did not attend. Nevertheless, Head Start remains politically very popular.

Educational Spending and Student Achievement

There is no reliable evidence that increased spending for public education improves student achievement. Public elementary and secondary school spending per pupil has risen dramatically over the years (see Figure 9–6). Yet SAT scores and other test measures of learning have failed to improve significantly (see Figure 9–2). The apparent failure of money alone, including federal aid, has directed the focus of educational improvement to new and sometimes controversial reforms.

NO CHILD LEFT BEHIND

At the urging of newly elected President George W. Bush, Congress passed comprehensive educational reform in the No Child Left Behind Act of 2001. While this act is officially only an amendment to Title I of the Elementary and Secondary Education Act of 1965, it really redefined the federal role in public education.

Testing

The No Child Left Behind Act (NCLB) relies primarily on testing as a means to improve performance of America's elementary and secondary schools. The preferred phraseology is "accountability"—requiring states to establish standards in reading and mathematics and undertaking to annually test all students in grades 3–8. (Testing under this act is in addition to the U.S. Department of Education's National Assessment of Educational Progress tests given each year to a sample of public and private school students in the fourth, eighth, and twelfth grades; results of these NAEP tests are frequently cited as indicators of educational achievement for the nation.) Among the goals of testing is to ensure that every child can read by the end of third grade.

Test results and school progress toward proficiency goals are published, including results broken out by poverty, race, ethnicity, disability, and limited-English proficiency, in order to ensure that no group is "left behind." School districts and individual schools that fail to make adequate yearly progress (AYP) toward statewide proficiency goals are to face "corrective action" and "restructuring measures" designed to improve their performance. Student achievement and progress are measured according to tests that are given to every child. Annual report cards on school performance give parents information about their child's school and all other schools in their district.

Parental Choice

Parents whose children attend schools that fail to make adequate yearly progress are given the opportunity to send their children to another public school or a public charter school within the school district. The school district is required to use its own money for transportation to the new school and to use Title I federal funds to implement school choice and supplemental educational services to the students. The objective is to ensure that no pupil is "trapped" in a failing school,

Educational Reform Remains on the Policy Agenda   President George W. Bush signs the No Child Left Behind Act in 2001. The Act won bipartisan support in the Congress including the late Democratic Senator Ted Kennedy (standing left) and the House Republican Leader John Boehner (standing right). But influential groups, including the National Education Association and the American Federation of Teachers, oppose many of the Act's key provisions, including the use of student achievement tests in evaluating schools and teachers.   (© Reuters/Corbis)

and in addition to provide an incentive for low-performing schools to improve. Schools that wish to avoid losing students, along with a portion of their annual budgets typically associated with these students, are required to make AYP. Schools that fail to make AYP for five years run the risk of "restructuring."

Flexibility

NCLB promises the states "flexibility in accountability." It allows the states themselves to design and administer the tests and decide what constitutes low performance and adequate yearly progress. The Act does *not* impose national achievement standards; standards are set by each state.

High-Stakes Testing

A number of states, including Texas and Florida, require all high school students, even after passing their courses, to pass a standardized statewide test to receive their diplomas. Supporters argue that such high-stakes testing guarantees that high school graduates have at least mastered basic skills, that they can read and do mathematics, and that they are reasonably well prepared to enter the work force or continue on to higher education. Opponents contend that it is unfair to students who have already earned all of their high school credits to subject them to the added pressure of a single test in order to obtain their diplomas. They also argue that with so much riding on the test results for both teachers and students, there is a tendency in the classroom to focus narrowly on basic drills rather than broader and more useful knowledge. And minority group leaders argue that low-income and minority students fail these tests at disproportionate rates and are denied their diplomas.

CONTROVERSIES OVER "NO CHILD"

Professional educators and teachers' unions have been vocal critics of No Child Left Behind. The federal drive for achievement testing may be popular among reformers, legislators, and parents, but it is decidedly unpopular in educational circles.

Teaching to the Test

Critics of NCLB contend that an emphasis on testing leads to "test-taking" education rather than broad preparation for life. Testing requires teachers to devote more time to coaching students on how to pass an exam than on preparing them for productive lives after graduation. Many teachers and school administrators have called for "multiple indicators" in lieu of test scores—allowing schools to evaluate student progress through alternative means, such as graduation rates, student "portfolios," and subjective evaluations. Another common recommendation is to expand testing to other subjects besides reading and mathematics—history and civics, for example.

Testing Teachers and Merit Pay

But while professional educators seek to modify the test-taking provisions of NCLB, others seek to strengthen these provisions, including controversial proposals to test teachers themselves and to base teachers' merit pay on student improvement on standardized tests. If students are to be tested, why not test teachers as well? Professional education groups strongly oppose teacher competency tests on the grounds that standardized tests cannot really measure performance in the classroom. The National Education Association and the American Federation of Teachers oppose both testing teachers and merit pay based on test results. While most states test teachers prior to certification, only a few states require all teachers to be tested. But where they have done so, the results have been disquieting. Large numbers of veteran classroom teachers have failed the tests.

Punishing Poorly Performing Schools

Many educators object to punishing schools that fail to meet annual yearly progress (AYP) for two or more years running. (Pupils in these schools must be given the opportunity to transfer to higher-performing schools.) Rather, many educators would prefer an approach that emphasizes additional aid to low-performing schools. But additional aid may be seen as a "reward" for poor performance.

Funding

Some supporters of NCLB complain that it is not adequately funded by either the federal government or the states. The costs of implementation have not been fully funded by the federal government, creating an "unfunded mandate" for states and school districts.

The Future of Educational Reform

Interest group conflict is likely to slow educational reform in the coming years. Teachers' unions—the National Education Association and the American Federation of Teachers—exercise considerable influence in the Obama Administration, as well as within Democratic majorities in the House and Senate. These unions have been highly critical of No Child Left Behind reforms. They generally oppose educational evaluations based upon test results, teacher testing, merit pay for teachers based on student performance, and school choice for parents whose children attend low-performing schools.

OBAMA EDUCATION AGENDA

The Obama Administration laid out an ambitious agenda for education—an agenda that envisions spending additional billions of dollars of federal monies for a wide variety of programs.[4] The bulk of this new spending is to go to poorer inner-city schools. Overseeing this new spending is President Obama's Secretary of Education, Arne Duncan, a longtime friend and adviser to the president and a former chief executive of the Chicago Public Schools.

Teacher Performance

Among the many recommendations are several dealing with incentives to recruit teachers and reward their performance. These proposals include the recruitment of new teachers through alternative certification programs and nontraditional channels. State education officials, colleges of education, and teachers' unions have traditionally been reluctant to certify as teachers people who have not acquired a formal accreditation through colleges of education. Less controversial are proposals to provide pay incentives to teachers who work in economically disadvantaged schools and to those who teach math and science.

President Obama has also voiced support for tying teacher compensation to measures of student performance. But education unions that supported Obama's election vigorously oppose any compensation schemes that are tied to student test results.

Standards and Assessments

Requiring states to develop and implement standards of student achievement—the idea behind the No Child Left Behind Act—remains on the Obama agenda. It is likely, however, that additional measures of student performance will be added to the assessment of school success, including problem-solving and critical thinking skills.

National Standards?

Under the current NCLB Act each state sets its own performance standards. States are required to set "proficiency" standards in reading and mathematics, but each state defines for itself what "proficiency" means. Comparisons among schools within each state are possible, as well as comparisons among racial and ethnic groups within states; yearly progress of pupils in schools within states can also be assessed. But a *national* system of standards and testing is required if we are to really evaluate state efforts in education. President Obama's Secretary of Education Arne Duncan has expressed support for national standards. But states themselves, including many state education officials and state legislators, have been cool to the notion of national testing. And teachers' unions and professional educators have been cool to testing itself. So this combination of interests is likely to subvert efforts to reform education through the adoption of national standards and testing.

Race to the Top

A key component of the Obama educational agenda is the Race to the Top—competition among the states for federal grants based upon their adoption of various reforms. The criteria for receiving Race to the Top grants include:

- Tying teacher and principal pay to student achievement in test scores
- Adopting national benchmark standards and assessments for student achievement
- Finding effective programs to turn around failing schools
- Building data systems that measure student success and track students throughout their educational careers
- Loosening legal requirements for charter schools

In practice, awards have been made to states with effective programs to turn around failing schools and to states with meaningful teacher evaluation systems linked to student achievement. Various reforms have been recommended as part of the competition—closing poor performing schools and reopening them as charter schools or transferring pupils to higher performing schools; evaluating students on "learning gains" observed in pre-and post-course exams; basing merit pay on student gains; and eliminating seniority as a basis for teacher retention and pay increases. But not all states have participated in the Race to the Top competition.

The Race to the Top is not without its critics. Teachers' unions—the National Education Association (NEA) and the American Federation of Teachers (AFT) and their state and local affiliates—have been reluctant partners in state competition for Race to the Top money. The unions generally oppose educational evaluations based on test results, teacher testing, merit pay for teachers based on student performance, the closing of low performance schools, and the establishment of charter schools. Yet support of the unions is one of the criteria the Obama administration uses to judge state applications for funding. Another source of opposition is from state officials who prefer to use their own student achievement standards rather than national standards, in part out of fear of a "federal takeover" of education in America. But the "dumbing down" of state standards is one of the concerns of reformers. Finally, educators worry that Race to the Top money may simply disappear into state budgets, rather than be directed specifically toward public schools.

PARENTAL CHOICE IN EDUCATION

Social science research suggests that educational performance is enhanced when the schools are perceived by children to be extensions or substitutes for their family.[5] Academic achievement and graduation rates improve for all students, but especially for students from disadvantaged backgrounds, in schools where there is a high expectation of achievement, an orderly and disciplined environment for learning, an emphasis on basic skills, frequent monitoring of students' progress, and teacher–parent interaction and agreement on values and norms. When parents choose schools for their children, as in the case of private and Catholic schools, these values are strengthened.[6]

Parental Choice

"Choice" is a key word in the movement to reform American education. Parental choice among schools and the resulting competition among schools for enrollment is said to improve academic achievement and graduation rates as well as increase parental satisfaction and teachers' morale. Principals and teachers are encouraged to work directly with parents to set clear goals, develop specialized curricula, impose discipline, and demand more from the students. Choice plans are said to do more than just benefit the parents who have the knowledge to choose schools wisely for their children. They also send a message to educators to structure their schools to give parents what they want for their children or risk losing enrollment and funding.[7]

Charter Schools

One way to implement parental choice is the charter school. Community educational groups sign a "charter" with their school district or state educational authority to establish their own school. They receive waivers from most state and school district regulations to enable them to be more innovative; in exchange for this flexibility they promise to show specific student achievement.

Magnet Schools

Another common reform proposal is the magnet school. High schools might choose to specialize, some emphasizing math and science, others the fine arts, others business, and still others vocational training. Some schools might be "adopted" by business, professional organizations, or universities. Magnet schools, with reputations for quality and specialized instruction, are frequently recommended for inner-city areas in order to attract white pupils and reduce racial isolation.

Educational Vouchers

A more controversial version of parental choice involves educational vouchers that would be given to parents to spend at any school they choose, public or private. State governments would redeem the vouchers submitted by schools by paying specified amounts—perhaps the equivalent of the state's per pupil educational spending. All public and private schools would compete equally for students, and state education funds would flow to those schools that enrolled more students. Competition would encourage all schools to satisfy parental demands for excellence. Racial, religious, or ethnic discrimination would be strictly prohibited in any private or public school receiving vouchers. Providing vouchers for private school education would be most effective for children from poor or disadvantaged homes. These children currently do not have the same options as children from more affluent homes of fleeing the public schools and enrolling in private academies.

Yet there is strong opposition to the voucher idea, especially from professional school administrators and state educational agencies. They argue that giving parents the right to move their children from school to school disrupts educational planning and threatens the viability of schools that are perceived as inferior. It may lead to a stratification of schools into popular schools that would attract the best students and less popular schools that would be left with the task of educating students whose parents were unaware or uninterested in their children's education. Other opponents of choice plans fear that public education might be undermined if the choice available to parents includes the option of sending their children to private, church-related schools. Public education groups are fearful that vouchers will divert public money from public to private schools. And, finally, there is the constitutional issue of whether vouchers—notably those given to parents who send their children to religiously affiliated schools—violate the First Amendment's prohibition against an "establishment of religion." We will return to this topic later in the chapter.

Vouchers Have *Not* Been Popular with Voters

In 1993 California voters soundly defeated a citizens' initiative that promised to "empower parents" by granting each schoolchild a "scholarship" (voucher) equal to about one-half of the average amount of state and local government aid per pupil in California. The money was to be paid directly to the schools in which parents chose to enroll their children. Either public or private schools could qualify as "independently scholarship-redeeming schools."

Opposition groups, including the powerful California Teachers Association, argued that the proposal would create "a two-tier system of schools, one for the haves, one for the have-nots." They portrayed vouchers as "an entitlement program offering wealthy families a private-school subsidy for their children, paid for by the taxpayers," noting that there was no means test for the vouchers. Opponents warned that public education would suffer grievously if both money and gifted students were removed from public schools.

BATTLES OVER SCHOOL FINANCES

Spending for education varies enormously across the United States. Nationwide over $10,000 per year is spent on the public education of each child. Yet national averages can obscure as much as they reveal about the record of the states in public education. In 2010, for example, public school expenditures for each pupil ranged from nearly $15,000 in New Jersey to less than $6,000 in Utah.[8] (See Table 5–5 in Chapter 5 for a ranking of the states in educational spending per pupil.) Why is it that some states spend more than twice as much on the education of each child as other states? Economic resources are an important determinant of a state's willingness and ability to provide educational services. Most of the variation among states in educational spending can be explained by differences among them in economic resources (see Chapter 5).

Inequalities Among School Districts

Another issue in the struggle over public education is that of distributing the benefits and costs of education equitably. Most school revenues are derived from *local* property taxes. In every state except Hawaii, local school boards must raise money from property taxes to finance their schools.

This means that communities that do *not* have much taxable property cannot finance their schools as well as communities that are blessed with great wealth.

School Inequalities as a Constitutional Issue

Do disparities among school districts within a state deny "equal protection of laws" guaranteed by the Fourteenth Amendment of the U.S. Constitution and similar guarantees found in most state constitutions? The U.S. Supreme Court ruled that disparities in financial resources among school districts in a state, and resulting inequalities in educational spending per pupil across a state, do *not* violate the Equal Protection Clause of the Fourteenth Amendment. There is no duty under the U.S. Constitution for a state to equalize educational resources within the state.[9]

However, in recent years *state courts* have increasingly intervened in school financing to ensure equality among school districts based on their own interpretation of *state* constitutional provisions. Beginning with an early California state supreme court decision requiring that state funds be used to help equalize resources among the state's school districts,[10] many state courts have pressured their legislatures to come up with equalization plans in state school grants to overcome disparities in property tax revenues among school districts. State court equalization orders are generally based on *state* constitutional provisions guaranteeing equality. To achieve equity in school funding among communities, an increasing number of state courts are ordering their legislatures to substitute state general revenues for local property taxes.

PUBLIC POLICY AND HIGHER EDUCATION

State governments have been involved in higher education since the colonial era. State governments in the Northeast frequently made contributions to private colleges in their states, a practice that continues today. The first state university to be chartered by a state legislature was the University of Georgia in 1794. Before the Civil War, northeastern states relied exclusively on private colleges, and the southern states assumed the leadership in public higher education. The antebellum curricula at southern state universities, however, resembled the rigid classical studies of the early private colleges—Greek and Latin, history, philosophy, and literature.

Growth of Public Universities

It was not until the Morrill Land Grant Act of 1862 that public higher education began to make major strides in the states. Interestingly, the eastern states were slow to respond to the opportunity afforded by the Morrill Act to develop public universities. The southern states were economically depressed in the post–Civil War period, and leadership in public higher education passed to the midwestern states. The philosophy of the Morrill Act emphasized agricultural and mechanical studies rather than the classical curricula of eastern colleges, and the movement for "A and M" education spread rapidly in the agricultural states. The early groups of midwestern state universities were closely tied to agricultural education, including agricultural extension services. State universities also took the responsibility for the training of public school teachers in colleges of education. The state universities introduced a broad range of modern subjects in the university curricula—business administration, agriculture, education, engineering. It was not until the 1960s that the eastern states began to emphasize public higher education, as evidenced by the expansion of the huge, multicampus State University of New York.

Over 18 million students are currently enrolled in institutions of higher education. About two-thirds of high school graduates enroll in college—universities, public and private; four-year

TABLE 9–1 Higher Education in America Over 18 million people are enrolled in more than 4,000 institutions of higher education.

Institutions	
Four-year colleges and universities	2,675
Two-year colleges	1,677
Faculty (thousands)	1,290
Percent full-time	52
Enrollment (thousands)	
Total	18,248
Four-year colleges and universities	11,630
Two-year colleges	6,618
Public	13,491
Private	4,757
Graduate	2,294
Undergraduate	15,604
Men	7,816
Women	10,432

SOURCE: *Statistical Abstract of the United States, 2010,* p. 173.

colleges; and two-year community colleges. Public higher education enrolls three-fourths of these college and university students (see Table 9–1). Women outnumber men—57 to 43 percent—on college campuses nationwide.

Funding Higher Education

Tuition and fees paid by students and their families cover only a small portion of the total cost of public higher education. The major sources of income for state colleges and universities and community colleges are state and local government appropriations (see Table 9–2). The federal government provides only about 16 percent of the costs of public higher education.

Traditionally, state appropriations made up the bulk of institutional revenue at public colleges and universities, but these appropriations are diminishing as a share of institutional revenue. The result has been increased tuitions and increased efforts by public institutions to solicit private donations from individuals and corporations.

Federal Aid

Although the federal government generally does not provide direct operational support to colleges and universities, federal funding for research contracts and grants is an important source of revenue for some institutions. And of course federal revenue comes with strings attached. In order for colleges and universities to participate in federally financed programs, they must comply with

TABLE 9–2   Funding Public Higher Education State and local governments provide the largest share of the income of public colleges and universities.

Sources of income for public institutions[1]	
Tuition and fees from students	16.5%
Federal government	15.8
State and local governments	37.2
Endowment/private gift income	1.8
Sales and other services	20.7
Other sources[2]	8.0

[1]Not including capital improvement revenue.
[2]Including investment income, auxiliary services, and independent operations.
SOURCE: American Council on Education, *A Brief Guide to U.S. Higher Education*, Washington, DC: ACE, 2007.

a wide range of requirements, including, for example, the Americans with Disabilities Act, laws governing the responsible experimental use of both animals and people, and Title IX regulations to ensure gender equity in intercollegiate athletics. Federal contracts and grants are closely monitored by the various federal agencies that fund them.

Historically, the Morrill Act of 1862 provided the groundwork for federal assistance to higher education. In 1890 Congress activated several federal grants to support the operations of the land-grant colleges, and this aid, although very modest, continues today. The GI bills following World War II and the Korean War (enacted in 1944 and 1952, respectively) were not, strictly speaking, aid-to-education bills but rather a form of assistance to veterans to help them adjust to civilian life. Nevertheless, these bills had a great impact on higher education because of the millions of veterans who were able to enroll in college. Congress continues to provide educational benefits to veterans but at reduced levels from the wartime GI bills. The National Defense Education Act of 1958 also affected higher education by assisting students, particularly in science, mathematics, and modern foreign languages.

Today, the federal government directly assists many colleges and universities through grants and loans for construction and improvement of facilities; and it supports the U.S. Military Academy (West Point), U.S. Naval Academy (Annapolis), U.S. Air Force Academy (Colorado Springs), U.S. Coast Guard Academy, U.S. Merchant Marine Academy, Gallaudet College, and Howard University.

Student Assistance

A major source of federal aid for higher education comes to colleges and universities from various forms of student assistance. Nearly half of all undergraduate students receive some form of federal aid. Basic Educational Opportunity Grants (commonly called Pell Grants for their original sponsor, U.S. Senator Claiborne Pell) provide college students in good standing with grants based on what their families could be expected to pay. In addition, the federal government now makes loans directly to students (Federal Direct Student Loan program) and to families (Federal

Family Education Loans). The Obama administration federalized these student loan programs in 2010; loans are now made directly by the U.S. Department of Education rather than by private banks. Repayment usually does not begin until after the student graduates or leaves college. A Perkins Loan program extends this guarantee to students from very low-income families. A Supplemental Educational Opportunity Grant program allows students to borrow from the financial aid offices of their own universities. Finally, the College Work-Study program uses federal funds to allow colleges and universities to employ students part time while they go to school.

Federal Research Support

Federal support for scientific research has also had an important impact on higher education. In 1950 Congress established the National Science Foundation (NSF) to promote scientific research and education. The NSF has provided fellowships for graduate education in the sciences, supported many specific scientific research projects, and supported the construction and maintenance of scientific centers. In 1965 Congress established a National Endowment for the Arts and a National Endowment for the Humanities but funded these fields at only a tiny fraction of the amount given to NSF. In addition to NSF, many other federal agencies have granted research contracts to universities for specific projects. Thus, with federal support, research has become a very big item in university life.

"DIVERSITY" IN HIGHER EDUCATION

Most colleges and universities in the United States—public as well as private—identify "diversity" as a goal, a term that refers to racial and ethnic representation in the student body and faculty.

Arguments over Diversity

University administrators as well as civil rights groups across the nation argue that students benefit when they interact with others from different cultural heritages. There is some evidence that students admitted under policies designed to increase diversity do well in their postcollege careers.[11] And there are claims that racial and ethnic diversity on the campus improves students' "self-evaluation," "social historical thinking," and "intellectual engagement."

But despite numerous efforts to develop scientific evidence that racial or ethnic diversity on the campus improves learning, no definitive conclusions have emerged. Educational research on this topic is rife with political and ideological conflict. There is very little evidence that racial diversity does in fact promote the expression of ideas on the campus or change perspectives or viewpoints of students.

Diversity and Affirmative Action

Even if diversity provides any educational benefits, the question arises as to how to achieve it. Diversity is closely linked to affirmative action programs on campuses throughout the nation. When affirmative action programs are designed as special efforts to recruit and encourage qualified minority students, they enjoy widespread public support. (See "Mass Opinion and Affirmative

Action" in Chapter 11.) But when affirmative action programs include preferences or quotas for racial minority applicants over equally or better-qualified nonminorities, public support disappears. Respondents in national polls, both faculty and students, oppose "relaxing standards" in order to add more minority students or faculty.[12]

Diversity as a Constitutional Question

The use of racial or ethnic classifications of applicants to colleges and universities in order to achieve "diversity" raises serious constitutional questions. The Fourteenth Amendment to the U.S. Constitution provides that "No State shall . . . deny to any person the equal protection of the laws." The Civil Rights Act of 1964, Title VI, prohibits discrimination based on race, color, or national origin by recipients of federal financial assistance (see Chapter 11).

The U.S. Supreme Court has held that the Fourteenth Amendment requires that racial classifications be subject to "strict scrutiny."[13] This means that race-based actions by governments—and any disparate treatment of racial or ethnic groups by federal, state, or local public agencies, including colleges and universities—must be found necessary to advance a "compelling government interest" and must be "narrowly tailored" to further that interest.

The U.S. Supreme Court held in 2003 that diversity may be a compelling government interest because it "promotes cross-racial understanding, helps to break down racial stereotypes, and enables [students] to better understand persons of different races." This opinion was written by Justice Sandra Day O'Connor in a case involving the University of Michigan Law School's affirmative action program. In the 5–4 decision, Justice O'Connor, writing for the majority, said the Constitution "does not prohibit the law school's narrowly tailored use of race in admissions decisions to further a compelling interest in obtaining the educational benefits of flow from a diverse student body."[14]

However, in a companion case involving the University of Michigan's affirmative action program for undergraduate admissions, the Supreme Court held that the admissions policy was "not narrowly tailored to achieve respondents' asserted interest in diversity" and therefore violated the Equal Protection Clause of the Fourteenth Amendment. The Court again recognized that diversity may be a compelling interest but rejected an affirmative action plan that made race the decisive factor for every minimally qualified minority applicant. "The University's current policy, which automatically distributes 20 points, or one-fifth of the points needed to guarantee admission, to every single underrepresented minority applicant solely because of race, is not narrowly tailored to achieve the interest in educational diversity that the respondents claim justifies their program."[15]

The Supreme Court restated its support for limited affirmative action programs that use race as a "plus" factor, a position the court has held since the *Bakke* case in 1978 (see Chapter 11 "The Supreme Court and Affirmative Action"). But the Court has consistently rejected numerical plans or quotas that automatically reject white applicants.

Race-Neutral Approaches to Diversity

There are a variety of ways of achieving diversity without using racial preferences in the admission of students. The U.S. Department of Education in the administration of President George W. Bush cited (1) preferences based on socioeconomic status; (2) recruitment and outreach efforts targeted at students from traditionally low-performing schools; and (3) admission plans for students who finish at the top of their high school classes without regard to their SAT or ACT scores.[16] Three states—Texas, California, and Florida—ended racial preferences in college and university admissions and substituted admission plans based on students' standings among graduates of their high schools. (Texas was ordered to end racial preferences by federal courts; California voters passed a constitutional initiative, Proposition 209, requiring the state to end racial preferences (see Chapter 14 "Mass Initiatives against Racial Preferences"); and Florida ended race-based admissions by order of Governor Jeb Bush.) The Texas Top-10 Percent Plan not only admits any student who graduates in the top 10 percent of their high school class but also considers hardships or obstacles that an applicant may have been obliged to overcome (employment during school, raising children, etc.). Florida's Talented Twenty Plan admits students to the state's higher education system who graduate in the top 20 percent of their high school class.

GROUPS IN HIGHER EDUCATION

There are many influential groups in public higher education—aside from the governors and legislators who must vote the funds each year.

Trustees

First, there are the boards of trustees (often called regents) that govern public colleges and universities. Their authority varies from state to state, but in nearly every state they are expected not only to set broad policy directions in higher education but also to insulate higher education from direct political involvement of governors and legislators. Prominent citizens who are appointed to these boards are expected to champion higher education with the public and the legislature.

Presidents

Another key group in higher education is made up of university and college presidents and their top administrative assistants. Generally, university presidents are the chief spokespersons for higher education, and they must convince the public, the regents, the governor, and the legislature of the value of state colleges and universities. The president's crucial role is to maintain support for higher education in the state; he or she frequently delegates administrative responsibilities for the internal operation of the university to the vice presidents and deans. Support for higher education among the public and its representatives can be affected by a broad spectrum of university activities, some of which are not directly related to the pursuit of knowledge. A winning football team can stimulate legislative enthusiasm and gain appropriations for a new classroom building. University service-oriented research—developing new crops or feeds, assessing the state's mineral resources, advising state and local government agencies on administrative problems, analyzing the state economy, advising local school authorities, and so forth—may help to convince the public of the practical benefits of knowledge. University faculties may be interested in advanced research and the education of future Ph.D.s, but legislators and their constituents are more interested in the quality and effectiveness of undergraduate teaching.

Faculty

The faculties of the nation's 4,000 colleges and universities traditionally identified themselves as professionals with strong attachments to their institutions. The historic pattern of college and university governance included faculty participation in policymaking—not only academic requirements but also budgeting, personnel, building programs, and so forth. But governance by faculty committee has proven cumbersome, unwieldy, and time-consuming in an era of large-scale enrollments, multimillion-dollar budgets, and increases in the size and complexity of academic administration. Increasingly, concepts of public accountability, academic management, cost control, and centralized budgeting and purchasing have transferred power in colleges and universities from faculties to professional academic administrators.

Full-time faculty are gradually being replaced by part-time "adjunct" faculty as a cost-cutting measure in colleges and universities throughout the nation. To date, *about half of all classes nationwide are taught by adjunct faculty or graduate students, rather than full-time faculty members.* Traditionally, college and university faculty aspired to "tenure"—protection against dismissal except for "cause," a serious infraction of established rules or dereliction of duty, shown in quasi-judicial administrative proceedings. Tenure was usually granted after five to seven years of satisfactory performance. Part-time adjunct faculty and graduate students cannot acquire tenure, nor do they usually receive medical, retirement, or other benefits.

Unions

The traditional organization of faculties has been the American Association of University Professors (AAUP); historically, this group confined itself to publishing data on salaries and officially censuring colleges or universities that violate long-standing notions of academic freedom or tenure. In recent years, the American Federation of Teachers (AFT) succeeded in convincing some faculty members that traditional patterns of individual bargaining over salaries, teaching load, and working conditions in colleges and universities should be replaced by collective bargaining in the manner of unionized labor. The growth of the AFT has spurred the AAUP on many campuses to assume a more militant attitude on behalf of faculty interests. The AAUP remains the largest faculty organization in the nation, but most of the nation's faculties are not affiliated with either the AAUP or the AFT.

Students

The nation's 18 million students are the most numerous yet least influential of the groups directly involved in higher education. Students can be compared to other consumer groups in society, which are generally less well organized than the groups that provide goods and services. American student political activism has been sporadic and generally directed toward broad national issues. Most students view their condition in life as a short-term one; organizing for effective group action requires a commitment of time and energy that most students are unwilling to subtract from their studies and social life. Nonetheless, students' complaints are often filtered through parents to state legislators or university officials.

Students and their parents appear to be most concerned about rapidly rising tuitions at both private and public institutions. The average tuition at private four-year universities rose from $7,000 in 1985 to over $30,000 in 2008; the average tuition at public four-year universities rose from $1,400 to over $7,000 in that same period. Average tution at public two-year colleges is about $2,050.[17] State government support for higher education has not kept up with increased enrollments and universities offer this explanation for their increases in tuition. Public universities now compete vigorously with private colleges for the financial support of alumni and philanthropic foundations.

Higher education in the United States is now open to virtually every high school graduate. Today about 64 percent of recent U.S. graduates enroll in a two-year or four-year college or university.

READING, WRITING, AND RELIGION

The First Amendment of the Constitution of the United States contains *two* important guarantees of religious freedom: (1) "Congress shall make no law respecting an establishment of religion . . ." and (2) "or prohibiting the free exercise thereof." The due process clause of the Fourteenth Amendment made these guarantees of religious liberty applicable to the states and their subdivisions (including school districts) as well as to Congress.

"Free Exercise"

Most of the debate over religion in the public schools centers on the "no establishment" clause of the First Amendment rather than the "free exercise" clause. However, it was respect for the "free exercise" clause that caused the Supreme Court in 1925 to declare unconstitutional an attempt by a state to prohibit private and parochial schools and to force all children to attend public schools. In the words of the Supreme Court, "The fundamental theory of liberty upon which all governments in this Union repose excludes any general power of the state to standardize its children by forcing them to accept instruction from public teachers only. The child is not the mere creature of the state."[18] It is this decision that protects the entire structure of private religious schools in this nation.

No "Establishment"

A great deal of religious conflict in America has centered on the meaning of the Establishment Clause, and the public schools have been the principal scene of this conflict. One interpretation of the clause holds that it does not prevent the government from aiding religious schools or encouraging religious beliefs in the public schools as long as it does not discriminate against any particular religion. Another interpretation is that the clause creates a "wall of separation" between church and state in America to prevent the government from directly aiding religious schools or encouraging religious beliefs in any way.

Government Aid to Church-Related Schools

The question of how much government aid can go to church schools and for what purposes is still largely unresolved. Proponents of public aid for church schools argue that these schools render a valuable public service by instructing millions of children who would have to be instructed by the state, at great expense, if the church schools were to close. There seem to be many precedents for public support of religious institutions: church property has always been exempt from taxation, church contributions are deductible from federal income taxes, federal funds have been appropriated for the construction of hospitals operated by religious organizations, chaplains are provided in the armed forces as well as in Congress, veterans' programs permit veterans to use their educational subsidies to finance college educations at church-related universities, and so on.

Opponents of aid to church schools argue that free public schools are available to the parents of all children regardless of religious denomination. If religious parents are not content with the type of school that the state provides, they should expect to pay for the operation of religious schools. The state is under no obligation to finance their religious preferences. Opponents also argue that it is unfair to compel taxpayers to support religion directly or indirectly. The diversion of any substantial amount of public funds to church schools would weaken the public school system. The public schools bring together children of different religious backgrounds and by so doing supposedly encourage tolerance and understanding. In contrast, church-related schools segregate children of different backgrounds, and it is not in the public interest to encourage such segregation. And so the dispute continues.

The "Wall of Separation"

Those favoring government aid to church-related schools frequently refer to the language found in several cases decided by the Supreme Court, which appears to support the idea that government can, *in a limited fashion*, support the activities of church-related schools. In *Everson* v. *Board of Education* (1947), the Supreme Court upheld bus transportation for parochial school children at public expense on the grounds that the "wall of separation between church and state does not prohibit the state from adopting a general program which helps *all* children." Interestingly in this case, even though the Court permitted the expenditure of public funds to assist children going to and from parochial schools, it voiced the opinion that the Establishment Clause of the First Amendment should constitute a "wall of separation" between church and state. In the words of the Court:

> Neither a state nor the federal government can set up a church. Neither can pass laws which aid one religion, aid all religions, or prefer one religion over another. Neither can force nor influence a person to go to or to remain away from church against his will, or force him to profess a belief or disbelief in any religion. No person can be punished for entertaining or professing religious beliefs or disbeliefs, for church attendance or nonattendance. No tax in any amount, large or small, can be levied to support any religious activities or institutions, whatever they may be called, or whatever form they may adopt to teach or practice religion. Neither a state nor the federal government can, openly or secretly, participate in the affairs of any religious organizations or groups, and vice versa.[19]

So the *Everson* case can be cited by those interests that support the allocation of public funds for assistance to children in parochial schools, as well as those interests that oppose any public support, direct or indirect, of religion.

Avoiding "Excessive Entanglement"

One of the more important Supreme Court decisions in the history of church-state relations in America came in 1971 in the case of *Lemon* v. *Kurtzman*.[20] The Supreme Court set forth a three-part *Lemon test* for determining whether a particular state law constitutes "establishment" of religion and thus violates the First Amendment. To be constitutional, a law affecting religious activity:

1. Must have a secular purpose.
2. As its primary effect, must neither advance nor inhibit religion.
3. Must not foster "an excessive government entanglement with religion."

Using this three-part test the Supreme Court held that it was unconstitutional for a state to pay the costs of teachers' salaries or instructional materials in parochial schools. The justices argued that this practice would require excessive government controls and surveillance to ensure that funds were used only for secular instruction and thus would create an "excessive entanglement between government and religion."

However, the Supreme Court has upheld the use of tax funds to provide students attending church-related schools with nonreligious textbooks, lunches, transportation, sign-language interpreting, and special education teachers. And the Court has upheld a state's granting of tax credits to parents whose children attend private schools, including religious schools.[21] The Court has also upheld government grants of money to church-related colleges and universities for secular purposes.[22] The Court has ruled that if school buildings are open to use for secular organizations, they must also be open to use by religious organizations.[23] And the Court has held that a state institution (the University of Virginia) not only can but must grant student activity fees to religious organizations on the same basis as it grants these fees to secular organizations.[24] But the Court held that a Louisiana law requiring the teaching of creationism along with evolution in the public schools was an unconstitutional establishment of a religious belief.[25]

Vouchers

Educational vouchers given to parents by governments to use as tuition at either public or private religiously affiliated schools raise the question of whether they violate the Establishment Clause of the First Amendment. In 2002 the Supreme Court, in a 5–4 decision, held that an Ohio program designed for needy students attending poor Cleveland schools did *not* violate the Establishment Clause, even though parents could use the vouchers for tuition at religiously affiliated schools.[26] Indeed, over 90 percent of the parents receiving vouchers chose to use them at religious schools. Nonetheless, the Supreme Court held that the program did not violate the Establishment Clause because (1) it had a valid secular purpose, (2) it was neutral with respect to religion (parents could send their children to nonreligious schools), and (3) the aid went to parents, who then directed it to religious schools "as a result of their own genuine and independent private choice." The vouchers were only an "incidental advancement of religion . . . attributable to individual aid recipients, not the government whose role ends with the distribution of the vouchers."

Prayer in Public Schools

Religious conflict also focuses on the question of prayer and Bible-reading ceremonies in public schools. Not too long ago the practice of opening the school day with such ceremonies was widespread in American public schools. Usually the prayer was a Protestant rendition of the Lord's Prayer and the reading was from the King James version of the Bible. To avoid the denominational aspects of the ceremonies, the New York State Board of Regents substituted a nondenominational prayer, which it required to be said aloud in each class in the presence of a teacher at the beginning of each school day: "Almighty God, we acknowledge our dependence upon Thee, and we beg Thy blessings upon us, our parents, our teachers, and our country."

New York argued that this prayer did not violate the Establishment Clause because it was denominationally neutral and because students' participation was voluntary. However, in *Engle* v. *Vitale* (1962), the Supreme Court stated that "the constitutional prohibition against laws respecting an establishment of a religion must at least mean in this country it is no part of the business of government to compose official prayers for any group of the American people to recite as part of a religious program carried on by government." The Court pointed out that making prayer voluntary did not free it from the prohibitions of the "no establishment" clause; that clause prevented the establishment of a religious ceremony by a government agency, regardless of whether the ceremony was voluntary or not:

> Neither the fact that the prayer may be denominationally neutral, nor the fact that its observance on the part of the students is voluntary can serve to free it from the limitations of the establishment clause, as it might from the free exercise clause, of the First Amendment, both of which are operative against the states by virtue of the Fourteenth Amendment. . . . The establishment clause, unlike the free exercise clause, does not depend on any showing of direct governmental compulsion and is violated by the enactment of laws which establish an official religion whether those laws operate directly to coerce nonobserving individuals or not.[27]

One year later, in the case of *Abbington Township* v. *Schempp*, the Court considered the constitutionality of Bible-reading ceremonies in the public schools.[28] Here again, even though the children were not required to participate, the Court found that Bible reading as an opening exercise in the schools was a religious ceremony. The Court went to some trouble in its opinion to point out that it was not "throwing the Bible out of the schools," for it specifically stated that the study of the Bible or of religion, when presented as part of a secular program of education, did not violate the First Amendment, but religious *ceremonies* involving Bible reading or prayer, established by a state or school district, did so.

State efforts to encourage "voluntary prayer" in public schools have also been struck down by the Supreme Court as unconstitutional. When the state of Alabama authorized a period of silence for "meditation or voluntary prayer" in public schools, the Court ruled that this was an "establishment of religion." The Court said that the law had no secular purpose, that it conveyed "a message of state endorsement and promotion of prayer," and that its real intent was to encourage prayer in public schools.[29] In a stinging dissenting opinion, Warren Burger, chief justice at the time, noted that the Supreme Court itself opened its session with a prayer, and that both houses of Congress opened every session with prayers led by official chaplains paid by the government. "To suggest that a moment of silence statute that includes the word *prayer* unconstitutionally endorses religion, manifests not neutrality but hostility toward religion." But Burger's view remains a minority view. The Court has gone on to hold that invocations and benedictions at public high school graduation ceremonies are an unconstitutional establishment of religion.[30] And it has held that a student-led prayer at a football game is unconstitutional because it was carried over the school's public address system at a school-sponsored event.[31]

SUMMARY

Let us summarize educational policy issues with particular reference to group conflicts involved:

1. American education reflects all of the conflicting demands of society. Schools are expected to address themselves to virtually all of the nation's problems, from racial conflict to drug abuse to highway accidents. They are also supposed to raise the verbal and mathematical performance levels of students to better equip the nation's work force in a competitive global economy. Various interests give different priorities to these diverse and sometimes conflicting goals.

2. In recent years, citizen groups, parents, taxpayers, and employers have inspired a back-to-basics movement in the schools, emphasizing reading, writing, and mathematical performance and calling for frequent testing of students' skills and the improvement of teachers' competency. Professional educators—school administrators, state education officials, and teachers' unions—have tended to resist test-oriented reforms, emphasizing instead the education of the whole child.

3. Conflict between citizens and professional educators is reflected in arguments over "professionalism" versus "responsiveness" in public schools. Parents, taxpayers, and locally elected school board members tend to emphasize responsiveness to citizens' demands; school superintendents and state education agencies tend to emphasize professional administration of the schools. Teachers' unions, notably state and local chapters of the NEA and AFT, represent still another group interest in education—organized teachers.

4. Professional educational groups and teachers' unions have long lobbied in Washington for increased federal financing of education. Federal aid to education grew with the Elementary and Secondary Education Act of 1965, but the federal share of educational spending never exceeded 10 percent. State and local governments continue to bear the major burden of educational finance. The creation of a cabinet-level Department of Education in 1979 also reflected the influence of professional educators.

5. There is little direct evidence that increased funding for schools improves the educational performance of students. Citizen groups and independent study commissions emphasized reforms in education rather than increased federal spending. The No Child Left Behind Act of 2001 relies heavily on testing to improve learning. Public school pupils are tested each year, and schools must show adequate yearly progress in average test scores or face the prospect of their students transferring to another school at the school district's expense.

6. Parental choice in education would empower parents and end the monopoly of public school administrators. But plans that allow parents to choose private over public schools threaten America's traditional reliance on public education. Choice *within* public school systems is somewhat less controversial, and various states have established charter and magnet schools.

7. Public higher education in the states involves many groups—governors, legislators, regents, college and university presidents, and faculties. State governments, through their support of state colleges and universities, bear the major burden of higher education in the United States. Federal support for research, plus various student loan programs, are an important contribution to higher education. Yet federal support amounts to less than 15 percent of total higher education spending.

8. A central issue in higher education today is achieving "diversity" on campus—the reference to racial and ethnic representation in the student body and faculty. The U.S. Supreme Court has recognized that diversity may be a "compelling government interest" that allows race to be considered in university admissions without violating the Fourteenth Amendment to the U.S. Constitution. However, the Court also held that race cannot be the sole or decisive factor in admissions.

9. Religious groups, private school interests, and public school defenders frequently battle over the place of religion in education. The U.S. Supreme Court has become the referee in the

group struggle over religion and education. The Court must interpret the meaning of the Establishment Clause of the First Amendment of the Constitution as it affects government aid to church-related schools and prayer in the public schools.

MySearchLab® EXERCISES

Apply what you learned in this chapter on MySearchLab (www.mysearchlab.com).

NOTES

1. *Statistical Abstract of the United States, 2010,* p. 143.

2. *Ibid.* p. 149.

3. National Commission on Excellence in Education, *A Nation at Risk* (Washington, DC: U.S. Government Printing Office, 1983).

4. Mark Green and Michelle Jolin, eds., *Change for America, a Progressive Blueprint for the 44th President* (New York: Basic Books, 2009), p. 141.

5. See James S. Coleman, Thomas Hoffer, and Sally Kilgore, *High School Achievement* (New York: Basic Books, 1982); John E. Chubb and Terry M. Moe, *Politics, Markets, and America's Schools* (Washington, DC: Brookings Institution Press, 1990); Chester E. Finn, Jr., *We Must Take Charge: Our Schools and Our Future* (New York: Free Press, 1991).

6. James S. Coleman and Thomas Hoffer, *Public and Private High Schools* (New York: Basic Books, 1987).

7. See John E. Chubb and Terry M. Moe, "Politics, Markets, and the Organization of Schools," *American Political Science Review* 82 (December 1988), 1065–1087.

8. *National Center for Education Statistics, http://nces.ed.gov*

9. *Rodriguez v. San Antonio Independent School District,* 411 U.S. 1 (1973).

10. *Serrano v. Priest,* 5 Cal. 584 (1971).

11. William G. Bowen and Derek Bok, *The Shape of the River* (Princeton, NJ: Princeton University Press, 2000).

12. Gallup poll, as reported in *USA Today,* June 24, 2003.

13. *Adarand v. Peña,* 515 U.S. 200 (1995).

14. *Grudder v. Bollinger,* 539 U.S. 306 (2003).

15. *Gratz v. Bollinger,* 539 U.S. 244 (2003).

16. U.S. Department of Education, Office for Civil Rights, "Race-Neutral Alternatives in Post Secondary Education," March, 2003.

17. Data in this paragraph from *Statistical Abstract of the United States, 2010,* p.185.

18. *Pierce v. The Society of Sisters,* 268 U.S. 510 (1925).

19. *Everson v. Board of Education,* 330 U.S. 1 (1947).

20. *Lemon v. Kurtzman,* 403 U.S. 602 (1971).

21. *Muebler v. Adams,* 463 U.S. 602 (1983).

22. *Tilton v. Richardson,* 403 U.S. 602 (1971).

23. *Lamb's Chapel v. Center Moriches Union Free School District,* 508 U.S. 384 (1993).

24. *Rosenberger v. University of Virginia,* 515 U.S. 819 (1995).

25. *Edwards v. Aguillard,* 482 U.S. 578 (1987).

26. *Zelman, Superintendent of Public Instruction of Ohio v. Simmons-Harris,* 536 U.S. 639 (2002).

27. *Engle v. Vitale,* 370 U.S. 421 (1962).

28. *Abbington Township v. Schempp,* 374 U.S. 203 (1963).

29. *Wallace v. Jaffree,* 472 U.S. 38 (1985).

30. *Lee v. Weisman,* 505 U.S. 577 (1992).

31. *Santa Fe Independent School District v. Doe,* 530 U.S. 290 (2000).

BIBLIOGRAPHY

BLOOM, ALLAN D. *The Closing of the American Mind.* New York: Simon & Schuster, 1987.

CHUBB, JOHN E., and TERRY M. MOE. *Politics, Markets, and America's Schools.* Washington, DC: Brookings Institution, 1990.

COLEMAN, JAMES S., and THOMAS HOFFER. *Public and Private High Schools.* New York: Basic Books, 1987.

HOWELL, WILLIAM G., and PAUL E. PETERSON. *The Education Gap: Vouchers and Urban Schools.* Washington, DC: Brookings Institution, 2005.

MOE, TERRY M. *School Vouchers and the American Public.* Washington, DC: Brookings Institution, 2002.

NATIONAL COMMISSION ON EXCELLENCE IN EDUCATION. *A Nation at Risk.* Washington, DC: U.S. Government Printing Office, 1983.

THERNSTROM, STEPHEN AND ABIGALE. *America in Black and White.* New York: Simon & Schuster, 1997.

WEB SITES

AMERICAN FEDERATION OF TEACHERS. The home page of the teachers' union, with information on a range of education issues. *www.aft.org*

CENTER FOR EDUCATION REFORM. Advocacy organization for school choice—vouchers, charter schools, etc. *www.edreform.org*

FIRE. The Foundation for Individual Rights in Education defends free speech on campus against "political correctness." *www.thefire.org*

NATIONAL CENTER FOR EDUCATION STATISTICS. Official site for all government statistics relating to education. *http://nces.ed.gov*

NATIONAL EDUCATION ASSOCIATION. Home page of the largest teachers' organization, with information on a variety of education issues. *www.nea.org*

U.S. DEPARTMENT OF EDUCATION. Official site of the Education Department, with information on laws, policies, and issues. *www.ed.gov*

AMERICAN COUNCIL ON EDUCATION. Organization representing major universities; includes policy positions on higher education. *www.acenet.org*

AMERICAN ASSOCIATION OF UNIVERSITY PROFESSORS. Organization representing university professors, with information on issues in higher education including salaries of faculty. *www.aaup.org*

NATIONAL ASSOCIATION OF SCHOLARS. Academic organization devoted to restoring individual merit and academic freedom in higher education. *www.nas.org*

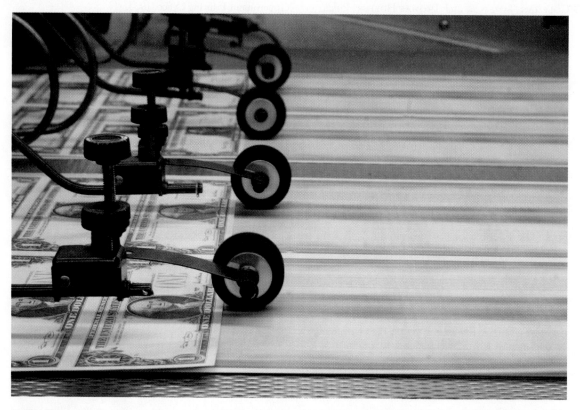

Making Money Printing money at the U.S. Bureau of Engraving and Printing. Currency (cash) makes up only a small portion of the nation's money supply, most of which is in the form of bank deposits. The Federal Reserve System (the Fed) influences the supply of money by making it easier for banks to lend money in recessions, or alternatively tightening the money supply when faced with inflation. Congress has granted the Fed considerable independence in its oversight of the nation's banking system and money supply. (AFP/Getty Images)

10

Economic Policy
Challenging Incrementalism

INCREMENTAL AND NONINCREMENTAL POLICYMAKING

Traditionally, fiscal and monetary policies were made *incrementally*; that is, decision makers concentrated their attention on modest changes—increases or decreases—in existing taxing, spending, and deficit levels, as well as the money supply and interest rates. Incrementalism was especially pervasive in annual federal budget making. The president and Congress did not reconsider the value of all existing programs each year or pay much attention to previously established expenditure levels. Rather last year's expenditures were considered as a base of spending for each program; active consideration of the budget focused on new items or increases over last year's base.

But crises often force policymakers to abandon incrementalism and reach out in *nonincremental* directions. In economic policy, the president and Congress and the Fed are pressured to "do something" in the face of a perceived economic crisis, even if there is little consensus on what should be done, or even whether there is anything the federal government can do to resolve the crisis. As we shall see later in this chapter, the "Great Recession" that began in 2008 caused policymakers to search for new policies and make dramatic changes in spending and deficit levels and to undertake unprecedented measures to prevent the collapse of financial markets and avoid a deeper recession.

FISCAL AND MONETARY POLICY

Economic policy is exercised primarily through the federal government's *fiscal policies*—decisions about taxing, spending, and deficit levels—and its *monetary policies*—decisions about the money supply and interest rates.

Fiscal policy is made in the annual preparation of the federal budget by the president and the Office of Management and Budget, and subsequently considered by Congress in its annual appropriations bills and revisions of the tax laws. These decisions determine overall federal spending levels, as well as spending priorities among federal programs. Together with tax policy decisions (see Chapter 11), these spending decisions determine the size of the federal government's annual deficits or surpluses.

Monetary policy is the principal responsibility of the powerful and independent Federal Reserve Board—"the Fed"—which can expand or contract the money supply through its oversight of the nation's banking system (see "The Fed at Work" later in this chapter). Congress established the Federal Reserve System and its governing Board in 1913 and Congress could, if it wished, reduce its power or even abolish the Fed altogether. But no serious effort has ever been undertaken to do so.

ECONOMIC THEORIES AS POLICY GUIDES

The goals of economic policy are widely shared: growth in economic output and standards of living, full and productive employment of the nation's work force, and stable prices with low inflation. But a variety of economic theories compete for preeminence as ways of achieving these goals. From time to time, economic policy has been guided by different theories; or worse, it has been guided by conflicting theories simultaneously.

Classical Theory

Classical economists generally view a market economy as a self-adjusting mechanism that will achieve an equilibrium of full employment, maximum productivity, and stable prices if left alone by the government. The price mechanism will adjust the decisions of millions of Americans to bring into balance the supply and demand of goods and labor. Regarding recessions, if workers are temporarily unemployed because the supply for workers exceeds the demand, wages (the price of labor) will fall; eventually it will again become profitable for businesses to have more workers at lower wages and thus end unemployment. Similarly, if the demand for goods (automobiles, houses, clothing, kitchenware, and so forth) falls, business inventories will rise and businesspeople will reduce prices (often through rebates, sales, etc.) until demand picks up again. Regarding inflation, general increases in prices will reduce demand and automatically bring it back into line with supply unless the government interferes. In short, classical economic theory relies on the free movement of prices to counter both recession and inflation.

Keynesian Theory

But the Great Depression of the 1930s shattered popular confidence in classical economics. During that decade, the average unemployment rate was 18 percent, rising to 25 percent in the worst year, 1933. But even in 1936, seven years after the great stock market crash in 1929, unemployment was still 18 percent of the work force, raising questions about the ability of the market to stabilize itself and ensure high employment and productivity.

According to the British economist John Maynard Keynes, economic instability was a product of fluctuations in demand. Both unemployment and lower wages reduced the demand for goods; businesses cut production and laid off more workers to adjust for lower demand for their goods, but cuts and layoffs further reduced demand and accelerated the downward spiral. Keynesian theory suggested that the economy could fall into a recession and stay there. Only government could take the necessary countercyclical steps to expand demand by spending more money itself and lowering taxes. Of course, the government cannot add to aggregate demand if it balances the budget. Rather, during a recession it must incur deficits to add to total demand, spending more than it receives in revenues. Government borrowing—and the national debt—would grow during recessions. Borrowed money would make up the difference (the deficit) between lowered revenues and higher spending. To counter inflationary trends, the government should take just the opposite steps. Thus government would "counter" economic cycles, that is, engage in "countercyclical" fiscal policies.

Supply-Side Economics

Supply-side economists argue that attention to long-term economic growth is more important than short-term manipulation of demand. Economic growth, which requires an expansion in the productive capacity of society, increases the overall supply of goods and services and thereby holds down prices. Inflation is reduced or ended altogether. More important, everyone's standard of living is improved with the availability of more goods and services at stable prices. Economic growth even increases government revenues over the long run.

Most supply-side economists believe that the free market is better equipped than government to bring about lower prices and more supplies of what people need and want. Government, they argue, is the problem, not the solution. Government taxing, spending, and monetary policies have promoted immediate consumption instead of investment in the future. High taxes penalize hard work, creativity, investment, and savings. The government should provide tax incentives to encourage investment and savings; tax rates should be lowered to encourage work and enterprise. Overall government spending should be held in check. Government regulations should be minimized to increase productivity and growth. The government should act to stimulate production and supply rather than demand and consumption.

MEASURING THE PERFORMANCE OF THE AMERICAN ECONOMY

Measures of the actual performance of the American economy include the gross domestic product (GDP), the unemployment rate, and the rate of inflation.

Economic Growth

The GDP is the nation's total production of goods and services for a single year valued in terms of market prices. It is the sum of all of the goods and services that people purchase, from wheat and corn to bicycles, from machine tools to maid service, from aircraft manufacturing to bus rides, from automobiles to chewing gum. GDP counts only final purchases of goods and services (that is, it ignores the purchase of steel by carmakers until it is sold as a car) to avoid double counting in the production process. GDP also excludes financial transactions (such as the sale of bonds and stocks) and income transfers (such as Social Security, welfare, and pension payments) that do not add to the production of goods and services. Although GDP is expressed in current dollar prices, it is often recalculated in constant dollar terms to reflect real values over time, adjusting for the effect of inflation. GDP estimates are prepared each quarter by the U.S. Department of Commerce; these figures are widely reported and closely watched by the business and financial community.

Economic recessions and recoveries are measured as fluctuations or swings in the growth of GDP (see Figure 10–1). Historical data reveal that periods of economic growth have traditionally been followed by periods of contraction, giving rise to the notion of economic cycles. The average annual GDP growth over the last half-century has been about 3 percent. But recessions (shown in Figure 10–1 as negative annual growth) have occurred periodically. The GDP in current dollars in 2012 is about $16 trillion.

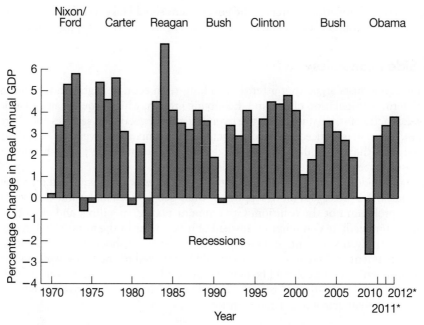

FIGURE 10–1 Economic Growth Annual growth in the GDP in recent years has averaged a little over 3 percent; recessions (when the economy actually contracts) have occurred periodically.
SOURCES: U.S. Bureau of Economic Analysis, www.bea.gov; *Budget of the United States Government, 2012.*
*Estimates.

Unemployment

The unemployment rate is the percentage of the civilian labor force who are looking for work or waiting to return to or begin a job. Unemployment is different from not working; people who have retired or who attend school and people who do not work because of sickness, disability, or unwillingness are not considered part of the labor force and so are not counted as unemployed. People who are so discouraged about finding a job that they have quit looking for work are also not counted in the official unemployment rate. Only people who are currently out of work and seeking a job are counted as unemployed. The unemployment rate fluctuates with the business cycle, reflecting recessions and recoveries (see Figure 10–2). Generally, unemployment lags behind GDP growth, often going down only after the recovery has begun. Following years of economic growth in the 1990s, the nation's unemployment rate fell to near record lows, below 5 percent. With the economic recession in 2008, unemployment rose again.

Inflation

Inflation erodes the value of the dollar because higher prices mean that the same dollars can now purchase fewer goods and services. Thus inflation erodes the value of savings, reduces the incentive to save, and hurts people who are living on fixed incomes. When banks and investors anticipate inflation, they raise interest rates on loans in order to cover the anticipated lower value

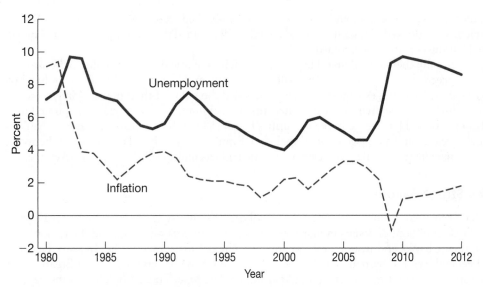

FIGURE 10–2 Unemployment and Inflation Unemployment rises with recessions; inflation is a problem during growth periods.

*Negative inflation—"deflation"—occured in 2009.

of repayment dollars. Higher interest rates, in turn, make it more difficult for new or expanding businesses to borrow money, for home buyers to acquire mortgages, and for consumers to make purchases on credit. Thus inflation and high interest rates slow economic growth.

Recession

Economists define a recession as two or more quarters of negative economic growth, that is, declines in the gross domestic product (In politics, a recession is often proclaimed when the economy only slows its growth rate or when unemployment rises). Recessions also entail a rise in unemployment and declines in consumer spending and capital investment. In some recessions, prices decline as well—"deflation." During the Great Depression of the 1930s the GDP fell by over 33 percent and the unemployment rate spiraled upward to a peak of 25 percent. The unemployment rate remained above 10 percent for nearly ten years, from 1930 to 1940. Compared to the Great Depression, the recession that began in 2008—the "Great Recession"—appears relatively mild.

FINANCIAL CRISIS AND NONINCREMENTAL POLICY CHANGE

For years Americans lived on easy credit. Families ran up credit card debt and borrowed heavily for cars, tuition, and especially home buying. Mortgage lenders approved loans for borrowers without fully examining their ability to pay. Loans were often made with little or no down payment. Some mortgages were "predatory," with the initial low payments followed by steep upward adjustable rates. Federally sponsored corporations, Fannie Mae and Freddie Mac, encouraged mortgage loans to low income and minority homebuyers. A nationwide market in "subprime mortgages" attracted financial institutions seeking quick profits. To make matters worse, banks and financial institutions bundled mortgages together and sold these mortgage-backed securities as "derivatives." Risks were frequently overlooked. Banks, insurers, and lenders all assumed that housing prices would inevitably rise. Housing construction boomed.[1]

Eventually the bubble burst. Housing prices fell dramatically. The number of houses for sale greatly exceeded the number of people willing to buy them. Homeowners found themselves holding "upside down" mortgages—mortgages that exceeded the value of their homes. Many were unable or unwilling to meet their mortgage payments. Foreclosures and delinquencies spiraled upward. Investors who held mortgage-backed securities began to incur heavy losses. Investment banks, such as Bear Stearns, and mortgage insurers, including Fannie Mae and Freddie Mac, found themselves in serious financial trouble. Bankruptcies and federal bailouts multiplied. The stock market plummeted.

Wall Street Bailout

In 2008 the credit crunch ballooned into Wall Street's biggest crisis since the Great Depression. Hundreds of billions of dollars in mortgage-related investments went bad, and the nation's leading investment banks and insurance companies sought the assistance of the Treasury Department and Federal Reserve System. The Fed acted to stave off the bankruptcy of Bear Stearns, and the Treasury Department took over Fannie Mae and Freddie Mac. The nation's largest insurance company, American International Group (AIG), was bailed out by the Fed. But the hemorrhaging continued, and it was soon clear that the nation was tumbling into a deep recession.

In September, President Bush sent Secretary of the Treasury Henry Paulson, accompanied by Federal Reserve Chairman Ben Bernanke, to Congress to plead for a massive $700 billion bailout of banks, insurance companies, and investment firms that held mortgage-backed "illiquid assets." They argued that their proposal was absolutely essential to safeguard the financial security of the nation. A full-blown depression might result if the federal government failed to purchase these troubled assets.

The nation's top leadership—President Bush, the Treasury secretary and Fed chairman, House and Senate Democratic and Republican leaders, and even the presidential candidates, Barack Obama and John McCain—all supported the bill. But polls show that most Americans opposed a "Wall Street bailout." Congress members were asked by their leaders to ignore the folks back home. The initial House vote stunned Washington and Wall Street: "nay" votes prevailed. The stock market plunged.

Predictions of economic catastrophe inspired a renewed effort to pass the bill. The Senate responded by passing it with a comfortable margin, while adding various sweeteners, mostly tax benefits to gain House support. Tensions were high when the House voted on the Senate version of the bill. In a sharp reversal of its earlier action, the House approved the Emergency Economic Stabilization Act of 2008. President Bush promptly signed it into law.

Treasury's TARP

The Treasury Department was given unprecedented power to bail out the nation's financial institutions. Secretary Paulson initially proposed to use the $700 billion appropriation by Congress to buy up "toxic assets"—mortgage-backed securities whose value had dropped sharply. The program was named the Troubled Asset Relief Program (TARP). But shortly afterward, Paulson reversed course and decided to use the TARP money to inject cash directly into banks by purchasing preferred shares of their stock. The nation's largest bank, Citigroup, was first in line, and other major banks and investment firms followed (see Table 10–1).

TABLE 10-1 Top Federal Bailout Recipients
American International Group
Citigroup
JPMorgan Chase
Wells Fargo
Bank of America
Goldman Sachs
Merrill Lynch
Morgan Stanley
PNC Financial Services
U.S. Bankcorp

Critics of the program noted that by accepting ownership shares in the nation's leading banks and investment houses, the government was tilting toward "socialism." Government ownership of the financial industry, that is, "nationalization" of the banks, would have been considered unthinkable before the crisis. The financial crisis had inspired a decidedly non-incremental policy change.

Mortgage Modification

Later, under President Obama's new Treasury Secretary, Timothy Geithner, banks receiving TARP assistance were obliged to adopt mortgage loan modification procedures to prevent foreclosures. This foreclosure modification program provided financial assistance to mortgage lenders as an incentive for them to modify home mortgages that were in danger of default. (To be eligible, borrowers had to show "hardship.") The intention was to help as many as 5 million mortgage borrowers refinance their loans at lower interest rates. Critics of the program expressed the fear of rising resentment among the millions of Americans who sacrificed to keep up with their mortgage payments.

Public–Private Investment Program

The key to loosening credit and jump-starting the economy appeared to be relieving the nation's banks of their "toxic" assets—securities backed by mortgages that were in foreclosure or default. President Obama's Secretary of the Treasury developed a Public-Private Investment Program that uses TARP money to leverage private purchases of toxic assets. The Federal Deposit Insurance Corp. and the Federal Reserve are to facilitate private purchases by providing low-interest loans to buyers of these assets. By relieving banks of these "nonperforming" loans, banks should be prepared to make new loans and thereby stimulate the economy. In effect, the government is creating a "yard sale" for junk securities at a cost of $500 billion to $1 trillion.

GM Bankruptcy

General Motors is an American institution, the biggest of the big three domestic automobile manufacturers—GM, Chrysler, and Ford. With federal supervision, GM and Chrysler sought bankruptcy protection in 2009; Ford managed to stay afloat by itself. Even before declaring bankruptcy, General Motors had received billions of federal dollars in loans and loan guarantees. Federal involvement forced out GM's chief executive officer. In bankruptcy the federal government took majority ownership of GM. President Obama declared that the federal government had no interest in the day-to-day operations of General Motors. Yet the White House issued guidelines for limiting the salaries of top executives of GM and of other institutions receiving TARP funds.

Fed Responses

In addition to the TARP bailouts, the Federal Reserve Board made a dramatic decision to pump over $1.25 *trillion* into the nation's financial system in order to unlock mortgage, credit card, college and auto lending. The Fed lowered its discount rate to less than 1 percent, and then later to zero percent, to encourage banks to make loans. But most of the Fed's efforts came in the form of loan guarantees to banks, credit unions, mortgage lenders, and automakers' financial arms. The objective was to lower interest rates on all forms of credit and thereby inspire consumers to borrow and lenders to lend, jump-starting the economy. But low-interest rates and easy credit do not guarantee that banks will lend money or that businesses and individuals will borrow money. As the recession deepened in early 2009, the president and Congress sought to provide additional economic "stimulus."

THE ECONOMIC STIMULUS PACKAGE

A massive economic stimulus plan, officially called the American Recovery and Reinvestment Act of 2009, was the centerpiece of President Barack Obama's early policy agenda. Its combination of spending increases and tax cuts totaled $787 billion—the largest single fiscal policy measure in American history. It was written in record time by a Democratic-controlled Congress; House Republicans were unanimous in opposition, and only three Republican senators supported the bill.

Spending Priorities

The stimulus package consisted of roughly two-thirds spending and one-third tax rebates. Democrats in the Congress used the package to increase spending in a wide variety of domestic programs—in education, Medicaid, unemployment compensation, food stamps, health technology, child tax credits, disability payments, higher education grants, renewable energy subsidies, and rail and transit transportation—as well as traditional spending for highways and bridge building (see Table 10–2). Republicans complained that much of the spending had little to do with stimulating the economy but rather increased government involvement in domestic policy areas favored by Democrats. Republicans had traditionally relied upon tax cuts to stimulate the economy.

"Making Work Pay"

The stimulus package also included a version of Obama's campaign promise of a middle-class tax cut. The tax "cuts" in the package, labeled "Making Work Pay," were actually payments of $400 to individuals with incomes under $75,000 and payments of $800 to couples with incomes under $150,000. These payments were to be made to anyone who paid Social Security taxes. It was not necessary to have paid any income taxes in order to receive these tax "cuts." Critics labeled these payments "welfare checks."

TABLE 10–2 The Stimulus Package   Major categories of items in the American Recovery and Reinvestment Act of 2009

- Tax payments: $400 to individuals with incomes under $75,000, and $800 to couples with incomes under $150,000

- State Medicaid assistance

- Education and job training aid to school districts

- Unemployment compensation: increase payments and extend to 33 weeks

- Highways and bridges: money to states for "shovel ready" projects

- Healthcare for unemployed: health insurance for unemployed for nine months

- Food stamp program increases

- Index the Alternative Minimum Tax for inflation

- Health technology grants and subsidies

- Renewable energy grants and subsidies

- Child care tax credits

- Pell Grant increases

- Health science research

- Extend Hope Scholarships from two years to four years

- Increase Title I education monies

- Increase aid for special education

- Rail transportation and public transit

- Total $787 billion

Financial Regulation

The near collapse of the nation's financial system in 2008, and the credit crisis that followed, inspired calls for greater regulation of the financial industry, including banks and bank holding companies, investment firms, credit unions, and insurance companies. Reversing years of banking "deregulation," President Obama and the Democratic-controlled Congress passed a sweeping overhaul of the nation's financial regulatory system-the Dodd-Frank Act of 2010.

Among its many provisions, the new law created a Financial Stability Oversight Council, chaired by the Secretary of the Treasury and including the Federal Reserve Board Chairman, the Comptroller of the Currency, the Securities and Exchange Commission Chairman, the Chairman of the Federal Deposit Insurance Corporation, among others. The Council is charged with the responsibility of monitoring national and international threats to the financial stability of the United States and recommending actions to its member regulators. The law set forth an "orderly liquidation" process under the supervision of the FDIC for failing financial institutions, including those previously considered "too big to fail."

The law also created a new Bureau of Consumer Financial Protection within the Federal Reserve to oversee consumer checking accounts, loans, credit cards and mortgages, to protect against unfair or deceptive practices. The new Office of Credit Ratings in the SEC oversees the operations of credit rating companies, such as Standard & Poor's and Moody's.

The law brings the market for "derivatives" under government regulation for the first time. These are financial instruments created out of mortgages, stocks, or commodities that are designed as a "hedge" against risk and often used for speculation.

Critics note that the new law fails to address the problems with Fanny Mae and Freddy Mac—the federal corporations that encouraged "subprime" mortgages that led to the financial collapse. They also charge that the law promises a federal bailout of firms that are considered "too big to fail" and that by doing so provides incentives for further risky behavior by these firms. Still other critics complain that excess regulation will make it more difficult for Americans to obtain loans, credit cards, and mortgages.

THE FED AT WORK

Most economically advanced democracies have central banks whose principal responsibility is to regulate the supply of money, both currency in circulation and bank deposits. And most of these democracies have found it best to remove this responsibility from the direct control of elected politicians. Politicians everywhere are sorely tempted to inflate the supply of money in order to fund projects and programs with newly created money instead of new taxes. The result is a general rise in prices and a reduction in goods and services available to private firms and individuals—inflation.

The Federal Reserve System

The task of the Fed is to regulate the money supply and by so doing to help avoid both inflation and recession. The Fed oversees the operation of the nation's twelve Federal Reserve Banks, which

Managing Money Federal Reserve Board Chairman Ben Bernanke testifies before the Senate Banking Committee at his confirmation hearing in December, 2009. President Obama nominated the former Princeton University economics professor for a second four-year term as Fed Chairman, praising his handling of the worst financial crisis in the United States since the Great Depression of the 1930s. The Fed was instrumental in stabilizing the nation's banking system, but high unemployment continued to plague American workers.   (© Zhang Jun/Xinhua Press/Corbis)

actually issue the nation's currency, called "Federal Reserve Notes." The Federal Reserve Banks are banker's banks; they do not directly serve private citizens or firms. They hold the deposits, or "reserves," of banks; lend money to banks at "discount rates" that the Fed determines; buy and sell U.S. Government Treasury bonds; and assure regulatory compliance by private banks and protection of depositors against fraud. The Fed determines the reserve requirements of banks and otherwise monitors the health of the banking industry. The Fed also plays an important role in clearing checks throughout the banking system.

Understanding Monetary Policy

Banks create money—"demand deposits"—when they make loans. Currency (cash) in circulation, together with demand deposits, constitute the nation's money supply—"M-1." But demand deposits far exceed currency; only about 5 percent of the money supply is in the form of currency. So banks really determine the money supply in their creation of demand deposits. However, the Fed requires that all banks maintain a reserve in deposits with a Federal Reserve Bank. If the Fed decides that there is too much money in the economy (inflation), it can raise the reserve requirement, reducing what a bank can create in demand deposits. Changing the "reserve ratio" is one way that the Fed can expand or contract the money supply.

The Fed can also expand or contract the money supply by changing the interest rate it charges member banks to borrow reserve. A bank can expand its demand deposits by borrowing reserve from the Fed, but it must pay the Fed an interest rate, called the "discount rate," in order to do so. By raising the discount rate, the Fed can discourage banks from borrowing reserve and thereby contract the money supply; lowering the discount rate encourages banks to expand the money supply. Interest rates generally—on loans to businesses, mortgages, car loans, and the like—rise and fall with rises and falls in the Fed's discount rate. Lowering rates encourages economic expansion; raising rates dampens inflation when it threatens the economy.

Finally, the Fed can also buy and sell U.S. Treasury bonds and notes in what is called "open market operations." The reserve of the Federal Reserve System consists of U.S. bonds and notes. If it sells more than it buys, it reduces its own reserve, and hence its ability to lend reserve to banks; this contracts the money supply. If it buys more than it sells, it adds to its own reserve, enabling it to lend reserve to banks and thereby expand the money supply.

Fed Independence

The decisions of the Federal Reserve Board are made independently. They need not be ratified by the president, Congress, the courts, or any other governmental institution. Indeed, the Fed does not even depend on annual federal appropriations, but instead finances itself. This means that Congress does not even exercise its "power of the purse" over the Fed. Theoretically, Congress could amend or repeal the Federal Reserve Act of 1913, but to do so would be politically unthinkable. The only changes to the act have been to *add to* the powers of the Fed. The Fed chairman often appears before committees of Congress and is given far more respect by committee members than other executive officials.

Fed Responses to Recession

In previous recessions, the monetary policies of the Federal Reserve Board succeeded fairly well in easing credit and encouraging recovery. But in the recession that began in 2008, Fed policies appeared to be insufficient by themselves in stimulating the economy. The Fed lowered the discount rate first to 1 percent and then later to zero. This unprecedented action was designed to encourage banks to borrow reserve and extend loans, thereby expanding the money supply. Later the Fed joined with the Treasury Departments TARP to help bail out the nation's financial institutions (see Table 10–1). And the Fed pumped over $1.25 trillion into the money supply in order to encourage lending, especially mortgage lending.

But *monetary policy* used to offset recession is often characterized as "trying to push with a string." Making available money at low interest rates does not guarantee that banks will lend more or that businesses and individuals will borrow more. Credit may remain "frozen" if banks and other lenders have lost confidence in the ability of businesses and individuals to repay loans. It is then advised that only *fiscal policy*—government increases in spending, reductions in taxes, and increases in deficits—can counter an especially deep recession.

THE GROWTH OF GOVERNMENT SPENDING

Government spending grows in all presidential administrations, regardless of promises to "cut government spending." Total federal spending grew from $480 billion in 1959 to $3.7 trillion in 2012 (see Table 10-3). At this level, federal government spending amounts to about 24 percent of the nation's gross domestic product.

TABLE 10–3 The Growth of Federal Government Spending Federal government spending of more than $3.8 trillion represents over 24 percent of the GDP.

	GDP (Billions)	Federal Government Spending (Billions)	Percentage of GDP
1959	480.2	92.1	19.2
1965	671.0	118.2	17.6
1970	985.4	195.6	19.8
1975	1,509.8	332.3	22.0
1980	2,644.1	590.9	22.3
1985	3,967.7	946.4	23.8
1992	5,868.6	1,381.8	23.5
1995	7,269.6	1,538.9	22.5
2000	9,872.9	1,789.2	18.4
2005	12,487.1	2,972.2	20.2
2008	14,394.1	2,983.0	20.7
2009	14,097.5	3,998.0	28.3
2010	14,508.2	3,456.2	23.8
2011	15,079.6*	3,818.8*	25.3*
2012	15,612.5*	3,728.7*	23.9*

SOURCES: *Statistical Abstract of the United States, 2011; Budget of the United States Government, 2012.*

*Estimates.

Challenging Incrementalism

For years federal government spending rose more or less incrementally, remaining close to 20 percent of the GDP. But the recession beginning in 2008 drove Congress and the president to increase spending to dramatically higher levels. In 2009 federal spending rose by almost $1 trillion from the previous year, the single largest year-to-year increase in history. Federal spending in that year rose to about 28 percent of the GDP. Federal revenues declined that year; the extra spending was financed through a $1.7 trillion deficit, the largest annual deficit in history. The bulk of this increase in spending and deficit levels can be attributed to the stimulus package designed to jump-start the sagging economy. But high levels of federal spending and deficits continued through 2012 (see Figure 10-3).

"Entitlement" Spending

The largest share of the federal government budget is devoted to "entitlements." These are spending items determined by past policies of Congress and represent commitments in future federal budgets. Entitlements provide classes of people with legally enforceable rights to benefits, and they account for about 60 percent of all federal spending, including Social Security, Medicare and Medicaid, welfare and food stamps, federal employees' retirement, and veterans' benefits. In addition to entitlements, other "mandatory" spending includes interest payments on the national debt. Only about 16 percent of the budget remains for "nondefense discretionary" spending (see Figure 10-4).

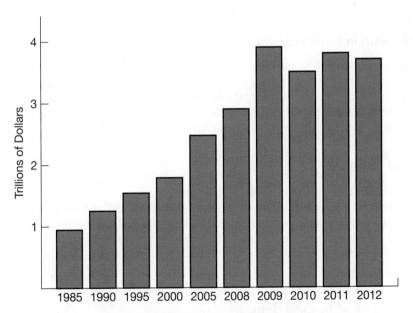

FIGURE 10–3   Federal Spending in Trillions Federal spending grew incrementally until 2009 when countercyclical "stimulus" efforts sent spending to unprecedented levels.
SOURCE: *Budget of the United States Government, 2012.*

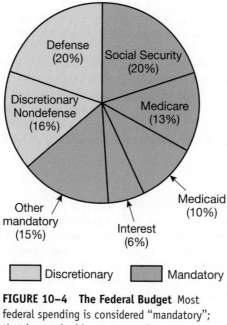

Discretionary   Mandatory

FIGURE 10–4   The Federal Budget Most
federal spending is considered "mandatory";
that is, required by past commitments.
SOURCE: *Budget of the United States Government,*
2012.

Incrementalism in Entitlements

Each year as more people become entitled to Social Security benefits and Medicare—the two
largest entitlement programs—government spending rises accordingly. It is true that, in theory,
Congress could change the basic laws establishing these programs and thereby avoid annual
increases in entitlement spending. But politically such a course of action is virtually unthinkable.
Reducing long-promised benefits would be regarded by voters as a failure of trust.

Indexing of Benefits

Another reason that spending increases each year is that Congress has authorized automatic
increases in benefits tied to increases in prices. Benefits are "indexed" to the Consumer Price Index
under Social Security, SSI, food stamps, and veterans' pensions. This indexing pushes up the cost
of entitlement programs each year. Indexing, of course, runs counter to federal efforts to restrain
inflation. Moreover, the Consumer Price Index generally overestimates real increases in the cost
of living.

Increasing Costs of In-Kind Benefits

Rises in the cost of major in-kind (noncash) benefits, particularly medical costs of Medicaid and
Medicare, also guarantee growth in federal spending. These in-kind benefit programs have risen
faster in cost than cash benefit programs.

Backdoor Spending

Some federal spending does not appear on the budget. For example, spending by the postal service is not included in the federal budget. No clear rule explains why some agencies are in the budget and others are not. But "off-budget" agencies have the same economic effects as other government agencies. Another form of backdoor spending is found in government-guaranteed loans. Initially government guarantees for loans—FHA housing, guaranteed student loans, veterans' loans, and so forth—do not require federal money. The government merely promises to repay the loan if the borrower fails to do so. Yet these loans create an obligation against the government.

GOVERNMENT DEFICITS AND THE NATIONAL DEBT

The federal government regularly spends more than it receives in revenues (see Figure 10–5). These annual deficits have driven up the accumulated debt of the United States government to over $15 trillion. The national debt now exceeds $45,000 for every man, woman, and child in the nation!

The national debt is owed mostly to American banks and financial institutions and private citizens who buy U.S. Treasury bonds. But an increasing share of the debt is held by foreign investors, notably China, who also buy U.S. Treasury bonds. As old debt comes due, the Treasury Department sells new bonds to pay off the old; that is, it continues to "roll over" or "float" the debt. The ability to float such a huge debt depends on public confidence in the U.S. government—confidence that it will continue to pay interest on its debt, that it will pay off the principal of bond issues when they come due, and that the value of the bonds will not decline over time because of inflation.

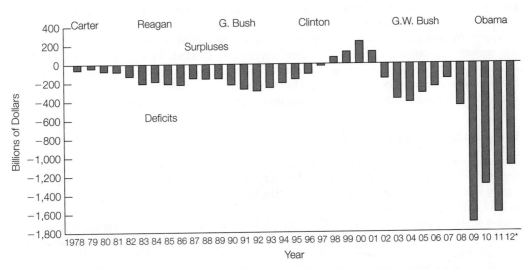

FIGURE 10–5　Annual Federal Deficits and Surpluses In only four years of the past four decades has the federal government enjoyed a surplus of revenues over expenditures; annual deficits have accumulated, creating a national debt of over $15 trillion dollars.
SOURCES: *Statistical Abstract of the United States, 2011; Budget of the United States Government, 2012.*
*Estimates.

Politics, Surpluses, and Deficits

Economic growth increases tax revenues. The nation's economic performance in the 1990s was much better than either politicians or economists expected. Tax revenues grew faster than government spending, and the federal government's annual deficits began to decline. President Clinton and a Democratic-controlled Congress passed a major tax increase in 1993 (see Chapter 11). After 1994, a Republican-controlled Congress slowed the growth of federal spending. Not surprisingly, both Democrats and Republicans claimed credit for ending forty years of deficits in 1998. For four years the federal government actually enjoyed surpluses of revenues over expenditures!

However, deficits returned in 2002 when economic growth slowed. Federal spending for national defense and homeland security increased after the terrorist attacks of September 11, 2001. And President Bush was committed to lowering federal income taxes. In his first year in office President Bush pushed Congress to enact a major tax reduction (see Chapter 11). Democrats argued that this tax reduction contributed to the return to deficit spending. Republicans argued that tax reductions stimulate the economy and that economic growth would eventually increase revenues and reduce deficits. Again in 2003 President Bush succeeded in getting Congress to enact further tax reductions. Large annual federal deficits continued through the end of the Bush Administration.

Deficits exploded under President Barack Obama. In his first budget message to Congress, he stated that the stimulus package would push the annual deficit for 2009 to $1.7 trillion, an amount over four times greater than any previous budget deficit. Budget deficits of over $1 trillion are projected far into the future.

The Burdens of Government Debt

Even if the federal government managed to balance its annual budgets, the accumulated national debt, and the interest payments that must be made on it, would remain obligations of current and future taxpayers. Interest payments on the national debt come from current taxes; interest payments soon will amount to about 10 percent of the federal government's budget. This means that for every dollar paid in federal taxes, taxpayers currently receive only 90 cents in government goods and services. Interest payments might otherwise be used for government programs in health, education, research, and so on. The burden of future interest payments is shifted to young people and future generations.

Bringing Spending Under Control?

The size and scope of government in America have grown dramatically in recent years. Federal spending, now about 24 of the nation's GDP, is being funded in large part with borrowed money, nearly half of it from foreign countries including China. Annual federal deficits have ballooned to $1.5 trillion; the accumulated debt of the United States now exceeds $15 trillion, an amount almost equivalent to the nation's GDP. This means that every man, woman and child in the country now owes about $45,000 in federal debt. "This debt is like a cancer that will truly destroy this country from within, if we don't fix it."[3]

How can we bring deficit spending under control? Nearly everyone in Washington, Democrats and Republicans and liberals and conservatives, agree that deficits must be reduced. Either government must curtail spending, or taxes must be increased, or both. But very few politicians are willing to accept responsibility for setting forth *specific* spending reductions or tax increases. In Washington, when politicians seek to avoid responsibility for unpopular proposals, they frequently resort to independent commissions to make the hard choices.

The President's Deficit Reduction Commission

President Barack Obama appointed a National Commission on Fiscal Responsibility and Reform (usually referred to as the president's deficit reduction commission) in 2010, and charged it with the responsibility for coming up with specific suggestions for reducing deficits. Among the Commission's recommendations:

Federal Employment: Cut the federal work force by 10 percent; freeze civilian salaries for three years; cut low-priority and underperforming programs; reduce congressional and White House spending by 15 percent.

Social Security: Raise the retirement age to 68 by 2050 and 69 by 2075; reduce annual cost-of-living increases; increase the amount of wage income subject to Social Security taxes; cut benefits to high income recipients.

Health Care: Limit cost increases in Medicare and Medicaid to no more than 1 percent above the growth rate of the economy; eliminate the tax-free status of employer-provided health benefits; cap jury awards in medical malpractice cases.

Taxes: Reduce or eliminate many popular deductions from income taxes, including the child credit, charity, and mortgage interest deductions, thereby allowing a reduction in individual tax rates; reduce the corporate tax rate from 35 percent to 26 percent to encourage corporations to remain in the United States; tax dividends and capital gains at ordinary income tax rates; increase the federal gasoline tax by 15 cents per gallon.

Defense: Cut Defense Department procurement spending; cancel a variety of new, expensive weapons programs; budget separately for overseas contingency operations (Iraq and Afganistan).

Congress: Eliminate all "earmarks" (special appropriations attached to spending bills by individual Congress members).

Ignoring the Commission's Report

President Obama ignored the recommendations of the Commission. His own 2012 *Budget of the United States Government* contained no reform recommendations regarding entitlement spending—Social Security, Medicare or Medicaid. It called for a five-year freeze on "non-security discretionary spending," including a two-year freeze on federal civilian worker pay. The president defended continued high levels of spending: "It would be shortsighted to cut spending across the board and thus deprive critical areas for growth and competitiveness—such as education, innovation, and infrastructure—or carelessly slash programs that protect the most vulnerable."[4]

Do the Commission's recommendations go far enough? Probably not. Even if all of them were enacted, annual federal deficits would continue. But predictably, reactions in Washington to the Commission's proposals were largely negative.

Republican "Path to Prosperity"

A Republican plan to reduce deficit spending, entitled "The Path to Prosperity," was offered in the House of Representatives in 2011 by the House Budget Committee Chairman Paul Ryan (R-WI). It promises to reduce annual federal spending to less than 20 percent of the gross domestic product. The plan involves reducing discretionary domestic spending to below 2008 levels; shrinking the federal work force; targeting inefficiencies in the Pentagon; converting Medicaid to a block grant to the states; placing Medicare recipients in private health plans with government premium support; and ending tax deductions and loopholes and lowering both top individual and corporate rates to 25 percent. But it is unlikely that any of these Republican policy recommendations could pass a Democratic-controlled Senate or escape President Obama's veto.

Obama's Response

President Obama responded to the Republican deficit reduction plan by renewing his call for an increase in the top marginal income tax rate to 39.6 percent. He also called for additional cuts in defense spending; limiting the growth of Medicare, including prescription drug spending; seeking greater "efficiencies" in Medicaid; and making modest cutbacks in discretionary domestic programs. He rejected Republican proposals to make fundamental changes in Medicare and Medicaid. And neither the Republican plan nor the president's response made any mention of Social Security reform.

Gridlock and Continued Deficit Spending

The need to raise the debt ceiling in August 2011 provided the House Republicans with an opportunity to attach conditions to their approval. They insisted on significant cuts in spending with no tax increases. Failure to raise the debt ceiling threatened default on US bonds. President Obama warned that August checks might not be issued for Social Security, military pay, and interest on the national debt. The Treasury Secretary warned of dire financial consequences for the nation resulting from a first-ever default on its debt. A last-minute compromise raised the debt ceiling until January 2013 (after the 2012 presidential election). It included minor spending cuts and a promise that a "super committee" of Congress would recommend ways to further reduce deficits.

A Balanced Budget Amendment?

A balanced budget amendment to the U.S. Constitution would limit federal government spending to an amount equal to or less than the revenue it receives each year. There would be exceptions, whereby Congress could spend more in times of war or recession or national emergency, if approved by a supermajority in both the House and Senate. The wording of proposed amendments varies. One simple version: "Outlays of the United States for any fiscal year shall not exceed receipts to the United States for that year, unless 3/5 of the whole number of both houses of Congress shall provide for a specific excess of outlays over revenues."

Controversy.   A balanced budget amendment challenges Keynesian economics, which teaches that federal spending and borrowing should counter economic cycles. The federal government should borrow money during recessions to stimulate the economy, and pay off the debt during upturns to hold down inflation. But politicians are loath to give up federal deficits, in either good times or bad, by either reducing spending of increasing taxes. It is easier to spend now, increase deficits, and place the burden of debt on future generations. Obligating taxpayers of tomorrow, our children and grandchildren, to pay for spending today may be morally indefensible, but it is politically attractive. Proponents of a balanced budget argue that only a constitutional amendment can protect future generations against the self-interested politicians. Or as one Congress member put it: "If you don't tie our hands, we'll keep stealing."[5]

But even proponents of an amendment recognize that wars, recessions or national emergencies can cause temporary imbalances of outlays over receipts. So most proposals for a balanced budget amendment include exceptions approved by supermajorities in both houses, that is a three-fifths or two-thirds vote.

One Vote Short.   Any constitutional amendment requires a two-thirds vote of both the House and Senate, as well as ratification by three quarters of the states. The states appear ready to ratify a balanced budget amendment if Congress can send it to them. Indeed, several states have petitioned Congress to pass such an amendment. In 1997 a balanced budget amendment fell one vote short in the U.S. Senate of the required two-thirds. This vote was inspired by the 1994 midterm Republican congressional election victory and pledge in the Republican "Contract with America" to pass the amendment. But the narrow defeat appeared to set back the balanced budget amendment movement for more than a decade.

Renewed Efforts.   U.S. Senator Orrin Hatch (R-UT) is a longtime advocate of the balanced budget amendment. In 2010 he renewed his effort by proposing a constitutional amendment that:

- Mandates that total outlays for any fiscal year cannot exceed revenues.
- Requires the president to submit a balanced budget to Congress each year.
- Waives these requirements if there is a formal declaration of war, or a military conflict threatening national security, or if two-thirds of both the House and Senate approves.

The Hatch proposal would go even further in limiting Congress in its fiscal powers. It would cap federal spending at 20 percent of GDP, and would require a two-thirds vote of both houses to raise taxes. The Hatch proposal would allow four years following notification by the necessary three-quarter of the states before taking effect. The purpose of the delay is to allow time for the federal government to adjust its fiscal policies. (Most observers believe that the states would quickly ratify a balanced budget amendment.)

A constitutional amendment does not require the president's signature. But achieving a two-thirds majority in both the House and Senate requires bipartisan support. Democrats must join with Republicans if the balanced budget amendment to the Constitution is ever to pass.

SUMMARY

Government influences the economy through fiscal policies—decisions about taxing, spending, and deficit levels—and monetary policy—decisions about the money supply and interest rates. Traditionally, fiscal and monetary policy decisions were made incrementally. But incrementalism fails to describe or explain policymaking during the economic crisis confronting the nation beginning in 2008.

1. Keynesian theory recommends government manipulation of aggregate demand to counter economic cycles—raising spending, lowering taxes, and incurring debt during recessions and pursuing the opposite policies during inflation. Supply-side economists argue that high government taxing and spending levels promote immediate consumption instead of investment in the future and penalize hard work, creativity, and savings.

2. Fiscal policymaking rests with the president, primarily in his preparation of the annual *Budget of the United States Government*, and with Congress, which actually appropriates all the funds to be spent by the federal government each year.

3. Monetary policy rests with the Federal Reserve Board—the "Fed"—which influences the supply of money in a variety of ways. It determines how much reserve banks must maintain and what interest rates banks must pay to borrow additional reserves. Through these decisions, the Fed can expand or contract the money supply to help counter recessions and inflation.

4. But traditional *monetary* policies appeared inadequate in coping with the "Great Recession" that began in 2008. The Fed dramatically increased the money supply in an effort to encourage banks and other lenders to make loans and jump-start the economy. The Fed also undertook to rescue many of the nation's leading financial institutions. But deepening recession caused the president and Congress to look to *fiscal* policy to stimulate the economy.

5. The economic "stimulus" package passed by Congress and signed by the president in early 2009 was a decidedly nonincremental response to a perceived economic crisis. It was the largest single fiscal policy measure in history—a combination of tax payments and spending increases that raised government deficits to unprecedented levels.

6. Entitlement spending accounts for over 60 percent of all federal government spending. These are spending items determined by past policies of Congress and represent commitments in future federal budgets. They provide classes of people with legally enforceable rights to benefits, including Social Security, Medicare, Medicaid, welfare and food stamps, federal employees' retirement, and veterans' benefits. Entitlement spending rises incrementally each year.

7. The accumulated annual federal deficits have resulted in a total national debt of nearly 15 *trillion* dollars. This debt is owed to banks and financial institutions and private citizens who buy U.S. Treasury bonds, including foreign governments, notably China. The Treasury Department continually "floats" the debt by issuing new bonds to pay off old bonds when they become due. Interest paid on the national debt will soon account for about 10 percent of total federal spending.

8. Serious deficit reduction efforts must include reform of entitlement programs, notably Social Security, Medicare and Medicaid. But recommendations of the president's Commission on Fiscal Responsibility and Reform were ignored by President Obama and poorly received in Washington. Deficit spending is projected to continue indefinitely into the future.

MySearchLab® EXERCISES

Apply what you learned in this chapter on MySearchLab (www.mysearchlab.com).

NOTES

1. See Michael Comiskey and Pawan Madhorgarthia, "Unraveling the Financial Crisis of 2008," *PS: Political Science & Politics*, vol. 42 (April, 2009), pp. 271–275.

2. William A. Niskanen, *Bureaucracy and Representative Government* (Chicago: Aldine, 1971).

3. Democrat Erskine Bowles, former Clinton White House Chief of Staff, co-chair with Alan Simpson, former U.S. Senator from Wyoming, of the National Commission on Fiscal Responsibility and Reform, quoted on November 11, 2010. The Commission report is available at *www.fiscalcommission.gov*

4. *Budget of the United States Government 2012*, p.20.

5. *Human Events* March 11, 2011, p.210.

BIBLIOGRAPHY

GREIDER, WILLIAM. *Secrets of the Temple: How the Federal Reserve Runs the Country.* New York: Simon & Schuster, 1987.

MIKESELL, JOHN. *Fiscal Administration,* 8th ed. Cengage, 2011.

NEIMAN, MAX. *Defending Government: Why Big Government Works.* New York: Longman, 2000.

RAHM, DIANNE. *United States Public Policy: A Budgetary Approach.* Cengage, 2004.

SCHICK, ALLEN. *The Federal Budget,* 3rd ed. Washington, DC: Brookings Institution, 2007.

SMITH, ROBERT W., and THOMAS D. LYNCH. *Public Budgeting in America,* 5th ed. New York: Longman, 2004.

WILDAVSKY, AARON, and NAOMI CAIDEN. *The New Politics of the Budgetary Process,* 5th ed. New York: Longman, 2004.

WEB SITES

FEDERAL RESERVE SYSTEM. Official site of the FRB (Federal Reserve Board), with information about the money supply, inflation, interest rates, etc. *www.federalreserve.gov*

U.S. OFFICE OF MANAGEMENT AND BUDGET. Official site of OMB, with the current Budget of the United States. *www.whitehouse.gov/omb*

U.S. CONGRESSIONAL BUDGET OFFICE. Official site of CBO, with reports on economic and budget issues. *www.cbo.gov*

U.S. DEPARTMENT OF TREASURY. Official Treasury site, with information on taxes, revenues, and debt. *www.treas.gov*

AFL-CIO. Home page of the AFL-CIO; includes information on unemployment, wages, strikes, and management salaries. *www.aflcio.org*

AMERICAN ENTERPRISE INSTITUTE. Moderate think tank, with reports on government taxing, spending, and deficits. *www.aei.org*

CONCORD COALITION. Organization devoted to balanced federal budgets. *www.concordcoalition.org*

INSTITUTE FOR POLICY INNOVATION. Organization advocating less government spending, lower taxes, and fewer regulations, with studies of policy options. *www.ipi.org*

Reporting to the IRS All income-earning Americans must report their taxable income to the Internal Revenue Service on its Form 1040 before April 15, "tax day," each year. Tax forms are so complex that a majority of taxpayers hire professional tax preparers. Roughly half of all personal income in the United States escapes income taxation through various exemptions, deductions, and special treatments in the tax laws. The complexity and inefficiency of the tax laws can be attributed largely to the influence of organized interest groups.   (2005 Getty Images)

11

Tax Policy
Battling the Special Interests

INTEREST GROUPS AND TAX POLICY

The interplay of interest groups in policymaking is often praised as "pluralism."[1] Public policy is portrayed by interest group theory as the equilibrium in the struggle between interest groups (see Chapter 2). While this equilibrium is not the same as majority preference, it is considered by pluralists to be the best possible approximation of the public interest in a large and diverse society.

But what if only a small proportion of the American people are organized into politically effective interest groups? What if the interest group system represents well-organized, economically powerful producer groups who actively seek immediate tangible benefits from the government? What if the interest group system leaves out a majority of Americans, particularly the less organized, economically dispersed consumers and taxpayers, who wish for broad policy goals such as fairness, simplicity, and general economic well-being?

There is no better illustration of the influence of organized interest groups in policy making than national tax policy. Every economics textbook tells us that the public interest is best served by a tax system that is universal, simple, and fair and that promotes economic growth and well-being. But the federal tax system is very nearly the opposite: it is complex, unfair, and nonuniversal. Over *one-half* of all personal income in the United States escapes income taxation through various exemptions, deductions, and special treatments in tax laws. Tax laws treat different types of income differently. They penalize work, savings, and investment and divert capital investment into nonproductive tax shelters and an illegal underground economy. The unfairness, complexity, and inefficiency of the tax laws can be attributed largely to organized interest groups.

THE FEDERAL TAX SYSTEM

The federal government derives its revenues from a variety of sources—the individual income tax; Social Security and Medicare payroll deductions; the corporate income tax; excise taxes on gasoline, liquor, tobacco, telephones, air travel, and other consumer items; estate and gift taxes; custom duties, and a wide variety of charges and fees (see Figure 11–1).

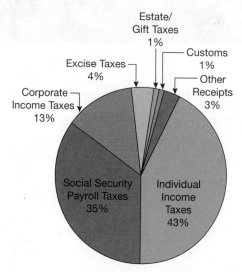

FIGURE 11–1   Sources of Federal Revenue The individual income tax provides the largest share of federal revenue, with Social Security payroll taxes close behind.
SOURCE: *Budget of the United States Government, 2012.*

Individual Income Taxes

More than 100 years ago, Supreme Court Justice Stephen J. Field, in striking down as unconstitutional a progressive income tax enacted by Congress, predicted that such a tax would lead to class wars: "Our political contests will become a war of the poor against the rich, a war constantly growing in intensity and bitterness."[2] But populist sentiment in the early twentieth century—the anger of midwestern farmers toward eastern railroad tycoons and the beliefs of impoverished southerners that they would never have incomes high enough to pay an income tax—helped secure the passage of the Sixteenth Amendment to the U.S. Constitution. The federal income tax that was passed by Congress in 1914 had a top rate of 7 percent; less than 1 percent of the population had incomes high enough to be taxed. Today the top rate is 35 percent, and about half of the population pays income taxes.

The personal income tax is the federal government's largest single source of revenue. Currently, personal income is taxed at six separate rates—10, 15, 25, 28, 33, and 35 percent. (A top rate of 39.6 percent was rejected in the comprehensive tax package passed in December, 2010. See "Compromise: The 2010 Tax Package" below.) These rates apply progressively to levels of income, or "brackets," that are indexed annually to reflect inflation.

The federal income tax is automatically deducted from the paychecks of employees. This withholding system is the backbone of the income tax. There is no withholding of non-wage income, but taxpayers with such income must file a Declaration of Estimated Taxes and pay this estimate in quarterly installments. On or before April 15 of each year, all income-earning Americans must report their taxable income to the Internal Revenue Service on its Form 1040.

Americans are usually surprised to learn that half of all personal income is *not* taxed. To understand why, we must know how the tax laws distinguish between *adjusted gross income* (which is an individual's total money income minus expenses incurred in earning it) and *taxable income* (that part of adjusted gross income subject to taxation). Federal tax rates apply only to taxable income. Federal tax laws allow many reductions in adjusted gross income in the calculation of taxable income.

Tax expenditures is a term meant to identify tax revenues that are lost to the federal government because of exemptions, deductions, and special treatments in tax laws. Table 11–1 lists the major tax expenditures in federal tax law. There is a continual struggle between proponents of special tax exemptions to achieve social goals and those who believe that the tax laws should be simplified and social goals met by direct expenditures.

Most working families pay no personal income taxes, although Social Security taxes are deducted from their paychecks. (A combination of the personal deduction and the standard deduction ensures that families of four with incomes under $40,000 pay little or no income taxes.) Moreover, most of these families are also entitled to an earned income tax credit (EITC)—a direct payment to low-income taxpayers who file for it (see "The Working Poor" in Chapter 7).

About 75 percent of all taxpayers take the standardized deduction; the 25 percent who itemize are middle- and upper-income taxpayers who have deductions exceeding the standardized amount.

To further complicate tax laws, an Alternative Minimum Tax requires taxpayers to compute a separate AMT tax in addition to their "regular" income tax. Taxpayers are required to pay whichever tax is higher. The AMT has a broader definition of taxable income and disallows many standard deductions. It was designed to ensure that higher income taxpayers with many exclusions

TABLE 11–1 Major "Tax Expenditures" in Federal Tax Policy   Exemptions, deductions, exclusions, and credits in tax laws are often referred to as "tax expenditures."

Personal exemptions and deduction for dependents

Deductibility of mortgage interest on owner-occupied homes

Deductibility of property taxes on first and second homes

Deferral of capital gains on home sales

Deductibility of charitable contributions

Credit for child-care expenses

Exclusion of employer contributions to pension plans and medical insurance

Partial exclusion of Social Security benefits

Exclusion of interest on public-purpose state and local bonds

Deductibility of state and local income and sales taxes

Exclusion of income earned abroad

Accelerated depreciation of machinery, equipment, and structures

Medical expenses over 7.5 percent of income

Tax credits for children

Tax credits for two years of college

Deductible contributions to IRAs and 401(k) retirement plans

Deductible contributions for education accounts

Deductions for health savings accounts

Deductions for hurricane losses

and deductions pay a minimum tax. It was originally passed by Congress in 1969, but it was not indexed to inflation. This means that increasing numbers of middle-class taxpayers are finding themselves subject to the AMT. But in recent years Congress has acted annually to protect many middle-class taxpayers from the AMT.

In addition to multiple means of tax *avoidance* (legal means), an "underground economy" that facilitates tax *evasion* (illegal means of dodging taxes) costs the federal government many billions of dollars. Independent estimates of the size of the underground economy place the loss at 15 percent of all taxes due.[3] Many citizens receive direct cash payments for goods and services, and it simply does not occur to them to report these amounts as income in addition to the wage statements they receive from their employer. Many others receive all or most of their income from cash transactions; they have a strong incentive to underreport their income. And, of course, illegal criminal transactions such as drug dealing are seldom reported on personal income tax forms. Hiding income becomes more profitable as tax rates rise.

Who Pays the Federal Income Tax?

The federal personal income tax is highly progressive. Its six tax brackets, together with personal and standard exemptions for families and earned income tax credits for low-income earners, combine to remove most of the tax burden from middle- and low-income Americans. Indeed, the lower 50 percent of income earners in America pay only 3 percent of all federal income taxes (see Figure 11–2). (However, the burden of Social Security payroll taxes falls mostly on these low- and

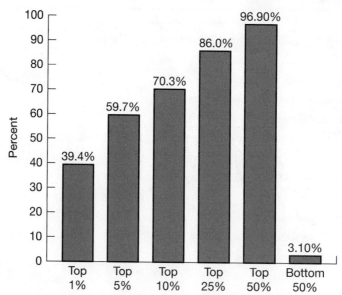

FIGURE 11–2   Who pays the Federal Income Tax? The federal income tax is steeply progressive in its effect. Almost all of it is paid by the upper half of income earners. Over two-thirds of it is paid by the top 10 percent of income earners.
SOURCE: National Taxpayers Union analysis of Internal Revenue Service data for tax year 2005.

middle-income workers.) The top 10 percent of income earners pay 70 percent of all personal income taxes, and the top 1 percent pay 39 percent.

Social Security Taxes

The second-largest source of federal revenue is social insurance payroll taxes. Social insurance payroll taxes include Social Security (OASDI, or Old Age Survivors and Disability Insurance) and Medicare (HI, or Health Insurance). Employers pay half of these taxes directly and withhold half from employees' wages. Over the years Social Security taxes rose incrementally in two ways: a gradual increase in the combined employer–employee tax rate (percent) and a gradual increase in the maximum earnings base of the tax (see Table 11–2). Today the OASDI tax (12.4 percent) and the HI tax (2.90 percent) are differentiated (total payroll tax–15.3 percent), with proceeds going to separate OASDI and HI "trust funds" in the federal treasury. The self-employed must pay the full 15.3 percent. (Employee payroll taxes were reduced by 2 percent for 2011 in the tax package passed by Congress in December, 2010.) The OASDI tax is limited to the first $106,800 (in 2011) in wage income; wages above that amount as well as nonwage income (profits, interest, dividends, rents, and so forth) are not subject to this tax. Thus, the OASDI tax is "regressive"—that is, it captures a larger share of the income of lower-income Americans than of higher-income Americans.

The taxes collected under Social Security are earmarked (by Social Security number) for the account of each taxpayer. Workers, therefore, feel that they are receiving benefits as a right rather than as a gift of the government. However, benefits are only slightly related to the earning record of the individual worker; there are both minimum and maximum benefit levels which prevent benefits from corresponding to payments. Indeed, for current recipients of Social Security, less

TABLE 11–2 Social Security Taxes The combined employee-employer Social Security tax rate is currently 15.3 percent of wages up to $106,800 (in 2011, a figure that increases each year with inflation).

	Combined Employee–Employer Tax Rate OASDI and HI	Maximum Wage Base OASDI
1937	2.0%	$ 3,000
1950	3.0	3,000
1960	6.0	4,800
1970	9.6	7,800
1980	12.26	25,900
1985	14.10	39,600
1990	15.3	67,600
2000	15.3	76,200
2006	15.3	94,200
2008	15.3	102,000
2011	15.3*	106,800

SOURCE: Social Security Administration, 2011.
*Employees' payroll tax reduced by 2 percent for 2011 in tax compromise package, passed in December, 2010.

than 15 percent of the benefits can be attributed to their prior contributions. Current taxpayers are paying more than 85 percent of the benefits being received by current retirees.

Corporate Income Taxes

The corporate income tax provides about 13 percent of the federal government's total income. The Tax Reform Act of 1986 reduced the top corporate income tax from 46 to 34 percent; Congress raised the corporate income tax rate to 35 percent in 1993.

The corporate income tax is notorious for its loopholes. Indeed, interest groups representing specific industries, and lobbyists representing individual corporations, have inserted so many exemptions, deductions, and special treatments into corporate tax laws that most corporate profits go untaxed.

Who pays the corporate income tax? Economists differ over whether this tax is "shifted" to consumers or whether corporations and their stockholders bear its burden. The evidence on the *incidence*—that is, who actually bears the burden—of the corporate income tax is inconclusive.[4]

Religious, charitable, and educational organizations, as well as labor unions, are exempt from corporate income taxes, except for income they may derive from "unrelated business activity."

Estate and Gift Taxes

Taxes on property left to heirs is one of the oldest forms of taxation in the world. Federal estate taxes now begin on estates of $5 million and levy a tax of 35 percent on amounts above this level. Because taxes at death could be easily avoided by simply giving estates to heirs while still alive, a federal gift tax is also levied.

Critics of the estate tax refer to it as "the death tax" and ridicule the federal government for "taxing people to die." Only a tiny proportion of all estates are subject to the tax. However, as the large baby-boom generation of voters reaches the age when their parents are passing away and leaving them estates, political pressure is building against the estate tax.

Excise Taxes and Custom Duties

Federal excise taxes on liquor, tobacco, gasoline, telephones, air travel, and other so-called luxury items account for only 4 percent of total federal revenue. Customs taxes on imports provide another 1 percent of total federal revenue.

TAXATION, FAIRNESS, AND GROWTH

The goal of any tax system is not only to raise sufficient revenue for the government to perform its assigned tasks, but also to do so simply, efficiently, and fairly, and in a way that does not impair economic growth. The argument on behalf of tax reform is that the federal tax system fails to meet *any* of these criteria:

- Tax forms are so complex that a majority of taxpayers hire professional tax preparers; an army of accountants and lawyers make their living from the tax code.
- Tax laws are unfair in treating various sources of income differently; the many exemptions, deductions, and special treatments are perceived as loopholes that allow the privileged to escape fair taxation.

- Tax laws encourage tax avoidance, directing investment away from productive uses and into inefficient tax shelters; whenever people make decisions about savings and investment based on tax laws instead of most productive use, the whole economy suffers.

- Tax laws encourage cheating and reduce trust in government; they encourage the growth of an underground economy, transactions that are never reported on tax forms.

- High marginal tax rates discourage work and investment; economic growth is diminished when individuals face tax rates of 50 percent or more (combined federal, state, and local taxes) on additional income they receive from additional work, savings, or investments.

But the goals of fairness, simplicity, and economic growth are frequently lost in the clash of special interests. Various interests define "fairness" differently; they demand special treatment rather than universality in tax laws; and produce a U.S. Tax Code of several thousand pages of provisions, definitions, and interpretations.

Deciding What's Fair

A central issue in tax politics is the question of who actually bears the heaviest burden of a tax—that is, which income groups must devote the largest proportion of their income to the payment of taxes. Taxes that require high-income groups to pay a larger percentage of their incomes in taxes than low-income groups are said to be *progressive*, and taxes that take a larger share of the income of low-income groups are called *regressive*. Taxes that require all income groups to pay the same percentage of their income in taxes are said to be *proportional*. Note that the *percentage of income* paid in taxes is the determining factor. Most taxes take more money from the rich than the poor, but a progressive or regressive tax is distinguished by the percentages of income taken from various income groups.

The federal income tax has a progressive rate structure. In 2011 tax rates rose from 10 to 35 percent through six brackets of increasingly taxable income. Rates apply to income in each bracket or for all taxpayers. For example, in 2011 a married taxpayer filing jointly with $400,000 in taxable income paid the 35 percent rate only on the amount over $379,150; that same taxpayer paid only 10 percent on the first $17,000, 15 percent on income between $17,000 and $69,000, and so on up through each bracket. (These are bracket figures for 2011; bracket figures change each year to reflect inflation. See Table 11–3.) A taxpayer with $400,000 in taxable income did not pay 35 percent of his or her total income in taxes; rather, this taxpayer paid approximately $119,000 in taxes, or about 30 percent of his or her total taxable income.

TABLE 11–3 Federal Income Tax Rates 2011

Taxable Income Over	But Not Over	Tax Rate
0	$17,000	10%
$17,000	$69,000	15%
$69,000	$139,500	25%
$139,500	$212,300	28%
$212,300	$379,150	33%
$379,150	—	35%

The Argument for Progressivity

Progressive taxation is generally defended on the principle of ability to pay; the assumption is that high-income groups can afford to pay a larger *percentage* of their incomes into taxes at no more of a sacrifice than that required of low-income groups to devote a smaller percentage of their income to taxation. This assumption is based on what economists call *marginal utility theory* as it applies to money: each additional dollar of income is slightly less valuable to an individual than preceding dollars. For example, a $10,000 increase in the income of an individual already earning $400,000 is much less valuable than a $10,000 increase to an individual earning only $20,000 or to an individual with no income. Hence, *added* dollars of income can be taxed at higher *rates* without violating equitable principles.

The Argument for Proportionality

Opponents of progressive taxation generally assert that equity can be achieved only by taxing everyone at the *same percentage of his or her income*, regardless of its size. A tax that requires all income groups to pay the same percentage of their income is called a *proportional* or *flat tax*. These critics believe that progressivity penalizes initiative, enterprise, and risk and reduces incentives to expand and develop the nation's economy. Moreover, by taking incomes of high-income groups, governments are taking money that would otherwise go into business investments and stimulate economic growth. Highly progressive taxes curtail growth and make everyone poorer.

Universality

Another general issue in tax policy is universality, which means that all types of income should be subject to the same tax rates. This implies that income earned from investments should be taxed at the same rate as income earned from wages. But traditionally federal tax laws have distinguished between "ordinary income" and *capital gains*—profits from the buying and selling of property, including stocks, bonds, and real estate. The top marginal rate on capital gains is only 15 percent. The argument by investors, as well as the real estate and securities industries, is that a lower rate of taxation on capital gains encourages investment and economic growth. But it is difficult to convince many Americans that income earned by *working* should be taxed at higher rates than income earned by *investing*. If it is true that high tax rates discourage investing, they must also discourage work, and both capital and labor are required for economic productivity and growth.

The principle of universality is also violated by the thousands of exemptions, deductions, and special treatments in the tax laws. It is true that most people wish to retain many widely used tax breaks—charitable deductions, child-care deductions, and home mortgage deductions. Proponents of these popular tax treatments argue that they serve valuable social purposes—encouraging charitable contributions, helping with child care, and encouraging home ownership. But reformers argue that tax laws should not be used to promote social policy objectives by granting a wide array of tax preferences.

Economic Growth

High tax rates discourage economic growth. Excessively high rates cause investors to seek "tax shelters"—to use their money not to produce more business and employment but rather to produce tax breaks for themselves. High tax rates discourage work, savings, and productive investment; they also encourage costly "tax avoidance" (legal methods of reducing or eliminating taxes) as well as "tax evasion" (illegal means of reducing or eliminating taxes).

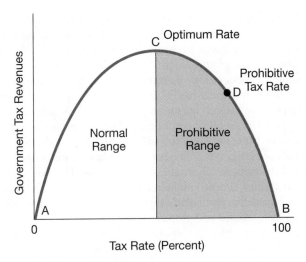

FIGURE 11–3   The Laffer Curve The "Laffer Curve" argues that when tax rates become too high, federal revenue actually declines because economic activity is discouraged.

According to supply-side economists (see "Economic Theories as Policy Guides" in Chapter 10), tax cuts do not necessarily create government deficits. Rather, they argue that if tax rates are reduced, the result may be to *increase* government revenue because more people would work harder and start new businesses, knowing they could keep a larger share of their earnings. This increased economic activity would produce more government revenue even though tax rates were lower.

Economist Arthur Laffer developed the diagram shown in Figure 11–3. If the government imposed a zero tax rate, of course, it would receive no revenue (point A). Initially, government revenues rise with increases in the tax rate. However, when tax rates become too high (beyond point C), they discourage workers and businesses from producing and investing. When this discouragement occurs, the economy declines and government revenues fall. Indeed, if the government imposed a 100 percent tax rate (if the government confiscated everything anyone produced), everyone would quit working and government revenues would fall to zero (point B). Laffer does not claim to know exactly what the optimum rate of taxation should be, but he (and the Reagan administration) clearly believed that the United States had been in the "prohibitive range" prior to the 1980s.

POLITICS AND TAX RATES

Tax Reform 1986

Nothing arouses interest groups more than the prospects of tax "reform," with its implied threats to their special exemptions, deductions, and treatments. The Tax Reform Act of 1986 was one of the most heavily lobbied pieces of legislation in the history of the Congress of the United States.[5] President Reagan offered this reform bill as a trade-off—a reduction in tax *rates* in exchange for the elimination of many tax *breaks*. The rate structure was reduced from 14 brackets, ranging from 11 to 50 percent, to two brackets of 15 and 28 percent. To make up for lost revenue, many exemptions, deductions, and special treatments were reduced or eliminated.

But powerful special interest groups fought hard against giving up their tax breaks in order to lower rates. The National Association of Home Builders strongly opposed the elimination of mortgage interest deductions for homeowners and for vacation homes as well. The real estate industry also wanted to preserve deductions for property taxes. The nation's large investment firms lobbied heavily to keep preferential treatment of capital gains—profits from the sales of stocks and bonds. And the investment firms joined with banks in arguing for the retention of tax-deferred Individual Retirement Accounts (IRAs). The nation's leading charities and foundations petitioned the president to retain deductions for charitable contributions. The AFL-CIO focused its opposition on the proposal to tax fringe benefits, including employer-paid health insurance. Lobbyists from state, county, and city governments, particularly those with high taxes, convinced Congress to retain deductibility of state and local income and property taxes. Interest from state and municipal bonds—"munies"—retained tax-free status. Nonetheless, the Tax Reform Act of 1986 was the most successful tax reform effort in modern history.

Breaking Promises

George H. W. Bush campaigned for the presidency in 1988 with an emphatic promise to veto any attempt to raise taxes—"Read my lips! No new taxes!" But the president's pledge did not last through his second year in office. In a budget summit with leaders of the Democratic-controlled Congress, President Bush announced his willingness to support a tax increase as part of a deficit reduction agreement. Once the Democratic leaders in Congress detected the irresolution of the Republican president, they proceeded to enact their own taxing and spending program while placing the political blame on Bush. The resulting budget plan made deep cuts in defense spending and token cuts in domestic spending, together with major tax increases.

Reversing the downward trend in top marginal tax rates, the Bush 1990 budget package raised the top rate from 28 to 31 percent (see Figure 11–4). The resulting rate structure became three-tiered—15, 28, and 31 percent. Democrats cheered the return to a more progressive rate structure. They ridiculed as "trickle-down economics" the arguments by supply-side theorists that high marginal tax rates would slow economic growth.

Raising Top Marginal Rates Again

President Bill Clinton's plan to reduce deficits centered on major tax increases on upper-income Americans. Specifically, Clinton succeeded in getting a Democratic-controlled Congress to add two new top marginal rates—36 and 39.6 percent. The corporate income tax was raised from 34 to 35 percent. But the special interests retained virtually all of their deductions, exemptions, and special treatments.

So-called targeted tax exemptions and deductions remain very popular in Washington. Targeted breaks—whether for the elderly, for education, for child care, for home buying, for investment income, or for a wide variety of particular industries—have strong, concentrated interest group support. In contrast, broad-based "across-the-board" tax reductions do not inspire the same kind of interest group enthusiasm or campaign contributions to Congress members. Indeed, cynics might argue that politicians deliberately enact high tax rates in order to inspire interest groups to seek special protections by making campaign contributions and otherwise providing for the comfort of lawmakers.

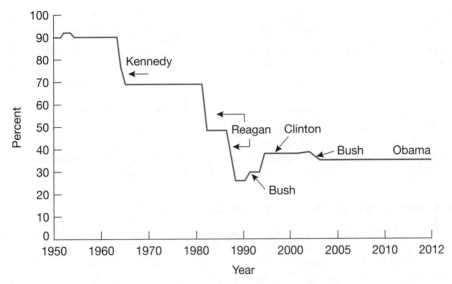

FIGURE 11–4   Maximum Income Tax Rates President Kennedy reduced the top income tax rate to 70 percent; President Reagan reduced it in two steps to 28 percent; Presidents Bush (the elder) and Clinton raised it to 39.6 percent; and President George W. Bush reduced it to 35 percent. President Barack Obama failed in his effort to raise the top marginal rate again to 39.6 percent.

The Bush Tax Cuts

George W. Bush came into office vowing *not* to make the same mistake as his father, raising tax rates to fight deficit spending. On the contrary, Bush was strongly committed to lowering taxes, arguing that doing so would revive the economy. He believed that federal deficits were the result of slow economic growth; tax reductions might temporarily add to deficits, but eventually the economic growth inspired by lower taxes would increase revenues and eliminate deficits.

In two separate tax reduction ("economic stimulus") packages in 2001 and 2003, Bush moved the Republican-controlled Congress to lower the top marginal rate from 39.6 to 35 percent. The Bush 2003 tax package also contained a variety of new targeted credits and special treatments:

Dividends. Corporate stock dividends were taxed at a low 15 percent rather than at the same rate as earned income. Bush and the Republicans in Congress initially proposed eliminating all taxes on dividends. They argued that corporations already paid taxes on corporate profits, and inasmuch as dividends come out of profits, taxing them as personal income amounted to "double taxation." They also recognized that nearly one-half of all American families now own stock or mutual funds, and they hoped that this new tax break would be politically popular. The 15 percent tax rate on dividends is less than half of the top marginal rate of 35 percent on earned income.

"Marriage penalty." For married couples the new law made the standard personal deduction twice that of a single person. This change corrected a flaw in the tax law that had long plagued married persons filing joint returns.

Child's tax credit. The per child tax credit was raised to $1,000 (from $600). This was a politically popular change supported by many Democrats as well as Republicans.

Capital gains. Finally, the Bush tax package chipped away again at the tax on capital gains—profits from the sale of investments held at least one year. The capital gains tax was reduced from 20 to 15 percent, a rate less than half of the top marginal rate on earned income of 35 percent.

The Bush tax package was approved in the Republican-controlled House and Senate on largely party line votes. Most Democrats opposed the package, arguing that it primarily benefited the rich, that it would do little to help the economy, and that it would add to the already growing annual federal deficits. Republicans argued that the package benefited all taxpayers, and inasmuch as the rich pay most of the taxes it is only fair that they should benefit from tax reductions.

Obama: Redistributing Income Via the Tax Code

President Barack Obama campaigned on a promise to lower taxes on the middle class, which he defined as 95 percent of taxpayers. But he also pledged to raise taxes on upper-income Americans, which he defined as families earning $250,000 a year or more. This combination of changes in taxation would have made the Tax Code more progressive.

A central item in the economic stimulus package of 2009 was "Making Work Pay"—tax payments of $400 to individuals with incomes under $75,000 and $800 to families with incomes under $150,000 (see Chapter 10). These payments were made to anyone who paid Social Security payroll taxes, whether or not they paid income taxes. These payments initially fulfilled Obama's campaign promise to lower taxes on the middle class.

The Bush tax cuts had been scheduled to expire at the end of 2010. (Republicans in Congress had agreed to this expiration date, believing that these tax cuts would eventually be made permanent; however, when Democrats captured control of Congress in 2006, Republicans were unable to make the tax cuts permanent.) President Obama urged Congress to allow the Bush tax cuts to expire, thus raising the top marginal tax rate from 35 to 39.6 percent. He also recommended a phaseout of deductions, including charitable contributions and mortgage payments, for families making over $250, 000. This combination of changes in the Tax Code—tax payments to families making less than $150,000 and an increase in the top tax rate to 39.6 percent—would have had the effect of redistributing after-tax income among Americans. Critics charged that income redistribution inspires class conflict; when a majority of Americans no longer have to pay income taxes, the incentive exists to raise taxes to prohibitive levels.

COMPROMISE: THE TAX PACKAGE OF 2010

Democrats and Republicans in Congress agreed that allowing the Bush tax cuts to expire during a recession would be a mistake. The effect would be to raise taxes, further depress buying power, and slow or reverse economic recovery. And both parties feared the political fallout from allowing taxes to rise. But President Obama and the Democratic leadership in the House and Senate, including Speaker Nancy Pelosi and Majority Leader Harry Reid, insisted on raising the top marginal tax rate to 39.6 percent. However, following the Republican victory in the midterm congressional election in 2010, Republicans in Congress united behind the notion of extending the Bush tax cuts to "every taxpayer," including those who paid the top rate. The issue threatened gridlock and an inability of the Congress to act in time to stave off the tax increases scheduled to begin January 2011. The issue fell to the Democratic-controlled "lame duck" Congress meeting in December to resolve.

Multiple Issues Inspire Compromise

Several other important issues were facing Congress in late 2010, in addition to the extension of the Bush tax cuts. Unemployment insurance payments were running out for persons who had been receiving benefits for 99 weeks. A bill to extend benefits was high on the agenda of the Democratic leadership. The federal estate tax, which had lapsed at the end of 2009, was also on the Democratic agenda for renewal. But the estate tax, previously set at a top rate of 45 percent for estates over $1 million, was attacked by Republicans as a "death tax." President Obama sought to continue his Making Work Pay payments to working families making $150,000 or less. And there was the recurring issue of the Alternative Minimum Tax (AMT) that increasingly affected middle-class families rather than only the very wealthy as intended. The variety of issues at stake appeared to improve the atmosphere in Washington for a grand compromise.

The Tax Package

The result of extended negotiations between the Democratic and Republican leadership in Congress and President Obama was a grand compromise involving a variety of issues.

- *Extending the Bush Tax Cuts.* The Bush tax cuts were extended for two years for *all* income levels. The top marginal tax rate remained at 35 percent. The child tax credit of $1000 was retained, as well as relief from the marriage penalty. A two-year "patch" was affixed to the AMT to prevent its application to millions of additional middle-class taxpayers.

Searching for Compromise   President Barack Obama meets with Democratic and Republican congressional leaders during the "lame duck" session of Congress in December, 2010, to work out a compromise package extending the Bush tax cuts for two years. Republicans succeeded in preserving the cuts for "every taxpayer," overcoming President Obama's effort to raise the top marginal income tax rate from 35 to 39.6 percent. Democrats succeeded in extending unemployment compensation benefits, reducing Social Security employees' contributions, and renewing the estate tax. But these controversial issues must be revisited by Congress at the end of 2012, a presidential election year.   (Getty Images)

- *Unemployment Insurance Extension.* An additional 13 months was added in unemployment compensation for jobless workers who have exhausted their benefits.

- *Estate Tax Renewal.* The federal estate tax was renewed but at a lower rate and with a larger exemption than in previous years. The current top rate is 35 percent with an exemption of $5 million.

- *Social Security Payroll Tax Reduction.* The employees' half of the Social Security payroll tax (FICA) was reduced by 2 percent. The Making Work Pay payments were ended.

It is important to note that these provisions are set to expire in two years, at the end of 2012. This guarantees that these battles will be fought again during the 2012 presidential election campaign.

THE CAPITAL GAINS CONTROVERSY

A capital gain is the profit made from buying and selling any asset—real estate, bonds, stocks, etc. Preferential tax treatment for capital gains appeals to a wide variety of interests, especially Wall Street brokerage houses and investment firms in the real estate industry. And, of course, it significantly reduces the tax burden on high income taxpayers—those most likely to have income from the sale of these assets (see Figure 11–5).

Preferential Treatment for Capital Gains

Why should income derived from investment be taxed at a lower rate than income made from work? A central reform in the Reagan Tax Reform Act of 1986 was the elimination of preferential treatment for income from capital gains. But when President George H. W. Bush and Congress

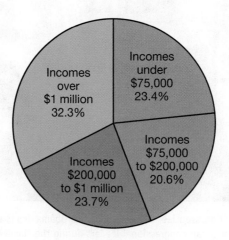

FIGURE 11–5   Who Benefits from Capital Gains? Capital gains, from buying and selling stocks, bonds, real estate, etc., go mainly to upper-income groups; these groups gain the most from reductions in capital gains taxes.
SOURCE: Congressional Budget Office.

agreed to increase the top marginal rate to 31 percent in 1990, they quietly made this increase applicable only to *earned* income; income from capital gains continued to be taxed at a top rate of 28 percent. This ploy succeeded in restoring preferential treatment to capital gains. The same tactic was employed again in 1993 when President Bill Clinton won congressional approval for an additional increase in the top marginal rate to 39.6 percent on earned income; the tax on income from capital gains remained at 28 percent.

Republicans continued to urge reductions in capital gains taxation. Following their congressional victory in the 1994 midterm elections, Republicans pushed through a 20 percent top rate on capital gains, about one half of the then-existing top rate on earned income. Again in 2003 Republicans in Congress, following President George W. Bush's lead, succeeded in lowering the capital gains tax rate again, this time to 15 percent.

President Obama campaigned on a promise to raise the capital gains tax. But in the compromise tax package of 2010 the Bush rate on capital gains was continued at 15 percent.

REPLACING THE INCOME TAX?

Special interest politics make comprehensive tax reform an unlikely prospect for America. Nonetheless, serious proposals have been offered in recent years to reform the nation's tax laws.

The Flat Tax

A "flat tax" has been recommended by economists over the years. It would eliminate all exemptions, exclusions, deductions, and special treatments, and replace the current progressive tax rates with a flat 19 percent tax on all forms of income.[6] This low rate would produce just as much revenue as the current complicated system, even excluding family incomes under $40,000. It would sweep away the nation's army of tax accountants and lawyers and lobbyists, and increase national productivity by relieving taxpayers of millions of hours of record keeping and tax preparation. A flat tax could be filed on a postcard form (see Figure 11–6). Removing progressive rates would create incentives to work, save, and invest in America. It would lead to more rapid economic growth and improve efficiency by directing investments to their most productive uses rather than to tax avoidance. It would eliminate current incentives to underreport income, overstate exemptions, and avoid and evade taxation. Finally, by including a generous personal and family allowance, the flat tax would be made fair.

However, many Americans support deductions for home mortgages and charitable contributions. This suggests a major political weakness in the flat tax idea: even if enacted, politicians would gradually erode the uniformity, fairness, and simplicity of a flat tax by introducing popular deductions. Lobbyists for special tax treatments would continue to pressure Congress, and, over time, deductions, exemptions, and exclusions would creep back into the tax laws.

Moreover, the flat tax violates the principle of progressivity described earlier. If it is true that added (marginal) income of higher-income recipients is less valuable to them than the income of lower-income recipients, then a flat tax appears unfair. A flat tax is also opposed by those who believe that government should undertake to reduce income differences among people.

The National Sales Tax

A national retail sales tax, similar to sales taxes currently levied by many states, could replace the federal income tax and "get the IRS completely out of our lives."[7] By taxing sales rather than income, it would penalize consumption rather than production. (A value-added tax or "VAT" is comparable

Your first name and initial (if joint return, also give spouse's name and initial)	Last name	Your Social Security number
Home address (number and street, including apartment number or rural route)		Spouse's Social Security number
City, town, or post office, state, and ZIP code		Your occupation
		Spouse's occupation

1 Wages and salary		1
2 Pension and retirement benefits		2
3 Total compensation *(line 1 plus line 2)*		3
4 Personal allowance		
(a) 0 $16,500 for married filing jointly		4a
(b) 0 $9,500 for single		4b
(c) 0 $14,000 for single head of household		4c
5 Number of dependents, not including spouse		5
6 Personal allowances for dependents *(line 5 multiplied by $4,500)*		6
7 Total personal allowances *(line 4 plus line 6)*		7
8 Taxable compensation *(line 3 less line 7, if positive; otherwise zero)*		8
9 Tax *(19% of line 8)*		9
10 Tax withheld by employer		10
11 Tax due *(line 9 less line 10, if positive)*		11
12 Refund due *(line 10 less line 9, if positive)*		12

FIGURE 11–6   Armey-Shelby Flat Tax Postcard Return
Hypothetically, a simple "flat tax" with no exemptions, deductions, or special treatments (except for a personal allowance for dependents) would result in a one-page "postcard" tax return.

in effect to a sales tax, but taxes are levied on each stage of a product's development rather than on retail sales.) By eliminating taxes on income, Americans would be encouraged to engage in all of the activities that produce income—working, investing, inventing, starting businesses, and so on. It would encourage people to save money by levying taxes on their *spending* rather than their savings. It would discourage people from borrowing to purchase goods. Increased savings and reduced borrowing would bring about lower interest rates, making it easier for people to buy homes and automobiles. A sales tax would also get at the underground economy; for example, drug dealers who do not report their income would pay a sales tax on their purchases of expensive homes, cars, and jewelry. It could be made more progressive (less regressive) by reducing or eliminating sales taxes on food, rent, medical care, or other necessities. Finally, collection costs, both in dollar terms and in lost freedom and privacy, would be greatly reduced by administering a sales tax rather than the income tax.

But a national sales tax is likely to be regressive, even if food, rent, and other basic necessities are excluded. Low-income groups spend almost all of their income, saving very little. This means that virtually all of their income would be subject to sales taxation. In contrast, higher-income groups save larger shares of their income, thereby avoiding sales taxation on the proportion saved.

A single national sales tax rate on all goods and services would violate the principle of progressivity. It would not satisfy liberals who believe that government tax policy should be shaped to serve social objectives, including the reduction of income inequality. And conservatives worry that such a tax might be adopted to supplement rather than replace an income tax. Finally, if different types of goods and services were taxed at different rates, interest groups would engage in a continuing frenzy of legislative activity seeking to lower the rate on their particular products.

Encouraging Savings

Various provisions in the tax laws currently encourage savings. Taxpayers can use Roth IRAs, traditional IRAs, 401(k) retirement plans, and 529 college plans to exclude limited amounts of savings from current taxation. Despite these plans, the percentage of personal income that Americans devote to savings has declined dramatically over the years. To encourage savings, the tax code could be changed to tax people only on the money they *spend*, that is, to exempt *all* savings from taxation. (This could be done incrementally by increasing amounts that could be contributed tax-free to IRA-type accounts.) Tax rates would rise on the money people spend. But again, excluding savings from taxation raises the issue of regressivity—wealthy taxpayers save a larger proportion of their income than less wealthy taxpayers.

Reining in the IRS

The Internal Revenue Service (IRS) is the most intrusive of all government agencies, overseeing the finances of every taxpaying citizen and corporation in America. It maintains personal records on more than 150 million Americans and requires them to submit more than a billion forms each year. It may levy fines and penalties and collect taxes on its own initiative; in disputes with the IRS, the burden of proof falls on the taxpayer, not the agency. Americans pay over $30 billion for the services of tax accountants and preparers, and they waste some $200 billion in hours of record keeping and computing their taxes.

The Internal Revenue Code (the tax law) contains about 10,000 pages, and the IRS has promulgated over 100,000 additional pages of rules and regulations. The result is a quagmire of confusion over compliance. The IRS itself is unable to provide accurate, consistent answers to tax questions. The U.S. General Accountability Office cites an "appallingly high error rate" in IRS handling of individual taxpayer questions. Submitting the exact same information to multiple tax experts almost always results in different computations of taxes owed. In 1998, Congress passed a "Taxpayers' Bill of Rights" that made it illegal for the IRS to establish quota systems for tax collections for its agents and sought to limit harassment of taxpayers and overly aggressive property seizures.

Simplifying the Tax Code

The dream of a simplified tax code remains just that, a dream. Tax reformers have dreamed for decades of tax filing on a postcard or through a simple Web site. But despite the lure of simplification, tax laws will remain complex. Powerful interests have a stake in maintaining the thousands of exemptions, deductions, exclusions, and special treatments that have accumulated in the tax code over decades. Accountants and tax lawyers live off the complexity of the tax code.

And Congress members themselves benefit directly from tax complexity. Complexity keeps the special interests coming to Capitol Hill and seeking to gain or maintain narrowly targeted tax provisions. They open their pocketbooks for campaign contributions to Congress members who assist them in their quests for preferential treatments. Members can boast to special interests in their states and district—farmers, ranchers, oil and gas producers, real estate investors, bankers, small business owners, and a host of others—that they have protected their existing tax breaks or have sponsored new ones. And every tax break necessitates greater complexity in the tax code. Even if some simplification could be achieved, as it was in 1986, interest group theory tells us that complexity would return over time.

SUMMARY

Modern pluralism praises the virtues of an interest group system in which public policy represents the equilibrium in the group struggle and the best approximation of the public interest. Yet it is clear that the interest group system puts broad segments of the American public at a disadvantage.

1. Tax reform to achieve fairness, simplicity, and economic growth is an elusive goal. The interest group system, designed to protect special privileges and treatments, especially in the tax code, frustrates efforts to achieve true tax reform.

2. Special interests can take advantage of the difficulties in defining fairness. Is fairness proportionality, with everyone paying the same percentage of income in taxes? Or is fairness progressivity, with the percentage of income paid in taxes increasing with increases in income?

3. Over half of the nation's total personal income escapes income taxation through exemptions, deductions, and special treatments.

4. The corporate income tax currently provides only 13 percent of total federal revenues. The individual income tax (43 percent) and Social Security payroll tax (35 percent) provide most of the federal government's revenue.

5. Supply-side economists are concerned about the impact of high marginal tax rates on economic behavior, including disincentives to work, save, and invest, and on inefficiencies created by tax avoidance activity. According to the Laffer curve, reducing high marginal tax rates increases government revenues by encouraging productivity.

6. The Tax Reform Act of 1986 was one of the most heavily lobbied pieces of legislation in the history of Congress. Powerful interests opposed significant tax reform. But President Ronald Reagan succeeded in getting Congress to reduce tax rates from 14 brackets, ranging from 11 to 50, to two brackets of 15 and 28 percent. Many exemptions, deductions, and special treatments were eliminated.

7. But the special interests never abandoned the battlefield. They won an important victory in 1990 when President George H. W. Bush agreed with the Democratic Congress to raise the top marginal rate on earned income to 31 percent, but to keep the tax on capital gains at 28 percent. President Clinton and Congress continued this preferential treatment for capital gains. Clinton's 1993 deficit reduction plan centered on major tax increases, including raising the top marginal income tax rate to 39.6 percent.

8. President George W. Bush inspired a Republican-controlled Congress to reduce taxes as an "economic stimulant." The top marginal rate was lowered from 39.6 to 35 percent, the marriage penalty was ended, and the child tax credit increased. Investors won a special low tax rate of 15 percent on dividends and capital gains. But the Bush tax cuts were scheduled to expire at the end of 2010.

9. In a grand compromise in late 2010, President Barack Obama and the Democratic and Republican leaders in Congress agreed to extend the Bush tax cuts for two years. Obama dropped his insistence on returning the top marginal rate back to 39.6 percent. Unemployment compensation was extended, and the estate tax was renewed, although at lower rates than in previous years. The Social Security FICA payroll tax on employees was reduced by 2 percent.

10. Major tax reform is regularly thwarted by special interest politics. Replacing the current federal income tax with a flat tax or a national sales tax is unlikely in the foreseeable future.

MySearchLab® EXERCISES

Apply what you learned in this chapter on MySearchLab (www.mysearchlab.com).

NOTES

1. Robert A. Dahl, *A Preface to Democratic Theory* (Chicago: University of Chicago Press, 1956), p. 124.

2. *Pollock v. Farmer's Loan*, 158 U.S. 601 (1895).

3. "The Underground Economy," National Center for Policy Analysis, 1998.

4. Joseph A. Pechman, *Federal Tax Policy*, 5th ed. (Washington, DC: Brookings Institution, 1987), Chap. 5.

5. For accounts of the politics surrounding the Tax Reform Act of 1986, see David A. Stockman, *The Triumph of Politics* (New York: Harper & Row, 1986), and Jeffrey H. Birnbaum and Alan S. Murray, *Showdown at Gucci Gulch* (New York: Random House, 1987).

6. See Dick Armey, *The Flat Tax* (New York: Fawcett, 1996).

7. Congressman Bill Archer, "Tear the Income Tax Out by Its Roots," *Madison Review* 1 (Spring 1996), pp. 17–21.

BIBLIOGRAPHY

ARMEY, DICK. *The Flat Tax*. New York: Ballantine Books, 1996.

BIRNBAUM, JEFFREY H., and ALAN S. MURRAY. *Showdown at Gucci Gulch*. New York: Random House, 1987.

GALE, WILLIAM G. *Rethinking Estate and Gift Taxation*. Washington, DC: Brookings Institution, 2001.

HALL, ROBERT E., and ALVIN RABUSHKA. *The Flat Tax*. Stanford, CA: Hoover Institution Press, 1985.

HOWARD, CHRISTOPHER. *The Hidden Welfare State: Tax Expenditures and Social Policies*. Princeton, NJ: Princeton University Press, 1997.

KENNEDY, DIANE. *Loopholes for the Rich*. New York: Warner Books, 2001.

ORSZAG, PETER R. *Taxing the Future*. Washington DC: Brookings Institution, 2006.

STEURLE, C. EUGENE. *Contemporary U.S. Tax Policy*. Washington, DC: Urban Institute Press, 2004.

STOCKMAN, DAVID A. *The Triumph of Politics*. New York: Harper & Row, 1986.

WEB SITES

TAX FOUNDATION. Information on taxes and tax burdens, including an explanation of "Tax Freedom Day." *www.taxfoundation.org*

NATIONAL TAXPAYERS UNION. Organization devoted to minimizing taxes, with information on tax policies and issues. *www.ntu.org*

NATIONAL CENTER FOR POLICY ANALYSIS. Conservative think tank, with information on tax and spending issues. *www.ncpa.org*

CITIZENS FOR TAX JUSTICE. Liberal organization favoring progressive income taxation and opposing tax cuts for the rich. *www.ctj.org*

AMERICANS FOR FAIR TAXATION. Organization opposed to federal income tax and supportive of national sales tax. *www.fairtax.org*

CITIZENS FOR AN ALTERNATIVE TAX SYSTEM. Organization devoted to eliminating Internal Revenue Service. *www.cats.org*

HOOVER INSTITUTION. Think tank devoted to issues of economic growth and free markets. *www.hoover.stanford.edu*

U.S. INTERNAL REVENUE SERVICE. Official site of IRS, with information on federal tax collections. *www.irs.gov*

U.S. DEPARTMENT OF TREASURY, OFFICE OF TAX POLICY. Presidential tax policy proposals; documents and studies of tax policy. *www.ustreas.gov/offices/tax-policy*

Illegal Immigration Challenges Border Enforcement A Border Patrol agent watches over a group of men caught attempting to cross illegally into the United States. Powerful industry groups that benefit from the availability of immigrant labor have led the fight in Washington to expand legal immigration and to weaken the enforcement of laws against illegal immigration. An estimated 10 to 15 million "undocumented" aliens currently live in the United States. (© Shaul Schwarz/Corbis)

12

International Trade and Immigration
Elite–Mass Conflict

The elite model portrays public policy as a reflection of the interests and values of elites. The model does not necessarily require that elites and masses be locked in conflict—conflict in which elites inevitably prevail at the expense of masses. Rather, the model envisions elites determining the direction of public policy, with the masses largely apathetic and poorly informed and/or heavily influenced by elite views. The model also acknowledges that elites may choose to pursue "public regarding" policies that benefit masses. Nonetheless, critics of the elite model often demand proof of elite–mass conflict over public policy and the subsequent shaping of policy to reflect elite preferences over mass well-being. Indeed, critics often demand proof that elites knowingly pursue policies that benefit themselves while hurting a majority of Americans. While this is not a fair test of elite theory, there is ample evidence that on occasion elites do pursue narrow, self-serving interests.

In describing immigration and international trade policy, we rely on the elite model. Arguably, U.S. policy, especially in international trade, serves the interests of the nation's largest multinational corporations at the expense of average American workers. We will argue that global trade policies have increased inequality in America. We will also argue that masses and elites have very different policy preferences regarding immigration.

THE GLOBAL ECONOMY

International trade—the buying and selling of goods and services between individuals and firms located in different countries—has expanded very rapidly in recent decades. Today, almost one-quarter of the *world's* total output is sold in a country other than the one in which it was produced. Today the United States exports about 12 percent of the value of its gross domestic product (GDP) and imports about 17 percent.[1] Exports and imports were only about 10 percent of GDP in 1980 (see Figure 12–1). (The recent "Great Recession" reduced both imports and exports in 2009). Global competition heavily impacts the American economy.

Currently, America's leading trading partners are Canada, Mexico, China, Japan, Germany, and Great Britain (see Figure 12–2). Note that some of these nations (Canada, Japan, Germany, for example) are advanced industrialized economies not unlike our own. But trade with developing countries (China and

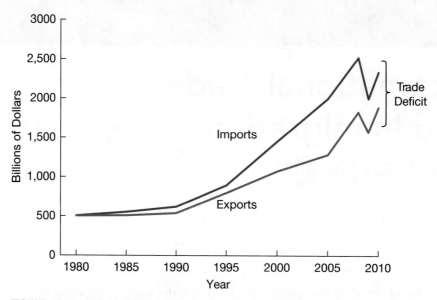

FIGURE 12–1 U.S. World Trade The "trade deficit"—the difference between what Americans import from abroad and what they export—has become wider over the years.
SOURCE: Bureau of Economic Analysis, *www.bea.gov*

Mexico, for example) is growing rapidly. And, as we shall see, it is trade with these nations that raises the most serious problems for America's labor force.

Years ago America's principal imports were oil and agricultural products not grown in the United States, for example, coffee. Today, however, our largest dollar-value imported products are automobiles, followed by office machinery, television sets, clothing, shoes, and toys. Our largest

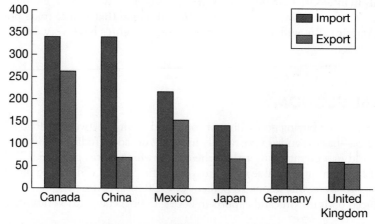

FIGURE 12–2 America's Leading Trading Partners Canada, China, and Mexico are our leading trading partners. The United States has a trade deficit with all of its major trading partners, especially China.
SOURCE: *Statistical Abstract of the United States, 2010*, p. 776.

dollar-value exports are aircraft, computers, power generators, and scientific instruments. The United States also exports wheat and corn, which can be harvested with high-tech machinery; it imports fruits, vegetables, and other agricultural products that require harvest by hand.

CHANGING ELITE PREFERENCES FOR WORLD TRADE

Historically, American business supported high tariffs, but as the U.S. economy matured and the costs of global transportation and communication declined, America's largest corporations began to look beyond the nation's borders.

Tariffs

Tariffs are simply taxes on foreign imports. Prior to World War II, U.S. tariffs on all imported goods averaged 30 to 50 percent in various decades. This suited U.S. manufacturers very well, eliminating most foreign competition from the U.S. market. U.S. firms enjoyed sheltered markets; they could raise prices to levels just below the price of imported goods with their high tariffs attached. Not only did this improve U.S. profit margins, but it also allowed U.S. firms that were less efficient than foreign producers to survive and prosper under the protection of tariffs. The pressure to cut wages and downsize work forces was less that it would be if U.S. firms had to face foreign corporations directly. American consumers, of course, paid higher prices than they otherwise would if foreign goods could enter the country without tariffs. But the U.S. steel, automobile, and electrical appliance industries grew powerful economically and politically.

Quotas

Trade quotas, in which foreign producers are prohibited from selling more than a specified number of units in the United States, also protect domestic manufacturers. To implement quotas, permits are granted by the U.S. State Department to favored firms in favored nations to sell specified amounts in the U.S. market. Note that quotas do not bring any revenue to the U.S. government as tariffs do; quotas allow the foreign firms exercising them to reap all of the benefits.

Protectionism

Today, supporters of open global markets refer to tariffs, quotas, and other barriers to free trade as "protectionism." Protectionism, they argue, is inefficient: it not only raises prices for American consumers, but it also directs American capital and labor away from their best uses into aging, inefficient industries. This reduces a nation's overall productivity and ultimately its standard of living. Moreover, they argue that protectionist policies initiated by the United States invite retaliatory actions by other nations. U.S. exporting industries may be adversely affected by the resulting trade wars.

Enter the Multinationals

After World War II, the American economy was the most powerful in the world. American manufacturing corporations had few international competitors in most industries. Given their dominant position in world trade, American corporations sought to lower trade barriers around the world. America's top exporting corporations dictated U.S. trade policy. The Council on Foreign Relations (see Chapter 3) and America's largest corporations lobbied Congress for reductions in U.S. tariffs in order to encourage other nations to reduce their own tariffs. The result was a rapid decline

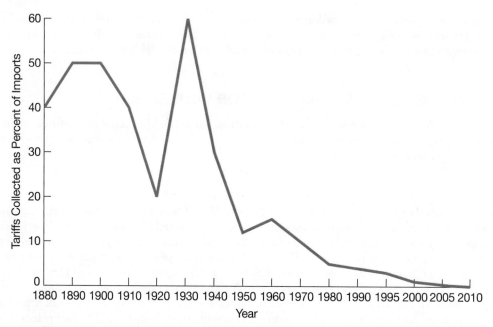

FIGURE 12–3   U.S. Tariff Policy over Time The U.S. followed a "protectionist" policy with high
tariff duties until the late 1940s when it gradually reduced tariffs, creating a virtually free market in
the U.S. for foreign goods.
SOURCE: U.S. Department of Commerce.

in average U.S. tariffs (see Figure 12–3). In effect, the United States became an open market.
Inasmuch as U.S. firms largely dominated their domestic markets in the 1950s and 1960s (steel,
automobiles, aircraft, drugs, electronics, appliances, agriculture, and so forth), they had little fear
of foreign competition. On the contrary, they expanded their own international sales, becoming
multinational corporations.

Prior to 1980 the United States incurred a *positive* trade balance, that is, exporting more goods
and services than it imported. But since 1980 the United States has incurred balance of trade
deficits every year. Nonetheless, today U.S. multinational corporations receive substantial revenues
from their exports. Moreover, most have manufacturing facilities as well as sales and distribution
staffs worldwide. They stand to gain much more from the globalization of trade than they might
lose from domestic competition from foreign firms.

ELITE GAINS FROM TRADE

The classic argument for free trade is based on the principle of "comparative advantage." If nations
devote more of their resources to the production of those goods that they produce most efficiently,
and trade for those goods that other nations produce more efficiently, then all trading nations benefit.

The "Comparative Advantage" Argument

Trade between two nations can improve efficiency even when one nation is much better
at producing aircraft and somewhat better at producing clothing than its trading partner.
Comparative advantage focuses on what each nation does *relatively* better than the other.

Trade shifts resources (investment capital, jobs, technology, raw materials, etc.) in each nation toward what each does best. (Imagine a lawyer who is also a faster typist than her secretary. Even though the lawyer is better than her secretary at both law and typing, it makes more sense for her to concentrate on law and leave the typing to her secretary. Their combined output of lawyering *and* typing will be greater than if each did some of the other's work.) Over time our nation will shift its resources to its aircraft industry and will import clothing from the other nation, and vice versa. Each nation will benefit more from trading than from trying to produce both airplanes and clothing.

Benefits from Trade

The efficiencies achieved by trading are said to directly benefit consumers by making available cheaper imported goods. Export industries also benefit when world markets are opened to their products. American exporters benefit directly from sales abroad, and they also benefit indirectly when foreign firms are allowed to sell in the American market. This is because sales of foreign goods in America provide foreigners with U.S. dollars which they can use to purchase the goods of America's exporting industries.

It is also argued that the pressure of competition from foreign-made goods in the American marketplace forces our domestic industries to become more efficient—cutting their costs and improving the quality of their own goods. Trade also quickens the flow of ideas and technology, allowing nations to learn from each other. Finally, trade expands the menu of goods and services available to trading countries. American consumers gain access to everything from exotic foods and foreign-language movies to Porsches, BMWs, and Jaguars.

The World Trade Organization

A multinational General Agreement on Tariffs and Trade (GATT) organization was created following World War II for the purpose of regulating international trade. Over the years GATT has been dominated by banking, business, and commercial interests in Western nations seeking multilateral tariff reductions and the relaxation of quotas. They have been especially successful over the years in opening the giant U.S. market to foreign goods. Indeed, average U.S. tariffs fell from more than 30 percent in 1947 to less than 1 percent today.

Through a series of GATT negotiations, known as rounds, a number of rules and regulations were developed that today run to some 30,000 pages. The first rounds dealt with tariffs and rules for trading in goods; later rounds dealt with services, including banking, insurance, telecommunications, hotels, and transportation, and finally with the protection of intellectual property—copyrights, patents, and trademarks.

The "Uruguay Round" in 1993 resulted in the creation of the World Trade Organization (WTO). The WTO was given power to adjudicate trading disputes among countries and monitor and enforce the trade agreements under GATT. Countries bring disputes to the WTO if they think their rights under the agreements are being infringed. Judgments by specially appointed independent experts are based on their interpretations of the agreements.

A "Doha Round" of WTO multinational trade negotiations (2001–2008) failed to produce a workable agreement on trade in agricultural and food products.

The WTO describes itself as a "democratic" organization that seeks to "improve the welfare of peoples of member countries" through trade liberalization. But the WTO's highest decision-making body is its Ministerial Conference which includes member nations' trade representatives.

Anti-globalization groups—a mix of labor, environmental, and human rights groups—have mounted demonstrations at various WTO meetings. They charge that the WTO has failed to enforce labor rights or correct labor abuses, that it has failed to protect the environment, and that it disadvantages poorer, less-developed countries.

International Monetary Fund and World Bank

The IMF's purpose is to facilitate international trade, allowing nations to borrow to stabilize their balance of trade payments. However, when economically weak nations incur chronic balance of trade deficits and perhaps face deferral or default on international debts, the IMF may condition its loans on changes in a nation's economic policies. It may require a reduction in a nation's government deficits by reduced public spending and/or higher taxes, or require a devaluation of its currency, making its exports cheaper and imports more expensive. It may also require the adoption of noninflationary monetary policies.

The World Bank makes long-term loans, mostly to developing nations, to assist in economic development. It works closely with the IMF in investigating the economic conditions of nations applying for loans and generally imposes IMF requirements on these nations as conditions for loans.

NAFTA

In 1993, the United States, Canada, and Mexico signed the North American Free Trade Agreement. Objections by labor unions in the United States (and 1992 and 1996 Reform Party presidential candidate Ross Perot) were drowned out in a torrent of support by the American corporate community, Democrats and Republicans in Congress, President Bill Clinton, and former President George H. W. Bush. NAFTA removed tariffs on virtually all products by all three nations over a period of 10 to 15 years. It also allowed banking, insurance, and other financial services to cross these borders (see Table 12–1). NAFTA has succeeded in increasing trade between all three nations. The jobs lost by the United States to Mexico have been in lower-paying industries, while the jobs gained have been in higher-paying industries.

Free Trade Area of the Americas

The United States and the nations of North, Central, and South America attempted to negotiate a free trade area throughout the Western Hemisphere. The Free Trade Area of the Americas (FTAA) was to resemble NAFTA. Barriers to trade and investment were to be progressively eliminated.

FTAA was supposed to be completed by 2005. But the agreement met with serious opposition with the election of an anti-American government in Venezuela, as well as opposition from other South American countries. Opponents argue that FTAA would drive down wages, erode labor union protections, destroy the environment, and increase poverty and inequality. These conditions would result from multinational corporations choosing to move their operations to countries with the lowest wages, fewest regulations, weakest unions, and lowest environmental standards—"a race to the bottom."

As FTAA negotiations stalled, the United States turned its attention to the creation of a Central America Free Trade Agreement (CAFTA). CAFTA was completed in 2008 and includes Costa Rica, the Dominican Republic, El Salvador, Guatemala, Honduras, and Nicaragua.

Anti-Dumping Policy

Dumping—the sale of foreign goods in the U.S. market at prices below those charged in the producing nation—presents a special trade problem. Dumping is often undertaken by foreign firms to introduce new products in the U.S. market; once Americans have accepted the product, prices

TABLE 12–1 Major Provisions of NAFTA NAFTA is the model of U.S.-backed free trade agreements.

Market Access

1. Within fifteen years after its implementation in 1994, all tariffs were to be eliminated on North American products traded among Canada, Mexico, and the United States.

2. Within five years after its implementation, 65 percent of all U.S. exports of industrial goods to Mexico were to enter tariff-free.

3. Mexico, immediately upon implementation of the treaty, eliminated tariffs on nearly 50 percent of all industrial goods imported from the United States.

4. Government procurement was to be opened up over ten years, with firms of the three countries able to bid on government contracts.

5. Tariffs were to be removed on car imports over a period of ten years. Mexico's import quota on cars was also to be lifted during the same period.

6. Most tariffs between the United States and Mexico on agricultural products were eliminated immediately after implementation of the agreement in 1994.

Investment

1. NAFTA gives U.S. companies the right to establish firms in Mexico and Canada or acquire existing firms.

2. Investors have the right to repatriate profits and capital; the right to fair compensation in the event of expropriation; and the right to international arbitration in disputes between investors and government that involve monetary damage.

3. NAFTA broadens investments to cover such areas as banking, real estate, legal services, consulting, publishing, and tourism.

4. Certain types of investments are restricted. Mexico prohibits foreign investment in petroleum and railroads; Canada prohibits investment in its cultural media; and the United States excludes investments in aviation transport, maritime, and telecommunications.

Intellectual Property Rights

1. NAFTA requires each country to provide for the enforcement of the rights of authors, artists, and inventors against infringement and piracy.

2. It ensures protection for North American producers of computer programs, sound recordings, motion pictures, encrypted satellite signals, and other creations.

3. It locks in the availability of patent protection for most technologies in Mexico, allowing U.S. firms to patent a broad range of inventions in Mexico.

SOURCE: Robert Langran and Martin Schnitzer, *Government, Business, and the American Economy* (Upper Saddle River, NJ: Prentice Hall, 2001), p. 285. Reprinted by permission of the author.

go up. This pattern has been regularly followed by Japanese automobile manufacturers. Dumping is also undertaken in order to destroy U.S. firms by underselling their products and forcing them out of business. Once foreign producers have driven out U.S. manufacturers, they raise their own prices. Dumping provides only temporary advantages to American consumers.

Dumping is officially illegal. The Trade Agreements Act of 1979 provides that special anti-dumping tariffs may be imposed when it is proven that a product is being sold in the United States at a price lower than that in the domestic market of a foreign producing nation. But it is a difficult and lengthy process for U.S. domestic firms to bring formal complaints to the U.S. government and obtain relief.

Trade Deficits

For many years the United States has imported a higher dollar value of goods than it has exported. The difference is referred to as a trade deficit (the area in Figure 12–1 between the exports and imports lines). The trade deficit is made up by the transfer of American dollars, government bonds, corporate securities, and so on, to foreign firms. U.S. banks as well as the U.S. Treasury actually benefit from the deficit because it means that foreigners are accepting U.S. paper—currency, bonds, and securities—in exchange for their products. This makes it easier for the U.S. government to fund its own huge debt—selling bonds to foreign investors. U.S. interest payments on this part of the national debt flow out of the country. China is the largest foreign holder of U.S. debt.

Retreat from Free Trade?

The Obama Administration voices its general support for free trade and open markets. Yet its support for trade agreements appears to be contingent upon the inclusion of worker protections and environmental safeguards in future trade agreements with foreign countries. Obama advisors recommend a "major review of trade policies" to ensure that trade agreements "include enforceable labor and environmental standards…and a new focus on ensuring that trade rules help combat climate change and do not impede the essential global energy transformation."[2] They also warn against unfair trade practices and currency manipulation, especially with regard to China. These concerns promise to complicate future trade negotiations with other countries.

"Fast Track" Authority

Like his predecessors, President Obama seeks "fast track" authority from Congress in negotiating trade agreements—a commitment from Congress to vote on negotiated trade agreements without amendments. It is argued that U.S. trade negotiators will not be taken seriously by other nations at the bargaining table unless Congress agrees to "fast track" agreements.

MASS LOSSES FROM TRADE

The global economy has produced growth and profit for America's largest corporations and amply rewarded the nation's highest skilled workers. Indeed, global trade has *raised aggregate income* for the nation. But at the same time, it has *worsened inequality* in America. Elite gains have been accompanied by mass losses.

Increased trade, especially with less developed economies such as Mexico, China, and India, with their huge numbers of low-wage workers, creates competition for American workers. It is difficult to raise the wage levels of American jobs, especially in labor intensive industries, in the face of such competition. American corporations may initially respond by increasing their investment in capital and technology, making American workers more productive and hence capable of maintaining their high wages. But over time developing nations are acquiring more capital and technology themselves. And U.S. corporations can move their manufacturing plants to low-wage countries, especially to northern Mexico where the transportation costs of moving finished products back to the U.S. market are minimal.

Worsening Inequality

U.S. export industries have thrived on international trade expansion, adding jobs to the American economy, and raising the incomes of their executives and their most highly skilled workers. But the combination of effects of international trade on the American economy—*lower* wages for less skilled workers and *higher* wages for executives and highly skilled workers—worsens inequality in the nation. Inequality can worsen even though the aggregate income of the nation rises.

Inequality in America is worsening. The percentage of the nation's total family income received by the poorest quintile (the lowest 20 percent of income earners) declined from 4.3 percent to 3.4 percent between 1975 and 2010 (see Table 12–2). Meanwhile the percentage of total family income of the highest income earners increased from 43.6 percent of total income to 50.3 percent. And the top 5 percent of income earners increased their share of total income from 16.5 to 21.7 percent in that same period.

Another view of worsening inequality in America is provided in Figure 12–4. The figure shows the percentage of losses and gains from 1975 to 2010 of households in each income class (fifths). The lowest income households lost 21 percent of their share of income over these years, while the highest income households gained 15 percent. The top 5 percent of households gained over 32 percent.

Policy Options

Both Democratic and Republican presidents over the past half-century have supported expanded world trade. The U.S. market is the largest in the world and the most open to foreign-made goods. Our policy has been to maintain an open American market while encouraging other nations to do the same. Indeed, the United States has led international efforts to liberalize world trade and investment and to eliminate foreign market barriers to American exports. The efforts include support for the WTO multinational trade agreement; NAFTA, the Canada, Mexico, and U.S. agreement; and a number of bilateral agreements with Japan and other Asian trading partners.

TABLE 12–2   Income Inequality in America Shares of Total Income Received by Each Fifth of Households and Top Five Percent. The highest one-fifth of income earners receive over 50 percent of aggregate household income, while the bottom one-fifth receive only 3.4 percent. And inequality has worsened over time.

	Percent Distribution & Aggregate Income				
	Lowest 5th	**Second 5th**	**Third 5th**	**Fourth 5th**	**Highest 5th**
1975	4.3	10.4	17.0	24.7	43.6
1980	4.2	10.2	16.8	24.7	44.1
1985	3.9	9.8	16.2	24.4	45.6
1990	3.8	9.6	15.9	24.0	46.6
1995	3.7	9.1	15.2	23.3	48.7
2000	3.6	8.9	14.3	23.0	49.8
2005	3.4	8.6	14.6	23.0	50.4
2010	3.4	8.6	14.6	23.2	50.3

SOURCE: www.census.gov/hhes/income/data/historical/inequality

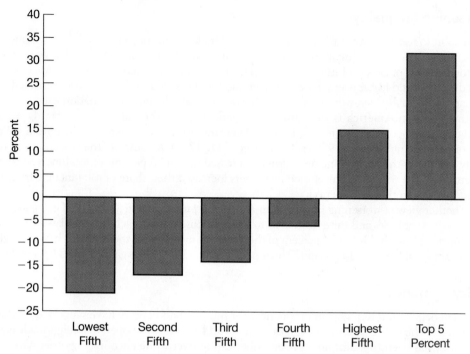

FIGURE 12–4 Worsening Inequality Change in Percent Distribution of Family Income by Quintile, 1975–2010. Inequality in income has risen in the U.S.; the highest income groups have increased their share of total family income, while lower income groups lost shares.
SOURCE: www.census.gov/hhes/income/data/historical/inequality

The elite response to wage inequality is to stress the need for American workers to improve their productivity through better education and increased training. The "solution" found in the *Economic Report of the President* reads as follows:

> Ultimately, the only lasting solution to the increase in wage inequality that results from increased trade is the same as that for wage inequality arising from any other source: better education and increased training, to allow low-income workers to take advantage of the technological changes that raise productivity.[3]

ELITE–MASS DIFFERENCES OVER IMMIGRATION

The United States accepts more immigrants than all other nations of the world combined. Officially about 1 million legal immigrants come to the United States each year. These are people who are granted permanent residence or "green cards." Unofficially, perhaps as many as 4 million legal and illegal immigrants cross the nation's borders each year.[4] Some cross the Mexican or Canadian borders surreptitiously or with false documentation. Others simply overstay their tourist or student visas. Immigration and Customs Enforcement (ICE) acknowledges about 33 million admissions to the United States each year. Most of these admissions are for tourists, business-people, and students. The government does *not* track visitors, nor does it systematically proceed against individuals who overstay their visas. Estimates of the number of illegal immigrants living in the United States range up to 15 million.

Most immigrants come to the United States for economic opportunity. Currently, the vast majority come from the less developed nations of Asia and Latin America (see Figure 12–5). Most personify the traits we typically think of as American: ambition, perseverance, initiative, and a willingness to work hard. As immigrants have always done, they frequently take dirty, low-paying, thankless jobs that other Americans shun. When they open their own businesses, they often do so in blighted, crime-ridden neighborhoods long since abandoned by other entrepreneurs.

The Immigration Surge

The nation's foreign-born or immigrant population (legal and illegal) reached a record high of nearly 38 million people in 2010 (see Figure 12–6). Immigrants now account for over 12 percent of the population. Earlier in the twentieth century, at the peak of the last great surge in immigration, there were fewer immigrants, although they accounted for almost 15 percent of the population.

The recession beginning in 2008 appears to have reduced the flow of immigration slightly. A weak job market discourages immigration. It has also increased the numbers of immigrants returning to their home countries.

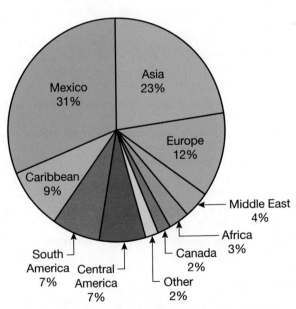

FIGURE 12–5 Sources of Immigration Currently most immigrants are coming to the United States from Mexico and other Latin American countries as well as from Asia. SOURCE: Data from the Center for Immigration Studies from the U.S. Bureau of the Census, *Current Population Survey*, 2007.

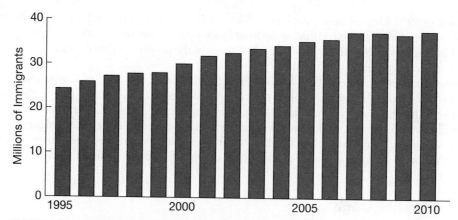

FIGURE 12-6 Immigrants Living in the United States Immigration has surged since 2000. Currently there are nearly 38 million immigrants living in the United States.
SOURCE: Center for Immigration Studies, *www.cis.org*

Cultural Conflict

The politics of immigration center on both cultural and economic issues. Elites, notably the nation's business and corporate leaders, tend to view immigration in economic terms, principally as an increase in the supply of low-wage workers in the United States. Most middle-class Americans view immigration in cultural terms, principally its impact on the ethnic composition of their communities.

While most Americans are themselves the descendants of immigrants (Native Americans constitute about 1 percent of the population), most believe that today's immigrants are different from earlier waves. Population projections based on current immigration and fertility (birth) rates suggest that the ethnic character of the nation will shift dramatically over time (see Figure 12–7).

America has always been an ethnically pluralist society, but all were expected to adopt American political culture—including individual liberty, economic freedom, political equality, and equality of opportunity—and to learn American history and traditions, as well as the English language. The nation's motto is "E Pluribus Unum" (from many, one), but opponents of large-scale immigration fear that it currently represents a threat to cultural and political unity.[5] There were always Italian, Irish, Polish, Chinese, and other ethnic neighborhoods in big cities. But the children of immigrants, if not immigrants themselves, quickly became "Americanized." In contrast, today policymakers are divided over whether to protect and preserve language and cultural differences, for example through bilingual education, bilingual language ballots, and "language minority" voting districts (all currently required by amendments and interpretations of the Civil Rights Act of 1964 and the Voting Rights Act of 1965).

Elite Support of Immigration

Powerful industry groups that benefit from the availability of legal and illegal immigrants have led the fight in Washington to keep America's doors open. They have fought not only to expand legal immigration but also to weaken enforcement of laws against illegal immigration.

Current U.S. immigration policy—the admission of more than 1 million *legal* immigrants per year and weak enforcement of laws against *illegal* immigration—is largely driven by industry

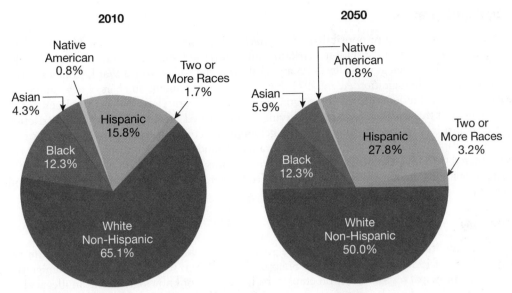

FIGURE 12–7   Projected Ethnic Changes in the United States over Time As a result of both immigration and differences in birthrates, the ethnic composition of the United States will change dramatically by 2050.
SOURCE: U.S. Census Bureau, 2011.

groups seeking to lower their labor costs. Agriculture, construction, restaurants, clothing, and hospitals, for example, all lobby heavily in Washington to weaken immigration laws and their enforcement. Large agribusinesses benefit from a heavy flow of unskilled immigrants who harvest their crops at very low wages. Clothing, textile, and shoe companies that have not already moved their manufacturing overseas are anxious to hire low-paid immigrants for their assembly lines. Even high-tech companies have found that they can recruit skilled computer analysts and data processors from English-speaking developing nations (India, for example) for wages well below those paid to American citizens with similar skills. These business interests frequently operate behind the scenes in Washington, allowing pro-immigration ethnic and religious groups to capture media attention. And indeed, large numbers of Americans identify with the aspirations of people striving to come to the United States, whether legally or illegally. Many Americans still have family and relatives living abroad who may wish to immigrate. Hispanic groups have been especially concerned about immigration enforcement efforts that may lead to discrimination against all Hispanic Americans. Foreign governments, especially Mexico, have also protested U.S. enforcement policies.

NATIONAL IMMIGRATION POLICY

America is a nation of immigrants, from the first "boat people," the Pilgrims, to the later Cuban "balseros" (rafters). Americans are proud of their immigrant heritage and the freedom and opportunity the nation has extended to generations of "huddled masses yearning to be free"—the words emblazoned upon the Statue of Liberty in New York's harbor. Today about 38 million people, or over 12 percent, of the U.S. population is foreign born.

Legal Immigration

Immigration policy is a responsibility of the national government. It was not until 1882 that Congress passed the first legislation restricting entry into the United States of persons alleged to be "undesirable" as well as virtually all Asians. Following the end of World War I, Congress passed a comprehensive Immigration Act of 1921 that established maximum numbers of new immigrants each year and set a quota for each foreign country at 3 percent (later reduced to 2 percent) of the number of that nation's foreign born living in the United States in 1890. These restrictions reflected anti-immigration feelings that were generally directed at the large wave of southern and eastern European, Catholic, and Jewish immigrants (Poland, Russia, Hungary, Italy, Greece) that had entered the United States prior to World War I. It was not until the Immigration Act of 1965 that national-origin quotas were abolished, replaced by preference categories for relatives and family members and professional and skilled persons.

Immigration "Reform"

Immigration "reform" was the announced goal of Congress in the Immigration Reform and Control Act of 1986, also known as the Simpson-Mazzoli Act. It sought to control immigration by placing principal responsibility on employers; it set fines for knowingly hiring an illegal alien. However, it allowed employers to accept many different forms of easily forged documentation and subjected them to penalties for discriminating against legal foreign-born residents. To win political support, the act granted *amnesty* to illegal aliens who had lived in the United States since 1982. Predictably, the act failed to reduce the flow of either legal or illegal immigrants.

Current Immigration Policy

Today, roughly 1 million people per year are admitted *legally* to the United States as "lawful permanent residents" (persons who have relatives who are U.S. citizens or lawful permanent residents, or who have needed job skills); or as "refugees," or "asylees" (persons with "a well-founded fear of persecution" in their country of origin). In addition, more than 33 million people are awarded visas each year to enter the United States for study, pleasure, or business. Federal law recognizes the following categories of noncitizens admitted into the United States:

- *Legal immigrants* (also "lawful permanent residents" or "permanent resident aliens"). These immigrants are admitted to the United States under a ceiling of 675,000 per year, with some admitted on the basis of job skills but most coming as family members of persons legally residing in the United States. Legal immigrants may work in the United States and apply for citizenship after five years of continuous residence.

- *Refugees and asylees.* These are persons admitted to the United States because of "a well-founded fear of persecution because of race, religion, nationality, political opinion, or membership in a social group." (Refugees are persons not yet in the United States; asylees are persons who have already arrived and apply for refugee protection.) They may work in the United States and are eligible for all federal assistance programs.

- *Parolees* (or persons enjoying "temporary protected status"). These are persons admitted to the United States for humanitarian or medical reasons or whose countries are faced with natural or man-made disasters.

- *Legalized aliens* (also called "amnesty aliens"). These formerly illegal aliens were given legal status (amnesty) under the Immigration Reform and Control Act of 1986. To qualify, they must show some evidence of having resided in the United States since 1982. They may work in the United States and are eligible for all federal assistance programs after five years.

- *Nonimmigrants* (also "nonresident legal aliens"). Over 33 million people are awarded visas to enter the United States for pleasure and business. Time limits are placed on these visas, usually by stamping a passport. Additionally, students, temporary workers and trainees, transient aliens, and foreign officials are eligible for temporary visas.

Illegal Immigration

The United States is a free and prosperous society with more than 5,000 miles of borders (2,000 with Mexico) and hundreds of international air- and seaports. In theory, a sovereign nation should be able to maintain secure borders, but in practice the United States has been unwilling and unable to do so. Estimates of illegal immigration vary wildly, from the official U.S. government estimate of 400,000 per year (about 40 percent of the legal immigration), to unofficial estimates ranging up to 4 million per year. The government estimates that about 4 million illegal immigrants currently reside in the United States; unofficial estimates range up to 15 million or more. Many illegal immigrants slip across U.S. borders or enter ports with false documentation, while many more overstay tourist or student visas.

As a free society, the United States is not prepared to undertake massive roundups and summary deportations of millions of illegal residents. The Fifth and Fourteenth Amendments to the U.S. Constitution require that every *person* (not just *citizen*) be afforded "due process of law." Immigration and Customs Enforcement (ICE) may turn back persons at the border or even hold them in detention camps. The Coast Guard may intercept boats at sea and return persons to their country of origin.[6] Aliens have no constitutional right to come to the United States. However, *once in the United States, whether legally or illegally, every person is entitled to due process of law and equal protection of the laws.* Once immigrants set foot on U.S. soil, they are entitled to a fair hearing prior to any government attempt to deport them. Aliens are entitled to apply for asylum and present evidence at a hearing of their "well-founded fear of persecution" if returned to their country. Localized experiments in border enforcement have indicated that illegal immigration can be reduced by half or more with significant increases in Border Patrol personnel and technology.

The Fence

The United States has attempted to stem the tide of illegal immigration by building a 700-mile security fence along portions of its border with Mexico. The U.S.–Mexican border extends approximately 2,000 miles, so a 700-mile fence leaves open most of the border area. The fence, however, is directed at sectors of frequent crossing.

Immigration and Federalism

Although the federal government has power over immigration policy, its decisions have very significant effects on states and communities—on their governmental budgets, on the use of their public services, and even on their social character. Immigration is by no means uniform across the states. On the contrary, legal and illegal immigration are concentrated in a relatively few states. California, Hawaii, New York, Florida, and Texas have the highest proportions of legal immigrants among their populations. And these states, together with Arizona, New Mexico, Colorado, Illinois, and New Jersey, probably have the highest numbers of illegal immigrants as well. Moreover, the populations of particular cities—such as Los Angeles, Miami, El Paso, and San Antonio—may be one-third to one-half foreign born.

The U.S. Supreme Court has mandated that state and local governments may not exclude either legal or *illegal* immigrants from public education, and—perhaps by implication—from any other benefits or services available to citizens.[7] Thus, federal immigration policy heavily impacts state and local budgets, especially in states with disproportionate numbers of immigrants. (Although family "sponsors" may have pledged support of immigrants, and immigrants who become a "public charge" may be deported legally, these provisions of the law are almost never enforced.) Indeed, some states have tried unsuccessfully to sue the federal government to recover the costs of providing services to immigrants.

The Arizona Immigration Law

The failure of the federal government to enforce existing federal immigration laws inspired Arizona to pass its own illegal immigration law in 2010. It makes it a *state* crime to be in the country illegally.

The key provision of the Arizona law states: "For any lawful contact made by a law enforcement officer . . . where reasonable suspicion exists that a person is an alien who is unlawfully present in the United States, a reasonable attempt shall be made when practicable to determine the immigration status of the person . . .".[8] A "lawful contact" presumably means that a police officer has stopped an individual for violating another law, most likely a traffic stop. "Reasonable suspicion" may involve a combination of circumstances, but the law specifically prohibits officers from using race or ethnicity as factors in determining reasonable suspicion. The law also states that if a person produces a state drivers' license or other state-issued identification, he or she is presumed to be here legally. Once identified as illegal immigrants, persons can be taken into custody, prosecuted for violating Arizona law, or turned over to federal Immigration and Customs Enforcement (ICE) for deportation.

The U.S. Justice Department filed suit against the Arizona law arguing that it violates the Supremacy Clause of the Constitution: "A state may not establish its own immigration policy or enforce state laws in a manner that interferes with federal immigration laws. The Constitution and federal immigration laws do not permit the development of a patchwork of state and local immigration policy throughout the country."[9] Although the Arizona law was written to ensure it was not in conflict with federal laws, federal courts must answer the question, "Do federal laws preempt state laws on immigration?"

Another constitutional question is whether the Arizona law poses a threat to the Fourteenth Amendment's Equal Protection Clause by encouraging racial profiling in its enforcement. Federal courts may find that the Arizona law is an invitation to harassment and discrimination against Hispanics. Despite the wording of the law prohibiting racial profiling, racial discrimination may be found to be inherent in its enforcement.

Immigration Reform

Conflict in Washington over immigration policy is intense. To date, conflicting interests have prevented any effective action to halt illegal immigration, or to determine the status of millions of illegal immigrants already living in the United States, or to decide how many immigrants should be admitted each year and what the criteria for their admission should be. Among the diverse interests with a stake in immigration policy are employers seeking to keep immigration as open as possible, millions of illegal immigrants seeking a legal path to citizenship, and citizens seeking border security and opposed to "amnesty" for illegal aliens.

Comprehensive Reform

"Comprehensive" immigration reform implies compromises among these interests. In 2007, Congress considered a comprehensive 789-page bill, cosponsored by Senators Edward M. Kennedy and John McCain, that included the following major provisions: strengthening border enforcement, including funding of 700 miles of fencing; granting legal status to millions of undocumented immigrants currently living in the country; providing a path to citizenship that included criminal background checks, paying fines and fees, and acquiring English proficiency; establishing a temporary (two-year) guest worker program; shifting the criteria for legal immigration from family-based preferences to a greater emphasis on skills and education. But opponents of one or another of these various provisions, both Democrats and Republicans, united to defeat the bill in the U.S. Senate.

Border Enforcement

It is argued that *no* program of immigration reform can be successful without first securing America's borders. Yet doing so involves some controversial measures. The U.S. Border Patrol must be increased in numbers and given improved technology. The current policy of "catch and release"—releasing illegal immigrants into the general population to await a court hearing—must be replaced by expanding the capacity to detain them until their hearings are held and expediting their judicial proceedings—a policy of "catch and return." Illegal immigrants convicted of a crime must be deported immediately after serving their prison sentences.

Workplace Enforcement

In addition to border enforcement efforts, additional measures could be put into place to deter businesses from hiring illegal immigrants. Congress has authorized the development of E-Verify—an Internet system that allows employers to quickly determine the eligibility of their employees to work in the United States. But participation in E-Verify is currently voluntary for most businesses. Reform efforts envision perfecting the system and making participation mandatory for all employers.

Dream Act

In 2010 Congress failed to pass a popular DREAM Act (an acronym for Development Relief and Education for Alien Minors) that would have provided permanent residency to children who arrived in the United States illegally. Beneficiaries of the Act must have arrived in the United States before age 16, resided here for five consecutive years, graduated from a U.S. high school or received a GED, graduated from a two-year community college or completed two years toward a four-year degree, or served two years in the U.S. military. The DREAM Act was not part of any comprehensive reform legislation; opponents argued that it provided a form of amnesty that would only encourage additional illegal immigration.

A Path to Citizenship

Immigration reform must deal with the millions of undocumented immigrants already in the country. And it must recognize the fact that immigrant labor plays an important role in our economy. Some legal channel must be devised for persons currently living illegally in the United States to win permanent residency and perhaps even the opportunity for citizenship after living and working in the country for a specified number of years. (The word *amnesty* is now politically unacceptable; some other term must be used to describe how current illegals can gain legitimate status.) And some sort of highly controlled temporary worker program must be devised to provide the labor that the nation seems to need. But again, these reforms cannot be put in place until the nation's borders are controlled.

Mass Opinion

Americans are more concerned that steps be taken to halt the flow of immigrants slipping in at the border than they are about the government developing a plan for dealing with the illegal immigrants already living here. Americans also believe that illegal immigration can be reduced by instituting tough penalties for businesses that hire illegal immigrants. But Americans also believe that undocumented immigrants currently living here should be given a path to citizenship (63 percent) as opposed to the more drastic action of deporting them (18 percent). Among those who support a path to citizenship, the most common requirements mentioned are: have a job (89 percent), learn to speak English (84 percent), pass a health screening test (83 percent), pay all taxes owed on past income earned in the United States (81 percent), and have lived in the United States for at least five years (67 percent).[10]

SUMMARY

The elite model portrays public policy as the preferences of elites. While the model does not assert that these preferences necessarily conflict with the welfare of the masses, it does imply that the elite preferences will prevail in public policy even when opposed by the masses in a democratic society.

1. The principal beneficiaries of the emergence of a global economy and the expansion of U.S. trade have been America's large multinational corporations.

2. Historically, American business supported high tariffs in order to disadvantage foreign competition in the U.S. market. But after World War II, American industry gained worldwide dominance and changed their policy preference. The United States led the worldwide effort to establish a global marketplace.

3. The principal instruments used to open world markets to U.S. goods were the General Agreement on Tariffs and Trade (GATT) later becoming the World Trade Organization (WTO), the International Monetary Fund (IMF), and the World Bank.

4. In 1993, elite support for the North American Free Trade Agreement (NAFTA) envisioning the removal of tariffs on virtually all goods traded between the United States, Canada, and Mexico, prevailed over the opposition of American labor unions.

5. The benefits of international trade are unevenly distributed between elites and masses in America. Average real inflation adjusted hourly wages of American workers have stagnated since 1970.

6. Global trade appears to have worsened inequality in the United States in recent years. Today, greater differences exist between well-educated and less-educated workers and high-skilled and low-skilled workers than 20 years ago. America's less-educated, low-skilled workers must now compete against low-wage workers in less developed countries around the world.

7. The United States accepts more immigrants than all other nations of the world combined. More than 1 million legal immigrants enter the United States each year, as well as 3 to 4 million illegal immigrants.

8. Immigration today is higher than at any other period in United States history. Most immigration today is from the less developed nations of Asia and Central and South America.

9. Powerful industry groups that benefit from the availability of low-wage workers lobby in Washington to maintain high levels of legal immigration and weaken efforts to reduce illegal immigration.

10. Immigration impacts the states differently, with California, Hawaii, New York, Florida, and Texas reporting the largest numbers of legal immigrants.

MySearchLab® EXERCISES

Apply what you learned in this chapter on MySearchLab (www.mysearchlab.com).

NOTES

1. *Statistical Abstract of the United States, 2010,* p. 427, p. 434, 805.
2. Mark Green and Michelle Jolin, eds. *Change for America* (New York: Basic Books, 2009), p. 148.
3. *Economic Report of the President 1995,* p. 232.
4. Center for Immigration Studies, 2008, *www.cis.org*
5. See Peter Brimelow, *Alien Nation* (New York: Random House, 1995); Samuel P. Huntington, *Who Are We? The Challenge to America's*
   National Identity (NewYork: Simon & Schuster, 2004).
6. *Sale v. Haitian Centers Council,* 125 L. Ed. 2d 128 (1993).
7. *Plyler v. Doe,* 457 U.S. 202 (1982).
8. Arizona SB 1070.
9. *United States v. State of Arizona* Federal District Court Brief, July 28, 2010.
10. Gallup opinion poll, April 7–9, 2006, *www.pollingreport.com*

BIBLIOGRAPHY

ALBA, RICHARD, and VICTOR NEE. *Remaking the American Mainstream: Assimilation and Contemporary Immigration.* Cambridge, MA: Harvard University Press, 2003.

BURTLESS, GARY. *Globaphobia: Confronting Fears About Open Trade.* Washington, DC: Brookings Institution, 1998.

DREZNER, DANIEL W. *U.S. Trade Policy.* New York: Council on Foreign Relations Press, 2005.

GILPIN, ROBERT, and JEAN M. GILPIN. *Global Political Economy.* Princeton, NJ: Princeton University Press, 2001.

HUNTINGTON, SAMUEL P. *Who Are We? The Challenges to America's National Identity.* New York: Simon & Schuster, 2004.

HUSTED, STEVEN, and MICHAEL MELVIN. *International Economics,* 8th ed. New York: Pearson, 2010.

STIGLITZ, JOSEPH E. *Globalization and Its Discontents.* New York: W. W. Norton, 2002.

TONELSON, ALAN. *The Race to the Bottom: Why a Worldwide Worker Surplus and Uncontrolled Free Trade Are Sinking American Living Standards.* New York: Westview Press, 2002.

WEB SITES

U.S. DEPARTMENT OF STATE. Official Web site of the State Department, with policies, press releases, speeches, news, etc. *www.state.gov*

U.S. TRADE AND DEVELOPMENT AGENCY. Official Web site of the U.S. agency responsible for promoting international trade, with policies, press releases, etc. *www.tda.gov*

UNITED NATIONS. Official Web site of the U.N., with links to all U.N. agencies, member nations, etc. *www.un.org*

WORLD TRADE ORGANIZATION. Official Web site of the WTO, with information on membership, trade agreements, and statistics on trade. *www.wto.org*

WORLD BANK. Official Web site of the World Bank, with information on policies, loans to various nations, etc. *www.worldbank.org*

INTERNATIONAL MONETARY FUND. The official Web site of the IMF, with information on currency transactions, national deficits, etc. *www.imf.org*

ORGANIZATION FOR ECONOMIC COOPERATION DEVELOPMENT. Official Web site of the OECD, with statistics on national GDP, imports and exports, etc. *www.oecdwash.org*

CENTER FOR IMMIGRATION STUDIES. Organization advocating control of U.S. borders, with policy studies, data on immigration, etc. *www.cis.org*

COUNCIL ON FOREIGN RELATIONS. Leading think tank supporting expansion of world trade. *www.foreignrelations.org*

OFFICE OF THE UNITED STATES TRADE REPRESENTATIVE. List of U.S trade agreements; current issues in trade policy. *www.ustr.gov*

U.S. CITIZENSHIP AND IMMIGRATION SERVICES (ICE). Formerly the Immigration and Naturalization Service (INS); maintains information on obtaining visas to the U.S., applying for asylum and refugee status, and applying for naturalization. *www.uscis.gov*

HIGH ANXIETY: Japan's Fukushima Daiichi reactor shows evidence of serious damage on March 15, 2011 Radioactive leakage following a devastating earthquake and tsunami inspired new fears about nuclear power. A less dangerous incident at Three Mile Island, Pennsylvania in 1979 brought nuclear plant construction in the United States to a halt. (© Tepco/ZUMA Press/Corbis)

13

Energy and the Environment
Externalities and Interests

PUBLIC CHOICE AND THE ENVIRONMENT

All human activity produces waste. As soon as we come to understand that we cannot outlaw pollution and come to see pollution as a cost of human activity, we can begin to devise creative environmental policies.

Environmental Externalities

Public choice theory views pollution as a "problem" when it is not a cost to its producer—that is, when producers can ignore the costs of their pollution and shift them onto others or society in general. An "externality" occurs when one individual, firm, or government undertakes an activity that imposes unwanted costs on others. A manufacturing firm or local government that discharges waste into a river shifts its own costs to individuals, firms, or local governments downstream, who must forgo using the river for recreation and water supply or else undertake the costs of cleaning it up themselves. A coal-burning electricity-generating plant that discharges waste into the air shifts its costs to others, who must endure irritating smog. By shifting these costs to others, polluting firms lower their production costs, which allows them to lower their prices to customers and/or increase their own profits. Polluting governments have lower costs of disposing their community's waste, which allows them to lower taxes for their own citizens. As long as these costs of production can be shifted to others, polluting individuals, firms, and governments have no incentive to minimize waste or develop alternative techniques of production.

Costs of Regulation

Environmental policies are costly. These costs are often ignored when environmental regulations are considered. Direct spending by business and government for pollution abatement and control has grown rapidly over recent years. Yet governments themselves—federal, state, and local governments combined—pay less than one-quarter of the environmental bill. Businesses and consumers pay over three-quarters of the environmental bill. Governments can shift the costs of their policies onto private individuals and firms by enacting *regulations* requiring pollution control. A government's own budget is unaffected by these regulations, but the costs are paid by society.

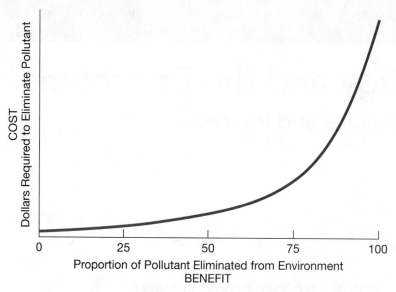

FIGURE 13–1   Cost Benefit Ratio in Environmental Protection Costs rise exponentially as society tries to eliminate the last measure of pollution.

Benefits in Relation to Costs

Public choice theory requires that environmental policies be evaluated in terms of their net benefits to society; that is, the costs of environmental policies should not exceed their benefits to society. It is much less costly to reduce the first 50 to 75 percent of any environmental pollutant or hazard than to eliminate all (100 percent) of it (see Figure 13–1). As any pollutant or hazard is reduced, the cost of further reductions rises, and the net benefits to society of additional reductions decline. As the limit of zero pollution or zero environmental risk is approached, additional benefits are minuscule, but additional costs are astronomical. Ignoring these economic realities simply wastes the resources of society, lowers our standard of living, and in the long run impairs our ability to deal effectively with any societal problem, including environmental protection.

ENVIRONMENTAL EXTERNALITIES

The air and water in the United States are far cleaner today than in previous decades. This is true despite growth in population and even greater growth in waste products. Nonetheless, genuine concern for environmental externalities centers on the disposal of solid waste (especially hazardous wastes), water pollution, and air pollution.

Solid Waste Disposal

Every American produces about 4.5 pounds of solid waste per day (see Table 13–1). The annual load of waste dumped on the environment includes 82 million tons of paper, 48 billion cans, 26 billion bottles and jars, 2 billion disposable razors, 16 billion disposable diapers, and 4 million automobiles and trucks. The nation spends billions of dollars annually on hauling all this away from homes and businesses.

TABLE 13–1 Growth in Solid Wastes Each day the average American produces more than four pounds of waste; about 33 percent of waste is recycled.

	1960	1970	1980	1990	2000	2008
Gross waste (million of tons)	87.50	120.50	151.2	205.2	239.1	249.6
Waste per person per day (lbs)	2.65	3.22	3.7	4.5	4.7	4.5
Percent recycled	NA	NA	9.6	16.4	29.0	33.2

SOURCE: *Statistical Abstract of the United States, 2011*, p. 229.

There are three methods of disposing of solid wastes—landfills, incineration, and recycling. Modern landfills have replaced town dumps nearly everywhere. Landfills are usually lined with clay so that potentially toxic wastes do not seep into the water system. Even so, hazardous wastes are separated from those that are not hazardous and handled separately. Given a reasonable site, there is nothing especially wrong with a landfill that contains no hazardous wastes. However, landfill sites need to meet strict standards, and people do not want landfills near their residences. These conditions combine to make it difficult to develop new landfills.

Another alternative is to burn the garbage. Modern incinerators are special plants, usually equipped with machinery to separate the garbage into different types, with scrubbers to reduce air pollution from the burning and often with electrical generators powered by heat from the garbage fire. Garbage is put through a shredder to promote even burning; metal is separated out by magnets, and the garbage is passed over screens that separate it further. At this point about half the garbage has been removed and hauled to a landfill. The remaining garbage is shredded still further into what is called fluff, or perhaps it is compressed into pellets or briquets. This material is then burned, usually at another site and perhaps together with coal, to produce electricity. The ash is handled by the public utility as it would handle any other ash, which often means selling it to towns to use on roads. One problem with this method is the substances emitted from the chimney of the incinerator or the utility that is burning the garbage. Another problem: because the garbage separated during the screening phase still has to be disposed of, the need for landfill sites is only reduced, not eliminated.

A third method of reducing the amount of solid waste is recycling. Recycling is the conversion of wastes into useful products. Most of the time, waste cannot be recycled into the same product it was originally but rather into some other form. Newspapers, for example, can be recycled into cardboard, insulation, animal bedding, and cat litter.

Overall, about 33 percent of all solid waste in the United States is recovered for reuse.[1] This is a notable improvement over the mere 10 percent that was recycled 30 years ago. Some materials lend themselves fairly well to recycling (e.g., aluminum cans, paper products), but other materials do not (e.g., plastics). At present there is more material available for recycling than plants can effectively use; millions of tons of recycled newspapers are either piled up as excess inventory in paper mills or dumped or burned. Nonetheless, recycling does have an effect in reducing the load on incinerators and landfills.

Hazardous Waste

Hazardous (toxic) wastes are those that pose a significant threat to public health or the environment because of their "quantity, concentration, or physical, chemical, or infectious characteristics."[2] The Resource Conservation and Recovery Act of 1976 gave the Environmental

Protection Agency (EPA) the authority to determine which substances are toxic, and the EPA has so classified several hundred substances. Releases of more than a specified amount must be reported to the National Response Center. Substances are considered hazardous if they easily catch fire, are corrosive, or react easily with other chemicals. Many substances are declared toxic by the EPA because massive daily doses administered to laboratory animals cause cancers to develop. Toxic chemical releases must also be reported annually. These reports show that toxic releases have been reduced substantially over the last decade.[3] Thus far, the United States has avoided any toxic releases comparable to the accident in Bhopal, India, in 1984, which killed almost 3,000 people.

Nuclear wastes create special problems. These are the wastes from nuclear fission reactors and nuclear weapons plants. Some have been in existence for 60 years. Because the waste is radioactive and some of it radioactive for thousands of years, it has proven very difficult to dispose of. Current plans to store some wastes in deep, stable, underground sites have run into local opposition. Most nuclear waste in the United States is stored at the site where it was generated, pending some long-term plan for handling it.

Hazardous wastes from old sites also constitute an environmental problem. These wastes need to be moved to more secure landfills. Otherwise, they can affect the health of people living near the waste site, often by seeping into the water supply. The EPA is committed to cleaning up such sites under the Superfund laws of 1980 and 1986. As a first step, it developed a National Priority List of sites that needs attention based on a hazard ranking system. The EPA listed about 1,300 hazardous waste sites. Cleanups have been done by the EPA itself, other federal state or local government agencies, or the company or party responsible for the contamination.

Water Pollution

Debris and sludge, organic wastes, and chemical effluents are the three major types of water pollutants. These pollutants come from (1) domestic sewage, (2) industrial waste, (3) agricultural runoff of fertilizers and pesticides, and (4) "natural" processes, including silt deposits and sedimentation, which may be increased by nearby construction. A common standard for measuring water pollution is biochemical oxygen demand (BOD), which identifies the amount of oxygen consumed by wastes. This measure, however, does not consider chemical substances that may be toxic to humans or fish. It is estimated that domestic sewage accounts for 30 percent of BOD, and industrial and agricultural wastes for 70 percent.

Primary sewage treatment—which uses screens and settling chambers, where filth falls out of the water as sludge—is fairly common. Secondary sewage treatment is designed to remove organic wastes, usually by trickling water through a bed of rocks 3 to 10 feet deep, where bacteria consume the organic matter. Remaining germs are killed by chlorination. Tertiary sewage treatment uses mechanical and chemical filtration processes to remove almost all contaminants from water. Some cities dump sewage sludge into the ocean after only primary treatment or no treatment at all. Although federal law prohibits dumping raw sewage into the ocean, it has proven difficult to secure compliance from coastal cities. Federal water pollution abatement goals call for the establishment of secondary treatment in all American communities. In most industrial plants, tertiary treatment ultimately will be required to deal with the flow of chemical pollutants. But tertiary treatment is expensive; it costs two or three times as much to build and operate a tertiary sewage treatment plant as it does a secondary plant.

Phosphates are major water pollutants that overstimulate plant life in water, which in turn kills fish. Phosphates run off from fertilized farm land. Farming is the major source of water pollution in the United States.

Waterfronts and seashores are natural resources. The growing numbers of waterfront homes, amusement centers, marinas, and pleasure boats are altering the environment of the nation's coastal areas. Marshes and estuaries at the water's edge are essential to the production of seafood and shellfish, yet they are steadily shrinking with the growth of residential-commercial-industrial development. Oil spills are unsightly. Although pollution is much greater in Europe than in America, America's coastal areas still require protection. Federal law makes petroleum companies liable for the cleanup costs of oil spills and outlaws flushing of raw sewage from boat toilets. The *EXXON Valdez* oil spill in Alaska in 1989 focused attention on the environmental risks of transporting billions of barrels of foreign and domestic oil each year in the United States. The British Petroleum (BP) Gulf Oil Spill in 2010 warned of the risks of drilling for oil in deep waters.

The federal government has provided financial assistance to states and cities to build sewage treatment plants ever since the 1930s. Efforts to establish national standards for water quality began in the 1960s and culminated in the Water Pollution Control Act of 1972. This "Clean Water Act" set "national goals" for elimination of all discharges of *all* pollutants into navigable waters; it required industries and municipalities to install "the best available technology"; it gave the EPA authority to initiate legal actions against pollution caused by firms and governments; it increased federal funds available to municipalities for the construction of sewage treatment plants.

Water quality in the United States has improved significantly over the years.[4] The problem, of course, is that removing *all* pollutants is neither cost-effective nor possible.

Air Pollution

The air we breathe is about one-fifth oxygen and a little less than four-fifths nitrogen, with traces of other gases, water vapor, and the waste products we put into it. Air pollution is caused, first of all, by the gasoline-powered internal combustion engines of cars, trucks, and buses. The largest industrial polluters are petroleum refineries, smelters (aluminum, copper, lead, and zinc), and iron foundries. Electrical power plants also contribute to total air pollutants by burning coal or oil for electric power. Heating is also a major source of pollution; homes, apartments, and offices use coal, gas, and oil for heat. Another source of pollution is the incineration of garbage, trash, metal, glass, and other refuse by both governments and industries.

Air pollutants fall into two major types: particles and gases. The particles include ashes, soot, and lead, the unburnable additive in gasoline. Often the brilliant red sunsets we admire are caused by large particles in the air. Less obvious but more damaging are the gases: (1) sulfur dioxide, which in combination with moisture can form sulfuric acid; (2) hydrocarbons—any combination of hydrogen and carbon; (3) nitrogen oxide, which can combine with hydrocarbons and the sun's ultraviolet rays to form smog; and (4) carbon monoxide, which is produced when gasoline is burned.

The EPA sets limits on fine particulate matter (soot, dust) in the air. But many large cities, for example, New York, Los Angeles, Chicago, and Washington, DC, exceed these limits. A recent federally financed study reported that "the risk of dying from lung cancer as well as heart disease in the most polluted cities was comparable to the risk associated with nonsmokers being exposed to second-hand smoke over a long period of time."[5]

The air we breathe is significantly cleaner today than thirty years ago (see Table 13–2). Federal clean air legislation (described later in this chapter) is generally credited with causing these

TABLE 13–2   Improvements in Air Quality Contrary to much popular opinion, the air is much cleaner today than in prior years.

| | Millions of Tons Per Year | | | | | | | |
	1980	1985	1990	1995	2000	2005	2008	Percent Change 1980–2008
Carbon Monoxide (CO)	178	170	144	120	102	91	77	−57
Lead	0.074	0.023	0.005	0.004	0.002	0.003	0.001	−99
Nitrogen Oxides (NO_x)	27	26	25	25	22	19	16	−41
Volatile Organic Compounds (VOCs)	31	27	24	22	17	18	16	−47
Particulate Matter (PM_{10})	6.2	3.6	3.2	3.1	2.3	2.6	2.5	−60
Sulfur Dioxide (SO_2)	26	23	23	19	16	15	12	−54

SOURCE: www.epa.gov/air/airtrends

improvements. The Environmental Protection Agency claims that the Clean Air Act of 1970 and subsequent amendments to it have resulted in an overall reduction in principal pollutants since 1970 of 57 percent. This improvement in air quality has come about despite increases in the gross domestic product (207 percent), vehicle miles traveled (179 percent), energy consumption (49 percent), and population growth (47 percent). (See Figure 13–2.)

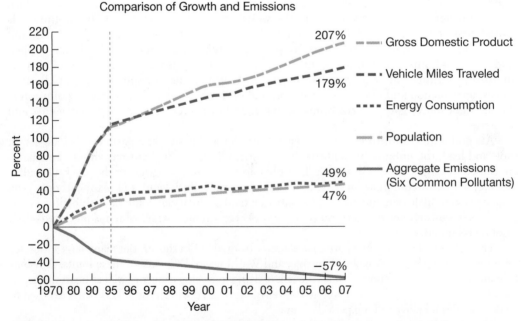

FIGURE 13–2   Comparison of Growth and Emissions Air pollution has decreased even while the economy has grown, the population has grown, more miles are traveled, and more energy is consumed.
SOURCE: Environmental Protection Agency, "Six Common Air Pollutants," www.epa.gov

POLITICIANS AND BUREAUCRATS: REGULATING THE ENVIRONMENT

Federal environmental policymaking began in earnest in the 1970s with the creation of the Environmental Protection Agency (EPA) and the passage of clean air and water acts. Potentially, the EPA is the most powerful and far-reaching bureaucracy in Washington today with legal authority over any activity in the nation that affects the air, water, or ground.

The Environmental Protection Agency

The EPA was created in an executive order by President Richard Nixon in 1970 to reorganize the federal bureaucracy to consolidate responsibility for (1) water pollution, (2) air pollution, (3) solid waste management, (4) radiation control, and (5) hazardous and toxic substance control. The EPA is a regulatory agency with power to establish and enforce policy. Its regulations can only be overturned by an act of Congress.

The National Environmental Protection Act

In 1970 Congress created the Council on Environmental Quality (CEQ) to advise the president and Congress on environmental matters. The CEQ is an advisory agency. However, the act requires all federal agencies as well as state, local, and private organizations receiving federal monies to file lengthy "environmental impact statements." If the CEQ wants to delay or obstruct a project, it can ask for endless revisions, changes, or additions in the statement. The CEQ cannot by itself halt a project, but it can conduct public hearings for the press, pressure other governmental agencies, and make recommendations to the president. The courts have ruled that the requirement for an environmental impact statement is judicially enforceable.

The Clean Air Act of 1970

The Clean Air Act of 1970 authorized the EPA to identify air pollutants that cause a health threat and to establish and enforce standards of emission. The EPA began by focusing on automobile emissions, requiring the installation of pollution equipment on all new cars. The EPA ordered lead removed from auto fuel and engines redesigned for lead-free gasoline. It also ordered the installation of emission controls in automobiles. The EPA was even more aggressive in pursuing stationary sources of air pollution with requirements for "smokestack scrubbers," low-sulfur coal, and other costly devices.

The Water Pollution Control Act of 1972

This act stiffened early antipollution laws, but it set an unrealistic goal: "that the discharge of pollutants into the navigable waters be eliminated by 1985." After a flood of lawsuits, the EPA was forced to abandon the zero-discharge standard. Forcing municipal governments to clean up their discharges proved more difficult than forcing industry to do so. Many municipalities remain in violation of federal water quality standards.

Endangered Species Act of 1973

This legislation authorizes the U.S. Fish and Wildlife Service to designate endangered species for federal protection and to regulate activities in their "critical habitat." Initially the law was widely praised as at least partially responsible for the survival of nationally symbolic species such as the bald eagle; but increasingly the law has been used to prevent landowners from using their property in order to protect obscure varieties of rodents, birds, and insects. Today more than 1,000 species are on the endangered species list, and there is virtually no land in the United States on which an endangered species does *not* live. The U.S. Fish and Wildlife Service has the potential to control any land in the nation under the Endangered Species Act.

Wetlands

In 1975 a federal court ruled that the Clean Water Act of 1972 also applied to "wetlands" adjacent to navigable waters. This gave the EPA control over millions of acres of land, estimated to be the equivalent of Ohio, Indiana, and Illinois combined. The result has been a bureaucratic nightmare for owners of land that is classified as wetlands.

Resource Conservation and Recovery Act of 1976

The act authorizes EPA to oversee the nation's solid waste removal and disposal, including the regulation of landfills, incinerators, industrial waste, hazardous waste, and recycling programs.

Toxic Substances Control Act of 1976

The Toxic Substances Control Act authorized the EPA to designate hazardous and toxic substances and to establish standards for their release into the environment.

The Comprehensive Environmental Response Act of 1980

The Comprehensive Environmental Response Act established a "Superfund" for cleaning up old toxic and hazardous waste sites. Out of 20,000 potential sites, the EPA has placed more than 1,200 on its National Priority List. The act specifies that EPA oversee the cleanup of these sites, assessing costs to the parties responsible for the pollution. If these parties cannot be found or have no money, then the government's Superfund is to be used. But over the years, cleanup efforts have been seriously hampered by the EPA's overly rigid site orders, lengthy lawsuits against previous owners and users, and complicated negotiations with local government over the cleanup of old landfill sites. The EPA also enforces "retroactive liability," holding owners liable for waste dumped legally before the law was enacted in 1980. Under current EPA policies, full cleanup of all hazardous waste sites on the National Priority List would cost many billions of dollars, far more than presidents or Congresses are likely to appropriate.

Clean Air Act of 1990

The Clean Air Act Amendments of 1990 enacted many new regulations aimed at a variety of perceived threats to the environment:

> *Acid rain.* Sulfur dioxide emissions were cut from 20 to 10 million tons annually, and nitrogen oxide emissions were cut by 2 million tons. Midwestern coal-burning utilities must burn low-sulphur coal and install added smoke-scrubbing equipment at increased costs to their consumers.

Ozone hole. Production of chlorofluorocarbons and hydrochlorofluorocarbons (aerosol sprays, insulating materials) was outlawed, and new regulations were placed on chemicals used in air conditioners and refrigerators.

Urban smog. Additional mandated pollution control equipment was required on new automobiles.

Toxic air pollutants. New definitions and regulations were enacted for more than 200 substances as "toxic air pollutants" released into the air from a wide variety of sources, from gas stations to dry cleaners. The EPA was given authority to require all of these sources to install "the best available control technology" and to provide "an ample margin of safety" for nearby residents.

INTEREST GROUP EFFECTS

Americans live longer and healthier lives today than at any time in their country's history. Life expectancy at birth is now 78.5 years (75.6 for males; 81.4 for females), up eight full years since 1970. Cancer deaths are up slightly but not because of environmental hazards. The primary causes of premature death are what they have always been: smoking, diets rich in fat and lean in fiber, lack of exercise, and alcohol abuse. Yet public opinion generally perceives the environment as increasingly contaminated and dangerous, and this perception drives public policy.

Interest Group Economics

Organized environmental interests must recruit memberships and contributions (see Table 13–3). They must justify their activities by publicizing and dramatizing environmental threats. When Greenpeace boats disrupt a U.S. Navy exercise, they are attracting the publicity required for a successful direct-mail fund-raising drive. The mass media, especially the television networks, welcome stories that capture and hold audiences' attention. Stories are chosen for their emotional impact, and threats to personal life and safety satisfy the need for drama in the news. Statistics that indicate negligible risks or scientific testimony that minimizes threats or presents ambiguous findings do not make good news stories. Politicians wish to be perceived as acting aggressively to protect citizens from any risk, however minor. Politicians want to be seen as "clean" defenders of the pristine wilderness. And government bureaucrats understand that the greater the public fear of environmental threat, the easier it is to justify expanded powers and budgets.

TABLE 13–3   Leading Environmental Organizations Environmental politics in Washington are heavily influenced by environmental interest groups.

National Wildlife Federation	Natural Resources Defense Council
Greenpeace	Environmental Defense Fund
National Audubon Society	Defenders of Wildlife
Sierra Club	Friends of the Earth
Wilderness Society	Union of Concerned Scientists

Shaping Public Opinion

Interest group activity and media coverage of environmental threats have succeeded in convincing most Americans that environmental pollution is getting worse. Evidence that the nation's air and water are measurably cleaner today than in the 1970s is ignored. Opinion polls report that 57 percent of Americans agree with this statement: "Protecting the environment is so important that requirements and standards cannot be too high, and continued environmental improvements must be made *regardless of cost.*"[6] If taken seriously, such an attitude would prevent either scientific or economic considerations from guiding policy. Environmentalism threatens to become a moral crusade that dismisses science and economics as irrelevant or even wicked. In such a climate of opinion, moral absolutism replaces rational public policy.

Interest Group Politics

Everyone is opposed to pollution. It is difficult publicly to oppose clean air or clean water laws—who wants to stand up for dirt? Thus the environmentalists begin with a psychological and political advantage: they are "clean" and their opponents are "dirty." The news media, Congress, and executive agencies can be moved to support environmental protection measures with little consideration of their costs—in job loss, price increases, unmet consumer demands, increased dependence on foreign sources of energy. Industry—notably the electric power companies, oil and gas companies, chemical companies, automakers, and coal companies—must fight a rearguard action, continually seeking delays, amendments, and adjustments in federal standards. They must endeavor to point out the increased costs to society of unreasonably high standards in environmental protection legislation. But industry is suspect; the environmentalists can charge that industry opposition to environmental protection is motivated by greed for higher profits. And the charge is partially true, although most of the cost of antipollution efforts is passed on to the consumer in the form of higher prices.

The environmentalists are generally upper-middle-class or upper-class individuals whose income and wealth are secure. Their aesthetic preferences for a no-growth, clean, unpolluted environment take precedence over jobs and income, which new industries can produce. Workers and small business people whose jobs or income depend on energy production, oil refining, forestry, mining, smelting, or manufacturing are unlikely to be ardent environmentalists. But there is a psychological impulse in all of us to preserve scenic beauty, protect wildlife, and conserve natural resources. It is easy to perceive industry and technology as the villain, and "man against technology" has a humanistic appeal.

NIMBY Power

Environmental groups have powerful allies in the nation's NIMBYs—local residents who feel inconvenienced or threatened by specific projects. Even people who otherwise recognize the general need for new commercial or industrial developments, highways, airports, power plants, pipelines, or waste disposal sites, nonetheless voice the protest "not in my back yard," earning them the NIMBY label. Although they may constitute only a small group in a community, they become very active participants in policymaking—meeting, organizing, petitioning, parading, and demonstrating. NIMBYs are frequently the most powerful interests opposing specific developmental projects and are found nearly everywhere. They frequently take up environmental interests, using environmental arguments to protect their own property investments.

Radical Environmentalism

At the extreme fringe of the environmental movement one finds strong opposition to economic development, to scientific advancement, and even to humanity. According to the Club of Rome (a radical environmental organization), "The real enemy, then, is humanity itself."[7] The "green" movement is international, with well-organized interest groups and even political parties in Western European nations. Its program to "Save the Planet" includes the deindustrialization of Western nations; reduction of the human population; elimination of all uses of fossil fuels, including automobiles; the elimination of nuclear power; an end to cattle raising, logging, land clearance, and so on; and the transfer of existing wealth from the industrialized nations to underdeveloped countries.[8]

GLOBAL WARMING/CLIMATE CHANGE

Gloomy predictions about catastrophic warming of the Earth's surface have been issued by the media and environmental interest groups in support of massive new regulatory efforts. Global warming is theorized to be a result of emissions of carbon dioxide and other gases that trap the sun's heat in the atmosphere. As carbon dioxide increases in the atmosphere as a result of increased human activity, more heat is trapped. Deforestation contributes to increased carbon dioxide by removing trees, which absorb carbon dioxide and produce oxygen. The dire predictions of greenhouse effects include droughts and crop destruction, melting of the polar ice caps, and ocean flooding.

Climate Change

It is true that the Earth's atmosphere creates a greenhouse effect; if not, temperatures on the Earth's surface would be like those on the moon—unbearably cold (−270°F) at night and unbearably hot (+212°F) during the day. The greenhouse gases, including carbon dioxide, moderate the Earth's surface temperature. And it is true that carbon dioxide is increasing in the atmosphere, an increase of about 25 percent since the beginning of the Industrial Revolution in 1850, and 13 percent since 1970 (see Figure 13–3).

It is also true that the Earth has been warming over the past century, since the beginning of the Industrial Revolution. Global average temperatures have risen about 1.4°F. Average sea levels have risen, and the northern hemispheric snow cover has diminished. Various computer simulations of the effect of increased dioxides in the atmosphere have predicted future increases in temperature ranging from 1° (not significant) to 8° (significant if it occurs rapidly).[9]

Global climate change is caused by a variety of factors: slight changes in the Earth's orbit, causing ice ages over millennia (the last ice age, when average temperatures were 9° cooler, ended 15,000 years ago.); solar activity including sun flares (a "little" ice age between 1500–1850 is estimated to have cooled the Earth by about 2°F); and volcanic activity, which tends to block sunlight and contribute to short-term cooling (a volcano in Indonesia in 1815 lowered global temperatures by 5°F, and historical accounts in New England described 1816 as "the year without a summer").

Is human activity contributing to global warming? Fossil fuels emit carbon dioxide (CO_2) into the atmosphere. Since the beginning of the Industrial Revolution, atmospheric carbon dioxide concentrations have increased by about 25 percent. This increase corresponds to an increase in average global temperature (see Figure 13–3). This correspondence does not prove causation, but it underlies the fundamental argument of global warming theory.

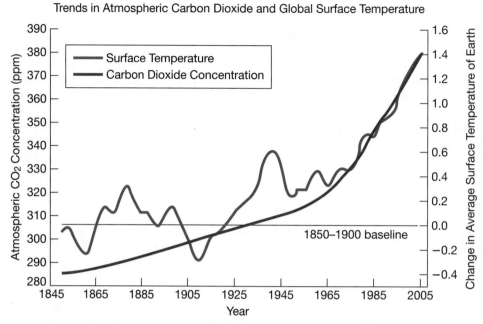

FIGURE 13–3   Trends in Atmospheric Carbon Dioxide and Global Surface Temperature Recent increases in atmospheric concentrations of carbon dioxide (CO_2) have corresponded with increases in average surface temperatures on Earth. The sharpest rises in CO_2 and temperatures have occurred since 1970.

SOURCE: Pew Center on Global Climate Change, *www.pewclimate.org*

International Panel on Climate Change

A United Nations-sponsored International Panel on Climate Change (IPCC) reported with "very high confidence" that human activity since the Industrial Revolution has contributed to increases in atmospheric concentrations of carbon dioxide, methane, and nitrous oxide.[10] The IPCC does not do its own research but rather assesses scientific reports from other bodies. Its *Fourth Assessment Report: Climate Change 2007* is widely cited by environmentalists: "Most of the observed increase in global average temperatures since the mid-20th century is very likely due to the observed increase in anthropogenic [caused by human activity] greenhouse gas concentrations." The popularity of the report was reflected in the awarding of a Nobel Prize to the IPCC and to its principal publicist, Al Gore, former vice president and author of *An Inconvenient Truth*, a study of global warming.

Greenhouse Gases

Carbon dioxide (CO_2) contributes about three-quarters of total greenhouse gas emissions; methane and nitrous oxide are also classified as greenhouse gases. The principal source of CO_2 emissions are power plants (30 percent), industrial processes (21 percent), transportation (19 percent), residential (13 percent), land use (9 percent), and other fossil fuel uses (8 percent). Any serious effort to reduce overall greenhouse gas emissions must deal with electric utilities, waste disposal facilities, natural gas producers, petroleum refineries, smelters, and motor vehicle emissions, among other sources.

Recently, China surpassed the United States as the largest single national contributor of atmospheric pollutants. Both nations together currently produce about 50 percent of the world's output of greenhouse gases. But China, together with India and Indonesia, contributes to the largest annual *increases* in greenhouse emissions. Whatever policies the United States adopts to limit its own emissions, the Earth's atmosphere will continue to be polluted by other nations. Environmentalists argue that the United States must act first in order to set an example for the world.

International Environmental Politics

Environmentalists argue that "drastic action" is required now to avert "catastrophic" global warming. Al Gore is a leading exponent of the view that governments cannot afford to wait until the scientific evidence demonstrates conclusively that human activity contributes to global warming. Rather, governments must immediately impose a system of "global environmental regulations" in order to "save the planet."[11] Inasmuch as developing nations are just beginning to industrialize, they pose the greatest threat of new sources of global pollution. But the industrialized nations are responsible for "undermining the Earth's life support system" (the United States is usually singled out as the primary culprit), and therefore they must compensate poorer nations in exchange for their pledge not to add to global pollution. The international environmental agenda includes massive transfers of wealth from industrialized nations to less developed countries.

The Rio Treaty

The Rio Treaty incorporates these ideas. It is a product of the "Earth Summit," officially the United Nations Conference on Environment and Development held in Rio de Janeiro, Brazil, in 1992. It was attended by 178 nations as well as hundreds of environmental interest groups, officially sanctioned as "nongovernmental organizations" or "NGOs." The conference produced a Global Climate Change Treaty, signed by President George H.W. Bush, but not ratified by the U.S. Senate, which declares, among other things, that "lack of scientific certainty shall not be used as a reason for postponing cost-effective measures to prevent environmental degradation"! The statement is, of course, a contradiction: without scientific information, it is impossible to determine cost-effectiveness.

The Kyoto Protocol

In 1997, a far-reaching amendment to the Rio Treaty, known as the Kyoto Protocol, was negotiated under the United Nations Framework Convention on Climate Change. Whereas the Rio Treaty set voluntary national goals for reducing greenhouse gases, the Kyoto agreement required the United States and other developed nations to reduce their emissions below 1990 levels sometime between 2008 and 2012. Reductions by developed nations were designed to offset expected increases in emissions by developing nations. The reduction mandated for the United States was

7 percent below its 1990 level—a reduction that would entail approximately a 40 percent reduction in fossil fuel use. The Clinton administration supported the Kyoto Protocol, but declined to submit it for ratification to the U.S. Senate in view of its likely defeat in that body. The Bush administration opposed the Protocol. The United States, China, Japan, and Russia, all remain outside of legally binding emission limits.

Copenhagen Conference

Governments and non-governmental organizations met in Copenhagen, Denmark in 2009 with the goal of developing a legally binding treaty to reduce worldwide carbon emissions. The negotiations were sponsored by the UN Framework Convention on Climate Change. The United States was among the 192 countries participating in the Conference; the United States favors the development of nonbinding pledges regarding carbon emissions, rather than legally binding emissions cuts. Less developed nations demanded compensation from the developed nations in exchange for limiting growth in their emissions. A weak, nonbinding "Copenhagen Accord" emerged from the conference, disappointing many participants.

Cancun Conference

A U.N. Climate Change Conference was held in Cancun, Mexico, in 2010. After weeks of sometimes rancorous discussions, participating countries reached a general agreement to worldwide emission cuts that would prevent average temperatures from rising more than 3.6°F for the rest of the century. They also agreed to the establishment of an international fund to assist developing nations in reducing emissions. Wealthy nations agreed to contribute $100 billion annually by 2020 to a "Green Climate Fund" administered by the World Bank to help developing countries switch to renewable energy sources. But it was not decided how this money was to be raised. Nor was it decided whether developing countries would have to meet emission requirements to access these funds. The Cancun Conference agreement is not a binding treaty.

ENERGY POLICY

Environmental policy and energy policy are closely intertwined. Currently, America gets most of its energy from fossil fuels—oil, natural gas, and coal (see Figure 13–4). These sources produce pollutants, including carbon dioxide emissions that appear related to global climate change. Despite heavy subsidization by the federal government, "renewable" energy sources—hydroelectric, geothermal, solar, wind, and biomass—account for only about 7 percent of the energy used in the United States.

Energy Consumption

Electric power plants account for the greatest share of energy produced in the United States (see Figure 13–4). About half of all electric generating plants are powered by coal; almost 20 percent are nuclear powered; most of the remainder are powered from oil or natural gas; less than 10 percent of electric power is derived from renewable energy sources. Transportation accounts for nearly 30 percent of total energy use in America, almost all of it from oil.

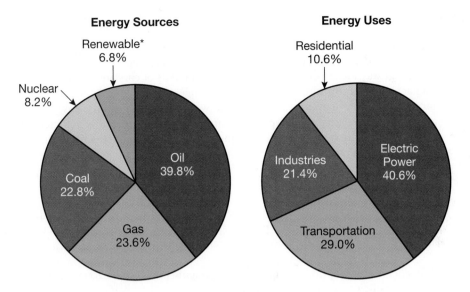

Energy Sources

Renewable*
6.8%

Nuclear
8.2%

Oil
39.8%

Coal
22.8%

Gas
23.6%

Energy Uses

Residential
10.6%

Electric
Power
40.6%

Industries
21.4%

Transportation
29.0%

*Hydroelectric, geothermal, solar, wind, biomass.

FIGURE 13–4   Energy Sources and Uses The U.S. gets most of its energy from oil, gas, and coal, all of which produce greenhouse gases. Clean nuclear and renewable sources provide relatively little energy for the country. Electric power plants and motor vehicles together use nearly 70 percent of the energy generated.
SOURCE: Data from Energy Information Administration, U.S. Department of Energy, *www.eia.doe.gov*

Energy consumption *per person* in United States has stabilized over the last thirty years. Growth in overall energy consumption has matched population growth. Energy consumption has actually *declined* relative to the gross national product, suggesting that America is becoming more efficient over time in energy use. And energy expenditures have declined as a share of the GDP. This good news is not widely reported in the mass media.

Energy Supply

Supply-side energy policies emphasize the search for more sources of energy. Domestic oil production can be increased through exploration and drilling in public lands and offshore waters. ("Drill, baby, drill" became a popular slogan at Republican campaign stops in 2008.) Drilling in the Alaska National Wildlife Refuge (ANWR) in Alaska is an especially controversial option. Natural gas is more plentiful than petroleum, but its widespread use would require a complete overhaul of the nation's automobile and truck fleets to run on natural gas rather than gasoline. Nuclear power promises a clean source of energy for electrical power plants, but to date political struggles have effectively foreclosed the nuclear option (see "Nuclear Industry Meltdown" later in this chapter). The federal government heavily subsidizes research and development into "renewable" energy sources—land, solar, geothermal, and biomass (including ethanol production from corn). But none of these sources appear to be commercially feasible on any significant scale. Nevertheless the call for greater reliance on these sources of energy remains politically very popular.

Fuel Efficiency

The federal government requires automobile manufacturers to maintain corporate average fuel efficiency (CAFE) standards in the production of automobiles and light trucks. These averages are calculated from highway miles-per-gallon figures for all models of cars and light trucks produced by each manufacturer. Determining CAFE standards engenders near constant political conflict in Washington, pitting auto manufacturers and auto workers' unions against environmental and consumer groups. The popularity of pickup trucks, minivans, and sports utility vehicles means that overall fuel efficiency on the roads is difficult to improve. Alternative fuel vehicles and hybrids—cars powered entirely or in part by electricity, natural gas, hydrogen, ethanol, etc.—constitute less than 5 percent of new vehicle sales.

Projections

The U.S. Department of Energy annually produces an "Energy Outlook" that projects energy use in greenhouse gas emissions to 2030. Among its current projections:[12]

- Growth in energy consumption and greenhouse gas emissions is likely to moderate as a result of government policies and high energy prices.
- Fossil fuels will continue to provide nearly 80 percent of total energy use.
- Energy efficiencies will cause declines in per capita energy use and declines in energy use per dollar of GDP.
- Hybrid motor vehicles—partly powered by electricity—are projected to increase significantly.
- Growth in electrical use will moderate with improved efficiency in homes and industry.
- Renewable energy sources will increase but remain less than 10 percent of total energy supply.
- Growth in energy-related carbon dioxide emissions will slow, along with slowing growth in energy use.

THE CAP AND TRADE CONTROVERSY

In his first budget message to Congress, President Barack Obama recommended an innovative approach to energy policy. In addition to pledging federal subsidies for research and development in "clean energy technologies," he proposed a carbon emissions trading program known as "cap and trade."

A Ceiling on Carbon Emissions

The cap and trade program envisions the EPA setting overall national ceilings on carbon emissions. The government would then hold a national auction in which polluting industries and firms could purchase tradable emission allowances (TEAs). The total amount of emission allowances auctioned off would not exceed the cap. In effect, industries would be purchasing allowances to pollute. These allowances could be traded on an open market, allowing polluting industries to keep polluting but at a price, and at the same time, encouraging industries to invest dollars in reducing carbon emissions. An industry that succeeded in reducing emissions below its allowance could then sell its allowance to other industries.

The cap and trade approach to reducing carbon emissions is recommended over direct regulatory control. Because it relies in part on a market mechanism, it is sometimes labeled free-market environmentalism. Setting the overall cap is a regulatory measure, but individual firms are free to choose how or if they will reduce their emissions. The system encourages innovation by individual firms. If they are successful in reducing their emissions, they can sell their allowances to other firms.

Costs to Consumers

The cost of the cap and trade program would be borne by all energy users. The federal government could actually make money from auction revenues. The costs to energy consumers would be largely invisible, passed on by industries in the form of price increases. Everything from gasoline prices to electric bills would incorporate the prices industries paid for emission allowances at auction or in trades.

Enforcement

The federal government would put in place a vast new bureaucracy to "track" the carbon emissions of individual industries and firms. It would be necessary to measure the "carbon footprint" of industries and firms to ensure that they are operating within the emission allowances purchased at auction or in trade.

A cap and trade program potentially could cover the entire economy—not just utilities, refineries, and heavy industries, but schools, hospitals and private homes as well. Everyone would be subject to a "carbon audit" by federal officials at the end of the year to ensure that their emissions were at or below their allowances. A less intrusive program might cover only utilities that generate electricity.

Opposition to "Cap and Tax"

The House of Representatives passed a version of Obama's cap and trade proposal in 2009. The Waxman-Markey bill, named for its sponsors, Henry Waxman (D-CA) and Edward Markey (D-MA), provided for an economy-wide emissions cap but included a host of concessions and exemptions for coal companies, utilities, refineries, heavy industries, and agribusinesses. Wall Street envisioned added business in nationwide trading of emission allowances. But the Senate failed to pass the bill. Opponents labeled the proposal as "cap and tax" and argued that it was a symbol of liberal intent to burden the economy with added taxes and regulations. Following the midterm congressional elections of 2010 in which Republicans captured control of the House, the future of cap and trade looked dim.

EPA Regulation of Carbon Dioxide

The Environmental Protection Agency issued an official finding in 2009 that carbon dioxide is a danger to human health and the environment, and therefore subject to EPA regulation under the Clean Air Act. This "endangerment finding" potentially allows the EPA to draw up regulations governing greenhouse gas emissions from all sources—from electric power plants, refineries, chemical plants, and motor vehicles, to schools, hospitals, homes, and apartment buildings.

Encouraged by the Obama Administration, and relying heavily on studies cited by the International Panel on Climate Change (see above), the EPA issued its finding. The Clean Air Act does not mention carbon dioxide. But earlier in 2007 the U.S. Supreme Court held that the Act "expressly authorized" the EPA to regulate air "pollutants," and the EPA agreed that carbon dioxide is a pollutant.[13]

The EPA proposes to achieve by regulation what the Obama Administration failed to do by legislation; that is, establish a nationwide cap and trade program. The EPA is constructing a comprehensive system for reporting emissions of carbon dioxide and other greenhouse gases produced by major sources in the United States. This reporting system will provide the data for comprehensive regulation envisioned by a cap and trade program.

THE NUCLEAR INDUSTRY MELTDOWN

Nuclear power is the cleanest and safest form of energy available. But the political struggle over nuclear power has all but destroyed early hopes that nuclear power could reduce U.S. dependence on fossil fuels. Nuclear power once provided about 20 percent of the nation's total energy. Many early studies recommended that the United States strive for 50 percent nuclear electric generation. But under current policies it is unlikely that nuclear power will ever be able to supply any more energy than it does today—less than 10 percent (see Figure 13–4). The nuclear industry itself has been in a state of "meltdown," and the cause of the meltdown is political, not technological.

History of Regulation

In its developmental stages, nuclear power was a government monopoly. The Atomic Energy Act of 1946 created the Atomic Energy Commission (AEC), which established civilian rather than military control over nuclear energy. The AEC was responsible for the research, development, and production of nuclear weapons, as well as the development of the peaceful uses of nuclear energy. The AEC contracted with the Westinghouse Corporation to build a reactor and with the Duquesne Light Company to operate the world's first nuclear power plant at Shippingport, Pennsylvania, in 1957. Under the Atomic Energy Act of 1954 the AEC granted permits to build, and licenses to operate, nuclear plants; the AEC also retained control over nuclear fuel.

The AEC promoted the growth of the nuclear industry for over 20 years. But opponents of nuclear power succeeded in the Energy Reorganization Act of 1974 in separating the nuclear regulatory function from the research and development function. Today a separate agency, the Nuclear Regulatory Commission (NRC), regulates all aspects of nuclear power. Only 104 nuclear power plants are currently operating in the United States (see Figure 13–5).

"No-nukes"

Nuclear power has long been under attack by a wide assortment of "no-nuke" groups. The core opposition is found among environmental activist groups. But fear plays the most important role in nuclear politics. The mushroom cloud image of the devastation of Japanese cities at the

U.S. Commercial Nuclear Power Reactors

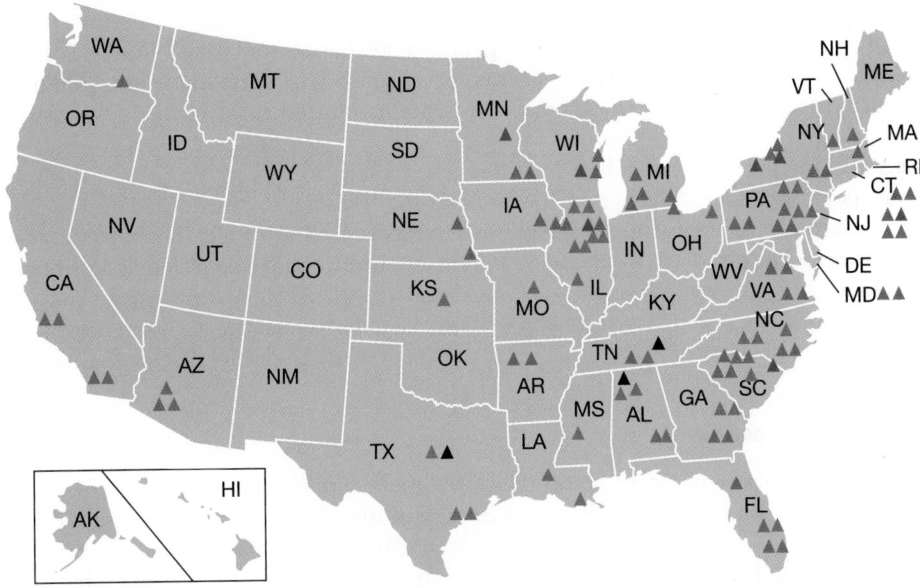

FIGURE 13–5 U.S. Commercial Nuclear Power Reactors The United States has 104 licensed nuclear power plants. Applications has been filed to open 19 new sites. But the accident at Japan's Fukushima Daiichi complex inspired new fears about reactor safety.
SOURCE: U.S. Nuclear Regulatory Commission.

end of World War II is still with us. The mass media cannot resist dramatic accounts of nuclear accidents. The public is captivated by the "China syndrome" story—an overheated nuclear core melts down the containing vessels and the plant itself and releases radioactivity that kills millions.

Nuclear power offers a means of generating electricity without discharging any pollutants into the air or water. It is the cleanest form of energy production. It does not diminish the world's supply of oil, gas, or coal. However, used reactor fuel remains radioactive for hundreds of years, and there are potential problems in burying this radioactive waste. Spent fuel is now piling up in storage areas in specially designed pools of water at nuclear power sites. When these existing storage places are filled to capacity, spent fuel will have to be transported somewhere else, adding to new complaints about the dangers of radioactive waste. There are many technical alternatives in dealing with waste, but there is no political consensus about which alternative to choose.

Safety

The nuclear power industry in the United States has a 60-year record of safety. No one has ever died or been seriously harmed by radioactivity from a nuclear power plant in the United States. This record includes 104 nuclear power plants operated in the United States and hundreds of nuclear-powered surface and submarine ships operated by the U.S. Navy. Despite sensational media coverage, the failure of the nuclear reactor at Three Mile Island, Pennsylvania, in 1979 did not result in injury to anyone or cause damage beyond the plant. There are about 450 nuclear power plants operating outside of the United States. France generates over 75 percent of its electricity by nuclear means. The worst nuclear accident in history occurred at Chernobyl in the Ukraine in 1986; it resulted in 31 immediate-term deaths from radiation.

Zero risk is an impossible standard, and the costs of efforts to approach zero risk are astronomical. Under popular pressure to achieve near-zero risk, the NRC has imposed licensing requirements that now make nuclear plants the most expensive means of generating electricity. No new nuclear plants have been built in over two decades, and private utilities have canceled dozens of planned nuclear plants.

The stated policy of the national government may be to keep open the nuclear power option, but the actual effect of nuclear regulatory policy over the last 30 years has been to foreclose that option.

A Nuclear Renaissance?

Can the nuclear power industry be revived? A "nuclear renaissance" may be inspired by a variety of factors: the U.S. Department of Energy projects that electricity demand will rise 25 percent by 2030, requiring the construction of hundreds of new power plants; oil price increases make nuclear power generation more competitive; concerns over global warming and pollution from fossil fuel use drive a new interest in nuclear power; and national security concerns regarding U.S. dependence on foreign oil suggest the need to develop reliable domestic power sources.

The Fukushima Effect

But Japan's devastating earthquake and tsunami in 2011, and the resulting damage to the Fukushima Daiichi nuclear power complex, renewed public fears about nuclear power. The official response in Washington was caution—resisting calls to reverse decisions on nuclear operating plant licenses and keeping the nuclear power option open. But public opinion shifted against nuclear power, and environmental groups were reenergized in their opposition to new or expanded nuclear plants.[14]

The Future of Nuclear Power

Reviving the nuclear energy industry will require, first of all, a streamlined and cost-conscious regulatory environment, one that encourages private companies to make the long-term capital investments required to bring new nuclear plants into operation. Secondly, the federal government must decide on, finance, and implement a nuclear waste management program, one that includes spent nuclear materials from both military and private power uses. Finally, nuclear power cannot be revived without federal subsidies and loan guarantees for private power companies to encourage them to move forward with building new nuclear plants. Yet even if Washington responded favorably to nuclear industry requirements, new plants are not likely to begin producing power in the United States for another 10 years.

SUMMARY

Public choice theory views environmental pollution as an externality of human activity. Individuals, firms, and governments frequently impose unwanted costs on others. The environment, especially air and water, is a common-pool resource: access is unrestricted; there are no clearly defined property rights to it; no one has the individual responsibility of caring for it; individuals, firms, and governments tend to use it to carry off waste materials, thus generating unwanted costs or externalities on everyone else. The government has a legitimate interest in managing environmental externalities. Public choice theory offers valuable guidelines in dealing with them.

1. Economic growth is not incompatible with environmental protection. On the contrary, increases in wealth and advances in technology provide the best hope for a cleaner environment.

2. Effective pollution control and risk reduction must be balanced against its costs. Environmental policies whose costs exceed benefits will impair society's ability to deal effectively with environmental problems.

3. The costs of removing additional environmental pollutants and risks rise as we approach zero tolerance. Total elimination of pollutants from air, water, or ground involves astronomical costs and wastes the resources of society.

4. Rational determination of benefits and costs requires scientific evidence. The deliberate rejection of scientific evidence on environmental issues, and the ideological or emotional inspiration to act even in the absence of scientific information, renders cost-effective policymaking impossible.

5. The air and water in the United States are significantly cleaner today than in 1970, when the first major environmental policies were enacted. Improvements in air and water quality have occurred despite growth in the population and growth in waste products.

6. Nonetheless, most Americans believe that pollution is growing worse. Interest group activity and media coverage of environmental "crises" have pushed environmental issues to the forefront of American politics. Predictions of global doom create a climate of opinion that precludes rational analyses of the benefits and costs of environmental policies.

7. Fossil fuels release carbon dioxide into the atmosphere. Increases in average global temperatures over the last century have corresponded to increases in atmospheric carbon dioxide. This correspondence underlies the argument of global warming theory.

8. A United Nations-sponsored International Panel on Climate Change (IPCC) reported with "very high confidence" that human activity is causing increasing atmospheric concentrations of greenhouse gases, including carbon dioxide. A United Nations-sponsored Rio Treaty in 1992 and a follow-up Kyoto Protocol in 1997 pledged the signing countries to reduce greenhouse gas emissions below 1990 levels. The United States has not ratified the Treaty or its Protocol. Less developed countries are demanding compensation from wealthy nations in return for their efforts at reducing emissions.

9. Energy consumption and greenhouse gas emissions have moderated in the United States in recent years. But most of the nation's energy continues to come from oil, gas, and coal. Clean, renewable energy sources, including hydroelectric, sun, wind, and biomass, produce very little of the nation's energy.

10. A cap and trade program envisions the EPA setting nationwide ceilings on carbon emissions and then auctioning off tradable emissions allowances (TEAs) to polluting industries. Individual firms could decide for themselves how to reduce emissions; then they could sell unused TEAs on the open market. Reliance on this partially based market system is thought to be preferable to direct regulation because it encourages firms to innovate in pollution control.

11. Congress failed to pass cap and trade in 2009, but the EPA proposes to establish it by regulation under the authority of the Clean Air Act. Enforcement of cap and trade entails a vast new regulatory bureaucracy, as well as increased costs to consumers.

12. Nuclear power is the cleanest and safest form of energy available. But under popular pressure to achieve zero risk, the Nuclear Regulatory Commission has made it so expensive to build nuclear plants that nuclear power has all but been foreclosed as an energy source of the future. Efforts to revive the nuclear power industry suffered a setback when an earthquake and tsunami destroyed the nuclear power complex, Fukushima Daiichi, in Japan in 2011.

MySearchLab® EXERCISES

Apply what you learned in this chapter on MySearchLab (www.mysearchlab.com).

NOTES

1. *Statistical Abstract of the United States, 2011,* p. 229.

2. Resource Conservation and Recovery Act, PL 94–580, Section 4001 (1976).

3. *Statistical Abstract of the United States, 2011,* p. 231.

4. Environmental Protection Agency, National Aquatic Resource Surveys, 2011. *www.epa.gov*

5. National Institute of Environmental Health Sciences, March 5, 2002.

6. CBS News/*New York Times* Survey, November 2002, As reported at *www.publicagenda.org*

7. Club of Rome, *The First Global Revolution* (New York: Pantheon Books, 1991), p. 115.

8. Christopher Manes, *Green Rage* (Boston: Little, Brown, 1990).

9. Hugh W. Ellsaesser et al., "Global Climate Trends as Revealed by Recorded Data," *Review of Geophysics* 24 (November 1986), 745–792; Patrick J. Michaels and David E. Stooksbury, "Global Warming: A Reduced Threat?" *Bulletin of the American Meteorological Society* 23 (October 1992), 1563–1577; Roy W. Spence and John R. Christy, "Precise Monitoring of Global Temperature Trends from Satellites," *Science* 247 (March 1990), 1558–1562.

10. International Panel on Climate Change, *Fourth Assessment Report: Climate Change 2007, www.ipcc.ch*

11. Al Gore, *Earth in the Balance* (Boston: Houghton Mifflin, 1992).

12. U.S. Department of Energy, *Annual Energy Review 2008, www.eia.doe.gov*

13. *Massachusetts v. EPA*, April 2, 2007.

14. "A Long Half-Life for Public's Fears," C. Q. Weekly, March 21, 2011, p. 618.

BIBLIOGRAPHY

Block, Ben, and Harold Lyons. *Apocalypse Not: Science, Economics, and Environmentalism.* Washington, DC: CATO Institute, 1993.

Gore, Al. *Earth in the Balance.* Boston: Houghton Mifflin, 1992.

Kraft, Michael E. *Environmental Policy and Politics,* 5th ed. New York: Longman, 2011.

Lipschutz, Ronnie D. *Global Environmental Politics.* Washington, DC: CQ Press, 2003.

Rosenbaum, Walter A. *Environmental Politics and Policy*, 8th ed. Washington, DC: CQ Press, 2010.

Vig, Norman J., and Michael E. Kraft. *Environmental Policy,* 7th ed. Washington, DC: CQ Press, 2009.

WEB SITES

U.S. ENVIRONMENTAL PROTECTION AGENCY. Official Web site of the EPA, with laws, regulations, key issues, press releases, etc. *www.epa.gov*

U.S. NATIONAL OCEANIC AND ATMOSPHERIC ADMINISTRATION. Official Web site of NOAA, with information on weather, climate, atmospheric research, etc., as well as real-time satellite imagery. *www.noaa.gov*

ENVIRONMENTAL DEFENSE FUND. Advocacy organization for environmental programs and spending. *www.environmentaldefense.org*

GREENPEACE. Home page of militant environmental organization opposed to world trade, whaling, fishing, deforestation, etc. *www.greenpeace.org*

NATIONAL WILDLIFE FEDERATION. Home page of moderate organization supporting wildlife conservation and environmental education. *www.nwf.org*

SIERRA CLUB. Advocacy organization for environmental protection, with information on issues, press releases, and voting records of Congress members. *www.sierraclub.org*

NATURAL RESOURCE DEFENSE COUNCIL. Advocacy organization that relies mainly on lawsuits to advance goals in clean air, clean water, nuclear waste, etc. *www.nrdc.org*

COMPETITIVE ENTERPRISE INSTITUTE. Advocacy organization opposed to centralize command approaches to environmental protection and favoring competitive free enterprise approaches. *www.cei.org*

INTERNATIONAL PANEL ON CLIMATE CHANGE. United Nations-Sponsored organization given responsibility for assessing global warming. *www.ipcc.ch*

NUCLEAR ENERGY INSTITUTE. News and information from the nuclear power industry. *www.nei.org*

NUCLEAR REGULATORY COMMISSION. Official NRC site with information on nuclear reactors, nuclear materials, radioactive wastes, and new and existing reactors in the United States. *www.nrc.gov*

"I Have a Dream" Martin Luther King, Jr. delivers his "I have a dream" speech to over 200,000 marchers at the Lincoln Memorial in Washington on August 28, 1963. "I have a dream. It is a dream deeply rooted in the American dream. I have a dream that one day this nation will rise up and live out the true meaning of its creed: 'We hold these truths to be self-evident, that all men are created equal.'" In response, President John F. Kennedy sent a strong civil rights bill to Congress, which passed the following year as the Civil Rights Act of 1964. (© Hulton-Deutsch Collection/Corbis)

14

Civil Rights
Elite and Mass Interaction

ELITE AND MASS OPINIONS AND RACE

Race has been a central issue in American politics over the long history of the nation. In describing this issue we have relied heavily on the elite model—because elite and mass attitudes toward civil rights differ, and public policy appears to reflect the attitudes of elites rather than masses. Civil rights policy is a response of a national elite to conditions affecting a minority of Americans rather than a response of national leaders to majority sentiments. Policies of the national elite in civil rights have met with varying degrees of mass resistance at the state and local levels. We will contend that national policy has shaped mass opinion more than mass opinion has shaped national policy.

Black–White Opinion Differences

The attitudes of white masses toward African Americans are ambivalent. Relatively few whites believe that there is much discrimination in society, or that discrimination is a very serious problem (see Table 14–1). In contrast, most blacks believe that discrimination is a very serious problem. However, whites and blacks agree that the election of Barack Obama as president will improve race relations.

Whites constitute a large majority of the nation's population. If public policy reflected the views of this *majority*, there would be very little civil rights legislation. Civil rights policy is *not* a response of the government to the demands of the white majority.

Mass Opinion Lags Behind Policy

White majority opinion has *followed* civil rights policy rather than inspired it. That is, public policy has shaped white opinion rather than white opinion shaping public policy. Consider the changes in opinion among whites toward school integration over the years. Between 1942 and 1985, samples of white Americans were asked this question: "Do you think white and black students should go to the same schools or separate schools?" (See Table 14–2.) In 1942, not one white American in three approved of integrated schools. In 1956, two years *after* the historic *Brown* v. *Topeka* court decision, white attitudes began to shift, although about half of all whites still favored segregation. By 1964, two out of every three whites supported

TABLE 14–1   White and Black Opinion about Discrimination White and black opinion differs on whether or not discrimination is a serious problem in America.

Q. *How serious do you think racial discrimination against blacks is in this country: a very serious problem, a somewhat serious problem, not too serious, or not at all serious?*

	Very Serious	Somewhat Serious	Not Too Serious	Not at All Serious
Whites	12%	45%	33%	9%
Blacks	56%	34%	9%	1%

Q. *How big a problem is racism in our society today?*

	A Big Problem	Somewhat of a Problem	A Small Problem	Not a Problem
Whites	22	49	23	5
Blacks	44	41	11	4

Q. *Do you think Barack Obama's election as president represents progress for all Blacks in America more generally, or do you think that it is only a single case that does not reflect broader progress for all Blacks overall?*

	Progress for All Blacks	Only a Single Case	Unsure
Whites	70	27	2
Blacks	66	29	5

Q. *Do you feel that racial minorities in this country have equal job opportunities as whites, or not?*

	Do	Do Not	Unsure
Whites	53	47	1
Blacks	17	81	2
Hispanics	34	62	3

SOURCE: Various polls, 2010, reported in *www.pollingreport.com*

TABLE 14–2   Changing White Attitudes toward School Integration Over time, white opinion regarding school integration changed from strong opposition to strong support.

Q. *"Do you think white students and black students should go to the same schools or to separate schools?"*

Same Schools

	Brown v. Topeka (1954)			Civil Rights Act (1964)			
	1942	1956	1964	1970	1972	1980	1985
Percent	30	48	62	74	80	86	92

SOURCE: General Social Survey, reported in Harold W. Stanley and Richard G. Niemi, *Vital Statistics on American Politics, 2007–2008* (Washington, DC: CQ Press, 2008), p. 161.

integrated schools. As public school integration proceeded in America, white parents became more accepting of sending their children to schools with substantial black enrollments. But, again, white opinion generally *follows* public policy rather than leads it.

Elite–Mass Differences

There is a wide gap between the attitudes of masses and elites on the subject of civil rights. The least favorable attitudes toward blacks are found among the less privileged, less educated whites. Whites of lower socioeconomic status are much less willing to have contact with blacks than those with higher socioeconomic status, whether it is a matter of using the same public restrooms, going to a movie or restaurant, or living next door. It is the affluent, well-educated white who is most concerned with discrimination and who is most willing to have contact with blacks. The political implication of this finding is obvious: opposition to civil rights legislation and to black advancement in education, jobs, income, housing, and so on is likely to be strongest among less educated and less affluent whites. Within the white community support for civil rights will continue to come from the educated and affluent.

THE DEVELOPMENT OF CIVIL RIGHTS POLICY

The initial goal in the struggle for equality in America was the elimination of discrimination and segregation practiced by governments, particularly in voting and public education. Later, discrimination in both public and private life—in transportation, theaters, parks, stores, restaurants, businesses, employment, and housing—came under legal attack.

The Fourteenth Amendment

The Fourteenth Amendment, passed by Congress after the Civil War and ratified in 1868, declares,

> All persons born or naturalized in the United States, and subject to the Jurisdiction thereof, are citizens of the United States and of the State wherein they reside. No State shall make or enforce any law which shall abridge the privileges or immunities of citizens of the United States; nor shall any State deprive any person of life, liberty, or property, without due process of law; nor deny to any person within its jurisdiction the equal protection of the laws.

The language of the Fourteenth Amendment and its historical context leave little doubt that its original purpose was to achieve the full measure of citizenship and equality for African Americans. During Reconstruction and the military occupation of the Southern states, some radical Republicans were prepared to carry out in Southern society the revolution this amendment implied. The early success of Reconstruction was evident in widespread black voting throughout the South and the election of blacks to federal and state offices. Congress even tried to legislate equal treatment in theaters, restaurants, hotels, and public transportation in the Civil Rights Act of 1875, only to have the Supreme Court declare the effort unconstitutional in 1883.[1]

Eventually Reconstruction was abandoned; the national government was not prepared to carry out the long and difficult task of really reconstructing society in the eleven states of the former Confederacy. In the Compromise of 1877, the national government agreed to end military occupation of the South, gave up its efforts to rearrange Southern society, and lent tacit approval to white supremacy in that region. In return, the Southern states pledged their support of the Union; accepted national supremacy; and agreed to permit the Republican candidate, Rutherford B. Hayes, to assume the presidency, even though his Democratic opponent, Samuel J. Tilden, had won more popular votes in the disputed election of 1876.

Segregation

The Supreme Court agreed to the terms of the compromise. The result was a complete inversion of the meaning of the Fourteenth Amendment so that it became a bulwark of segregation. State laws segregating the races were upheld. The constitutional argument on behalf of segregation under the Fourteenth Amendment was that the phrase "equal protection of the laws" did not prevent state-enforced *separation* of the races. Schools and other public facilities that were "separate but equal" won constitutional approval. This separate but equal doctrine became the Supreme Court's interpretation of the Equal Protection Clause of the Fourteenth Amendment in *Plessy* v. *Ferguson* in 1896.[2]

However, segregated facilities, including public schools, were seldom if ever equal, even in physical conditions. In practice, the doctrine of segregation was separate and *unequal*. The Supreme Court began to take notice of this after World War II. Although it declined to overrule the segregationist interpretation of the Fourteenth Amendment, it began to order the admission of individual blacks to white public universities when evidence indicated that separate black institutions were inferior or nonexistent.[3]

NAACP

Leaders of the newly emerging civil rights movement in the 1940s and 1950s were not satisfied with court decisions that examined the circumstances in each case to determine if separate school facilities were really equal. Led by Roy Wilkins, executive director of the National Association for the Advancement of Colored People (NAACP), and Thurgood Marshall, chief counsel for the NAACP, the civil rights movement pressed for a court decision that segregation *itself* meant inequality within the meaning of the Fourteenth Amendment, whether or not facilities were equal in all tangible respects. In short, they wanted a complete reversal of the separate but equal interpretation of the Fourteenth Amendment and a ruling that laws separating the races were unconstitutional.

The civil rights groups chose to bring suit for desegregation to Topeka, Kansas, where segregated black and white schools were equal in buildings, curricula, qualifications, salaries of teachers, and other tangible factors. The object was to prevent the Court from ordering the admission of blacks because tangible facilities were not equal and to force the Court to review the doctrine of segregation itself.

Brown v. Topeka

The Court rendered its historic decision in *Brown* v. *Board of Education of Topeka, Kansas*, on May 17, 1954:

> Segregation of white and colored children in public schools has a detrimental effect upon the colored children. The impact is greater when it has the sanction of law, for the policy of separating the races is usually interpreted as denoting the inferiority of the Negro group.[4]

Note that this first great step toward racial justice in the twentieth century was taken by the *nonelective* branch of the federal government. Nine men, secure in their positions with lifetime appointments, responded to the legal arguments of highly educated black leaders, one of whom— Thurgood Marshall—would later become a Supreme Court justice himself. The decision was made by a judicial elite, not by the people or their elected representatives.

MASS RESISTANCE TO DESEGREGATION

Although the Supreme Court had spoken forcefully in the *Brown* case in declaring segrega-tion unconstitutional, from a political viewpoint the battle over segregation was just beginning. Segregation would remain a part of American life, regardless of its constitutionality, until effective elite power was brought to bear to end it. The Supreme Court, by virtue of the American system of federalism and separation of powers, has little direct force at its disposal. Congress, the president, state governors and legislatures, and even mobs of people can act more forcefully than the federal judiciary. The Supreme Court must rely largely on the other branches of the federal government and on the states to enforce the law of the land.

Segregationist States

In 1954 the practice of segregation was widespread and deeply ingrained in American life (see Figure 14–1). Seventeen states *required* the segregation of the races in public schools:

Alabama	Mississippi	Texas	Maryland
Arkansas	North Carolina	Virginia	Missouri
Florida	South Carolina	Delaware	Oklahoma
Georgia	Tennessee	Kentucky	West Virginia
Louisiana			

The Congress of the United States required the segregation of the races in the public schools of the District of Columbia. Four additional states—Arizona, Kansas, New Mexico, and Wyoming—authorized segregation on the option of local school boards.

Thus, in deciding *Brown* v. *Topeka*, the Supreme Court struck down the laws of 21 states and the District of Columbia in a single opinion. Such a far-reaching decision was bound to meet with difficulties in implementation. In an opinion delivered the following year, the Supreme Court declined to order immediate nationwide desegregation but instead turned over the responsibility for desegregation to state and local authorities under the supervision of federal district courts. The way was open for extensive litigation, obstruction, and delay by states that chose to resist.

The six border states with segregated school systems—Delaware, Kentucky, Maryland, Missouri, Oklahoma, West Virginia—together with the school districts in Kansas, Arizona, and New Mexico that had operated segregated schools chose not to resist desegregation formally. The District of Columbia also desegregated its public schools the year following the Supreme Court's decision.

State Resistance

However, resistance to school integration was the policy choice of the 11 states of the Old Confederacy. Refusal of a school district to desegregate until it was faced with a federal court injunction was the most common form of delay. State laws that were obviously designed to evade

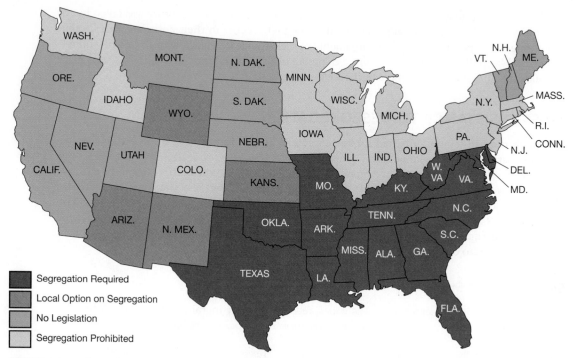

FIGURE 14–1   Segregation Laws in the United States in 1954 Prior to *Brown* v. *Topeka* in 1954, segregation was required in 21 states and the District of Columbia; four additional states gave local school districts the option of segregation.

constitutional responsibilities to end segregation were struck down in federal courts; but court suits and delays slowed progress toward integration. On the whole, those states that chose to resist desegregation were quite successful in doing so from 1954 to 1964. In late 1964, 10 years after the *Brown* decision, only about 2 percent of the black schoolchildren in the 11 southern states were attending integrated schools.

Presidential Use of Force

The historic *Brown* decision might have been rendered meaningless had President Dwight Eisenhower not decided to use military force in 1957 to secure the enforcement of a federal court order to desegregate Little Rock's Central High School. Governor Orval Faubus had posted state units of the Arkansas National Guard at the high school to prevent federal marshals from carrying out federal court orders to admit black students. President Eisenhower officially called the Arkansas National Guard units into federal service, ordered them to leave the high school, and replaced them with units of the U.S. 82nd Airborne Division under orders to enforce desegregation. Eisenhower had not publicly spoken on behalf of desegregation, but the direct threat to national power posed by a state governor caused the president to assert the power of the national elite. President John F. Kennedy also used federal troops to enforce desegregation at the University of Mississippi in 1962.

Congress and the Power of the Purse

Congress entered the civil rights field in support of court efforts to achieve desegregation in the Civil Rights Act of 1964. Title VI provided that every federal department and agency must take action to end segregation in all programs or activities receiving federal financial assistance. It was specified that this action was to include termination of financial assistance if states and communities receiving federal funds refused to comply with federal desegregation orders. Thus, in addition to court orders requiring desegregation, states and communities faced administrative orders, or "guidelines," from federal executive agencies threatening loss of federal funds for noncompliance.

Unitary Schools

The last legal excuse for delay in implementing school desegregation collapsed in 1969 when the Supreme Court rejected a request by Mississippi school officials for a delay in implementing school desegregation in that state. The Court declared that every school district was obligated to end dual school systems "at once" and "now and hereafter" to operate only unitary schools.[5] The effect of the decision, 15 years after the original *Brown* case, was to eliminate any further legal justification for the continuation of segregation in public schools.

RACIAL BALANCING IN PUBLIC SCHOOLS

After over a half century of efforts at desegregation by law, de facto segregation—black children attending public schools in which more than half the pupils are black—continues to characterize American education. Indeed, nationwide, roughly two-thirds of all black public school pupils attend schools with a black majority. One-third of black pupils attend schools with 90 to 100 percent minority enrollment.[6] Years ago, the U.S. Civil Rights Commission reported that even when segregation was de facto—that is, a product of segregated housing patterns and neighborhood school attendance—the adverse effects on black students were still significant.[7]

Ending racial isolation in the public schools often involves busing schoolchildren into and out of segregated neighborhoods. The objective is to achieve a racial balance in each public school, so that each has roughly the same percentage of blacks and whites as is found in the total population of the entire school district. Indeed, in some large cities where blacks make up the overwhelming majority of public school students, ending racial isolation may require city students to be bused to the suburbs and suburban students to be bused to the core city.

Federal Court Intervention

Federal district judges enjoy wide freedom in fashioning remedies for past or present discriminatory practices by governments. If a federal district court anywhere in the United States finds that any actions by governments or school officials have contributed to racial imbalances (e.g., by drawing school district attendance lines), the judge may order the adoption of a desegregation plan to overcome racial imbalances produced by official action.

In the important case of *Swann v. Charlotte-Mecklenburg County Board of Education* (1971), the Supreme Court upheld (1) the use of racial balance requirements in schools and the assignment of pupils to schools based on race, (2) "close scrutiny" by judges of schools that are predominantly of one race, (3) gerrymandering of school attendance zones as well as "clustering" or "grouping" of schools to achieve equal balance, and (4) court-ordered busing of pupils to achieve racial balance.[8] The Court was careful to note, however, that racial imbalance in schools is not itself grounds for ordering these remedies, unless it is also shown that some present or past government action contributed to the imbalance.

However, in the absence of any government actions contributing to racial imbalance, states and school districts are *not* required by the Fourteenth Amendment to integrate their schools. For example, where central-city schools are predominantly black and suburban schools are predominantly white because of residential patterns, cross-district busing is not required unless some official action brought about these racial imbalances. Thus, in 1974, the Supreme Court threw out a lower federal court order for massive busing of students between Detroit and fifty-two suburban school districts. Although Detroit city schools were 70 percent black, none of the Detroit-area school districts segregated students within their own boundaries. Chief Justice Burger, writing for the majority, said, "Unless [Detroit officials] drew the district lines in a discriminatory fashion, or arranged for the white students residing in the Detroit district to attend schools in Oakland or Macomb counties, they were under no constitutional duty to make provision for Negro students to do so."[9] In a strong dissent, Justice Thurgood Marshall wrote, "In the short run it may seem to be the easiest course to allow our great metropolitan areas to be divided up each into cities—one white, the other black—but it is a course, I predict, our people will ultimately regret."

Racial isolation continues to characterize public schools in many of the nation's largest cities; racial isolation is especially prevalent in cities with majority African American populations; for example, Atlanta, Baltimore, Cleveland, Detroit, Memphis, New Orleans, Newark, St. Louis, and Washington, DC.[10]

An End to Racial Balancing

Racial balancing in public elementary and secondary schools may be nearing an end. With regard to schools with a history of segregation (Southern schools), the Supreme Court has begun to address the question of when desegregation has been achieved and therefore when racial balancing plans can be abandoned. In the 1990s the Court began to free school districts from direct federal court supervision and court-ordered racial balancing. When the last vestiges of state-sanctioned discrimination have been removed "as far as practicable," the Supreme Court has allowed lower federal courts to dissolve racial balancing plans even though imbalances due to residential patterns continue to exist.[11]

The Supreme Court has also held that all racial classifications by governments for whatever purpose are subject to "strict scrutiny" by the courts.[12] This means that racial classifications must be "narrowly tailored" to achieve a "compelling government interest." When a Seattle, Washington, school district voluntarily adopted student assignment plans that relied on race to determine which schools certain children would attend, the Supreme Court held that the district had violated the Fourteenth Amendment's guarantee of equal protection of the laws.[13] Inasmuch as the Seattle district had no history of segregation, its racial balancing was subject to the strict scrutiny test. The Court went on to reason that achieving "diversity" in the student body was not proven to be a compelling interest in public elementary and secondary schools. Moreover, the Seattle district's racial balancing plan was not narrowly tailored; the district had failed to consider race-neutral assignment plans that might achieve the same outcome as racial classifications. The Court noted that the Seattle plan considered race exclusively and not in a broader definition of "diversity." The effect of the decision is to force school districts across the country to reconsider voluntary racial balancing plans.

THE CIVIL RIGHTS MOVEMENT

The early goal of the civil rights movement in America was to prevent discrimination and segregation by *governments*, particularly states, municipalities, and school districts. But even while important victories for the civil rights movement were being recorded in the prevention of discrimination by governments, particularly in the *Brown* case, the movement began to broaden its objectives to include the elimination of discrimination in *all* segments of American life, private as well as public. Governments should not only cease discriminatory practices of their own, they should also act to halt discrimination by private firms and individuals.

The goal of eliminating discrimination in private life creates a positive obligation of government to act forcefully in public accommodations, employment, housing, and many other sectors of society. When the civil rights movement turned to combating private discrimination, it had to carry its fight into the legislative branch of government. The federal courts could help end discrimination by state and local governments and school authorities, but only Congress, state legislatures, and city councils could end discrimination practiced by private owners of restaurants, hotels and motels, private employers, landlords, real estate agents, and other individuals who were not government officials.

The Montgomery Bus Boycott

The leadership in the struggle to eliminate discrimination and segregation from private life was provided by a young African American minister, Martin Luther King, Jr. His father was the pastor of one of the South's largest and most influential congregations, the Ebenezer Baptist Church in Atlanta, Georgia. Martin Luther King, Jr., received his doctorate from Boston University and began his ministry in Montgomery, Alabama. In 1955, the African American community of Montgomery began a year-long boycott, with frequent demonstrations against the Montgomery city buses over segregated seating. The dramatic appeal and the eventual success of the boycott in Montgomery brought nationwide attention to its leader and led to the creation in 1957 of the Southern Christian Leadership Conference.

Nonviolent Direct Action

Under King's leadership the civil rights movement developed and refined political techniques for minorities in American politics, including nonviolent direct action, a form of protest that involves breaking "unjust" laws in an open, nonviolent fashion. The general notion of civil disobedience is not new; it has played an important role in American history, from the Boston Tea Party to the abolitionists who illegally hid runaway slaves, to the suffragettes who demonstrated for women's voting rights, to the labor organizers who formed the nation's major industrial unions, to the civil rights workers of the early 1960s who deliberately violated segregation laws. The purpose of the nonviolent direct action is to call attention, or to "bear witness," to the existence of injustice. In the words of King, civil disobedience "seeks to dramatize the issue so that it can no longer be ignored."[14]

There should be no violence in true civil disobedience, and only "unjust" laws are broken. Moreover, the law is broken "openly, lovingly" and with a willingness to accept the penalty. Punishment is actively sought rather than avoided since it will help to emphasize the injustice of the law. The object is to stir the conscience of an elite and win support for measures that will eliminate the injustices. By willingly accepting punishment for the violation of an unjust law, one demonstrates the strength of one's convictions. The dramatization of injustice makes news, the public's sympathy is won when injustices are spotlighted, and the willingness of demonstrators to accept punishment is visible evidence of their sincerity. Cruelty or violence directed against the demonstrators by police or others plays into the hands of the protesters by further emphasizing the injustices they are experiencing.

Martin Luther King, Jr.

In 1963 a group of Alabama clergymen petitioned Martin Luther King, Jr., to call off mass demonstrations in Birmingham. King, who had been arrested in the demonstrations, replied in his famous "Letter from Birmingham City Jail":

> In no sense do I advocate evading or defying the law as the rabid segregationist would do. This would lead to anarchy. One who breaks an unjust law must do it *"openly, lovingly"* (not hatefully as the white mothers did in New Orleans when they were seen on television screaming "nigger, nigger, nigger") and with a willingness to accept the penalty. I submit that an individual who breaks a law that conscience tells him is unjust, and willingly accepts the penalty by staying in jail to arouse the conscience of the community over its injustice, is in reality expressing the very highest respect for law.[15]

It is important to note that King's tactics relied primarily on an appeal to the conscience of white elites. The purpose of demonstrations was to call attention to injustice and stimulate established elites to remedy the injustice by lawful means. The purpose of civil disobedience was to dramatize injustice; only *unjust* laws were to be broken, and punishment was accepted to demonstrate sincerity. King did *not* urge black masses to remedy injustice themselves by any means necessary; and he did *not* urge the overthrow of established elites.

In 1964, Martin Luther King, Jr., received the Nobel Peace Prize in recognition of his unique contributions to the development of nonviolent methods of social change.

"I Have a Dream"

The culmination of the nonviolent philosophy was a giant, yet orderly, march on Washington, held on August 28, 1963. More than 200,000 blacks and whites participated in the march, which was endorsed by many labor leaders, religious groups, and political figures. The march ended at the Lincoln Memorial where King delivered his most eloquent appeal, entitled "I Have a Dream": "I have a dream. It is a dream deeply rooted in the American dream. I have a dream that one day this nation will rise up and live out the true meaning of its creed: 'We hold these truths to be self-evident, that all men are created equal.'" In response President

Kennedy sent a strong civil rights bill to Congress, which was passed after his death—the famous Civil Rights Act of 1964.

The Civil Rights Act of 1964

The Civil Rights Act of 1964 passed both houses of Congress by better than a two-thirds favorable vote; it won the overwhelming support of both Republican and Democratic members of Congress. It was signed into law by President Lyndon B. Johnson on July 4, 1964. It ranks with the Emancipation Proclamation, the Fourteenth Amendment, and *Brown* v. *Topeka* as one of the most important steps toward full equality for blacks in America. Among its most important provisions are the following:

Title II: It is unlawful to discriminate or segregate persons on the grounds of race, color, religion, or national origin in any public accommodation, including hotels, motels, restaurants, movies, theaters, sports arenas, entertainment houses, and other places that offer to serve the public. This prohibition extends to all establishments whose operations affect interstate commerce or whose discriminatory practices are supported by state action.

Title VI: Each federal department and agency shall take action to end discrimination in all programs or activities receiving federal financial assistance in any form. This action shall include termination of financial assistance.

Title VII: It shall be unlawful for any employer or labor union to discriminate against any individual in any fashion in employment because of his race, color, religion, sex, or national origin, and that an Equal Employment Opportunity Commission shall be established to enforce this provision by investigation, conference, conciliation, persuasion, and if need be, civil action in federal court.

The Civil Rights Act of 1968

For many years fair housing had been considered the most sensitive area of civil rights legislation. Discrimination in the sale and rental of housing was the last major civil rights problem on which Congress took action. Discrimination in housing had not been mentioned in any previous legislation—not even in the comprehensive Civil Rights Act of 1964. Prohibiting discrimination in the sale or rental of housing affected the constituencies of northern members of Congress more than any of the earlier, southern-oriented legislation.

The prospects for a fair housing law were not very good at the beginning of 1968. However, when Martin Luther King, Jr., was assassinated on April 4, the mood of Congress and the nation changed dramatically. Congress passed a fair housing law as tribute to the slain civil rights leader.

The Civil Rights Act of 1968 prohibited the following forms of discrimination:

Refusal to sell or rent a dwelling to any person because of his race, color, religion, or national origin.

Discrimination against a person in the terms, conditions, or privileges of the sale or rental of a dwelling.

Advertising the sale or rental of a dwelling indicating a preference or discrimination based on race, color, religion, or national origin.

PUBLIC POLICY AND AFFIRMATIVE ACTION

The gains of the early civil rights movement were primarily gains in *opportunity* rather than in *results*. Racial politics today center on the actual inequalities between whites and minorities in incomes, jobs, housing, health, education, and other conditions of life.

Continuing Inequalities

The problem of inequality is often posed as differences in the "life chances" of whites and minorities (see Table 14–3). The average income of a black family is only 61 percent of the average white family income. More than 25 percent of all black families fall below the recognized poverty line, while only about 12 percent of white families live in poverty. The black unemployment rate is more than twice

TABLE 14–3 Minority Life Chances Continuing inequalities are revealed in income, poverty, education, and unemployment.

Median Income of Families (Constant 2008 Dollars)				
Race	1980	1990	2000	2008
White	54,493	58,952	66,302	65,000
Black	31,530	34,212	42,105	39,879
Hispanic	36,611	37,419	43,063	40,466

Persons Below Poverty Level					
Race	1980 (%)	1990 (%)	2000 (%)	2008 (%)	2009 (%)
White	10.2	10.7	9.5	10.6	12.3
Black	32.5	31.9	22.5	24.9	25.8
Hispanic	25.7	28.1	21.5	21.8	25.3

Persons Over 25 Completing, 2009		
Race	High School (%)	Bachelor's Degree (%)
White	87.1	30.0
Black	84.1	19.3
Hispanic	61.9	13.2

Unemployment Rate			
Race	1992	2000	2010
White	5.5	2.6	8.7
Black	11.0	5.4	16.0
Hispanic	9.8	4.4	12.5

SOURCES: *Statistical Abstract of the United States, 2011*, pp. 455, 466, 150; Bureau of Labor Statistics, *www.bls.gov*

as high as the white unemployment rate. The civil rights movement of the 1960s opened up new opportunities for black Americans, but equality of opportunity is not the same as equality of results.

Opportunity Versus Results

Most Americans are concerned more with equality of opportunity than equality of results. *Equality of opportunity* refers to the ability to make of oneself what one can; to develop one's talents and abilities; and to be rewarded for work, initiative, and achievement. It means that everyone comes to the same starting line with the same chance of success, that whatever differences develop over time do so as a result of abilities, talents, initiative, hard work, and perhaps good luck. *Equality of results* refers to the equal sharing of income, jobs, contracts, and material rewards regardless of one's condition in life. It means that everyone starts and finishes the race together, regardless of ability, talent, initiative, or work.

Equal Opportunity Versus Affirmative Action

The earlier emphasis of government policy, of course, was nondiscrimination, or equal employment opportunity. "It was not a program to offer special privilege to any one group of persons because of their particular race, religion, sex, or national origin."[16] This appeared to conform to the original nondiscrimination approach, beginning with President Harry Truman's decision to desegregate the armed forces in 1946 and carrying through Title VI and Title VII of the Civil Rights Act of 1964 to eliminate discrimination in federally aided projects and private employment.

Gradually, however, the goal of the civil rights movement shifted from the traditional aim of *equality of opportunity* through nondiscrimination alone to affirmative action to establish "goals and timetables" to achieve *equality of results* between blacks and whites. While avoiding the term *quota*, the notion of affirmative action tests the success of equal employment opportunity by observing whether blacks achieve admissions, jobs, and promotions in proportion to their numbers in the population.

Affirmative action programs were initially products of the federal bureaucracy. They were not begun by Congress. Instead, they were developed by the federal executive agencies that were authorized by the Civil Rights Act of 1964 to develop "rules and regulations" for desegregating activities receiving federal funds (Title VI) and private employment (Title VII). President Lyndon B. Johnson gave impetus to affirmative action with Executive Order No. 11246 in 1965, which covered employment and promotion in federal agencies and businesses contracting with the federal government. In 1972 the U.S. Office of Education issued guidelines that mandated "goals" for university admissions and faculty hiring of minorities and women. The Equal Employment Opportunity Commission, established by the Civil Rights Act of 1964 (Title VII) to eliminate discrimination in private employment, has carried the notion of affirmative action beyond federal contractors and recipients of federal aid into all sectors of private employment.

THE SUPREME COURT AND AFFIRMATIVE ACTION

Affirmative action programs pose some important constitutional questions. Do these programs discriminate against whites in violation of the Equal Protection Clause of the Fourteenth Amendment? Do these programs discriminate against whites in violation of the Civil Rights Act of 1964, which prohibits discrimination "on account of race," not just discrimination against African Americans?

The Bakke Case

In an early case, *Regents of the University of California* v. *Bakke* (1978), the Supreme Court struck down a special admissions program for minorities at a state medical school on the grounds that it excluded a white applicant because of his race and violated his rights under the equal protection clause.[17] Allan Bakke applied to the University of California Davis Medical School two consecutive years and was rejected; in both years black applicants with significantly lower grade point averages and medical aptitude test scores were accepted through a special admissions program that reserved 16 minority places in a class of 100.* The University of California did not deny that its admissions decisions were based on race. Instead, it argued that its racial classification was "benign," that is, designed to assist minorities, not to hinder them. The special admissions program was designed (1) to "reduce the historical deficit of traditionally disfavored minorities in medical schools and the medical profession," (2) to "counter the effects of societal discrimination," (3) to "increase the number of physicians who will practice in communities currently underserved," and (4) to "obtain the educational benefits that flow from an ethnically diverse student body."

The Court held that these objectives were legitimate and that race and ethnic origin may be considered in reviewing applications to a state school without violating the Equal Protection Clause. However, the Court also held that a separate admissions program for minorities with a specified quota of openings that were unavailable to white applicants did violate the Equal Protection Clause. The Court ordered Bakke admitted to medical school and the elimination of the special admissions program. It recommended that California consider developing an admissions program that considered disadvantaged racial or ethnic background as a "plus" in an overall evaluation of an application, but did not set numerical quotas or exclude any persons from competing for all positions.

Affirmative Action as a Remedy for Past Discrimination

However, the Supreme Court has approved affirmative action programs where there is evidence of past discriminatory actions. In *United Steelworkers of America* v. *Weber* (1979), the Court approved a plan developed by a private employer and a union to reserve 50 percent of higher-paying, skilled jobs for minorities. Kaiser Aluminum Corporation and the United Steelworkers Union, under federal government pressure, had established a program to get more African Americans into skilled technical jobs. When Weber was excluded from the training program and African Americans with less seniority and fewer qualifications were accepted, he filed suit in federal court claiming that he had been discriminated against because of his race in violation of Title VII of the Civil Rights Act of 1964. But the Supreme Court held that Title VII of the Civil Rights Act of 1964 "left employers and unions in the private sector free to take such race-conscious steps to eliminate manifest racial imbalances in traditionally segregated job categories. We hold that Title VII does not prohibit such . . . affirmative action plans." Weber's reliance on the clear language of Title VII was "misplaced." According to the Court, it would be "ironic indeed" if the Civil Rights Act were used to prohibit voluntary, private race-conscious efforts to overcome the past effects of discrimination.[18]

---

*Bakke's grade point average was 3.51; his MCAT scores were verbal 96, quantitative 94, science 97, general information 72. The *average* for the special admissions students were grade point average 2.62, MCAT verbal 34, quantitative 30, science 37, general information 18.

Despite changing membership over time, the Supreme Court has not altered its policy regarding affirmative action as a remedy for past discrimination. In *United States v. Paradise* (1987), the Court upheld a rigid 50 percent African American quota system for promotions in the Alabama Department of Safety, which had excluded blacks from the ranks of state troopers before 1972 and had not promoted any blacks higher than corporal before 1984. In a 5-to-4 decision, the majority stressed the long history of discrimination in the agency as a reason for upholding the quota system. Whatever burdens were imposed on innocent parties were outweighed by the need to correct the effects of past discrimination.[19]

Cases Questioning Affirmative Action

Yet in the absence of past discrimination, the Supreme Court has expressed concern about whites who are directly and adversely affected by government action solely because of their race. In *Firefighters Local Union v. Stotts* (1984), the Court ruled that a city could not lay off white firefighters in favor of black firefighters with less seniority.[20] In *Richmond v. Crosen* (1989), the Court held that a minority set-aside program in Richmond, Virginia, which mandated that 30 percent of all city construction contracts go to "blacks, Spanish-speaking, Orientals, Indians, Eskimos, or Aleuts," violated the Equal Protection Clause of the Fourteenth Amendment.[21]

However, the Supreme Court has never adopted the *color-blind doctrine* first espoused by Justice John Harlan in his dissent from *Plessy v. Ferguson*—that "our constitution is color-blind and neither knows nor tolerates classes among citizens."[22] If the Equal Protection Clause required that the laws of the United States and the states be truly color-blind, then *no* racial preferences, goals, or quotas would be tolerated. This view has occasionally been expressed in minority dissents and concurring opinions.[23]

Proving Discrimination

The Civil Rights Act of 1964, Title VII, bars racial or sexual discrimination in employment. But how can persons who feel that they have been passed over for jobs or promotions go about the task of proving that discrimination was involved? Evidence of direct discrimination is often difficult to obtain. Can underrepresentation of minorities or women in a work force be used as evidence of discrimination, in the absence of any evidence of direct discriminatory practice? If an employer uses a requirement or test that has a "disparate effect" on minorities or women, who has the burden of proof that the requirement or test is relevant to effective job performance?

The Supreme Court responded to both of these questions in its interpretation of the Civil Rights Act in *Wards Cove Packing Co., Inc. v. Atonio* (1989).[24] In a controversial 5-to-4 decision, the Court held that statistical imbalances in race or gender in the workplace were *not* sufficient evidence by themselves to prove discrimination. The Court also ruled that it was up to the plaintiffs to prove that an employer had no business reason for requirements or tests that had an adverse impact on minorities or women. This decision clearly made it more difficult to prove job discrimination.

Civil rights groups were highly critical of what they regarded as the Supreme Court's "narrowing" of the Civil Rights Act protections in employment. They turned to Congress to rewrite portions of the Civil Rights Act to restore these protections. Business lobbies, however, believed that accepting statistical imbalances as evidence of discrimination or shifting the burden of proof to employers would result in hiring by "quotas" simply to avoid lawsuits. After nearly two years of negotiations on Capitol Hill and a reversal of President George H.W. Bush's initial opposition, Congress crafted a policy in its Civil Rights and Women's Equity Act of 1991. Among the more important provisions of the act are the following:

> *Statistical imbalances:* The mere existence of statistical imbalance in an employer's work force is not, by itself, sufficient evidence to prove discrimination. However, statistical imbalances may be evidence of employment practices (rules, requirements, academic qualifications, tests) that have a "disparate impact" on minorities or women.

> *Disparate employment practices:* Employers bear the burden of proof that any practice that has a "disparate impact" is necessary and has "a significant and manifest relationship to the requirements for effective job performance."

"Strict Scrutiny"

In 1995, the Supreme Court held that racial classifications in law must be subject to "strict scrutiny." This means that race-based actions by government—any disparate treatment of the races by federal, state, or local public agencies—must be found necessary to remedy past proven discrimination, or to further clearly identified legitimate and "compelling" government objectives. Moreover, it must be "narrowly tailored" so as not to adversely affect the rights of individuals. In striking down a federal construction contract set-aside program for small businesses owned by racial minorities, the Court expressed skepticism about governmental racial classifications: "There is simply no way of determining what classifications are 'benign' and 'remedial' and what classifications are in fact motivated by illegitimate notions of racial inferiority or simple racial politics."[25]

Affirmative Action in Higher Education

College and university efforts to achieve "diversity" in higher education; that is, efforts to recruit more minority students and faculty are also subject to "strict scrutiny." In practice, diversity is another term for affirmative action. (See "Diversity in Higher Education" in Chapter 9.) The U.S. Supreme Court ruled in 2003 that diversity may be "a compelling government interest."[26] However, programs to achieve diversity must be "narrowly tailored" to that purpose. They must not establish race as the "decisive factor" in university admissions.[27]

Mass Initiatives Against Racial Preferences

"Direct democracy," in which the people themselves initiate and decide on policy questions, has always been viewed with skepticism by America's elite. James Madison believed that "such democracies have ever been spectacles of turbulence and contention." Policy should be made "through the medium of a chosen body of citizens, whose wisdom may best discern the true interests of their country."[28] There is no provision in the U.S. Constitution for national referenda. But the Progressive Era of the late nineteenth and early twentieth centuries brought with it many popular reforms, including the initiative and referendum. Currently, 18 states provide for state constitutional initiatives—allowing citizens to place amendments on the ballot by petition—followed by a referendum vote—allowing citizens to adopt or reject the amendment.[29]

Challenging Affirmative Action Barbara Grutter and Jennifer Gratz contested the affirmative action policies of the University of Michigan. The Supreme Court rejected Grutter's challenge, holding that the law school's admission policy was "narrowly tailored" to achieve a "compelling interest"—diversity. But the high court upheld Gratz's claim that making race the "decisive factor" in undergraduate admissions was unconstitutional.   (Associated Press)

California's Proposition 209

Mass opposition to affirmative action has been expressed in several states through the popular initiative device. California voters led the way in 1996 with a citizens' initiative (Proposition 209) that added the following phrase to that state's constitution:

> Neither the state of California nor any of its political subdivisions or agents shall use race, sex, color, ethnicity or national origin as a criterion for either discriminating against, or granting preferential treatment to, any individual or group in the operation of the State's system of public employment, public education or public contracting.

Supporters of the "California Civil Rights Initiative" argued that this initiative leaves all existing federal and state civil rights protections intact. It simply extends the rights of specially protected groups to all of the state's citizens. Opponents argued that it sets back the civil rights movement, that it will end the progress of minorities in education and employment, and that it denies minorities the opportunity to seek assistance and protection from government. The initiative was approved by 54 percent of California's voters.

Following the adoption of the California initiative, opponents filed suit in federal court arguing that it violated the Equal Protection Clause of the U.S. Constitution because it denied minorities and women an opportunity to seek preferential treatment by governments. But a federal Circuit Court of Appeals upheld the constitutionality of the initiative: "Impediments to preferential treatment do not deny equal protection."[30] The court reasoned that the Constitution allows some race-based preferences to correct past discrimination, but it does not prevent states from banning racial preferences altogether.

State Initiatives Banning Racial Preferences

The success of the California Civil Rights Initiative inspired similar mass movements in other states: Washington adopted a similarly worded state constitutional amendment in 1998, and Michigan approved a statewide ban on racial preferences in public education, employment, and state contracts in 2006. (In Michigan this initiative was opposed by elites in the political, business, and academic worlds, including both Democratic and Republican gubernatorial candidates. Nonetheless, 58 percent of Michigan voters favored banning racial preferences.) Nebraska voters approved a ban on racial preferences in 2008, and Arizona votes did so in 2010. Colorado voters narrowly defeated such a ban in 2008, making Colorado the only state to reject a ban on racial preferences in a popular referendum vote.

PUBLIC POLICY AND HISPANIC AMERICANS

Hispanic Americans are now the nation's largest minority. The experience of Hispanics—a term that the U.S. Census Bureau uses to refer to Mexican Americans, Puerto Ricans, Cubans, and others of Spanish-speaking ancestry and culture—differs significantly from that of African Americans. It is true, of course, that the Equal Protection Clause of the Fourteenth Amendment protects "any person" and the Civil Rights Act of 1964 specifically identifies "national origin" as a category coming under its protection. Thus, the Constitution and laws of the United States offer Hispanics protection against discrimination.

Elite Exploitation

Some Mexican Americans are descendants of citizens who lived in the Mexican territory annexed by the United States in 1848, but most have come to the United States in accelerating numbers in recent decades. For many years, agricultural businesses encouraged immigration of Mexican farm labor willing to endure harsh conditions for low pay. Farm workers were not covered by the federal National Labor Relations Act; thus, they were not guaranteed a minimum wage or protected in the right to organize labor unions. It was not until the 1960s that civil rights activity among Hispanic farm workers, under the leadership of Cesar Chávez and the United Farm Workers union, began to make improvements in the wages and living conditions of Mexican farm workers. The movement (often referred to as *La Raza*) encouraged Mexican Americans throughout the Southwest to engage in political activity.

However, inasmuch as many Mexican American immigrants were noncitizens, and many were *indocumentados* (undocumented residents or illegal aliens), they were vulnerable to exploitation by employers. Many continued to work in sub-minimum wage jobs with few or no benefits and under substandard conditions.

Inequalities between Hispanics and whites ("Anglos") can be observed in overall statistics on employment, income, and education (see Table 14–3 earlier in this chapter). Hispanics are included in affirmative action program protections. However, the federal Equal Employment Opportunity Commission receives fewer complaints from Hispanics than from African Americans or women.

Most Hispanics today believe that they confront less prejudice and discrimination than their parents. Nonetheless, in 1994, California voters approved a referendum, Proposition 187, that would have barred welfare and other benefits to persons living in the state illegally. Most Hispanics opposed the measure, believing that it was motivated by prejudice. A federal court later declared major portions of Proposition 187 unconstitutional. Moreover, the U.S. Supreme Court has held that a state may not bar children of illegal immigrants from attending public schools.[31]

Voting Rights

The Voting Rights Act of 1965, as later amended and as interpreted by the U.S. Supreme Court, extends voting rights protections to "language minorities." Following redistricting after the 1990 census, Hispanic representation in Congress rose substantially. Today about 4 percent of the U.S. House of Representatives are Hispanic, still well below the nation's 15 percent Hispanic population.

THE CONSTITUTION AND GENDER EQUALITY

Although the historical context of the Fourteenth Amendment implies its intent to guarantee equality for newly freed slaves, the wording of its Equal Protection Clause applies to "any person." Thus the text of the Fourteenth Amendment *could* be interpreted to bar any gender differences in the law. However, the Supreme Court has never interpreted the Equal Protection Clause to give the same level of protection to gender equality as to racial equality. Indeed, the Supreme Court in the nineteenth century specifically rejected the argument that this clause applied to women; the Court once upheld a state law banning women from practicing law, arguing that "The natural and proper timidity and delicacy which belongs to the female sex evidently unfits it for many of the occupations of civil life."[32]

Early Feminist Politics

The first generation of feminists learned to organize, hold public meetings, and conduct petition campaigns in the pre–Civil War antislavery movement. Following the Civil War, women were successful in changing many state laws that abridged the property rights of married women and otherwise treated them as chattel (property) of their husbands. Activists were also successful in winning some protections for women in the workplace, including state laws improving hours of work, working conditions, and physical demands. At the time, these laws were regarded as progressive. Feminist efforts of the 1800s also centered on the protection of women in families. The perceived threats to women's well-being were their husbands' drinking, gambling, and consorting with prostitutes. Women led the Anti-Saloon League and succeeded in outlawing gambling and prostitution in every state except Nevada and provided the major source of moral support for the Eighteenth Amendment (Prohibition).

The feminist movement in the early twentieth century concentrated on women's suffrage—the drive to guarantee women the right to vote. The early suffragettes employed mass demonstrations, parades, picketing, and occasional disruption and civil disobedience—tactics similar to those of the civil rights movement of the 1960s. The culmination of their efforts was the 1920 passage of the Nineteenth Amendment to the Constitution: "The right of citizens of the United States to vote shall not be denied or abridged by the United States or by any state on account of sex."

Judicial Scrutiny of Gender Classifications

The Supreme Court became responsive to arguments that sex discrimination might violate the Equal Protection Clause of the Fourteenth Amendment in the 1970s. It ruled that sexual classifications in the law "must be reasonable and not arbitrary, and must rest on some ground of difference having fair and substantial relation to . . . important governmental objectives."[33] Thus, for example, the Court has ruled (1) that a state can no longer set different ages for men and women to become legal adults[34] or purchase alcoholic beverages;[35] (2) women cannot be barred from police or firefighting jobs by arbitrary height and weight requirements;[36] (3) insurance and retirement plans for women must pay the same monthly benefits (even though women on the average live longer);[37] and (4) public schools must pay coaches in girls' sports the same as coaches in boys' sports.[38]

Court Recognition of Gender Differences

Yet the Supreme Court has continued to recognize some gender differences in law. For example, the Court has upheld statutory rape laws that make it a crime for an adult male to have sexual intercourse with a female under the age of 18, regardless of her consent. The Court has upheld Congress's draft registration law for men only, and it has declined to intervene in U.S. Defense Department decisions regarding the assignments of women in the military.

Equal Rights Amendment

At the center of feminist activity in the 1970s was the Equal Rights Amendment (ERA) to the Constitution. The amendment stated simply, "Equality of rights under the law shall not be denied or abridged by the United States or by any state on account of sex." The ERA passed Congress easily in 1972 and was sent to the states for the necessary ratification by three-fourths (38) of them. The amendment won quick ratification in half the states, but a developing "Stop ERA" movement slowed progress and eventually defeated the amendment itself. In 1979, the original seven-year time period for ratification—the period customarily set by Congress for ratification of constitutional amendments—expired. Proponents of the ERA persuaded Congress to extend the ratification period for three more years, to 1982. But despite heavy lobbying efforts in the states and public opinion polls showing national majorities favoring it, the amendment failed to win ratification by the necessary 38 states.*

PUBLIC POLICY AND GENDER EQUALITY

Today, women's participation in the labor force is not much lower than men's, and the gap is closing over time. More than 78 percent of married women with school-age children are working; and about 68 percent of married women with children under 6 years of age are working.[39] The movement of women into the American work force shifted feminist political activity toward economic concerns—gender equality in education, employment, pay, promotion, and credit.

Civil Rights Laws

The Civil Rights Act of 1964, Title VII, prevents sexual (as well as racial) discrimination in hiring, pay, and promotions. The Equal Employment Opportunity Commission (EEOC), the federal agency charged with eliminating discrimination in employment, has established guidelines barring stereotyped classifications of "men's jobs" and "women's jobs." The courts have repeatedly struck down state laws and employer practices that differentiate between men and women in hours, pay, retirement age, and so forth.

The Federal Equal Credit Opportunity Act of 1974 prohibits sex discrimination in credit transactions. Federal law prevents banks, credit unions, savings and loan associations, retail stores, and credit card companies from denying credit because of sex or marital status. However, these businesses may still deny credit for a poor or nonexistent credit rating, and some women who have always maintained accounts in their husbands' name may still face credit problems if they apply in their own name.

---

*By 1982, 34 states had ratified the ERA. Three of them-Idaho, Nebraska, and Tennessee-subsequently voted to "rescind" their ratification, but the U.S. Constitution does not mention rescinding votes. The states that had not ratified it by 1982 were Nevada, Utah, Arizona, Oklahoma, Illinois, Indiana, Missouri, Arkansas, Louisiana, Mississippi, Alabama, Georgia, Florida, North Carolina, South Carolina, and Virginia.

The Education Act Amendment of 1972, Title IX, deals with sex discrimination in education. This federal law bars discrimination in admissions, housing, rules, financial aid, faculty and staff recruitment, pay, and—most troublesome of all—athletics. Athletics has proven very difficult because men's football and basketball programs have traditionally brought in the money to finance all other sports, and men's football and basketball have received the largest share of school athletic budgets. But the overall effect of Title IX has been to bring about a dramatic increase in women's participation in sports.

The Earnings Gap

Overall, women's earnings remain less than men's earnings, although the gap has narrowed over the years. Today, on average, women earn about 78 percent of men's earnings.

The earnings gap is not so much a product of direct discrimination; that is, women in the same job with the same skills, qualifications, experience, and work record being paid less than men. This form of direct discrimination has been illegal since the Civil Rights Act of 1964. Rather, the earnings gap is primarily a product of a division in the labor market between traditionally male and female jobs, with lower salaries paid in traditionally female occupations.

The initial efforts of the women's movement were directed toward ensuring that women enjoyed equal access to traditionally male "white-collar" occupations, for example, physician, lawyer, and engineer. Success in these efforts would automatically narrow the wage gap. And indeed, women have been very successful over the last several decades in increasing their representation in prestigious white-collar occupations (see Table 14–4), although most of these occupational fields continue to be dominated by men.

Dual Labor Market

Nonetheless, evidence of a "dual" labor market, with male-dominated "blue-collar" jobs distinguishable from female-dominated "pink-collar" jobs, continues to be a major obstacle to economic equality between men and women. These occupational differences may be attributed to cultural stereotyping, social conditioning, and premarket training and education, which narrow the choices available to women. Progress has been made in recent years in reducing occupational sex segregation (a majority of bartenders are now women). Women are reaching parity as college and university professors; women also constitute about half of law and medical school students today, suggesting parity in the future in these professions (see Table 14–4).

The Glass Ceiling

Relatively few women have climbed the ladder to become president or chief executive officer or director of the nation's largest industrial corporations, banks, utilities, newspapers, or television networks. Large numbers of women are entering the legal profession, but few have made it to senior partner in the nation's largest and most prestigious law firms. Women are more likely to be found in the president's cabinet than in the corporate boardroom.

The barriers to women's advancement to top positions are often very subtle, giving rise to the phrase *the glass ceiling*. There are many explanations for the absence of women at the top, and all of them are controversial: women choose staff assignments rather than fast-track, operating-head assignments. Women are cautious and unaggressive in corporate politics. Women have lower expectations about peak earnings and positions, and these expectations become self-fulfilling. Women bear children, and even during relatively short maternity absences they fall behind their male counterparts. Women are less likely to want to change locations than men,

TABLE 14–4   The Dual Labor Market Gender differences in occupational fields are changing very slowly, with women still concentrated in lower-paying jobs.

"White Collar"

Women are increasingly entering white-collar occupation fields traditionally dominated by men.

	1960	1983	2009
Architects	3	13	25
College and university professors	28	36	49
Engineers, mechanical	1	6	6
Lawyers and judges	4	16	32
Physicians	10	16	32

"Pink Collar"

Women continue to be concentrated in occupational fields traditionally dominated by women.

	1970	1980	2009
Secretaries	98	99	97
Waitresses and waiters	91	88	72
Nurses	97	96	92
Office clerks	75	82	82

"Blue Collar"

Women continue to be excluded from many blue-collar occupational fields traditionally dominated by men, although women bartenders now outnumber men.

	1970	1980	2009
Truck drivers	1	2	5
Carpenters	1	1	2
Auto mechanics	1	1	2
Bartenders	21	44	56

SOURCES: U.S. Department of Labor, *Employment in Perspective: Working Women* (Washington, DC: U.S. Government Printing Office, 1983); National Research Council, National Academy of Sciences, *Women's Work, Men's Work* (Washington, DC: National Academy Press, 1985); *Statistical Abstract of the United States, 2011,* pp. 393–396.

and immobile executives are worth less to a corporation than mobile ones. Women executives in sensitive positions come under even more pressure than men in similar posts. Women executives believe that they get much more scrutiny than men and must work harder to succeed. Finally, it is important to note that affirmative action efforts by governments, notably the EEOC, are directed primarily at entry-level positions rather than senior management posts.

Sexual Harassment

The specific phrase "sexual harassment" does not appear in the Civil Rights Act of 1964. However, Title VII protects employees from sexual discrimination "with respect to compensation, terms, conditions, or privileges of employment." The Supreme Court held in 1986 that "discriminatory intimidation" of employees could be "sufficiently severe" to alter the "conditions" of employment and therefore violate Title VII.

Discriminatory intimidation based on sex (sexual harassment) may take various forms. There seems to be little doubt that it includes (1) conditioning employment or promotion or privileges of employment on the granting of sexual favors by an employee and (2) "tangible" acts of touching, fondling, or forced sexual relations. But sexual harassment has also been defined to include (3) a "hostile working environment." This phrase may include offensive utterances, sexual innuendos, dirty jokes, the display of pornographic material, and unwanted proposals for dates. Several problems arise with this definition. First, it would appear to include speech and hence raise First Amendment questions regarding how far speech may be curtailed by law in the workplace. Second, the definition depends more on the subjective feelings of the individual employee about what is "offensive" and "unwanted" rather than on an objective standard of behavior that is easily understood by all. The Supreme Court wrestled with the definition of a "hostile work environment" in *Harris* v. *Forklift* in 1993. It held that a plaintiff need not show that the utterances caused psychological injury but only that a "reasonable person" would perceive the work environment as hostile or abusive. Presumably a single incident would not constitute harassment; rather, courts should consider "the frequency of the discriminatory conduct," "its severity," and whether it "unreasonably interferes with an employee's work performance."[40]

ABORTION AND THE RIGHT TO LIFE

Abortion is not an issue that can easily be compromised. The arguments touch on fundamental moral and religious principles. Supporters of abortion rights, who often refer to themselves as "pro-choice," argue that a woman should be permitted to control her own body and should not be forced by law to have unwanted children. They cite the heavy toll in lives lost in criminal abortions and the psychological and emotional pain of an unwanted pregnancy. Opponents of abortion, who often refer to themselves as "pro-life," generally base their belief on the sanctity of life, including the life of the unborn child, which they believe deserves the protection of law—"the right to life." Many believe that the killing of an unborn child for any reason other than the preservation of the life of the mother is murder.

Early State Laws

Historically, abortions for any purpose other than saving the life of the mother were criminal offenses under state law. About a dozen states acted in the late 1960s to permit abortions in cases of rape or incest or to protect the physical health of the mother, and in some cases her mental health as well. Relatively few abortions were performed under these laws, however, because of the red tape involved—review of each case by several concurring physicians, approval of a hospital board, and so forth. Then, in 1970, New York, Alaska, Hawaii, and Washington enacted laws that in effect permitted abortion at the request of the woman involved and the concurrence of her physician.

Roe v. Wade

The U.S. Supreme Court's 1973 decision in *Roe* v. *Wade* was one of the most important and far-reaching in the Court's history.[41] The Court ruled that the constitutional guarantee of "liberty" in the Fifth and Fourteenth Amendments included a woman's decision to bear or not to bear a child. The Court also ruled that the word *person* in the Constitution did *not* include the unborn child. Therefore, the Fifth and Fourteenth Amendments to the Constitution, guaranteeing "life, liberty, and property," did not protect the "life" of the fetus. The Court also ruled that a state's power to protect the health and safety of the mother could not justify *any* restriction on abortion in the first three months of pregnancy. Between the third and sixth months of pregnancy, a state could set standards for abortion procedures to protect the health of women, but a state could not prohibit abortions. Only in the final three months could a state prohibit or regulate abortion to protect the unborn.

Government Funding of Abortions

The Supreme Court's decision did not end the controversy over abortion. Congress defeated efforts to pass a constitutional amendment restricting abortion or declaring that the guarantee of life begins at conception. However, Congress, in what is known as the "Hyde Amendment," banned the use of federal funds under Medicaid (medical care for the poor) for abortions except to protect the life of a woman. The Supreme Court upheld the constitutionality of laws denying tax funds for abortions. Although women retained the right to an abortion, the Court held that there was no constitutional obligation for governments to pay for abortions;[42] the decision about whether to pay for abortion from tax revenues was left to Congress and the states.

Abortions in the United States

About 1.2 million abortions are currently performed each year in the United States. There are approximately 300 abortions for every 1,000 live births.[43] This abortion rate has *declined* since 1990. About 85 percent of all abortions are performed at abortion clinics; others are performed in physicians' offices or in hospitals, where the cost is significantly higher. Most of these abortions are performed in the first three months; about 10 percent are performed after the third month.

Abortion Battles

Early efforts by the states to limit abortion ran into Supreme Court opposition. The Court held that states may not interfere with a woman's decision to terminate a pregnancy. However, opponents of abortion won a victory in *Webster* v. *Reproductive Health Services* (1989), when the Supreme Court upheld a Missouri law restricting abortions.[44] The right to abortion under *Roe* v. *Wade* was not overturned, but the Court held that Missouri could deny public funds for abortions that were not necessary for the life of the woman and could deny the use of public facilities or employees in performing or assisting in abortions. More important, the Court upheld the requirement for a test of "viability" after 20 weeks and a prohibition on abortions of a viable fetus except to save a woman's life. The Court recognized the state's "interest in the protection of human life when viability is possible."

The effect of the *Webster* decision was to rekindle contentious debates over abortion in virtually all state capitols. Various legal restrictions on abortions have been passed in some states, including (1) prohibitions on public financing of abortions; (2) requirements for a test of viability and prohibitions on abortions of a viable fetus; (3) laws granting permission to doctors and hospitals to refuse to perform abortions; (4) laws requiring humane and sanitary disposal of fetal remains; (5) laws requiring physicians to inform patients about the development of the fetus and the availability of assistance in pregnancy; (6) laws requiring that parents of minors seeking abortion be informed; (7) laws requiring that late abortions be performed in hospitals; (8) laws setting standards of cleanliness and care in abortion clinics; (9) laws prohibiting abortion based on the gender of the fetus; (10) laws requiring a waiting period.

Reaffirming *Roe* v. *Wade*

Abortion has become such a polarizing issue that pro-choice and pro-life groups are generally unwilling to search out a middle ground. Yet the Supreme Court appears to have chosen a policy of affirming a woman's right to abortion while upholding modest restrictions.

When Pennsylvania enacted a series of restrictions on abortion—physicians must inform women of risks and alternatives; a 24-hour waiting period is required; minors must have consent of parents or a judge; spouses must be notified—these restrictions reached the Supreme Court in the case of *Planned Parenthood of Pennsylvania* v. *Casey* in 1992. Justice Sandra Day O'Connor took the lead in forming a moderate, swing bloc on the Court; her majority opinion strongly reaffirmed the fundamental right of abortion:

> Our law affords constitutional protection to personal decisions relating to marriage, procreation, contraception, family relationships, child rearing, and education. . . .These matters, involving the most intimate and personal choices a person may make in a lifetime, choices central to personal dignity and autonomy, are central to the liberty protected by the Fourteenth Amendment. . . . A woman's liberty is not so unlimited, however, that from the outset the State cannot show its concern for the life of the unborn, and at a later point in fetal development the State's interest in life has sufficient force so that the right of the woman to terminate the pregnancy can be restricted. We conclude the line should be drawn at viability, so that before that time the woman has a right to choose to terminate her pregnancy.[45]

Justice O'Connor went on to establish a new standard for constitutionally evaluating restrictions: They must not impose an "undue burden" on women seeking abortion or place "substantial obstacles" in her path. All of Pennsylvania's restrictions were upheld except spousal notification.

Medicaid and Abortion

Pro-choice and pro-life forces battle in Congress as well as in the courts. Pro-choice forces regularly attempt to repeal the Hyde Amendment that prevents states from using federal Medicaid funds to pay for abortions. A Democratic-controlled Congress responded in a limited fashion in 1993 by making abortions in cases of rape and incest eligible for Medicaid payments.

"Partial Birth Abortion"

Following a long and emotional battle, Congress outlawed an abortion procedure known as "partial birth" abortion in 2003. This procedure, which is used in less than 1 percent of all abortions, involves partial delivery of a living fetus feet-first, then vacuuming out the brain and crushing the skull to ease complete removal. In 2000 the Supreme Court declared a Nebraska law prohibiting the procedure to be an unconstitutional "undue burden" on a woman's right to an abortion.[46]

The Court noted that the Nebraska law failed to make an exception to preserve the life and health of the mother. Congress designed its law to meet the Supreme Court's objections (although Congress failed to make an exception for the health of the mother).

In 2007 the Supreme Court *upheld* Congress's ban on partial birth abortions.[47] The court reaffirmed the principle of the Casey decision—that the government has an interest in preserving the life of a viable fetus.

PUBLIC POLICY AND SEXUAL ORIENTATION

In recent years gays and lesbians have made considerable progress in winning public acceptance of their lifestyle and in changing public policy. Discrimination based on sexual orientation is not prohibited in *federal* civil rights acts, but many states and cities have enacted laws prohibiting discrimination based upon sexual orientation. Nonetheless, many gay-lesbian issues remain on the nation's political agenda.

Securing Privacy Rights

Historically, "sodomy" was defined as "an act against the laws of human nature" and criminalized in most states. As late as 1986, the U.S. Supreme Court upheld a Georgia law against sodomy holding that "the Constitution does not confer a fundamental right upon homosexuals to engage in sodomy."[48] But the Supreme Court reversed its position in 2003 in *Lawrence v. Texas* holding that consenting adults "engaged in sexual practices common to a homosexual lifestyle.... are entitled to respect for their private lives.... Their right to liberty under the Due Process Clause gives them the full right to engage in their conduct without intervention by the government."[49] The Court noted that since its earlier decision, most of the states had repealed their laws on sodomy. *Lawrence v. Texas* is a landmark decision that is likely to affect every type of case involving sexual orientation including employment, marriage, child custody, and adoption.

However, the U.S. Supreme Court has refused to interfere with private or religious organizations that ban homosexuals. The Court upheld a Boy Scout prohibition against homosexuals becoming scout leaders in 2003.[50] It also upheld the decision by the organizers of New York's annual St. Patrick's Day Parade to exclude a gay-lesbian marching contingent.

Ending "Don't Ask, Don't Tell"

Historically, the U.S. military banned homosexuals from the services. Upon taking office in 1993, President Bill Clinton announced his intention to overturn this ban. Gay-rights groups had donated heavily to the Clinton campaign. But military professionals at the time strongly objected to this move. Clinton was eventually obliged to compromise the issue and the policy of "Don't Ask, Don't Tell" emerged. The military would no longer inquire into the sexual orientation of service personnel or recruits as long as they did not make their orientation public. Gays and lesbians were still subject to dismissal from the Armed Forces if they were to "come out of the closet" or were caught in homosexual acts. But President Obama made a campaign pledge in 2008 to end the policy and to allow gays and lesbians to serve openly in the military. After lengthy Department of Defense studies and even a poll of people serving in the military, in 2010 Congress acted to repeal "Don't Ask, Don't Tell." Gays and lesbians may now serve openly in the armed forces.

Same-Sex Marriage

Most states prohibit same-sex marriage. Many of these state prohibitions have come about as a result of popular initiative and referendum. But Vermont decided in 2000 to sanction "civil unions" between same-sex couples. Several other states followed, granting same-sex couples the benefits, protections, and responsibilities that are granted to married couples. In 2003 the Massachusetts Supreme Court ruled that same-sex couples had a right to *marriage* under the Massachusetts state constitution.[51] Several other states followed Massachusetts and began issuing marriage licenses to same-sex couples. New York approved same-sex marriage in 2011.

Defense of Marriage Act

Anticipating that some states might pass laws allowing same-sex marriage, or that some state courts might rule that such marriages were constitutionally protected in their states, Congress passed a Defense of Marriage Act in 1996. This Act declared that marriage is between a man and a woman, and that "no state... shall be required to give effect to any public act, record, or judicial proceeding of any other state respecting a relationship between persons of the same sex that is treated as a marriage." This provision is designed to circumvent the Full Faith and Credit Clause of Article IV of the Constitution that requires each state to recognize the "public acts, records, and judicial proceedings of every other state." (Article IV does however include a provision that Congress may "prescribe the manner in which such acts, records, and proceedings shall be proved, and the effect thereof.")

The gay-rights movement is bitterly opposed to the Defense of Marriage Act, and President Barack Obama has pledged to use his influence to have Congress overturn it. It is likely that the issue of same-sex marriages will be thrashed out in federal courts.

AIDS

The gay-rights movement was threatened in the early 1980s by the spread of the HIV virus and the deadly disease, acquired immune deficiency syndrome, or AIDS. Gay men were identified as one of the high-risk groups in the United States. The medical consensus was that the disease is spread through a sexual activity especially prevalent among male homosexuals, as well as through the sharing of contaminated needles among intravenous drug users and through blood transfusions. Casual contact (touching, kissing, using common utensils, etc.) does not transmit the disease. But the gay-rights movement was successful in its campaign to convince Americans that "anyone could get AIDS," and over time it won the sympathy and support of the American public. Funding for AIDS research rose dramatically. The Center for Disease Control (CDC) gave priority to the search for antidotes to the virus, and at the same time, instituted a public education effort aimed at changing sexual behavior. Gay organizations across the nation distributed material describing safe sex practices. Over time, deaths from AIDS declined, and the feared epidemic was held in check.

State Laws

Much of the conflict over gay rights occurs at the state level—in referenda, legislative enactments, and court decisions—yielding a complex mosaic of laws involving sexual orientation throughout the nation. Among the issues confronting the states:

- *Adoption.* Should gay and lesbian couples be allowed to adopt children?
- *Hate Crimes.* Should hate crime laws also protect homosexuals?

- *Health.* Should health insurance companies be required to extend benefits to homosexual spouses?
- *Employment.* Should laws against job discrimination be extended to protect homosexuals?
- *Housing.* Should laws against discrimination in housing be extended to protect homosexuals?
- *Marriage.* Should gay and lesbian couples be allowed to marry?
- *Civil Unions.* Should gay and lesbian couples be allowed to legally form civil unions giving them many of the rights of married couples?

State laws differ on each of these issues, although recent changes have generally benefited gays and lesbians.[52]

PUBLIC POLICY AND THE DISABLED

The Americans with Disabilities Act (ADA) of 1990 is a sweeping law that prohibits discrimination against disabled people in private employment, government programs, public accommodations, and telecommunications. The act is vaguely worded in many of its provisions, requiring "reasonable accommodations" for disabled people that do not involve "undue hardship." This means disabled Americans do not have exactly the same standard of protection as minorities or women, who are protected from discrimination *regardless* of hardship or costs. Specifically the ADA includes the following protections:

Employment: Disabled people cannot be denied employment or promotion if, with "reasonable accommodation," they can perform the duties of the job. Reasonable accommodation need not be made if doing so would cause "undue hardship" on the employer.

Government programs: Disabled people cannot be denied access to government programs or benefits. New buses, taxis, and trains must be accessible to disabled persons, including those in wheelchairs.

Public accommodations: Disabled people must enjoy "full and equal" access to hotels, restaurants, stores, schools, parks, museums, auditoriums, and the like. To achieve equal access, owners of existing facilities must alter them "to the maximum extent feasible"; builders of new facilities must ensure that they are readily accessible to disabled persons unless doing so is structurally impossible.

Communications: The Federal Communications Commission is directed to issue regulations that will ensure telecommunications devices for hearing- and speech-impaired people are available "to the extent possible and in the most efficient manner."

But the ADA, as interpreted by the Equal Employment Opportunity Commission and federal courts, has begun to generate considerable controversy. Persons who are "learning disabled" have successfully sued colleges and universities, and even state bar associations, not only for admission but also to gain extra time and assistance in passing examinations. Persons claiming various mental disorders have successfully sued employers for being dismissed for chronic tardiness, inability to concentrate on the job, uncooperative and hostile attitudes toward supervisors, and the like.

SUMMARY

The following propositions are consistent with elite theory and help describe the development of civil rights policy:

1. Elites and masses in America differ in their attitudes toward minorities. Support for civil rights legislation has come from educated, affluent whites in leadership positions.

2. Mass opinion toward civil rights has generally *followed* public policy and not led it. Mass opinion did not oppose legally segregated schools until after elites had declared national policy in *Brown* v. *Topeka* in 1954.

3. The greatest impetus to the advancement of civil rights policy in the twentieth century was the U.S. Supreme Court's decision in *Brown* v. *Topeka*. Thus, it was the Supreme Court, nonelected and enjoying life terms in office, which assumed the initiative in civil rights policy. Congress did not take significant action until 10 years later.

4. The elimination of legal discrimination and the guarantee of equality of opportunity in the Civil Rights Act of 1964 were achieved largely through the dramatic appeals of middle-class black leaders to the consciences of white elites. Black leaders did not attempt to overthrow the established order but rather to increase opportunities for blacks to achieve success within the American system.

5. Elite support for equality of opportunity does not satisfy the demands of black masses for equality of results. Inequalities between blacks and whites in life chances—income, education, employment, health—persist.

6. Affirmative action programs are pressed on governments, universities, and private employers by federal agencies seeking to reduce inequalities. But white masses generally reject preferences or quotas, which they believe to put working-class and middle-class white males at a disadvantage.

7. The Supreme Court has approved affirmative action programs with racial quotas when there is evidence of current or past discriminatory practices and when the program is narrowly defined to remedy the effects of previous discrimination. The Court has upheld some claims that racial preferences by governments violate the Fourteenth Amendment's guarantee of equal protection of laws when white males are excluded altogether solely on the basis of race, and when there is no "compelling" government objective in classifying people by race.

8. Hispanic Americans are now the nation's largest minority. For many years, elites, especially in agribusiness, encouraged legal and illegal immigration of Mexicans in order to obtain cheap labor.

9. Although representing over half of the nation's population, the women's movement has had to rely on the tactics of minorities—demonstrations, parades, occasional civil disobedience—to convince governing elites to recognize women's rights. Women did not secure the right to vote in the U.S. Constitution until 1920. Women failed to secure ratification of the Equal Rights Amendment by three-quarters of states. The protection of women's rights relies primarily on the Civil Rights Act of 1964, together with subsequent laws of Congress prohibiting gender discrimination.

10. Abortion was prohibited by most states until the Supreme Court decided in *Roe* v. *Wade* in 1973 that women have a constitutional right to terminate pregnancies. Thus, the Court established as a constitutional right what pro-choice forces had failed to gain through political processes. Despite heated battles over abortion policy, the Supreme Court has steered a moderate policy, affirming a woman's right to abortion while upholding restrictions that do not impose an "undue burden" on women. The court has recognized the government's interest in preserving the life of a viable fetus.

11. Most states ban same-sex marriage and Congress did so in the Defense of Marriage Act in 1996. But the Massachusetts Supreme Court held that marriage prohibition on same-sex marriage violated the state's Constitution. The gay rights movement has turned to federal courts to overturn bans.

MySearchLab® EXERCISES

Apply what you learned in this chapter on MySearchLab (www.mysearchlab.com).

NOTES

1. *Civil Rights Cases*, 100 U.S. 3 (1883).

2. *Plessy v. Ferguson*, 163 U.S. 537 (1896).

3. *Sweatt v. Painter*, 339 U.S. 629 (1950).

4. *Brown v. Board of Education of Topeka, Kansas*, 347 U.S. 483 (1954).

5. *Alexander v. Holmes County Board of Education*, 396 U.S. 19 (1969).

6. Harold W. Stanley and Richard G. Niemi, *Vital Statistics on American Politics, 2005–2006* (Washington, DC: CQ Press, 2006), p. 380.

7. U.S. Commission on Civil Rights, *Racial Isolation in the Public Schools* (Washington, DC: U.S. Government Printing Office, 1966).

8. *Swann v. Charlotte-Mecklenburg County Board of Education*, 402 U.S. 1 (1971).

9. *Milliken v. Bradley*, 418 U.S. 717 (1974).

10. *Statistical Abstract of the United States, 2007*, p. 39.

11. *Board of Education v. Dowell*, U.S. (1991), 111 S. Ct. 630.

12. *Adarand Construction v. Pena*, 515 U.S. 200 (1995).

13. *Parents Involved in Community Schools v. Seattle School District*, June 28, 2007.

14. For an inspiring essay on nonviolent direct action and civil disobedience, read Martin Luther King, Jr., "Letter from Birmingham City Jail," April 16, 1963.

15. Ibid.

16. See David H. Rosenbloom, "The Civil Service Commission's Decision to Authorize the Use of Goals and Timetables in Federal Equal Employment Opportunity Programs," *Western Political Quarterly* 26 (June 1973), pp. 236–251.

17. *Regents of the University of California v. Bakke*, 438 U.S. 265 (1978).

18. *United Steelworkers v. Weber*, 443 U.S. 193 (1979).

19. *United States v. Paradise*, 480 U.S. 149 (1987).

20. *Firefighters Local Union v. Stotts*, 467 U.S. 561 (1984).

21. *Richmond v. Crosen*, 109 S. Ct. 706 (1989).

22. *Plessy v. Ferguson*, 163 U.S. 537 (1896), dissenting opinion.

23. See Justice Antonin Scalia's dissenting opinion in *Johnson v. Transportation Agency of Santa Clara County*, 480 U.S. 616 (1987).

24. *Wards Cove Packing Co., Inc. v. Atonio*, 490 U.S. 642 (1989).

25. *Adarand Construction v. Pena*, 515 U.S. 200 (1995).

26. *Grutter v. Bollinger*, 539 U.S. 306 (2003).

27. *Gratz v. Bollinger*, 539 U.S. 244 (2003).

28. *The Federalist*, Number 20.

29. Council of State Governments, *Book of the States*, annual publication.

30. *Coalition for Economic Equity v. Wilson*, Ninth Circuit Court of Appeals, April 1997.

31. *Plyer v. Doe*, 457 U.S. 202 (1982).

32. *Bradwell v. Illinois*, 16 Wall 130 (1873).

33. *Reed v. Reed*, 404 U.S. 71 (1971).

34. *Stanton v. Stanton*, 421 U.S. 7 (1975).

35. *Craig v. Borden*, 429 U.S. 190 (1976).

36. *Dothard v. Rawlinson*, 433 U.S. 321 (1977).

37. *Arizona v. Norris*, 103 S. Ct. 3492 (1983).

38. *EEOC v. Madison Community School District*, 55 U.S.L.W. 2644 (1987).

39. *Statistical Abstract of the United States, 2011*, p. 385.

40. *Harris v. Forklift*, 510 U.S. 17 (1993).

41. *Roe v. Wade*, 410 U.S. 113 (1973).

42. *Harris v. McRae*, 448 U.S. 297 (1980).

43. *Statistical Abstract of the United States, 2011*, p. 74.

44. *Webster v. Reproductive Health Services*, 492 U.S. 111 (1989).

45. *Planned Parenthood v. Casey*, 112 S. Ct. 2791 (1992).

46. *Stenburg v. Carhart*, 530 U.S. 914 (2004).

47. *Gonzales v. Carhart*, 550 U.S. 124 (2007).

48. *Bowers v. Hardwick*, 478 U.S. 186 (1986).

49. *Lawrence v. Texas*, 539 U.S. 558 (2003).

50. *Boy Scouts of America v. Dale*, 530 U.S. 640 (2000).

51. *Goodridge v. Department of Public Health*, 798 N.E. 2d 941 (2003).

52. Jeffrey R. Lax and Justin H. Phillips, "Gay Rights in the States," *American Political Science Review* vol. 103 (August, 2009) pp. 367–386.

BIBLIOGRAPHY

CONWAY, M. Margaret. *Women and Public Policy*, 3rd ed. Washington, DC: CQ Press, 2004.

MCGLEN, NANCY E., et al. *Women, Politics, and American Society*, 5th ed. New York: Longman, 2011.

NATIONAL URBAN LEAGUE. *The State of Black America*. New York: National Urban League, 2000.

ROSE, MELODY. *Safe, Legal, and Unavailable? Abortion Politics in the United States*. Washington, DC: CQ Press, 2006.

THERNSTORM, STEPHEN, AND ABIGAIL THERNSTORM. *America in Black and White*. New York: Simon & Schuster, 1997.

WALTON, HANES JR., and Robert C. Smith. *American Politics and the African-American Quest for Universal Freedom*, 6th ed. New York: Longman, 2012.

WHITAKER, LOIS DUKE. *Women in Politics*, 5th ed. New York: Longman, 2011.

WEB SITES

CENTER FOR AMERICAN WOMEN AND POLITICS. Information on women in national and state elected office. *www.rci.rutgers.edu/~cawp*

NATIONAL ASSOCIATION FOR THE ADVANCEMENT OF COLORED PEOPLE (NAACP). Oldest civil rights organization working on behalf of African Americans. Information on political, social, and economic equality issues. *www.naacp.org*

NATIONAL COUNCIL OF LA RAZA. National organization working on behalf of civil rights and economic opportunities for Hispanics. Information on issues confronting Hispanic Americans. *www.nclr.org*

NATIONAL URBAN LEAGUE. Social service and civil rights organization, with information on issues confronting minorities. *www.nul.org*

CENTER FOR EQUAL OPPORTUNITY. Organization opposed to racial preferences. Policy briefs on issues relating to race, ethnicity, and public policy, including affirmative action. *www.ceousa.org*

AMERICAN CIVIL RIGHTS INITIATIVE. Advocacy organization seeking an end to racial preferences. Provided leadership for California Civil Rights Initiative. *www.acri.org*

JOINT CENTER FOR POLITICAL AND ECONOMIC STUDIES. Information on black elected officials in national and state office. *http://jointcenter.org*

War fighting in difficult terrain A U.S. Marine descends a mountainside at the end of a combat operation near the Hindu Kush in Afghanistan's eastern Kunar Province. The stated goal of U.S. military operations in Afghanistan is to "disrupt, dismantle, and defeat Al Qaeda." (© Ed Darack/Science Faction/Corbis)

15

Defense Policy
Strategies for Serious Games

NATIONAL SECURITY AS A SERIOUS GAME

Game theory provides an interesting way of thinking about defense policy. The defense policies of major world powers are interdependent. Each nation must adjust its own defense policies to reflect not only its own national objectives but also its expectations of what other powers may do. Outcomes depend on the combination of choices made in world capitals. Moreover, it is not unreasonable to assume that nations strive for rationality in defense policymaking. Nations choose defense strategies (policies) that are designed to achieve an optimum payoff even after considering all their opponents' possible strategies. Thus, national defense policymaking conforms to basic game theory notions. Our use of game theory is limited, however, to suggesting interesting questions, posing dilemmas, and providing a vocabulary for dealing with policymaking in a competitive, interdependent world.

A rational approach to the formulation of defense policy begins with a careful assessment of the range of threats to the nation and its interests. Once major threats have been identified, the next step is to develop strategies designed to counter them and protect the nation's interests. Once strategies have been devised, defense policymaking must determine the appropriate forces (military units, personnel, weapons, training, readiness, and so forth) required to implement them. Finally, budgets must be calculated to finance the required force levels. Thus, a rational game plan proceeds from:

Threat Assessments

to

Strategies

to

Force Levels

to

Budget Requests

Of course, differences and uncertainties arise at each step in this process—differing assessments of the nature and magnitude of the threats facing the nation, the right strategies to confront these threats, the force levels necessary to implement the strategies, and the funds required to provide these forces.

And too often in Washington political pressures intervene to skew rational processes in defense policymaking. Threats may be exaggerated in order to justify preferred levels of forces or higher budget requests. More often, however, the rational process is reversed: Congress and the president first decide how much money is to be spent on defense and then they tailor force levels and strategies to conform to budget requests. Defense and intelligence officials are then pressured to evaluate threats downward in order to conform to predetermined force levels and spending decisions. In short, politics poses a challenge to rationalism in defense policy.

CONFRONTING NUCLEAR THREATS

For more than four decades, following the end of World War II in 1945, the United States and the former Union of Soviet Socialist Republics (USSR) confronted each other in a superpower struggle as intense as any in the history of nations. Indeed, nuclear weaponry made the Cold War more dangerous than any national confrontation in the past. The nuclear arsenals of the United States and the former USSR threatened a human holocaust. Yet paradoxically, the very destructiveness of nuclear weapons caused leaders on both sides to exercise extreme caution in their relations with each other. Scores of wars, large and small, were fought by different nations during the Cold War years, yet American and Soviet troops never engaged in direct combat against each other.

Deterrence

To maintain nuclear peace, the United States relied primarily on the policy of deterrence. Deterrence is based on the notion that a nation can dissuade a *rational* enemy from attacking by maintaining the capacity to destroy the enemy's society *even after* the nation has suffered a well executed surprise attack by the enemy. It assumes that the worst may happen—a surprise first strike against our own nuclear forces. It emphasizes *second-strike* capability—the ability of a nation's forces to survive a surprise attack by the enemy and then to inflict an unacceptable level of destruction on the enemy's homeland in retaliation. Deterrence is really a psychological defense against attack; no effective physical defenses against a ballistic missile attack exist even today. The strategy of deterrence maintains peace through fear of retaliation.

Strategic Weapons

To implement the deterrence strategy, the United States relied on a TRIAD of weapons systems: (1) land-based intercontinental ballistic missiles (ICBMs), (2) submarine-launched ballistic missiles (SLBMs), and (3) manned bombers. Each "leg" of the TRIAD was supposed to be an independent, survivable, second strike force. Thus, each leg posed separate and unique problems for an enemy who sought to destroy the U.S. second strike deterrent.

ARMS CONTROL GAMES

The United States and the Soviet Union engaged in negotiations over strategic arms for many years. They began in 1970 under President Richard Nixon and his national security advisor, Henry Kissinger, and were originally labeled the Strategic Arms Limitation Talks (SALT).

Salt I

SALT I, in 1972, was a milestone in that it marked the first effort by the superpowers to limit strategic nuclear weapons. It consisted of a formal treaty halting further development of antiballistic missile systems (ABMs) and an executive agreement placing numerical limits on offensive missiles. The ABM treaty reflected the theory that the populations of each nation should remain undefended from a ballistic missile attack in order to hold them hostage against a first strike by either nation. This MAD theory (mutual assured destruction) was based on the idea that no rational government would order an attack on another nuclear superpower knowing that its own population would be wiped out in a retaliatory attack.

Salt II

After seven more years of difficult negotiations, the United States and the Soviet Union signed the lengthy and complicated SALT II Treaty in 1979. It set an overall limit on "strategic nuclear launch vehicles"—ICBMs, SLBMs, and bombers with cruise missiles—at 2,250 for each side. It also limited the number of missiles that could have multiple warheads (MIRVs). When the Soviet Union invaded Afghanistan, President Carter withdrew the SALT II Treaty from Senate consideration. However, Carter, and later President Reagan, announced that the United States would abide by the provisions of the unratified SALT II treaty as long as the USSR did so too.

Start

In negotiations with the Soviets, the Reagan administration established three central principles of arms control—*reductions, equality,* and *verification.* The new goal was to be reductions in missiles and warheads, not merely limitations on future numbers and types of weapons, as in previous SALT negotiations. To symbolize this new direction, President Reagan renamed the negotiations the Strategic Arms Reductions Talks, or START.

Start I

The long-awaited agreement on long-range strategic nuclear weapons was finally signed in Moscow in 1991 by Presidents George H. W. Bush and Mikhail Gorbachev. The START I Treaty reduced the total number of deployed strategic nuclear delivery systems (ICBMs, SLBMs, and manned bombers) to no more than 1,600, a 30 percent reduction from the SALT II level. The total number of strategic nuclear warheads were reduced to no more than 6,000, a reduction of nearly 50 percent. Verification included on-site and short-notice inspections, as well as "national technical means" (satellite surveillance).

Start II

The end of the Cold War was confirmed by the far-reaching START II agreement between President George H. W. Bush and Russian President Boris Yeltsin. This agreement promised to eliminate the threat of a first-strike nuclear attack by either side. Its most important provision called for the elimination of all multiwarhead (MIRV) land-based missiles. It also called for the reduction of overall strategic warheads to 3,500, slashing the nuclear arsenals of both nations by more than two-thirds from Cold War levels (see Figure 15–1).

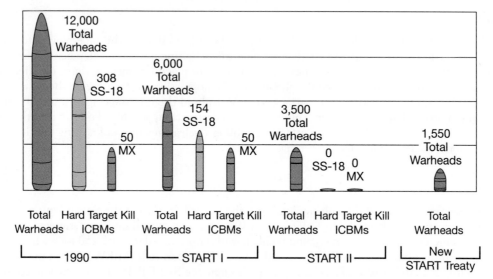

FIGURE 15–1 Strategic Nuclear Arms Reductions Post–Cold War treaties between the United States and Russia have dramatically reduced the number of nuclear warheads held by both nations.

Strategic nuclear arms reductions progressed further with the Treaty of Moscow, signed by Russian President Vladimir Putin and U.S. President George W. Bush in 2002. This treaty called for an overall limit of nuclear warheads at 1,700–2,200 by 2012.

The New START Treaty

The New START Treaty was negotiated by Russian President Dmitry Medvedev and U.S. President Barack Obama in Prague, Czech Republic, in 2010. The U.S. Senate ratified this formal treaty in the same year. New START reduces overall nuclear warheads for each side to 1550. Each side is allowed a combination of 700 missile silos and bombers. Each side can determine for itself the composition of its strategic forces—long-range bombers, land-based missiles, submarines-based missiles—consistent with these limits. The effect of this Treaty, together with earlier reductions in strategic nuclear weapons, is to reduce the nuclear warhead arsenals of the former adversaries by over 85 percent from Cold War levels. Both sides resolved to seek even deeper cuts in nuclear weapons, but no agreement was reached on the development of ballistic missile defense systems.

Nuclear Testing and Nonproliferation

The United States and the former Soviet Union reached an agreement in 1963—the Limited Test Ban Treaty—that prohibited nuclear testing in the atmosphere, under water, or in outer space. The effect was to allow only underground testing, which was believed to reduce radioactivity in the atmosphere. A Threshold Test Ban Treaty was signed in 1974 that prohibited tests of nuclear weapons with explosive power greater than 150 kilotons (equivalent to 150,000 tons of conventional explosives).

In 1992 the Russian government under President Yeltsin announced that it would discontinue *all* nuclear testing if the United States would do the same. President George H. W. Bush declined to make this pledge, but later President Bill Clinton placed a moratorium on U.S. nuclear testing.

President Bill Clinton signed a Comprehensive Nuclear Test Ban Treaty in 1996, a multi-lateral agreement that prohibits all nuclear testing. Many nonnuclear-armed nations signed this treaty. But in 1999 the U.S. Senate voted against ratification. Opponents of the treaty noted that testing verified the safety and reliability of weapons, and that several other potentially threatening nuclear nations had refused to sign the treaty, including North Korea, Iran, India, and Pakistan.

Yet another multilateral treaty, the nuclear Nonproliferation Treaty, was signed by the United States and the former Soviet Union in 1968. It prohibits nuclear-armed nations from transfer-ring weapons and technologies to nonnuclear nations. Nonnuclear signing nations pledged not to "receive, manufacture, or otherwise acquire nuclear weapons." But the Nonproliferation Treaty has been largely ignored, not only by nations that went on to acquire nuclear weapons (including India, Pakistan, China, and North Korea), but also by nations that have transferred nuclear tech-nology to nonnuclear nations (including France and Russia).

MISSILE DEFENSES: THE LIMITS OF DETERRENCE

For over a half century, since the terrible nuclear blasts of Hiroshima and Nagasaki in Japan in 1945, the world has avoided nuclear war. Peace has been maintained by deterrence—by the threat of devastating nuclear attacks that would be launched in retaliation to an enemy's first strike. Nuclear peace has depended on rational leaders who would not endanger their own populations.

Nuclear Terrorism and Nondeterrable Threats

But even as the threat of a large-scale nuclear attack recedes, the threats arising from "nondeterrable" sources are increasing. Today, the principal nondeterrable nuclear threats are estimated to be (1) missiles launched by a terrorist nation, possibly Iran or North Korea, or a "rogue" nation whose leaders are prepared to sacrifice their own people to a retaliatory strike, and (2) missile launches by terrorist groups who have acquired nuclear weapons and the means of delivering them. Over time, global nuclear and ballistic missile proliferation steadily increases the likelihood of these types of threats. Attacks by rogue nations and terrorist groups are considered nondeterrable because the threat of nuclear retaliation is largely meaningless.

"Star Wars"

In 1993, President Ronald Reagan urged that instead of deterring war through fear of retaliation, the United States should seek a technological defense against nuclear missiles:

> Our nuclear retaliating forces have deterred war for forty years. The fact is, however, that we have no defense against ballistic missile attack. . . . In the event that deterrence failed, a president's only recourse would be to surrender or to retaliate. Nuclear retaliation, whether massive or limited, would result in the loss of millions of lives. . . .[1]

Reagan's Strategic Defense Initiative (SDI) was a research program designed to explore means of destroying enemy nuclear missiles in space before they could reach their targets. Following President Reagan's initial announcement of SDI in March 1983, the press quickly labeled the effort "Star Wars." In theory, a ballistic missile defense (BMD) system could be based in space, orbiting over enemy missile-launching sites. Should an enemy missile get through the space-based defense, a ground-based BMD system would attempt to intercept warheads as they reentered the atmosphere and approached their targets. SDI included research on laser beams, satellite surveillance, computerized battle-management systems, and "smart" and "brilliant" weapons systems. SDI under President Reagan was a very ambitious program with the goal of creating an "impenetrable shield" that would protect not only the population of the United States but the populations of our allies as well.

Protecting Against Nuclear Terrorism

The end of the Cold War refocused missile defense research away from a massive Russian missile attack to much more limited, yet more likely, threats. Today the principal nuclear threats are missiles launched by terrorist groups or a "rogue state." President George W. Bush notified the Russians in 2002 that the United States was withdrawing from provisions of the SALT I Treaty of 1972 that prohibited the development, testing, or deployment of new ballistic missile defense systems.

Advanced testing has met with both successes and failures. Intercepting an incoming missile has been compared to "hitting a bullet with a bullet." Even this daunting challenge is further complicated by the likelihood of enemy decoys masking the real warhead; a reliable ballistic missile defense must be able to discriminate between decoys and actual warheads. In early 2008 the U.S. Navy successfully intercepted and destroyed a falling reconnaissance satellite with a sea-based anti-ballistic missile.

The actual deployment of a limited number of ground-based and sea-based missile interceptors began in 2004. This initial missile defense capability is designed "to meet the near-term threat to our homeland, our deployed forces, and our friends and allies."[2] It is directed at potential attacks from terrorist states. Currently the U.S. has BMDs based in Alaska, presumably to defend against missiles from North Korea. And the United States deploys Aegis ballistic missile defense warships around the world.

President George W. Bush proposed to deploy BMD sites in Poland and the Czech Republic in order to defend Europe against missiles from Iran. But Russia vigorously opposed such a deployment. In 2009 President Barack Obama canceled this deployment, hoping that in exchange Russian President Dmitry Medvedev would help in preventing Iran from acquiring nuclear weapons.

NATO AND EUROPEAN SECURITY

The preservation of democracy in Western Europe was the centerpiece of U.S. foreign and military policy for most of the twentieth century. The United States fought in two world wars to preserve democracy in Europe.

Origins of NATO

In response to aggressive Soviet moves in Europe after World War II, the United States, Canada, Belgium, Britain, Denmark, France, Iceland, Italy, Luxembourg, the Netherlands, Norway, and Portugal joined in the North Atlantic Treaty Organization (NATO). Each nation pledged that "an armed attack against one . . . shall be considered an attack against them all." Greece and Turkey joined in 1952 and West Germany in 1955. To give this pledge credibility, a joint NATO military command was established with a U.S. commanding officer (the first was General of the Army Dwight D. Eisenhower). After the formation of NATO, the Soviets made no further advances in Western Europe. The Soviets themselves, in response to NATO, drew up a comparable treaty among their own Eastern European satellite nations—the Warsaw Pact. It included Poland, Hungary, Czechoslovakia, Romania, Bulgaria, and the German Democratic Republic (the former East Germany).

Collapse of Communism in Eastern Europe

The dramatic collapse of the communist governments of Eastern Europe in 1989—Poland, Hungary, Romania, Bulgaria, and East Germany—vastly reduced the threat of a military attack on Western Europe. The dismantling of communist governments came about as a direct result of President Mikhail Gorbachev's decision to renounce the use of Soviet military force to keep them in power. For over 40 years, the communist governments of Eastern Europe were supported by Soviet tanks; bloody Soviet military operations put down civilian uprisings in Hungary in 1956 and Czechoslovakia in 1968. The threat of Soviet military intervention crushed the Solidarity movement in Poland in 1981, yet that same movement became the government of Poland in 1989. Any effort today by a Russian leader to reimpose control over Eastern European nations would probably result in widespread bloodshed.

Germany United

The collapse of the Berlin Wall in 1989 and the formal unification of Germany in 1990 rearranged the balance of military power in central Europe. Today Germany is the strongest military power in Western Europe. It remains a member of NATO.

Collapse of the Warsaw Pact and the USSR

The Warsaw Pact collapsed following the ouster of communist governments in the Eastern European nations and was officially dissolved in 1991. Its former members requested the withdrawal of Russian troops from their territory; the Russian government complied, although withdrawals were slowed by economic conditions in that nation.

At the same time, strong independence movements emerged in the republics of the USSR. Lithuania, Estonia, and Latvia—Baltic Sea nations that had been forcibly incorporated into the Soviet Union in 1939—led the way to independence in 1991. Soon all 15 republics declared their independence, and the Union of Soviet Socialist Republics officially ceased to exist after December 31, 1991. Russian President Boris Yeltsin took over the offices of former Soviet Union President Mikhail Gorbachev. The red flag with its banner and sickle atop the Kremlin was replaced by the flag of the Russian Republic.

NATO and Western Europe

If Russia, Ukraine, and the other republics of the former Soviet Union make a full transition to democracy and capitalism, the twenty-first century promises much more peace and prosperity for the peoples of the world than the twentieth century. The residual threat to Western Europe posed by Russian forces, even under a hostile regime, is very weak. However, the total withdrawal of U.S. military forces from Western Europe would probably mean an end to the NATO alliance. Proponents of a continued U.S. military presence in Europe argue that it provides reassurance and stability as democracy emerges in Eastern Europe; they note that both our old allies and new friends in Europe have urged the United States to remain involved in European security. Opponents counter that the Western European nations are now quite capable of shouldering the burden of their own security.

NATO Expansion

Despite Russian objections, NATO extended its membership eastward in 1997 by admitting Poland, Hungary, and the Czech Republic. Proponents of NATO expansion argued successfully that a historic opportunity existed to solidify freedom and democracy in Eastern Europe by admitting those nations to NATO. Russia was reassured that it would be "consulted" on NATO policies, but was given no veto powers over these policies or no guarantee that other Eastern European nations might also be admitted to NATO in the future. Indeed, in 2003 NATO admitted seven former Communist countries of Eastern Europe—Estonia, Latvia, and Lithuania, together with Bulgaria, Romania, Slovakia, and Slovenia. NATO now includes a total of 26 nations (see Figure 15–2).

NATO and Ethnic Conflicts in the Balkans

Traditionally, NATO forces were never deployed outside of Western Europe. Yet ethnic wars in the former communist nation of Yugoslavia, and the media coverage of the hardships endured by the people there, inspired NATO to intervene and deploy troops to Bosnia in 1995 to halt conflict raging among Serbs, Croats, and Muslims. The United States provided about one-third of the ground troops deployed in Bosnia as "peacekeepers." Yet some argued that U.S. national security interests were not at stake in southeastern European ethnic conflicts and therefore American troops should not be exposed to the dangers of intervention.

NATO again acted militarily to halt ethnic conflict in Kosovo in 1999. NATO's objective was to force Serbian troop withdrawal from the largely Muslim province. NATO relied exclusively on bombing from the air to force the Serbian withdrawal. Despite some controversy, even among NATO nations, as well as denunciations from Russia and China, NATO aircraft and missiles hit targets in both Kosovo and Serbia itself. (Even the Chinese embassy in the Serbian capital of Belgrade was bombed, apparently by mistake.) Eventually, Serbian troops were withdrawn from Kosovo.

NATO in Afghanistan

The United States turned over command of its military forces in Afghanistan to NATO in 2003. NATO created an International Security Assistance Force (ISAF), officially under U.N. auspices, "to assist the Islamic Republic of Afghanistan in creating a stable and secure environment for the people of Afghanistan." Over 40 nations contribute troops to this Force, but the United States contributes the largest number. (See "Using Military Force: Afghanistan," later in this chapter.)

FIGURE 15–2 NATO Nations of Europe* NATO was originally created to protect the nations of Western Europe from Soviet expansion; the collapse of the Soviet Union in 1991 has led to the expansion of NATO into Eastern European nations formerly dominated by the old Soviet Union.
*NATO members United States and Canada not shown.

WHEN TO USE MILITARY FORCE?

All modern presidents have acknowledged that the most agonizing decisions they have made were to send U.S. military forces into combat. These decisions cost lives. The American people are willing to send their sons and daughters into danger—and even to see some of them wounded or killed—but *only* if a president convinces them that the outcome "is worth dying for." A president must be able to explain why they lost their lives and to justify their sacrifice.

To Protect Vital Interests

The U.S. military learned many bitter lessons in its long, bloody experience in Vietnam. Secretary of State Colin Powell was among the younger officers who served in Vietnam. Later, General Powell became national security adviser to President Ronald Reagan and then chief of staff during the Gulf War under President George H. W. Bush; still later he would serve as secretary of state under President George W. Bush. The lessons of Vietnam were summarized by the "Powell Doctrine":[3]

- The United States should commit its military forces only in support of vital national interests.
- If military forces are committed, they must have clearly defined military objectives—the destruction of enemy forces and/or the capture of enemy-held territory.
- Any commitment of U.S. forces must be of sufficient strength to ensure overwhelming and decisive victory with the fewest possible casualties.
- Before committing U.S. military forces, there must be some reasonable assurances that the effort has the support of the American people and their representatives in Congress.
- The commitment of U.S. military forces should be a last resort, after political, economic, and diplomatic efforts have proven ineffective.

These guidelines for the use of military force are widely supported within the U.S. military itself. Contrary to Hollywood stereotypes, military leaders are extremely reluctant to go to war when no vital interest of the United States is at stake, where there are no clear-cut military objectives, without the support of Congress or the American people, or without sufficient force to achieve speedy and decisive victory with minimal casualties. They are wary of seeing their troops placed in danger merely to advance diplomatic goals, to engage in "peacekeeping," to "stabilize governments," or to "build democracy." They are reluctant to undertake humanitarian missions while being shot at. They do not like to risk their soldiers' lives under "rules of engagement" that limit their ability to defend themselves.

In Support of Important Political Objectives

In contrast to military leaders, political leaders and diplomats often reflect the view that "war is a continuation of politics by other means"—a view commonly attributed to nineteenth-century German theorist of war Carl von Clausewitz. Military force may be used to protect interests that are important but not necessarily vital. Otherwise, the United States would be rendered largely impotent in world affairs. A diplomat's ability to achieve a satisfactory result often depends on the expressed or implied threat of military force. The distinguished international political theorist Hans Morganthau wrote: "Since military strength is the obvious measure of a nation's power, its demonstration serves to impress others with that nation's power."[4]

Currently, American military forces must be prepared to carry out a variety of missions in addition to the conduct of conventional war:

- Demonstrating U.S. resolve in crisis situations
- Demonstrating U.S. support for democratic governments
- Protecting U.S. citizens living abroad

- Peacemaking among warring factions or nations
- Peacekeeping where hostile factions or nations have accepted a peace agreement
- Providing humanitarian aid, often under warlike conditions
- Assisting in international efforts to halt drug trafficking

In pursuit of such objectives, recent U.S. presidents have sent troops to Lebanon in 1982 to stabilize the government (Reagan), to Grenada in 1983 to rescue American medical students and restore democratic government (Reagan), to Panama in 1989 to oust drug-trafficking General Manuel Antonio Noriega from power and to protect U.S. citizens (Bush), to Somalia in 1992–1993 to provide emergency humanitarian aid (Bush and Clinton), to Haiti in 1994 to restore constitutional government (Clinton), and to Bosnia in 1995 for peacekeeping among warring ethnic factions and to force Serbian withdrawal from Kosovo in 1999 (Clinton) (see Table 15–1).

TABLE 15–1   Major Deployments of U.S. Military Forces since World War II Every president since World War II has found it necessary to deploy U.S. troops abroad.

Year	Area	President
1950–53	Korea	Truman
1958	Lebanon	Eisenhower
1961–64	Vietnam	Kennedy
1962	Cuban waters	Kennedy
1965–73	Vietnam	Johnson, Nixon
1965	Dominican Republic	Johnson
1970	Laos	Nixon
1970	Cambodia	Nixon
1975	Cambodia	Ford
1980	Iran	Carter
1982–83	Lebanon	Reagan
1983	Grenada	Reagan
1989	Panama	Bush
1990–91	Persian Gulf	Bush
1992–93	Somalia	Bush, Clinton
1994–95	Haiti	Clinton
1995–96	Bosnia	Clinton
1999	Kosovo	Clinton
2002–	Afghanistan	Bush, Obama
2003–11	Iraq	Bush, Obama
2011	Libya	Obama

Proponents of these more flexible uses of U.S. military forces deny any intent to be the "world's policeman." Rather, they argue that each situation must be judged independently on its own merits—weighing the importance of U.S. goals against expected costs. No military operation is without risk, but some risks may be worth taking to advance important political interests even though these interests may not be deemed "vital" to the United States. The media, particularly television, play an influential role in pressuring the president to use military force. Pictures of torture and killing, starvation and death, and devastation and destruction from around the world provide a powerful emotional stimulus to U.S. military intervention.

Generally a president can count on an initial "rally 'round the flag" surge in popular support for a military action, despite overall poor public knowledge of international politics. But if casualties mount during an operation, if no victory or end appears in sight, then press coverage of body bags coming home, military funeral services, and bereaved families create pressure on a president to end U.S. involvement. Unless the U.S. military can produce speedy and decisive results with few casualties, public support for military intervention wavers and critical voices in Congress arise.

President Barack Obama committed U.S. military forces to Libya in 2011 to protect the civilian population from attacks by forces of the strongman Muammar Gaddafi. The president justified the commitment on humanitarian grounds, citing a U.N. resolution establishing a no-fly zone over Libya, as well as an appeal for help by the Arab League. Then Secretary of Defense Robert Gates admitted that "no vital interest" of the United States was at stake in Libya. After an initial bombardment by U.S. air and naval forces, Obama turned over operational command to NATO. He vowed that no U.S. ground troops would be sent to Libya.

Critics charged that Obama's humanitarian justification amounted to a new "Obama doctrine" for the use of force—implying future U.S. obligations to protect popular uprisings from brutal regimes. They also complained that Obama failed to consult with Congress, and that he failed to state clearly the goals of the military action. Early on, Obama said, "Gaddafi must go!", implying regime change as the goal of the operation. But the U.S. military was constrained by the limits of the U.N. resolution to only protect civilian populations. There was no "rally 'round the flag" boost in public opinion; Americans were divided over the wisdom of initiating a third war while U.S. troops were heavily involved in Iraq and Afghanistan.

In Support of the War on Terrorism

The War on Terrorism creates new conditions for the use of military force.[5] Currently U.S. forces are prepared for:

- Direct attacks against terrorist forces to capture or kill them. These operations may be carried out by highly trained Special Operations Forces, or may be undertaken by sophisticated drones that can find and destroy isolated targets.

- Attacks on nations that harbor terrorists, allow terrorists to maintain bases, or supply and equip terrorist organizations. In 1986, the United States struck at Libya in a limited air attack in response to various Libyan-supported acts of terrorism around the world. In 1993, the United States struck Iraq's intelligence center in Baghdad in response to a foiled plot to assassinate former President George H. W. Bush. In 2001, the United States relied principally on Special

Forces working in conjunction with tribal forces in Afghanistan to attack Al Qaeda terrorists and to topple the Taliban government that had harbored and supported Al Qaeda (see below).

- Preemptive attacks on regimes that threaten to use weapons of mass destruction—chemical, biological, or nuclear weapons—against the United States or its allies, or to supply terrorist organizations with these weapons. Preemptive military action represents a reversal of traditional U.S. policy. Historically, the United States acted militarily only in response to a direct attack on its own forces or those of its allies. But it is argued that the terrorist attacks of 9/11 initiated the current War on Terrorism and that American military actions in the Middle East, including those in Afghanistan and Iraq, are related to the 9/11 attacks on America. The argument for preemptive military action was summarized by President Bush's National Security Adviser Condoleezza Rice: "We cannot wait until the smoking gun becomes a mushroom cloud."

During the Bush administration the *National Security Strategy* noted that "if necessary under long-standing principle of self defense, we do not rule out the use of force before attacks occur."[6] But under the Obama administration, in the same publication in a segment headed "Use of Force," it was asserted that "while the use of force is sometimes necessary, we will exhaust other options before war whenever we can, and carefully weigh the costs and risks of action against the costs and risks of inaction." These subtle changes in wording suggest a less aggressive war fighting posture.

THREATS, STRATEGIES, AND FORCES

Overall, military force levels in the United States should be threat-driven, that is, determined by the size and nature of the perceived threats to national security. It is true that particular weapons systems or base openings or closings may be driven by political forces such as the influence of defense contractors in Congress or the power of a member of Congress from a district heavily affected by defense spending. And not everyone in the White House and Congress, or even the Defense Department, agrees on the precise nature of the threats confronting the United States now or in the future. Yet defense policy planning and the "sizing" of U.S. military forces should begin with an assessment of the threats confronting the nation.

The End of the Cold War

The end of the Cold War rationalized deep cuts in military forces and defense budgets in the 1990s. Active duty military personnel declined from 2.1 million to 1.4 million. The Army was reduced to ten active combat divisions and the Air Force to twelve fighter wings (a U.S. Army division includes 15,000 to 18,000 troops; and an Air Force fighter wing includes approximately 70 combat aircraft). The Navy was reduced to twelve and later eleven carrier battle groups (a carrier battle group typically includes one aircraft carrier with 65 to 75 aircraft, plus defending cruisers, destroyers, frigates, attack submarines, and support ships). The Marine Corps retained all three of its Marine expeditionary forces (each MEF includes one Marine division, one Marine air wing, and supporting services) (see Table 15–2). National Guard and Reserve forces were assigned a larger and more active role. There are an additional 1.2 million persons in the Army, Navy, Air Force, and Marine reserve forces. Military deployments in Iraq and Afghanistan required many of these reserve units to be called to active duty.

TABLE 15–2   Military Force Level Military force levels declined rapidly after the end of the Cold War, igniting criticism that American troops are spread "too thin."

	1990	2000	2010
Active duty personnel (in millions)	2.1	1.4	1.4
Army divisions	18	10	10 (45 BCTs)
Navy carrier battle groups	15	12	11
Marine expeditionary forces	3	3	3
Air Force fighter wings	24	12	(10 AEFs)

SOURCE: Office of the Secretary of Defense.

NOTE: BCT = Brigade Combat Team; AEF = Aerospace Expeditionary Forces.

The Army continues to maintain the equivalent of ten active duty divisions. However, the Army has been reorganized into 45 Brigade Combat Teams (BCTs). Each BCT includes about 3,500 soldiers; BCTs may be armored (tanks), mechanized infantry, airborne (paratroopers), air assault (helicopter borne), or Stryker (combined arms). The Air Force has been reorganized into ten Aerospace Expeditionary Forces (AEFs). Each AEF combines bomber, fighter, attack, refueling, and reconnaissance aircraft.

Confronting Regional Threats

Following the Gulf War in 1991, U.S. military planning focused on the possibility of *two* regional aggressors attacking at the same time. If U.S. troops were heavily engaged in one regional conflict similar to the Gulf War, defense strategists worried about a second aggressor taking advantage of the U.S. military commitment to launch its own military action elsewhere against the United States or its allies or interests. The most common scenario for simultaneous regional threats was a heavy U.S. military involvement in the Middle East, and the possibility that an Asian regional power would be tempted to take advantage of that commitment to launch its own aggression (for example North Korea against South Korea, China against Taiwan). While officially recognizing the "Two Major Theaters of War" threat as late as 2002, the United States never possessed the forces to prevail in major conflicts in the Middle East and Asia simultaneously. Current force levels make it unlikely that the United States could do more than "hold" in one conflict while pursuing victory in another, and then later shifting forces to the second conflict. The United States is most deficient in airlift and sealift forces—the cargo, supply, and weapons and troop-carrying capability required to move combat forces around the world.

Fighting Terrorism

Confronting terrorism brought a new emphasis in defense policy on nonconventional forces and tactics. Special Operations Forces played a central role in ousting the Taliban regime from Afghanistan. Special Operations Forces on the ground, together with manned and unmanned surveillance aircraft in the skies, provided the targeting intelligence for U.S. air attacks from carriers in the Arabian Sea, attack aircraft based in the Middle East, and even long-range bombers based in the continental United States. These attacks allowed Afghan forces opposed to the regime to capture the capital, Kabul, two months after the initiation of Operation Enduring Freedom.

Asymmetrical Warfare of the Future

Traditionally the United States structured its military tactics and forces to confront conventional threats—national armies with heavy armor, tanks and artillery, mechanized infantry, and combat aircraft. During the Cold War, U.S. forces were designed to confront heavy Soviet armor and artillery in Central Europe, in a manner similar, albeit more violent, to the armies that fought in World War II. The Gulf War in 1991 demonstrated the superiority of American forces in large-scale conventional operations.

The war on terror requires the United States to reshape its military planning to confront unconventional (or asymmetrical) wars—lightly armed irregular enemy forces engaging in tactics such as ambushes, hidden explosives, suicide bombings, and hostage takings. America's enemies are fully aware of the overwhelming firepower of conventional U.S. military forces. Consequently, they seek to minimize U.S. advantage in firepower in a variety of ways. They choose terrain that inhibits the use of conventional tank, artillery, and air power—jungles and mountains where these conventional forces cannot operate as effectively as in open country. They also choose built-up urban areas where civilian populations inhibit U.S. forces from employing their full firepower. They avoid direct confrontations with large American units, blending in with the population and seeming to disappear in the presence of U.S. combat forces.

Asymmetrical warfare is the approach of a weaker foe trying to overcome the advantages of a force that is superior in conventional forms of warfare. Traditionally, the U.S. Army preferred that its opponents face it and massed formations on conventional battlefields where overwhelming American power could be brought to bear to destroy the opponent. But an inferior opponent would be foolhardy to cooperate in its own destruction by fighting the war that Americans prefer to fight. Guerrilla warfare, which United States encountered in Vietnam, is one form of asymmetrical warfare. Terrorism is another, which includes consciously targeting civilians.

Counterinsurgency Emphasis

Former Secretary of Defense Robert Gates expressed his belief that "asymmetric warfare will remain the mainstay of the contemporary battlefield for some time." The experiences in Afghanistan and Iraq are currently shaping U.S. military planning. Among the current developments:

- Expansion of the size of the Army and Marine Corp in recognition of the need for more "boots on the ground."
- Transformation of a division-based Army into one organized into Brigade Combat Teams.
- Heavier reliance on Army Reserve and National Guard units. (Some of these units were called for multiple tours of duty in Afghanistan and Iraq.)
- Introduction of new equipment, including mine resistant and ambush protection vehicles (MAPVs) and unmanned aerial vehicles (UAVs), capable of both reconnaissance and attack missions.

- Overhaul of the counterinsurgency doctrine to shift operations away from "enemy-centric" armed conflict toward a "population-centric" approach, emphasizing political goals and the importance of social and cultural factors in military operations.

While many military leaders agree with the new emphasis on asymmetrical threats, others argue that the true lesson of Afghanistan and Iraq is that U.S. forces should avoid protracted commitments to "peacekeeping" and "nation building" and instead undertake only those military operations that promise rapid, decisive results.

Peacekeeping/Nation Building

U.S. military forces are currently deployed in more than 120 countries around the world. The largest deployments are in South Korea and Afghanistan, but large numbers of U.S. forces are deployed in Qatar, Bahrain, Saudi Arabia, Kuwait, Bosnia, Kosovo, Philippines, Japan, Cuba (Guantanamo), Colombia, Honduras, and the NATO countries, including Great Britain, Germany, Italy, Ireland, and Turkey.

Traditionally, U.S. military forces were trained for combat, not "peacekeeping" or "nation building". Currently, however, the U.S. military is tailoring more of its training, doctrine, and equipment to these missions. This means increasing the numbers of military police, language specialists, civil affairs units, local force trainers, and humanitarian relief supply units.

Stretched Too Thin?

Over the years, U.S. military forces have been assigned increasing numbers of missions—war-fighting, peacekeeping, nation building, counterinsurgency, and humanitarian aid. Yet force levels have remained minimal.

Experience has taught the U.S. military that casualties can be kept low only when overwhelming military force is employed quickly and decisively. Lives are lost when minimal forces are sent into combat, when they have inadequate air combat support, or when they are extended over too broad a front. Current numbers of Army and Air Force combat units and the limited transport and support services available to the military are inadequate for two major regional conflicts. Potential regional foes—for example, Iran and North Korea—deploy modern heavy armor and artillery forces. Commitments of U.S. troops to peacekeeping and humanitarian missions divert resources, training, and morale away from war-fighting. Morale is also affected when U.S. military forces are deployed abroad for long periods of time; this is especially true for National Guard and Reserve troops.

USING MILITARY FORCE: THE GULF WAR

Saddam Hussein's invasion of Kuwait in August, 1990, was apparently designed to restore his military prestige after a long and indecisive war against Iran; to secure additional oil revenues to finance the continued buildup of Iraqi military power; and to intimidate (and perhaps invade) Saudi Arabia and the Gulf states, thereby securing control over a major share of the world's oil reserves. Early in the crisis President George H. W. Bush committed U.S. forces to the Gulf region for the military defense of Saudi Arabia. The president described the early U.S. military deployment as "defensive." But he soon became convinced that neither diplomacy, UN resolutions, nor an economic blockade would dislodge Saddam from Kuwait. He ordered his military commanders to prepare an "offensive" plan that would force the withdrawal of Iraqi forces from Kuwait.

The top military commanders—including the Chairman of the Joint Chiefs of Staff, General Colin Powell, and the commander in the field, General Norman Schwarzkopf—were reluctant to go into battle without the full support of the American people. If ordered to fight, they wanted to employ *overwhelming and decisive military force*; they wanted to avoid gradual escalation, protracted conflict, target limitations, and political interference in the conduct of the war. Accordingly, they presented the president with a plan that called for a very large military buildup. More than 500,000 U.S. military personnel were sent to the Gulf region.

In November, 1990, Secretary of State James Baker won the support of the UN Security Council for a resolution authorizing the "use of all necessary means" against Iraq to force its withdrawal from Kuwait. Following a lengthy debate in Congress, in January 1991, President Bush won a similar resolution in the House (250–183) and in the Senate (52–47). President Bush succeeded in putting together a large coalition of nations in support of military action. The British and French sent significant ground combat units, and smaller units from Gulf Arab states also participated.

From Baghdad, CNN reporters were startled on the night of January 16, 1991, when Operation Desert Storm began with an air attack on key installations in the city. After five weeks of air war, intelligence estimated that nearly half of Iraq's tanks and artillery had been destroyed, that demoralized troops were hiding in deep shelters, and that the battlefield had been isolated and prepared for ground operations. On the night of February 24, the ground attack began. Marines breached ditches and minefields and raced directly to the Kuwait airport. Army helicopter assaults lunged deep into Iraq; armored columns raced northward across the desert to outflank Iraqi forces and attack them from the West; and a surge in air attacks kept Iraqi forces holed up in their bunkers. Iraqi troops surrendered in droves, highways from Kuwait City became a massive junkyard of Iraqi vehicles, and Iraqi forces that tried to fight were quickly destroyed. After one hundred hours of ground fighting, President Bush ordered a cease-fire.

The United States had achieved a decisive military victory quickly and with remarkably few casualties. The president resisted calls to expand the original objectives of the war and to go on to capture Baghdad or to kill Saddam, although it was expected that his defeat would lead to his ouster. President Bush chose to declare victory and celebrate the return of American troops. But the results of the war were mixed. In retrospect, the president's decision to end the war after only one hundred hours of ground operations appears to have been premature. With his surviving forces, Saddam maintained his cruel grip on the country and proceeded to attack his regime's opponents brutally, even using chemical weapons against the Kurdish minority in northern Iraq. Tens of thousands of Iraqis were killed in Saddam's retribution following the departure of American troops.

USING MILITARY FORCE: IRAQ

At the end of the Gulf War in 1991, the Iraqi regime of Saddam Hussein agreed to destroy all of its chemical and biological weapons and to end its efforts to acquire nuclear weapons. United Nations inspectors were to verify Iraqi compliance with these conditions. But Saddam's regime refused to cooperate: in 1998 he ordered the inspectors out of the country. Over a twelve-year period Iraq violated at least a dozen UN resolutions. Following a U.S. military buildup in the region in late 2002, Saddam allowed UN inspectors to return but continued to obstruct their work. On March 19, 2003, after giving Saddam a 48-hour warning to leave Iraq, the United States and Great Britain launched air strikes designed to eliminate Saddam and his top command.

Operation Iraqi Freedom

At different times President George W. Bush stated the purposes of Operation Iraqi Freedom as (1) the elimination of Iraq's weapons of mass destruction, (2) a "regime change" for Iraq to end the threat that Saddam posed for his neighbors and to free the Iraqi people from his oppressive rule, and (3) to ensure that Saddam would not harbor or assist terrorist organizations. But President Bush and Secretary of State Colin Powell failed to secure UN Security Council approval for military action. Among the permanent members of the Security Council, only the British, with the strong support of Prime Minister Tony Blair, were prepared to offer significant military support for the war against Saddam. Public opinion in America supported military action, but public opinion in Europe opposed it. France and Germany led the diplomatic opposition; Turkey refused to let U.S. troops use its territory to attack Iraq; and the United States was obliged to rely primarily on Kuwait, Qatar, and the other smaller Gulf states for regional support.

The U.S. military wanted to wage war in the fashion of the successful Gulf War—a period of heavy air bombardment to "prepare the battlefield," followed by a massive ground attack using overwhelming military force. But Secretary of Defense Donald Rumsfeld wanted a "leaner" fighting force in Iraq. He deployed fewer than half of the air, ground, and naval forces that had been used in the Gulf War. And he began the air and ground attacks simultaneously.

American and British soldiers and Marines took just 21 days to sweep the 350 miles from the Kuwait border to downtown Baghdad. The British 3rd Armored Division with Australian support captured the port city of Basra; the U.S. 3rd Infantry Division moved up the west side of the Euphrates River; and the U.S. 1st Marine Division moved up the east side. Special Operations Forces together with elements of the 101st Airborne Division joined Kurdish forces in northern Iraq. Special Operations Forces also acted quickly to secure Iraq's oil fields and prevent their destruction. At first, progress was hindered by the requirement that soldiers wear heavy chemical protection gear and carry decontamination equipment. But neither chemical nor biological weapons were used against U.S. forces. The advance on Baghdad was speeded up, and the city was captured with precious few U.S. casualties.

President Bush announced "the end of major combat" on May 1, 2003, but the real war in Iraq had just begun.

WHAT WENT WRONG IN IRAQ?

The war in Iraq was a "preemptive" strike against terrorism, consistent with the declarations of the Bush administration about the necessity of fighting terrorists on their own ground rather than on American soil. American, British, and other intelligence services reported that Iraq had chemical and biological weapons and was in the process of acquiring enriched uranium for the construction of nuclear weapons. Initially public opinion in America supported military action. Yet much of what had been learned at a high cost in Vietnam and summarized by the Powell Doctrine (described above) was ignored.

Limits on the Number of Troops

Early on, Defense Secretary Donald Rumsfeld decided to place severe limits on the number of troops sent to Iraq. This decision was part of his broader vision of a "lean" military force. And indeed, this force was able to quickly capture Baghdad. Within weeks, however, an insurgent movement developed that soon inflicted far more casualties on U.S. troops than were experienced in the capture of Iraq's capital. U.S. troops were stretched so thin across Iraq that they could not hold cities or neighborhoods after they had been captured. Supply lines could not be defended, and the insurgents quickly learned to plant IEDs—improvised explosive devices—along routes commonly used by U.S. troops. More casualties were inflicted by these devices than by any other means; the U.S. did not have enough troops to guard supply routes.

American Troops Used for "Nation Building"

The American occupation of Iraq started out poorly and proceeded over time to become worse. Planning for postwar Iraq appeared nonexistent. The U.S. administrator for Iraq, L. Paul Bremer, began by dismissing the entire Iraqi Army, sending thousands of well-armed, unemployed young men into the streets. The United States promised to restore infrastructure—water, electricity, roads, etc.—yet Bremer pursued a policy of dismissing virtually all Iraqi managers and technicians on the grounds that they had been Baathists (Saddam's ruling party members). Later, the United States would be obliged to begin recruiting and training an Iraqi Army and police force and bringing in U.S. contract workers, managers, and technicians. Bremer was fired after one year.

Soon, Iraqi street mobs that had earlier torn down Saddam's statue began demonstrations against the American presence. An insurgent movement seemed to surprise Secretary of Defense Donald Rumsfeld. He steadfastly refused to send additional U.S. troops to Iraq to handle the insurgency and insisted that a new Iraqi government could eventually recruit and train enough troops to contain the insurgency.

No weapons of mass destruction were found despite an intensive search. Saddam himself was captured and turned over to the Iraqis. After a bizarre show trial, he was convicted of mass murder and executed by hanging.

Iraq held its first nationwide election in fifty years in 2003, despite violence and threats of violence. Nearly 60 percent of the population participated, many proudly displaying their blue-inked thumbs to signal that they had voted. The result was a new constitution that was approved in a second vote that year. However, a substantial number of Sunnis boycotted the elections, fearing a loss of their power and the ascendancy of the Shiites. The United States officially turned over sovereignty to a new Iraqi government in 2004.

Involvement in Civil Strife

The population of Iraq is composed of three major factions: the Kurds, who occupy most of northeastern Iraq; the Shiites, who occupy most of southern Iraq; and the Sunnis, who occupy central Iraq. Baghdad itself is divided between Sunni and Shiite neighborhoods. The Sunnis have long dominated Iraq. Saddam's family was Sunni. Yet the Shiites are the largest faction, with more than half of the total population of Iraq. Over the years, the Kurds have fought for a separate outcome strongly opposed by neighboring Turkey.

By 2006, most of the violence in Iraq was occurring among various factions; thousands of Iraqi were victims of sectarian killings. The Shiites, the majority of Iraq's population, gained power for the first time in more than 1000 years. Above all, the Shiites are interested in preserving that power. The Sunnis fear displacement and the loss of their traditional position of power in Iraq. The Kurds seek, at a minimum, quasi-independence and control over the oil resources in their region. The Shiites also seek control over oil in southern Iraq. But the areas with the largest Sunni population lack oil resources, so the Sunni fight to maintain control of all of Iraq. Corruption is rampant throughout Iraq, the judiciary is weak, oil production is down, and the U.S.-backed government is unable to produce an acceptable plan of national reconciliation.[7]

Costs to the U.S. Military

American military forces suffered a gruesome toll in lives and limbs. By 2006 over 4,000 American troops had been killed, many from "improvised explosive devices." U.S. Army and Marine forces approached the "breaking point." Nearly every Army and Marine combat unit, and several National Guard and Reserve units, were rotated into Iraq more than once. The strain on U.S. forces worldwide became clearly evident, with both personnel and equipment wearing down.

"Clear, Hold and Build"

U.S. policy in Iraq focused primarily on security. The key phrase was "clear, hold, and build." U.S. military forces were to clear neighborhoods, cities, towns, and regions of insurgents, then to hold the cleared areas with U.S. trained and equipped Iraqi army and police forces; and then to begin to rebuild infrastructure. U.S. forces were able to "clear" many areas, but there were too few troops to "hold" these areas. Iraqi forces were unable or unwilling to halt insurgents from reoccupying these areas after American troops left. Very little "building" took place. Many members of the Iraqi security forces remained loyal to their sectarian—Shiite or Sunni—goals, rather than the agenda of the national government. Many of these units simply refused to carry out assigned missions.

Nevertheless, President Bush continued to argue that the war in Iraq was central to the world-wide war against terrorism. He argued that an abrupt withdrawal ("cut and run") would encourage radical Islamic terrorists around the world.

> Failure is not an option. Iraq would become a safe haven from which terrorists could plan attacks against American interests abroad, and our allies. Middle East reformers would never again fully trust American assurances of support for democtacy in human rights in the region. Iraq is the central front in the global war on terror.[8]

The "Surge"

The sweeping Democratic victory in the congressional elections of 2006 was widely attributed to popular disaffection with the war in Iraq. Democrats gained control of both the House and the Senate. Many of their supporters expected them to end the war by cutting off funds for the prosecution of the war. At a minimum, opponents of the war wanted Congress to set a timetable for the reduction of U.S. troops in Iraq. But when staring directly at the prospect of cutting off funds for troops in the field, Congress blinked. Resolutions to end the war failed, as did efforts to set a timetable for troop withdrawal.

Instead, President Bush announced a "surge" in troop strength designed to improve security in Iraq and allow the Iraqi government to reach "benchmarks" in resolving civil strife. The "surge" involved increasing U.S. troop levels in Iraq from roughly 138,000 to 160,000. In January, 2007, the president appointed a new commander for Iraq, General David Petraeus. Petraeus was unanimously confirmed by the Senate, but Congress stipulated that in September, 2007, the general was to report on progress in Iraq.

Petraeus reported to Congress that the "surge" was working, that progress was being made in stabilizing Iraq and training Iraqi forces, that U.S. troop levels could be reduced to pre-surge levels, but that some U.S. forces may be needed in Iraq many more years. He argued that a timetable for troop reductions would be counterproductive.

Loss of Public Support

Americans demand quick victory in war. With the exception of World War II, American public support for wars, notably Korea (1950–53) and Vietnam (1965–73), declined steadily as casualties rose and no end appeared in sight. The initial "rally 'round the flag" support for military action begins to wane after the first year of combat. Quick victories with few casualties, as in the Gulf War (1991), inspire support for the president and his decision to go to war. Prolonged stalemates with mounting casualties gradually erode public support for war.

Shortly after the war in Iraq began, most Americans thought Iraq was worth going to war over. Indeed, this opinion climbed to 76 percent immediately following the capture of Baghdad. But as American casualties mounted and no end to the fighting appeared in sight, mass opinion in support of the war declined rapidly. By late 2004, the majority of Americans believed that Iraq was "not worth going to war" (see Figure 15–3).

Withdrawal of Combat Forces

In the presidential campaign of 2008, Barack Obama pledged to end the war in Iraq "responsibly." He warned against "an occupation of undetermined length, with undetermined costs and undetermined consequences." Upon taking office in January, 2009, Obama ordered the U.S. military to plan for a phased withdrawal of American combat forces from Iraq. The expectation was that the United States could "redeploy" combat brigades at a pace of one to two per month over a sixteen-month period, ending in the summer of 2010. A "residual force" was to remain in Iraq—to conduct targeted counterterrorism missions against Al Qaeda and to protect American diplomatic and civilian personnel. This residual force would continue to train and support Iraqi security forces "as long as Iraqi leaders move toward political reconciliation and away from sectarianism."[9]

A Mixed Outcome

The U.S. military officially ceased combat missions in Iraq in August 2010, leaving primary responsibility for the maintenance of order in that country to the Iraqi security forces. The U.S. military had already withdrawn from Iraq's cities and towns in 2009 in accordance with a Status of Forces Agreement (SOFA) negotiated between the Iraqi and American governments in the last days of the George W. Bush administration. The SOFA also set a deadline for all U.S. forces to be removed from the country by December 31, 2011. The number of remaining U.S. military advisers and trainers, if any, remains undetermined.

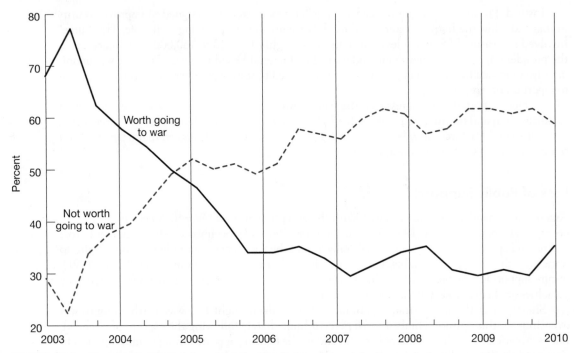

FIGURE 15–3   Changing Public Opinion about the War in Iraq Support for the war in Iraq among the American people declined over time.
SOURCE: *www.pollingreport.com*

The American public remains unconvinced that military intervention in Iraq was worth the heavy price paid: over 4,500 American service members killed and 35,000 wounded. Sporadic violence continues in Iraq, and the future of democracy in that embattled country remains in doubt.

USING MILITARY FORCE: AFGHANISTAN

The military phase of the war on terrorism began October 7, 2001, less than one month after September 11. U.S. Air Force and Navy aircraft began attacks on known Al Qaeda bases in Afghanistan, and U.S. Special Forces organized and led anti-Taliban fighters, including several tribal groups calling themselves the Northern Alliance, in a campaign against the Taliban regime. A coalition of nations participated in Operation Enduring Freedom; some, including Britain and Canada, contributed troops, while others, including Pakistan, Saudi Arabia, and Uzebekistan, informally allowed U.S. forces to base operations on their territory. Kabul, the capital of Afghanistan, was occupied by anti-Taliban forces on November 13, 2001.

President Bush made it clear that the United States was prepared to act militarily against governments that harbored or gave sanctuary to terrorists. The Taliban regime was ousted from power. By April 2002—six months into Operation Enduring Freedom—Al Qaeda and Taliban forces had been scattered into small groups in the mountainous areas of Afghanistan and neighboring Pakistan. Osama bin Laden himself, however, escaped capture.

The United States through the United Nations and NATO created an International Security Assistance Force (ISAF) in 2002 to conduct comprehensive population-centric counterinsurgency operations, to support the development of the Afghan National Security Forces, and to provide a secure environment for the development of legitimate governance in Afghanistan.

A meeting in Bonn, Germany, of various Afghan political and military groups produced general agreement on the installation of a new government in Kabul, headed by Hamid Karzai. The Karzai government has less than full control over Afghanistan. Various tribal military chiefs, or "warlords," exercise independent power throughout the country.

Al Qaeda and Taliban Resurgence

While campaigning for the presidency in 2008, Barack Obama drew a sharp distinction between the war in Iraq and the war in Afghanistan. Iraq, he claimed, had diverted America's attention away from the greater dangers posed by Al Qaeda and Taliban forces in Afghanistan. It was Al Qaeda that was responsible for the September 11, 2001, attacks on the New York World Trade Center and the Pentagon, and it was the Taliban regime in Afghanistan that provided Al Qaeda with a safe haven. And evidence was mounting of a resurgence of Al Qaeda and its Taliban allies in the southern and eastern mountainous areas of Afghanistan and across the border in neighboring Pakistan.

Obama's War

Shortly after entering the White House, President Obama ordered a strategic review of the situation in Afghanistan and Pakistan. The review concluded that the situation was "increasingly perilous," with Al Qaeda and its Taliban allies controlling large sections of both Afghanistan and Pakistan. Additional combat brigades were to be sent to the region as well as thousands of trainees for Afghanistan army and police forces. The United States was also to make a heavy financial investment in the economic development of both countries.

Afghanistan became the Obama administration's principal military effort. In December, 2009, President Obama ordered a substantial increase in U.S. combat forces in Afghanistan. Yet, at the same time he pledged that "our troops will begin to come home" in the summer of 2011. He qualified this pledge by citing the need to build Afghan capacity for maintaining security "to allow for a responsible transition of our forces out of Afghanistan." A further qualification came from a NATO Lisbon Summit in 2010 in which leaders planned to begin handing over security responsibilities to the Afghan government in 2011, with a view to completing the transition by 2014.

Counterinsurgency Operations

The announced goal of U.S. policy is to "disrupt, dismantle, and defeat" Al Qaeda in both Afghanistan and Pakistan. The policy suggests that Al Qaeda will no longer find a safe haven across the border in Pakistan. Economic and military aid to Pakistan is to be contingent upon that country's commitment to its own security and its willingness to "confront violent extremists." Afghanistan will offer a test of the U.S. military's concept of asymmetrical (counterinsurgency) warfare.

Limited Objectives

U.S. policy recognizes that Afghanistan's 25 million people are divided along ethnic lines. The central government in Kabul exercises little control over a country the size of Texas. U.S. strategy appears to be to win over local tribes and leaders, including Taliban forces that are not allied to Al Qaeda. The objective of U.S. policy is not necessarily to bring Western-style democracy to Afghanistan, but rather to ensure that the country does not become a safe haven for Al Qaeda and its terrorist allies.

In an *Afghanistan-Pakistan Security Review* in 2011, the Obama administration attempted to clarify the overall goal of the mission in that area: "It is not to defeat every last threat to the security of Afghanistan, because, ultimately it is Afghans who must secure their country. And it is not nation building, because it is Afghans who must build their nation. Rather, we are focused on disrupting, dismantling and defeating Al Qaeda in Afghanistan and Pakistan, and preventing its capacity to threaten America and our allies in the future." The transition to Afghan security control "will begin in 2011 and conclude in 2014."[10] It is not clear whether "conditions on the ground" will interfere with this timetable.

ISAF Buildup

By 2011, ISAF forces consisted of about 131,000 troops, 90,000 from the United States and the remainder from 20 NATO and 28 non-NATO nations. Some 9,500 troops are from the United Kingdom, and contingents of 1000 or more are from Poland, Romania, Spain, Germany, France, Italy, Canada, Australia, and Turkey. However, some U.S. allies have expressed a desire to withdraw from Afghanistan at an early date.

Prior to 2009, U.S. forces were often able to clear Taliban from various areas, but inadequate force levels led to a subsequent abandonment of these areas. The Taliban were able to re-occupy towns, with dire consequences for Afghan officials and civilians who had cooperated with the Americans. But increased U.S. combat capability beginning in 2009 enabled ISAF forces not only to clear but to hold cities and towns in disputed provinces. Modest successes were reported in ISAF attacks on Taliban leadership. Successes in these counterinsurgency operations frequently depends upon real-time intelligence, often supplied by unmanned aerial vehicles (UAVs). Restrictions on the use of heavy weapons artillery and airstrikes have reduced civilian casualties. But this "disciplined use of force" means increased risk for U.S. and ISAF troops.

American and ISAF troops face a determined enemy in Al Qaeda and the Taliban. The strength of the Taliban lies in part in the perception by the Afghan people that the United States will leave the country soon and that Taliban victory is inevitable. This allows the Taliban to play the waiting game. The Taliban seek to inflict casualties on ISAF forces and Afghan civilians who cooperate with them, hoping to provoke overreaction and further alienation of the Afghan people to foreign intervention. The Taliban insurgency is based primarily on ethnic Pashtons, most of whom are found in the south and east of the country, notably in the Helmand and Kandahar provinces. The Taliban appear divided between contending groups, including the Quetta Taliban led by Mullah Omar based in Quetta, Pakistan, and the Haggani Network responsible for many attacks in the eastern region and in Kabul, the capital. Both the Afghan government and the ISAF have declared a willingness to allow Taliban fighters deemed to be "reconcilable" to become reintegrated into Afghan society. But to date no large-scale, durable reconciliation has been achieved.

SUMMARY

Decisions about defense policy in Washington and in other capitals are interdependent—strategies, force levels, and spending decisions depend on perceived threats posed by other major powers. Game theory provides a way of thinking rationally about decision making in competitive, interdependent situations.

1. During the long Cold War, deterrence strategy prevented nuclear war by making the consequences of a nuclear attack unacceptable to a rational enemy. Deterrence emphasized *second-strike* capability—the ability of a nation's forces to survive an attack and inflict unacceptable levels of destruction on the attacker in retaliation.

2. The end of the Cold War resulted in a decline in overall strategic nuclear forces by two-thirds. The START agreements slashed total nuclear warheads on both sides and required the elimination of all land-based MIRV missiles. The resulting force levels on both sides virtually eliminated the possibility of launching a rational first strike. The New START Treaty of 2010 reduces nuclear warheads of both sides to 1550 each, a reduction of over 85 percent from Cold War levels.

3. Current strategic debate focuses on nondeterrable threats—missiles launched by terrorist nations or by terrorist groups. Global nuclear proliferation increases the likelihood of these threats. President Ronald Reagan began a large-scale research program, the Strategic Defense Initiative (SDI), or "Star Wars," to develop a capability to intercept and destroy incoming ballistic missiles. President George W. Bush redirected missile defense from large-scale Russian attacks to smaller attacks by terrorist nations. He withdrew the United States from the SALT I Treaty banning the deployment of missile defenses. The U.S. currently deploys limited land-based (Alaska) and sea-based anti-ballistic missiles.

4. In the NATO alliance the United States and Western European nations pledged that an armed attack against one would be considered an armed attack against all. A joint NATO military command is designated to implement this pledge. The collapse of communist governments in Eastern Europe, the unification of Germany, and the dissolution of the Soviet Union greatly diminished the threat to European security. NATO has expanded to 28 countries including countries formerly in the Soviet orbit.

5. The United States has never adopted clear policy guidelines regarding when to use military force. Most military leaders argue that troops should be used only to protect vital national interests, with clearly defined military objectives, and with the support of Congress and the American people. Furthermore, military force should only be used with sufficient force to achieve speedy and decisive victory with minimum casualties, and only as a last resort.

6. In contrast, many political and diplomatic leaders argue that troops may be used in support of important political objectives and humanitarian goals. These may include demonstrating U.S. resolve in crisis situations, U.S. support for democratic governments, peacemaking among warring factions or nations, peacekeeping where hostile parties have agreed to a settlement, and the provision of humanitarian aid. President Obama justified U.S. military action in Libya in 2011 on U.N.-sponsored humanitarian grounds.

7. The war on terrorism added to the responsibilities of the military, including direct attacks against terrorist forces and attacks against nations that harbor terrorists or that seek to develop weapons of mass destruction.

8. The war in Iraq, beginning in 2002, was expected to eliminate weapons of mass destruction (WMDs), end the regime of Saddam Hussein, and ensure that Iraq would not threaten its neighbors or become a haven for terrorists. Following the rapid capture of Baghdad, however, no WMDs were found and an insurgency grew that eventually caused far more casualties among U.S. and British troops than the capture of Baghdad. Conflict between Shia and Sunni sects threatened civil war.

9. By 2004, a majority of Americans had turned against the War in Iraq, declaring in polls that

it was "not worth" the sacrifice in American casualties. A troop "surge" in 2007 appeared to reduce overall violence. Following victories in the 2006 congressional elections, Democrats tried but failed to set dates for the withdrawal of U.S. troops from Iraq.

10. Upon taking office, President Barack Obama ordered the phased withdrawal of American combat forces from Iraq. A Status of Forces Agreement with the new Iraqi government set a deadline for the removal of all U.S. forces from Iraq by December 31, 2011.

11. The initial U.S. attack in Afghanistan in 2001 was successful in dislodging the Taliban regime that had assisted Al Qaeda terrorists in mounting the September 11, 2001, attacks on the World Trade Center in New York and the Pentagon in Washington. But over time Al Qaeda and the Taliban regrouped in the mountainous border areas with Pakistan.

12. An International Security Assistance Force (ISAF) in Afghanistan was created in 2002 with both NATO and non-NATO nations contributing troops. ISAF eventually included over 40 nations with 131,000 troops; 90,000 from the United States.

13. The Obama Administration increased U.S. forces in Afghanistan in 2009, but at the same time pledged that U.S. troops would begin coming home in 2011. A NATO London Summit announced the intention to complete security transition to the Afghan National Army by 2014.

14. The stated goal of the United States in Afghanistan is not nation building, but rather "disrupting, dismantling, and defeating Al Qaeda."

MySearchLab® EXERCISES

Apply what you learned in this chapter on MySearchLab (www.mysearchlab.com).

NOTES

1. President Ronald Reagan, *The President's Strategic Defense Initiative*, The White House, January 3, 1985.

2. Office of the President, *National Security Strategy of the United States, 2002* (Washington, DC: U.S. Government Printing Office, 2002).

3. General Colin Powell, testimony before the Budget Committee of the U.S. Senate, February 1992.

4. Hans Morgenthau, *Politics among Nations* (New York: Knopf, 1973), p. 27.

5. Donald M. Snow, *National Security for a New Era* (New York: Pearson, 2008), p. 309.

6. Quotations from Department of Defense, *National Strategic Review* 2006; Department of Defense, *National Strategic Review* 2009; see International Institute for Strategic Studies, *The Military Balance 2011*, London: IISS, 2011.

7. *The Iraq Study Group Report* (New York: Vintage Books, 2006).

8. President George W. Bush, *National Strategy in Victory in Iraq*, November 1, 2005, *www.whitehouse.gov*

9. *www.whitehouse.gov/agenda/Iraq*

10. U.S. Department of Defense, *Afghanistan-Pakistan Review* 2011, as reported in International Institute for Strategic Studies, *The Military Balance 2011*. London: IISS, 2011, p. 42.

BIBLIOGRAPHY

Combs, Cynthia C. *Terrorism in the 21st Century*, 6th ed. New York: Longman, 2011.

Editors of *Time. 21 Days to Baghdad*. New York: Time Books, 2003.

Office of the President. *Quadrennial Defense Review*. Washington, DC: U.S. Government Printing Office, 2003.

Snow, Donald M. *National Security for a New Era*, 4th ed. New York: Longman, 2011.

Summers, Harry G., Jr. *On Strategy II: A Critical Analysis of the Gulf War*. New York: Dell, 1992.

The Iraq Study Group. New York: Vintage, 2006.

The Military Balance. London: International Institute for Strategic Studies, annually.

WEB SITES

U.S. Department of Defense. Official Web site of the Defense Department, with news column photos, and links to Army, Navy, Air Force, and Marine Web sites, and Web sites of all Unified Commands. *www.defenselink.gov*

Central Intelligence Agency. Official Web site of the CIA, with history, news, press releases, and links to its *World Factbook* and *Factbook on Intelligence* and other publications. *www.cia.gov*

North Atlantic Treaty Organization. Official Web site of NATO, with history, membership, facts, and current issues. *www.nato.int*

Council on Foreign Relations. Home page of the CFR, with information on world trade, globalization, national security and defense, etc. *www.cfr.org*

National Security Council. Official site of the NSC, with membership, functions, press releases, and information on national security issues. *www.whitehouse.gov/nsc*

United Nations. Official site of the UN, with news, resolutions, agenda issues, and links to all UN agencies. *www.un.org*

Global Security. News and information about weapons, forces, and military conflicts around the world. *www.globalsecurity.org*

American Security Council. Organization providing summary information on national security threats. *www.ascusa.org*

Missile Defense Agency. Summary of U.S. ballistic missile defense systems and technology. *www.mda.mil*

9/11 launches the war on terror Historic photo of New York's World Trade Center twin towers just prior to their collapse, September 11, 2001. On that date Al Qaeda terrorists hijacked four airliners, intentionally crashing two of them into the twin buildings, and crashing a third into the Pentagon in Washington. The fourth crashed in rural Pennsylvania after passengers and crew bravely fought to retake the aircraft. Nearly 3,000 people died in the attacks. (© Beth Dixson/Alamy)

16

Homeland Security
Terrorism and Nondeterrable Threats

THE NATURE OF TERRORISM

Maintaining peace and security through deterrence assumes *rational* enemies—enemies who are *unwilling* to bring death and destruction upon themselves, their own people, or their own nation, in response to their own aggression. For a half-century, before the terrorist attacks on America, September 11, 2001, the defense of the homeland of the United States relied primarily on deterrence—convincing potential enemies that an attack on our nation would result in devastating losses to themselves and their people. But "9/11" awakened America to the threat of terrorism—deliberate attacks on civilian targets by enemies who are willing to sacrifice themselves and their people to their cause.

The attack of "9/11" resulted in over 3,000 deaths in New York, Washington, and Pennsylvania. Commercial airliners with civilian passengers were hijacked and flown at high speeds directly into the symbols of America's financial and military power—the World Trade Center in New York and the Pentagon in Washington. Televised images of the collapse of New York City's largest buildings left a lasting impression on Americans.

The Goals of Terrorism

Terrorism is political violence directed against innocent civilians.* As barbaric as terrorism appears to civilized peoples, it is not without a rationale. Terrorists are not "crazies." Their first goal is to announce in the most dramatic fashion their own grievances, their commitment to violence, and their disregard for human life, often including their own. In its initial phase the success of a terrorist act is directly related to the publicity it receives. Terrorist groups jubilantly claim responsibility for their acts. The more horrendous, the more media coverage, the more damage, the more dead—all add to the success of the terrorists in attracting attention to themselves.

A prolonged campaign of terrorism is designed to inspire pervasive fear among people, to convince them that their government cannot protect them, and to erode their confidence in their nation's

---

*Title 22 of the U.S. Code, Section 2656 (d): "The term 'terrorism' means premeditated, politically motivated violence perpetrated against noncombatant targets by subnational groups or clandestine agents, usually intended to influence an audience."

leadership. (The Latin root of the term, *terrere*, means "to frighten.") The horror of terrorist acts and their unpredictability add to public fear—people can neither anticipate nor prepare for tragedies inflicted upon them. Terrorists hope that people will eventually conclude that submission to the terrorists' demands is preferable to living in a continuing climate of anxiety and uncertainty.

Democratic leaders are particularly vulnerable to terrorism. They must respond quickly and effectively to maintain the confidence of their people. But in doing so they are almost always forced to sacrifice some of the very liberties they are dedicated to protect—increased surveillance with cameras, wiretaps, and other detection devices; stopping and searching citizens without cause; searches at airports, terminals, and public gatherings; detention of persons for long periods without trial; crackdowns on immigrants; and other restrictive measures.

Global Terrorism

Global terrorism has evolved over the years into highly sophisticated networks operating in many countries. The most notable terrorist attacks extend back over 30 years (see Table 16–1). Prior to the attacks on New York's World Trade Center and the Pentagon on September 11, 2001, most Americans thought of terrorism as foreign. Terrorist acts on American soil had been rare; the most destructive attack—the Oklahoma City bombing of a federal building in 1995—had been carried out by a domestic terrorist. But the 9/11 attacks were on an unprecedented scale, and they revealed a sophisticated global plot against America.

A loose-knit network of terrorist cells (Al Qaeda) organized by a wealthy Saudi Arabian, Osama bin Laden, was engaged in global terrorism. Their political grievances included America's support of Israel in Middle East conflicts and an American presence in Islamic holy lands, notably Saudi Arabia. Several nations share these grievances and, more important, provided support and

TABLE 16–1 Selected Global Terrorist Acts Major terrorist attacks occur regularly around the world.

Date	Number of People Killed	Description	Prime Suspect(s)
September 5, 1972	17	Israeli athletes are killed during the Olympics in Munich, Germany	Black September, a Palestinian guerrilla group
April 18, 1983	63	The American Embassy in Beirut, Lebanon, is bombed	Hezbollah (Party of God)
October 23, 1983	299	Two truck bombs kill U.S. Marines and French paratroopers in Beirut, Lebanon	U.S. blames groups aligned with Iran and Syria
June 23, 1985	329	An Air India jet explodes over the Atlantic Ocean, off the coast of Ireland	The Royal Canadian Mounted Police charge Ajaib Singh Bagri and Ripudaman, two Sikh dissidents, in 2000
November 29, 1987	115	A Korean Air Lines jet explodes over the Burma coast	South Korea suspects North Korean involvement
December 21, 1988	270	Pan Am 103 explodes over Lockerbie, Scotland	One Libyan intelligence officer is convicted in a trial in the Hague in 2001; another is acquitted

TABLE 16–1   Continued

Date	Number of People Killed	Description	Prime Suspect(s)
February 26, 1993	6	A van filled with explosives explodes in the garage of the World Trade Center, leaving more than 1,000 people wounded	Ramzi Yousef receives a life sentence plus 240 years in 1998; the FBI suspects Osama bin Laden is behind the plot
April 19, 1995	168	Oklahoma City truck bomb destroys Alfred P. Murrah federal building	Timothy McVeigh executed June 11, 2001
August 7, 1998	224	Car bombs destroy U.S. embassies in Nairobi, Kenya, and Dar Es Salaam, Tanzania	Al Qaeda (Osama bin Laden) suspected
October 12, 2000	17	Rubber boat filled with explosives detonates next to USS *Cole* in Yemen	Al Qaeda (Osama bin Laden) suspected
September 11, 2001	2,999	Four U.S. commercial airliners hijacked. Two destroy World Trade Center, one hits the Pentagon, one crashes in Pennsylvania	Al Qaeda (Osama bin Laden) suspected
March 11, 2004	191	Bombing of train in Madrid, Spain	Al Qaeda suspected
September 3, 2004	355 (155 children)	Chechen terrorists attack school in Russia	Chechens
July 7, 2005	58	Four bombs set off in London transit system	Unknown
July 11, 2006	209	Mumbai (Bombay) India train bombings	Kashmir muslims
December 27, 2007	22	Benizar Bhutto, Pakistan opposition leader assasinated in bombing	Unknown
November 26, 2008	164	Mumbai (Bombay), India multiple attacks	Lashkar-e-Taiba Pakistani-based group
November 5, 2009	13	Fort Hood, Texas	Radical Islamic Army officer Nidal Hasan
March 29, 2010	40	Moscow metro	Chechens
January 24, 2011	35	Moscow Airport bombing	Chechens suspected

SOURCE: U.S. National Counterterrorism Center, 2011. *www.nctc.gov*

haven to Al Qaeda and similar terrorist organizations. The U.S. State Department lists as terrorist-sponsoring states: Syria, Iran, Iraq, Sudan, Cuba, and North Korea. Countries on the State Department watch list are Pakistan, Lebanon, and Yemen. But the principal base of support and sanctuary for Al Qaeda was the repressive and violent Taliban regime of Afghanistan.

POST–9/11 RESPONSE

On the evening of September 11, 2001, President George W. Bush spoke to the American people from the Oval Office in a nationally televised address:

> The pictures of airplanes flying into buildings, fires burning, huge structures collapsing, have filled us with disbelief, terrible sadness, and a quiet, unyielding anger. These mass murders were intended to frighten our nation into chaos and retreat. But they failed, our country is strong... These deliberate and deadly attacks were more than acts of terror. They were acts of war.[1]

The president outlined a broad "response to terrorism" to be fought both at home and abroad through diplomatic, military, financial, investigative, homeland security, and humanitarian means. He warned that the new "war on terrorism" would require a long-term sustained effort.

Aviation Security

The 9/11 attacks frightened many airline travelers. The first response of Congress was the Aviation and Transportation Security Act of 2001. Congress and the president agreed to create a new Transportation Security Agency that, among other things, would federalize all airport baggage and passenger screening, require all checked baggage to be screened, authorize the presence of federal marshals on domestic and international flights, and tighten airport security throughout the United States. The Transportation Security Agency is now part of the Department of Homeland Security.

The USA Patriot Act

But an even more sweeping enactment followed: the USA Patriot Act of 2001, officially the Uniting and Strengthening America Act by Providing Appropriate Tools Required to Intercept and Obstruct Terrorism. President Bush and Attorney General John Ashcroft successfully lobbied Congress to increase the federal government's powers of searches, seizures, surveillance, and detention of suspects. The concerns of civil libertarians were largely swept aside. The American public generally supported new restrictions on their liberty. The act was passed nearly unanimously in the Senate (98–1) and overwhelmingly in the House (337–66), with the support of both Democrats and Republicans.

Among the key provisions of the Patriot Act:

- *Roving Wiretaps.* Allows wiretaps of any telephones that suspects might use, instead of requiring separate warrants for each line.
- *Internet Tracking.* Allows law enforcement authorities to track Internet communications, that is, to "surf the Web" without obtaining warrants.
- *Business Records.* Allows investigators to obtain information from credit cards, bank records, consumer purchases, libraries, schools and colleges, and so on.
- *Foreign Intelligence Surveillance Court.* A special Foreign Intelligence Surveillance Court (FISA) may issue search warrants on an investigator's assertion that the information sought is relevant to a terrorist investigation. No showing of "probable cause" is required. The warrant is not made public, in order to avoid "tipping off" the subject.

- *Property Seizure*. Authorizes the seizure of the property of suspected terrorists. Persons whose property is seized bear the burden of proof that the property was not used for terrorist purposes in order to secure the return of their property.
- *Detention*. Allows the detention of suspected terrorists for lengthy periods.
- *Aliens Reporting and Detention*. Authorizes the Immigration and Customs Enforcement (ICE) to require reporting by aliens of selected nations and indefinite detention of illegal aliens suspected of terrorist connections.
- *Prohibits Harboring of Terrorists*. Creates a new federal crime: knowingly harboring persons who have committed, or are about to commit, a terrorist act.

PATRIOT Reauthorizations

Several key provisions of the PATRIOT Act are subject to expiration dates, including: roving wiretaps to permit surveillance of multiple phones; seizure of business and banking and property records in antiterrorist investigations, and surveillance of so-called lone wolf persons engaged in terrorism but not part of a recognized terrorist group. These provisions were reauthorized with various modifications for limited time periods in 2005, 2006, and 2010. President Barack Obama secured their reauthorization again in 2011, but continued debates may be expected as reauthorization bills come up in Congress.

Surveillance Powers

Congress passed a Foreign Intelligence Surveillance Act (FISA) in 1978 that established a special court to oversee requests for surveillance warrants against suspected domestic terrorists and foreign intelligence agents operating inside the United States. The FBI is the principal agency requesting FISA warrants. The FISA court is a "secret court"—hearings are closed and records are not available to the public.

The National Security Agency (NSA) has the responsibility for monitoring foreign electronic intelligence. NSA is an important component of the intelligence community (see Figure 16–1 later in this chapter). NSA is not authorized to undertake surveillance of domestic targets. But controversy arose following the 9/11 attacks regarding NSA surveillance of international calls between one party located within the United States and another party in a foreign country.

President George W. Bush authorized NSA to intercept international telephone calls made to and from the United States. These intercepts were done without warrants from the FISA court. President Bush argued that obtaining warrants from the FISA court was too slow, and that the president, as commander in chief during wartime, could authorize the gathering of intelligence by means of his choosing. But critics charged that the president acted lawlessly in authorizing warrantless telephone intercepts.

At President Bush's urgent request, Congress passed a Protect America Act in 2007. It authorizes warrantless surveillance of electronic communications of targets "reasonably believed" to be outside of the United States. It authorizes warrantless intercepts of calls and e-mails between overseas targets and persons located within the United States. It also allows warrantless monitoring of foreign communications that travel through telecommunications equipment located in the United States. Domestic-to-domestic communications still cannot be intercepted without a FISA warrant. Congress also dismissed lawsuits against communications companies that had cooperated earlier in the president's surveillance program.

Enemy Combatants

The U.S. military detains hundreds of "enemy combatants." These include people captured in the fighting in Afghanistan and Iraq as well as terrorists captured in other nations. Traditionally, prisoners of war are not entitled to rights under the U.S. Constitution; but they are protected by the Geneva Convention. They may be detained for the duration of a war. However, detainees in the war on terrorism are not uniformed soldiers of a sovereign nation and therefore are not officially prisoners of war. Some have been detained for many years without trial and without prospects for release.

Habeas Corpus

The U.S. Supreme Court held in 2004 that detainees in the war on terrorism, even those captured on foreign battlefields and held outside the United States, are entitled to a judicial hearing under the Constitution's guarantee of the writ of habeas corpus.[2] And in a controversial 2008 decision the Supreme Court held that detainees at Guantánamo "have the constitutional privilege of habeas corpus"—access to federal courts to challenge their detention. Although the Constitution recognizes that habeas corpus can be suspended "in cases of Rebellion or Invasion" this Suspension Clause does not apply to current enemy combatants. "Some of the petitioners have been in custody for six years with no definitive judicial determination as to the legality of their detention. Their access to the writ [of habeas corpus] is a necessity to determine the lawfulness of their status...."[3] In a stinging dissent, Justice Scalia wrote: "Today for the first time in our nation's history, the Court confers a constitutional right to habeas corpus on alien enemies detained abroad by military forces in the course of an ongoing war....It will almost certainly cause more Americans to be killed."[4]

Guantánamo

Shortly after taking office, President Barack Obama ordered the prison at the U.S. naval base in Guantánamo, Cuba, to be closed within a year. The U.S. military had held hundreds of enemy combatants in the prison since 2002; approximately 250 detainees remained at the time of the president's order. But it soon became clear that Guantánamo could not be closed. Congress cut off funds for the transfer of prisoners to the United States. Among the detainees were persons deemed to be extremely dangerous—persons who were likely to resume terrorist activities if released. Many could not be convicted in jury trials in federal courts because of problems in assembling evidence. Nor could they be safely repatriated or resettled in another country. The president's announced intention to close Guantánamo and to try terrorists in civilian courts collapsed in the face of bipartisan opposition in the Congress.

In an embarrassing reversal, President Obama issued a new executive order in early 2011 ordering indefinite detention of prisoners at Guantánamo who continue to pose a threat to national security. The Obama Administration now argues that it has the authority to hold enemy combatants judged to be a danger to national security until the cessation of hostilities. The original Authorization for the Use of Force, passed within days of the 9/11 attack, grants the president the authority to "use all necessary and appropriate" force against those responsible for the attack and to prevent any future acts of terrorism against the United States. Detainees will continue to have habeas corpus petition rights in federal courts where the government must show cause for their detention.

Military Commissions

President Obama also ordered new military commission trials for certain Guantánamo detainees. The Congress authorized military commission trials under the Bush administration, but Obama initially insisted that terrorists be tried in civilian courts. Perhaps the most notorious of the detainees at Guantánamo is Kalid Shiekh Mohammed (KSM), the self-proclaimed mastermind of the attacks of 9/11. Attorney General Eric Holder initially announced that KSM and his co-conspirators would be tried in federal court in New York City. But the prospects of his being set free on procedural grounds aroused a storm of protest. (Was he read his Miranda rights? Were his confessions coerced? Was evidence against him obtained illegally? Can an impartial jury be found in New York?) In 2011 Attorney General Holder reluctantly announced that KSM and other terrorists would be tried in Guantánamo by military commissions.

Interrogation

Following national security crises, the CIA and FBI come under intense pressure both to find terrorist perpetrators and to prevent subsequent attacks. After "9/11" the CIA was pressured to break terrorist suspects and obtain information through "enhanced interrogation techniques," including sleep deprivation and simulated drowning ("water boarding"). (Accounts vary regarding how successful these techniques were in identifying terrorists and heading off new attacks.) The Justice Department's Office of Legal Council ruled that various techniques did not violate laws and treaties banning "torture," in effect granting approval for the use of these techniques. But civil libertarians objected, and when the Obama Administration came to Washington, the president issued an order against the future use of these techniques.

THE DEPARTMENT OF HOMELAND SECURITY

Presidents often create new bureaucratic organizations to symbolize their commitment to a policy direction. On October 8, 2001, less than one month after the 9/11 terrorist attacks, President George W. Bush issued an executive order establishing the Office of Homeland Security. Then later, in 2002, in response to growing criticism that he had not done enough to reassure the American public of the federal government's commitment to protect them from terrorism, President Bush proposed a new *Department* of Homeland Security.

Organization

The creation of the Department of Homeland Security involved a significant reorganization of the federal bureaucracy. The new department incorporated the U.S. Customs Service (formerly part of the Department of Treasury), the Immigration and Naturalization Service and the Border Patrol (formerly parts of the Department of Justice), the Transportation Security Administration (formerly part of the Department of Transportation), the United States Coast Guard (formerly part of the Department of Treasury), the Secret Service (formerly part of the Department of Treasury), and FEMA, the Federal Emergency Management Agency (formerly an independent agency).

Effectiveness

Reorganization alone seldom solves policy problems. The agencies transferred to the Department of Homeland Security remain largely intact, each with its own continuing problems. In all, some 22 agencies employing nearly 200,000 workers were moved into the new department; it was the largest federal reorganization in more than a half-century. Indeed, the administrative problems created by reorganization may overshadow the mission of the department—fighting terrorism.

But perhaps the greatest obstacle to effectiveness is that the federal agencies with the greatest involvement in homeland security—the Federal Bureau of Investigation (FBI), the Central

Intelligence Agency (CIA), and intelligence and anti-terrorist units of the Department of Defense—remain independent of each other and beyond the scope of the Department of Homeland Security. Rather, the new Secretary of Homeland Security is charged with the responsibility for "coordinating" with these agencies. This requires integrated analysis of all foreign and domestically collected threat information—a daunting task. Indeed, bureaucratic obstacles to the flow of information between federal intelligence agencies may have contributed to the "9/11" disaster.[5] It is by no means certain that the new department can gain access to all the sources of intelligence relating to the threats of terrorism against the U.S. homeland.

FIGHTING TERRORISM WITH INTELLIGENCE

Success in the war on terrorism requires actions to prevent terrorist attacks before they occur. A proactive war on terrorism requires the collection, analysis, and dissemination of relevant foreign and domestic information to federal, state, and local government agencies, and to the American people. This is the responsibility of America's intelligence community.

The Intelligence Community

The intelligence community refers to a broad array of organizations within the federal government that collect, analyze, and disseminate information to intelligence "consumers"—from the president and other top Washington policymakers to battlefield commanders (see Figure 16–1). The principal components of the intelligence community are as follows:

Director of National Intelligence.   The Director of National Intelligence (DNI) oversees the entire intelligence community. (The DNI replaced the CIA director's role as the principal intelligence advisor to the president. The CIA director now concentrates on the responsibilities of the CIA itself.) The DNI must unify the budget for national intelligence as well as approve and submit nominations for individuals to head various agencies of the intelligence community. The DNI also manages the nation's counterterrorism effort, with the assistance of a new National Counterterrorism Center, which assembles and analyzes information on terrorists gathered both at home and abroad.

Central Intelligence Agency.   The Central Intelligence Agency (CIA) is the lead agency in assembling, analyzing, and disseminating intelligence from all other agencies in the intelligence community. It prepares the President's Daily Briefing (PDB), which summarizes all intelligence reports from all agencies for the president each day. The CIA also prepares National Intelligence Estimates (NIEs)—more thorough studies of specific topics, for example, North Korea's nuclear capabilities. In addition, the CIA is charged with responsibility for human intelligence collection (recruiting agents around the world and supervising their work), and it also oversees covert operations, including paramilitary special operations, with a special "presidential finding" authorizing such operations.

AGENCIES WITHIN THE DEPARTMENT OF DEFENSE

Defense Intelligence Agency (DIA)—provides timely and objective military intelligence to warfighters, policymakers, and force planners.

National Security Agency (NSA)—collects and processes foreign electronic signals and intelligence information for our nation's leaders and warfighters, and protects critical U.S. information security systems from compromise.

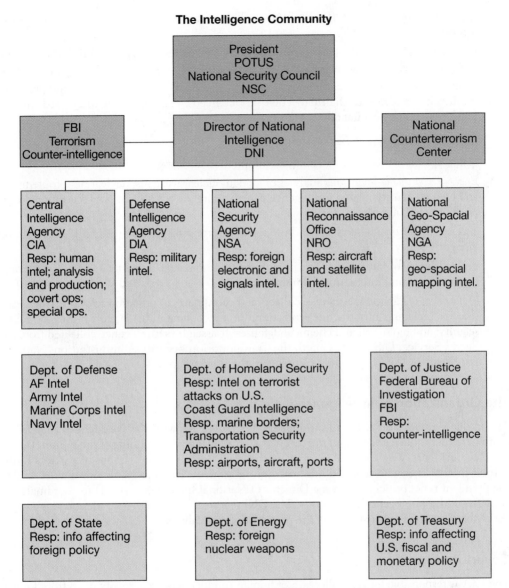

The Intelligence Community

FIGURE 16–1 The Intelligence Community The "intelligence community" includes a variety of agencies, now under the direction of the Director of National Intelligence who reports to the president. NOTE: The CIA, DIA, NSA, NRO, and NGA are concerned exclusively with intelligence. The Departments of Defense, Homeland Security, Justice, State, Energy, and Treasury are concerned primarily with other missions, but do have intelligence responsibilities.

National Reconnaissance Office (NRO)—collects information from airplane and satellite reconnaissance.

National Imagery and Mapping Agency (NIMA)—provides timely, relevant, and accurate geospatial intelligence in support of national security.

Army, Navy, Air Force, and Marine Corps Intelligence Agencies—each collects and processes intelligence relevant to their particular service needs. Each is closely integrated with its respective military commands.

AGENCIES WITHIN OTHER DEPARTMENTS

State Department—collects and analyzes information affecting U.S. foreign policy.

Energy Department—performs analyses of foreign nuclear weapons, nuclear nonproliferation, and energy-security related intelligence issues in support of U.S. national security policies, programs, and objectives.

Treasury Department—collects and processes information that may affect U.S. fiscal and monetary policy.

Federal Bureau of Investigation—deals with counterespionage, domestic and foreign terrorist organizations, and international criminal cases.

Department of Homeland Security—collects and coordinates information relevant to domestic security, including infrastructure protection, Internet communication protection, technology security, and biological and chemical defenses. It assembles intelligence collected from the Secret Service, U.S. Coast Guard, the Transportation Security Administration, National Bio-Weapons Defense Analysis Center, and the Border Patrol.

The Organization of Intelligence

The ultimate responsibility for all intelligence activities rests with the President of the United States. Presidents have undertaken intelligence activities since the founding of the nation. During the Revolutionary War, General George Washington nurtured small groups of patriots living behind British lines who supplied him with information on Redcoat troop movements. Today, the president relies principally on the Director of National Intelligence (DNI) to coordinate the activities of the Intelligence Community. The DNI reports directly to the president and is a member of the National Security Council, the president's inner cabinet.

Covert Actions

The CIA is responsible for the collection of human intelligence—reports obtained from foreign sources by CIA caseworkers around the world. The CIA's responsibilities also include supervision of all covert actions—activities in support of the national interest of the United States that would be ineffective or counterproductive if their sponsorship by the United States were to be made public. Most covert actions consist of routine transfers of economic aid and military training and equipment to pro–U.S. forces that do not wish to acknowledge such aid publicly. (For example, one of the largest covert actions ever taken by the United States was the support for nearly 10 years of the Afghan rebels fighting Soviet occupation of their country from 1978 to 1988. These rebels did not wish to acknowledge such aid in order to avoid being labeled as "puppets" of the United States.)

Integrating Foreign and Domestic Intelligence

Perhaps the most troublesome problem in intelligence and counterterrorism in the past had been the lack of coordination between the CIA and the FBI. Fighting global terrorism requires close surveillance of individuals and terrorist organizations both within and outside of the United States. But in the original National Security Act of 1947 that established the CIA, this agency was specifically prohibited from engaging in any activities, including surveillance of individuals and organizations, *inside the borders of the United States*. Only the FBI has the authority to act against terrorists inside the United States. Intelligence reorganization encouraged greater cooperation between these agencies, and the Patriot Act now permits both agencies to undertake surveillance of communications relevant to terrorism both within the United States and abroad. However, the FBI and the intelligence community continue to operate largely separately from each other, and it is not clear whether their communication and coordination problems have been resolved.

The congressional Joint Inquiry into the 9/11 tragedy concluded:

> ...prior to September 11, the Intelligence Community was neither well organized nor equipped, and did not adequately adapt to meet the challenge posed by global terrorists focused on targets within the domestic United States... Within the Intelligence Community, agencies did not share relevant counterterrorism information... not only between different Intelligence Community agencies but also within individual agencies, and between the intelligence and the law-enforcement agencies. Serious problems in information sharing also persisted between the Intelligence Community and other federal agencies as well as state and local authorities.[6]

FBI Counterterrorist Activity

The principal responsibility for combating domestic terrorism rests with the FBI. Indeed, the FBI has specifically designated counterterrorism as its top priority. (Previously, its top priorities were federal crimes, drug trafficking, public corruption, civil rights protection, and the support of state and local law enforcement.) The FBI has established Joint Terrorism Task Forces in all of its regional offices; these forces include members of other agencies such as the Immigration and Customs Enforcement (ICE), and the Bureau of Alcohol, Tobacco and Firearms (ATF) as well as state and local law enforcement. The FBI also sponsors a National Joint Terrorism Task Force and promises to integrate its intelligence activities with the CIA and the Department of Homeland Security.

However, the traditional missions and methods of the FBI may not be well suited to fighting terrorism. It is widely acknowledged that counterterrorism must be preventative. Investigation and apprehension of terrorists *after* a terrorist act has been committed is not enough. Rather, terrorist attacks must be preempted. Preemption frequently requires the identification and surveillance of suspected terrorists, undercover penetration of suspected terrorist organizations, "watch lists" of persons who may be connected to terrorist organizations, and the preventative disruption of terrorist plans. These kinds of activities raise issues of personal liberty and privacy.

The FBI operates under congressional restraints on its methods. Following a congressional investigation in the 1970s of FBI surveillance of anti-Vietnam War and civil rights groups, Congress enacted a series of laws restricting FBI surveillance of individuals and organizations. The Foreign Intelligence Surveillance Act of 1978 requires the FBI to obtain warrants from a special Foreign Intelligence Surveillance Court in order to watch or wiretap aliens living in the United States. Warrants to place U.S. citizens under surveillance must be obtained from federal courts; law enforcement agencies seeking such warrants must set forth "probable cause" to believe that a crime has been committed. The Patriot Act relaxed some of these restrictions, but the FBI continues to confront criticism from civil rights groups for undertaking surveillance of individuals and groups who have not (yet?) committed any crimes.

SECURITY VERSUS LIBERTY

The war on terrorism promises to be a long one. Americans must become accustomed to greater restrictions on their travel, increased surveillance of their activities, and new intrusions into their privacy. With the tragedy of 9/11 fresh in their minds, most Americans approved of increased restrictive measures. But over time Americans became increasingly concerned with the losses of personal liberty inspired by the war on terrorism.

Historic Trade-Offs

Historically, threats to national security have resulted in challenges to individual liberty. Abraham Lincoln suspended the writ of habeas corpus (the requirement that authorities bring defendants before a judge and show cause for their detention) during the Civil War. (Only after the war did the U.S. Supreme Court hold that he had no authority to suspend the writ.[7]) In the wake of World War I, Congress passed the Espionage Act, which outlawed "any disloyal, profane, scurrilous, or abusive language intended to cause contempt, scorn, contumely, or disrepute" to the government. Socialist presidential candidate Eugene V. Debs was imprisoned for speaking against the war and the draft: his conviction was upheld by the U.S. Supreme Court, as were the convictions

Security Versus Privacy   A Transportation Security Administration (TSA) agent performs a pat down on an airline passenger at a security checkpoint at the Phoenix, Arizona International Airport. The TSA was created in November, 2001, in response to the 9/11 attacks; it is now part of the Department of Homeland Security. Passengers who decline a full body scan or who set off a scanner are subject to pat downs. Critics charge that indiscriminate pat downs are unnecessary invasions of privacy. (Getty Images)

of other antiwar protesters of that era.[8] In February, 1942, shortly after the Japanese attack on Pearl Harbor, President Franklin D. Roosevelt authorized the removal and internment of Japanese Americans living on the West Coast. The U.S. Supreme Court upheld this flagrant violation of the Constitution.[9] Not until 1988 did the U.S. Congress vote to make reparations and public apologies to the surviving victims. During the Cold War, the U.S. government prosecuted top leaders of the Communist party for violating the Smith Act, which made it unlawful "to knowingly and willfully advocate, abet, advise, or teach the duty, necessity, or propriety of overthrowing any government in the United States by force or violence." Again, the U.S. Supreme Court upheld their convictions.[10] Not until the 1960s did the Court begin to reassert freedom of expression including the advocacy of revolution. Only when the perceived crisis appears to fade do American elites again reassert their commitment to fundamental liberties.

The Costs to Liberty

The war on terrorism has inspired a new arsenal of anti-terrorist weapons—laws, executive orders, and military actions—many of which raise serious questions about individual liberty. Yet there is evidence in opinion polls that Americans generally support many restrictions on personal liberty in the fight against terrorism.[11]

What do you think is more important right now: for the federal government to investigate possible terrorist threats even if that intrudes on personal privacy; or for the federal government not to intrude on personal privacy, even if it limits its ability to investigate possible terrorist threats?

	Investigate threats	Not intrude on liberty	Unsure
2010	68%	26%	6%

Americans remain fearful of another terrorist attack.

How likely is it that there will be further acts of terrorism in the United States over the next several weeks?

	Very Likely	Somewhat Likely	Not too Likely	Not at all Likely
2010	14%	41%	31%	12%

Americans generally take a hard line in support of airport security measures, even with long lines at security checkpoints, hassles with carry-on baggage and shoes, and full body scans and pat downs.

We would like you to think about any loss of personal privacy air travelers may experience from going through a full body scan or a full body pat down. Do you think that loss of personal privacy is worth it or not worth it as a method to prevent acts of terrorism?

	Worth It	Not Worth It	Unsure
2010	71%	27%	2%

In another approach, would you support or oppose the TSA profiling people, using available information about passengers in order to determine who gets selected for extra security at airports?

	Support	Oppose	Unsure
2010	70%	25%	5%

And Americans support the continued use of the U.S. prison at Guantánamo, and the trial of suspected terrorists by military courts rather than civilian courts:

As you may know the United States has been holding a number of suspected terrorists at a U.S. military prison in Guantánamo Bay Cuba. Based on what you have heard or read, do you think the U.S. should continue to operate the prison, or do you think the U.S. should close the prison and transfer the prisoners somewhere else?

	Continue to Operate	Close the Prison	Unsure
2010	55%	32%	13%

Which do you think is more important: to try 9/11 terror suspects in open trial in civilian court so the world can see how the American system works; or to try 9/11 terror suspects in military courts to better assure security of trials?

	Civilian courts	Military courts	Unsure
2010	35%	59%	6%

In short, the threat of terrorism in the minds of Americans justifies many restrictions on individual liberty.

SUMMARY

1. The United States traditionally relied on deterrence to protect itself, including protection against a direct attack on its homeland. However, the attacks on the U.S. on September 11, 2001, demonstrated that terrorism is a nondeterrable threat. Terrorists deliberately attack civilian targets and sacrifice themselves and their people to their cause.

2. Terrorism is political violence directed against innocent civilians. It is designed to inspire fear in people and erode their confidence in the ability of their government to protect them. Global terrorism has developed over the years into highly sophisticated networks operating in many countries.

3. The American people initially responded to the 9/11 attacks with strong support for the nation's leadership and for security measures designed to reduce the threat of terrorism.

4. The USA Patriot Act was supported in Congress by large majorities of both parties. It gave federal law enforcement authorities sweeping new powers of searches, seizures, surveillance, and detention of suspects in fighting the war on terrorism.

5. A new Department of Homeland Security was created, reorganizing the federal bureaucracy. The new department includes the Customs and Border Protection, Citizenship and Immigration Services, Immigration and Customs Enforcement, Coast Guard, Federal Emergency Management Agency, Secret Service, and the Transportation Security Administration.

6. Success in fighting terrorism depends heavily on intelligence—information that allows government authorities to act to prevent terrorist attacks before they occur. The U.S. intelligence community refers to a broad array of organizations of the federal government, not all of which have effectively communicated with each other in the past.

7. The war on terrorism has placed greater restrictions on the liberties of Americans. As in the past, Americans have tolerated restrictions on their liberties when confronted with perceived serious threats. As the threat recedes, they are less willing to sacrifice individual liberties.

MySearchLab® EXERCISES

Apply what you learned in this chapter on MySearchLab (www.mysearchlab.com)

NOTES

1. President George W. Bush, Remarks to the Nation, September 11, 2001.
2. *Rasul v. United States*, 542 U.S. 466 (2004).
3. *Boumediene v. Bush*, June 12, 2008.
4. Ibid.
5. *The 9/11 Commission Report* (New York: Norton, 2005).
6. Senate Select Committee on Intelligence and House Permanent Select Committee on Intelligence Joint Inquiry into the Terrorist Attacks of September 11, 2001, *Final Report* (Washington, DC: U.S. Government Printing Office, 2003).
7. *Ex Parte Milligan* (1866).
8. *Debs v. United States*, 249 U.S. 211 (1919); *Schenk v. United States*, 249 U.S. 47 (1919).
9. *Korematsu v. United States*, 323 U.S. 214 (1944).
10. *Dennis v. United States*, 341 U.S. 494 (1951).
11. Various polls as reported in *The Polling Report*, *www.pollingreport.com*. Accessed March, 2011.

BIBLIOGRAPHY

Department of Homeland Security. *Strategic Plan 2008–2013*. Washington, DC: U.S. Government Printing Office, 2008.

Gertz, Bill. *Breakdown: How America's Intelligence Failures Led to September 11*. New York: Regnery, 2002.

Gunaratna, Rohan. *Inside Al Queda*. New York: Columbia University Press, 2002.

Kettl, Donald F. *System Under Stress: Homeland Security and American Politics*, 2nd ed. Washington, DC: CQ Press, 2006.

Lowenthal, Mark M. *Intelligence: From Secrets to Policy*, 4th ed. Washington, DC: CQ Press, 2008.

National Commission on Terrorist Attacks upon the United States. *The 9/11 Commission Report*. New York: Norton, 2005.

White, Jonathan R. *Terrorism and Homeland Security*, 7th ed. Cengage Learning, 2012.

WEB SITES

Department of Homeland Security. Official government site for homeland security, with information on travel, transportation, immigration, threats, and homeland protection. *www.dhs.gov*

U.S. Immigration and Customs Enforcement. The official government site (of agency replacing INS), with immigration laws, regulations, etc. *www.ice.gov*

Federal Emergency Management Agency. Official site of FEMA, with information on current disasters, how to get help, etc. *www.fema.gov*

Institute for Homeland Security. Private think tank devoted to research, education, and public awareness of homeland security issues. *www.homelandsecurity.org*

Electronic Privacy Information Center. Advocacy organization for privacy rights, opposed to many homeland security measures. *www.epic.org*

American Civil Liberties Union. Advocacy organization for civil liberties, opposed to homeland security measures believed to violate civil rights. *www.aclu.org*

Senate Select Committee on Intelligence and House Permanent Select Committee on Intelligence Joint Inquiry. Report of activities of U.S. intelligence community in connection with attacks of September 11, 2001. *www.gpoaccess.gov/serialset/creports/all*

Credits

PHOTO CREDITS

Chapter 1

p. 2: © Brooks Kraft/Corbis; p. 6: © Michael Reynolds/epa/Corbis

Chapter 2

p. 14: © Rick D'Elia/Corbis; p. 18: Fotalia;
p. 26: © Andrew Davies/Specialist Stock/Corbis

Chapter 3

p. 32: © Brooks Kraft/Corbis; p. 40: © Brooks Kraft/Corbis

Chapter 4

p. 62: © Benjamin J. Myers/Corbis; p. 72: Washington Post/Getty Images

Chapter 5

p. 82: © Ted Soqui/Corbis; p. 94: © prettyfoto/Alamy

Chapter 6

p. 106: Getty Images; p. 121: © Shannon Stapleton/Reuters/Corbis

Chapter 7

p. 140: © Randy Pench/ZUMA Press/Corbis

Chapter 8

p. 160: © Wendy Stone/Corbis; p. 169: © Martin H. Simon/Corbis

Chapter 9

p. 174: © Will & Deni McIntyre/Corbis;
p. 186: © Reuters/Corbis

Chapter 10

p. 206: AFP/Getty Images; p. 217: © Zhang Jun/Xinhua Press/Corbis

Chapter 11

p. 228: 2005 Getty Images; p. 241: Getty Images

Chapter 12

p. 248: © Shaul Schwarz/Corbis

Chapter 13

p. 268: © Tepco/ZUMA Press/Corbis

Chapter 14

p. 292: © Hulton-Deutsch Collection/Corbis;
p. 309: Associated Press

Chapter 15

p. 324: © Ed Darack/Science Faction/Corbis

Chapter 16

p. 352: © Beth Dixson/Alamy; p. 364: Getty Images

TEXT CREDITS

Chapter 3

p. 45, 47, and 52: Center for Responsive Politics (OpenSecrets.org)

Chapter 12

p. 255: Langran, Robert; Schnitzer, Martin, Government, Business, and The American Economy, © 2001. Reprinted by permission of the author.

Index